Musical Groups in the Movies, 1929–1970

Roy Liebman

McFarland & Company, Inc., Publishers
Jefferson, North Carolina, and London

LIBRARY OF CONGRESS CATALOGUING-IN-PUBLICATION DATA

Liebman, Roy.
Musical groups in the movies,
1929–1970 / Roy Liebman.
p. cm.
Includes bibliographical references and index.

ISBN 978-0-7864-3484-8
softcover : 50# alkaline paper ∞

1. Motion picture music — Bio-bibliography — Dictionaries.
2. Musical groups — Dictionaries. 3. Motion pictures and music.
I. Title.
ML102.M68L54 2009   780.92'2 — dc22   2008037715

British Library cataloguing data are available

©2009 Roy Liebman. All rights reserved

*No part of this book may be reproduced or transmitted in any form
or by any means, electronic or mechanical, including photocopying
or recording, or by any information storage and retrieval system,
without permission in writing from the publisher.*

Cover photograph: The Mills Brothers, circa 1940s–1950s (Photofest)

Manufactured in the United States of America

*McFarland & Company, Inc., Publishers
Box 611, Jefferson, North Carolina 28640
www.mcfarlandpub.com*

Janine, Marissa and Hannah — and the friends
who have made The Big Decision worthwhile

Contents

Preface
1

MUSICAL GROUPS IN THE MOVIES
7

Appendix One:
Other United Kingdom Bands
201

Appendix Two:
Dance Teams, Skaters and Other Specialty Acts
202

Bibliography
205

Index
207

Preface

During the reign of silent movies, music was always present to underscore the onscreen action. Of course, it did not come from the screen itself unless it was one of the early, unsuccessful experiments in sound, of which there were many. In the often shabby nickelodeon "theaters" (usually storefronts) the music may have been produced by a tinny piano. As the great art of silent films matured, the music could be played by full orchestras in magnificent movie palaces.

Films usually reflect the era in which they are made and the 1920s was, after all, the Jazz Age. So even though they were silent, such motion pictures as *Jazz Cinderella*, *The Jazz Girl*, *The Jazz Hounds*, *Jazz Mad*, *Jazzland* and *Jazzmania* were seen in theaters. There may have been jazz bands pictured in them but their music was soundless and was interpreted off-screen.

Several years before all movies officially "talked" (which was a fait accompli almost everywhere by 1930) music did actually emanate from the screen — or, more technically, from a synchronized turntable. Beginning in the summer of 1926, this was primarily due to the success of the Vitaphone sound-on-disc technology introduced by Warner Brothers studio. More sophisticated technology soon produced sound-on-film.

Almost from the first, musical groups were part of the sound revolution that initially encompassed films running one or two reels. Appearing in one of the short subjects in the very first Vitaphone program, which accompanied the 1926 feature *Don Juan*, was the 107-member strong New York Philharmonic Orchestra playing the overture to Richard Wagner's *Tannhauser*. Other pioneering shorts included the Dixie Jubilee Singers and the Metropolitan Opera Chorus accompanying opera star Anna Case, the singing/instrumental group the Four Aristocrats, Vincent Lopez and his orchestra, and many others.

It was Al Jolson's epochal *The Jazz Singer*, released in October 1927, which energized the emergence of full-length sound features. It had very little talking (and that largely accidental) but several songs. During the next year several part-talking films and a few all-talkies were released, some with songs, but apparently none included musical groups. In 1928 Jolson's part-talkie *The Singing Fool* was a massive hit, further encouraging the production of sound films.

The year 1929 saw musical films in full flower and the emergence of musical groups as part of that blossoming. Hordes of singers and musical ensembles were enticed from radio, records, opera, Broadway and vaudeville. Every kind of singing act seemingly had its turn. If a group could get anywhere near the right notes it was put into pictures.

Established Hollywood silent movie old-timers like Bebe Daniels, Walter Pidgeon, John Boles, Bessie Love, Janet Gaynor and Marion Davies suddenly found themselves warbling onscreen. Greta Garbo only *talked* but they *sang*. For a couple of years it was to be "All-singing! All-dancing! All-talking!" *all* the time, until a weary public said it was *all* too much.

Among the very first musical ensembles to be heard in features were the three Brox Sisters, Patricia, Lorayne and Dagmar, who co-introduced "Singin' in the Rain" in MGM's *The Hollywood Revue of 1929*. They were precursors to such female close-harmony acts of the 1930s as the Boswell, Pickens and Andrews Sisters.

Not too long thereafter the enormously popular (and enormously-girthed) Paul Whiteman had the 1930 film *King of Jazz* built around his ample frame. It was one of the last films to celebrate the Jazz Age and use that word in its title. It seems probable, though, that Fred Waring was the first bandleader to be featured in a film, 1929's *Syncopation*.

Innumerable music groups also appeared in the thousands of short subjects that were made well into the 1950s by nearly all the major studios. Many of these groups were never seen in full-length features and thus are rarely encountered today, even on recordings, having for all intents and purposes disappeared into (perhaps) undeserved obscurity.

There was even a way to see many of them in short films *outside* of theaters. To meet the public demand for entertainment just before, during, and a little while after World War II, the Panoram, a kind of coin-operated juke box/video machine, could be found in venues like bars and nightclubs and even some restaurants. For ten cents the machines played short (usually three minutes) black-and-white musical films known as "soundies" that featured many of the top bands and singers of the time.

Some of these shorts were a bit more "far out" than Hollywood product and they were shot at minimal cost as well. It is estimated there were some 1,800 produced and lately there has been a concerted effort to preserve these almost-neglected slices of Americana which were the precursors of music videos.

Since Hollywood has always been better at following, exploiting and capitalizing on trends than setting them, the musical groups used in feature films largely reflected the popular taste of the day. For that reason, it is instructive to see and hear them in the context of their films, however silly some of the movies were and however badly some of the groups were utilized.

In features, for the most part, groups were inserted into a film for momentary diversion, not as integral parts of the plot; often multiple ensembles appeared in the same film. Even in that limited role they could still increase a picture's profitability. This was certainly true in the case of the dominant music of the 1930s and '40s, the Big Band Era. And it was also true of the other dominant music of those two decades, western swing, heard on the radio and in that staple of neighborhood movie houses, the "B" western.

A few of the big bands had long-term contracts with studios, among them those of Tommy Dorsey and Xavier Cugat at MGM and Harry James at 20th Century–Fox. Fans flocked to their films even though their favorites usually had only brief screen time. This may have been the start of Hollywood's great appeal to teenagers because they formed the backbone of the Big Bands' fan base.

Occasionally film plots would revolve around a bandleader such as Glenn Miller (as the thinly-disguised "Gene Morrison") in *Orchestra Wives* and Kay Kyser in several films. Usually orchestra leaders and most other music personalities played "themselves"; i.e., their public personas, if indeed they were called upon to act at all. This was partly due to the fact that few of them *could* really act beyond delivering a few woodenly-spoken lines. Some, like Harry James, took acting lessons— or so the publicity said.

Because diversion for the home front was so important during World War II these few years probably marked the epitome of on-screen music groups. Musicals were at the height of their popularity and nearly every studio, from MGM and 20th Century–Fox at the more prestigious end (they usually made theirs in blazing Technicolor) to the less exalted Universal produced a string of them. The latter studio generally starred lesser-known young and bouncy performers in their minor "A" black-and-white programmers, usually with short running times.

The end of World War II brought about the beginning of the end of the Big Bands for several reasons. Among them were changing musical tastes and the economics of maintaining such large-sized groups when the public no longer flocked to see them. However the genesis of their decline probably came during the war itself when the draft took many if not most of the best players.

Hollywood, behind the curve as usual, decided about ten years later that the era's legacy was worth preserving. Such celebratory films as *The Glenn Miller Story*, *The Eddy Duchin Story*, *The Benny Goodman Story*, *The Gene Krupa Story* and *The Five Pennies* (about Red Nichols) came to the screen, usually with miscast stars as the title characters. The earliest of these fictionalized biopics did come at the tail end of Big Band Era, *The Fabulous Dorseys* made in 1947. It was not, however, a fabulous film.

During the heyday of the so-called singing western from the mid–1930s to the early '50s, it was not only the oater stars like Gene Autry and Roy Rogers who warbled. Almost all of these films had a group of musicians in the cast who doubled as the "boys," i.e., ranch hands, deputies and other secondary characters who often had no spoken lines but were usually ubiquitous. It seems that job responsibilities in Hollywood's version of the West always included singing and/or playing at least two or three songs.

So-called "western swing" had slowly evolved from traditional country music and by the early 1930s such bands as the Light Crust Dough Boys, Bob Wills and the Texas Playboys and Milton Brown and His Brownies were popularizing it regionally in the Southwest. It contained elements of blues, Dixieland, jazz and even ragtime. The term western swing itself gained currency in the early 1940s and is often attributed to musician Spade Cooley.

Although it never gained much popularity east of the Appalachians, western swing did spread to the West Coast and ultimately to the notice of Hollywood. Los Angeles became the home base to many western and even hillbilly bands (e.g., the original Beverly Hill Billies). By the 1950s so-called western bop and rockabilly had become subgenres of western swing music.

There were of course economic reasons for even the most cheaply-made westerns to provide musical interludes. For one, western-style music increased the box office take in areas like the South and Southwest where it was very popular. Secondly, there were major cowboy stars who could not themselves sing, among them Charles "Durango Kid" Starrett, William "Hopalong Cassidy" Boyd and Johnny Mack Brown.

Another reason was simple padding; the plots of these films were usually very similar and musical interludes made for a welcome diversion and filled out the running time. If a film needed to be cut for some reason, as for television viewing, the extraneous musical numbers could often be eliminated. Perhaps the simple bottom line was that cowboy heroes needed their sidekicks and if they could sing so much the better!

Sometimes one or more of the "boys" had lines and were even second male leads, like Bob Nolan of the Sons of the Pioneers. And sometimes the songs they played became considerable hits among a much larger audience than went to see "B" westerns. Some of their songs, indeed, have lived on long after the forgettable movies in which they were first heard.

Nearly always, though, the individual members of musical ensembles remained anonymous onscreen. They were usually not given lines to speak except in the case of top-billed performers like the Andrews Sisters, and even then very sparingly. Sometimes one member would break from the bunch to launch a successful solo career. Among them were Bing Crosby who emerged from the Rhythm Boys, Judy Canova, who split from her family's singing hillbilly act, Jo Stafford (the Stafford Sisters) and Andy Williams (the Williams Brothers).

For a few years after the postwar decline of the Big Bands, easy-listening ballads were chart-toppers. There was really no dominant musical movement and the movies reflected this accordingly; many of the early 1950s musicals harked back to an earlier time. This largely changed in 1955 with the release of *The Blackboard Jungle,* featuring the feverish Bill Haley song "Rock Around the Clock" on its soundtrack. It did not take long for Hollywood to notice the emerging rock-and-roll culture.

It was a repeat of the 1920s, only with "Rock" instead of "Jazz" frequently appearing in film titles. In a short time a movie titled *Rock Around the Clock* appeared followed by, among others, *Rock, Pretty Baby, Rock All Night, Don't Knock the Rock, Mister Rock and Roll, Shake, Rattle and Rock,* and inevitably *Rock, Rock, Rock.* For the next fifteen years or so the studios continued to follow the mostly teen trends in music.

When a new dance craze emerged there were generally at least a couple of movies to capitalize on it, *Twist Around the Clock, Don't Knock the Twist* and *Calypso Heat Wave* being examples. Country, Latin-American and folk music also had their cycle of pictures, the former mostly popular in rural areas, the latter two mostly in urban ones. Even classical music groups had had their day in films like *One Hundred Men and a Girl* and *Carnegie Hall.*

The plots of the rock pictures were minimal: the older folks disapproved of rock-and-roll and thought the kids were hoodlums, although they only really wanted to have a bit of fun. Mainly the plots were just thin frameworks on which to hang the music. When the popular "beach" films emerged in the early 1960s their premises were mostly an excuse to go surfing. They were also crammed with "now" musical groups like the Beach Boys and the Supremes, as were the "ski" pictures that followed.

The British Invasion beginning in 1964 gave the movies more material with which to exploit the popular music of the day. The Beatles and more transitory British groups had films devoted to them, usually produced by British companies. Several Brit bands appeared in American films and a few U.S. groups were seen in British films. The 1970s saw the featuring of musical groups diminish to almost the vanishing point, but many rock bands appeared in hard-edged documentaries like *Don't Look Back, Monterey Pop, Gimme Shelter* and *Woodstock.*

Television took its turn keeping the flame of musical ensembles burning. With great fanfare, variety shows like that of Ed Sullivan featured the top musical acts of the day as did teen magnets like *American Bandstand, Hullaballoo!* and *Shindig.* Interestingly, the so-called "girl groups" were rarely seen on mainstream shows like Ed Sullivan's, presumably because of their more blatant sexuality, but frequently were guests on *American Bandstand.* On record charts the girl groups, most of them African-American, accounted for the highest proportion of hits before the British Invasion but were not so well-represented in movies.

Trends rarely die a permanent demise, however. After the time covered in this book such ensembles as The Village People and the Ramones appeared in pictures; more recently the Spice Girls had their turn. The success of such stage shows as *Dreamgirls* (also a movie), *Forever Plaid* and *Jersey Boys* shows a continuing nostalgia for the "good old days" of golden oldies. And of course Hollywood has produced many films about fictional musical groups ranging from the mockumentary *This Is Spinal Tap* to *That Thing You Do!* to *Velvet Goldmine.*

There will probably never be a time when Hollywood does not hope to strike box office gold, so perhaps very popular "flavor of the month" groups will make films in the future.

There is no question that some of the music groups that did appear in features seemed eminently forgettable, and at the time were only considered to be passing entertainment. But it would be a mistake to completely overlook them.

Now we understand that they were part of the history of musical entertainment and even somewhat of the social history of their time. For those that performed prior to the days of modern media, their films (if they are not lost), old stills and photographs are all we have to preserve their visual existence. As for their sounds, scratchy recordings may have to suffice if indeed they even exist. Perhaps as important, when we do get a glimpse of them they can still have the power to entertain us.

* * *

The book is arranged according to the way groups were actually billed in films; e.g., Cab Calloway and His Band, *not* Calloway, Cab, and His Band. Commonly-occurring alternate forms of billing like Hal Grayson and His Orchestra and Hal Grayson's Orchestra appear together.

Ample "*see*" references are supplied, such as Night Jumpers *see* Jimmy Bryant and the Night Jumpers. In cases where a "*see*" reference leads to more than one form of billing, the name is followed by an ellipsis: Hall, Juanita *see* Juanita Hall... (and not *see* Juanita Hall Singers and Juanita Hall Choir).

In a relatively few cases disparate groups that were led by the same performer have been placed together for the reader's convenience, not because they are alternate forms of billing. Example: Herb Jeffries and the Four Tones and Herb Jeffries' Calypsomaniacs. Other disparate-sounding groups are placed together because they may have changed their names over time, or had many of the same members, and thus are more closely related than it might appear; for example, those under the heading of Jimmie Davis.

If it is known what movie song(s) a group performed, the title or titles follow the name of the film in the filmographies at the end of each entry. The great majority of films listed are features but there are some documentaries included. While most groups made only features, a small number made a mixture of features and documentaries and a few made only documentaries. It was deemed useful not to omit major musical ensembles because they can be seen only in fact-based films.

In a relatively few instances there seems no reliable way of confirming what the nature of the group was. In cast lists and reviews they simply appear as "Specialty" or "Specialty act" or the even more unhelpful "Themselves." Thus there may be some non-singing/non-instrumental groups inadvertently included. In cases of doubt the word "unknown" in brackets follows the group's name, as: Two Fat Men [unknown].

A relatively few British groups have been included because, as mentioned above, some bands from Great Britain appeared in American movies. They are meant to be a representative sampling and not all may have appeared in U.S. films. Appendix One contains a more comprehensive listing of British bands that appeared in films, but it is also not intended to be a complete accounting.

Finally, Appendix Two has a lengthy list of groups that were neither singers nor instrumentalists but, to the audience's enjoyment, caused music to issue from the screen. These are primarily dance duos (but sometimes larger ensembles), skaters and other specialties. It is not meant to include performers like Fred Astaire and Ginger Rogers who were primarily actors teamed together to dance for given films.

Musical Groups in the Movies

Abe Lyman and His Band; Abe Lyman and His Californians; Abe Lyman and His Orchestra

Abe Lyman (Abraham Simon, Chicago, Illinois, 1897–1957)

Having begun as a nickelodeon and club drummer in his mid-teens, Abe Lyman brought his musicality to his own orchestra The Californians beginning in 1921. They began making records a couple of years later, among the first to record on the West Coast. Not surprisingly, "California, Here I Come" was their theme song.

Lyman gave up the band a while later to tour in vaudeville but eventually re-constituted it and it became a fixture at the famed Cocoanut Grove nightclub in Hollywood. The orchestra was in the right place at the right time to appear in several early talkies, and it remained popular into the mid–1940s.

Among the band's successful recordings were "Shake That Thing" and "California Blues." Abe Lyman himself was not considered a particularly talented bandleader but he had a personal style that appealed to audiences. He was also a noted songwriter with such standards as "I Cried for You," "After I Say I'm Sorry" and "Mandalay."

Hold Everything (1930) * *Pardon My Gun* (1930) * *Madam Satan* (1930) * *Ten Cents a Dance* (1931) * *Broadway Thru a Keyhole* (1933) * *Sweet Surrender* (1935) * *Junior Prom* (1946)

Ace of Cups

Denise Kaufman; Mary Ellen Simpson; Maria Hanson; Mary Gannon; Diane Vitalich

One of the very few all-female bands of the 1960s, the Ace of Cups was a San Francisco group which performed locally for most of its career and opened for acts that included the Jefferson Airplane. They disbanded in 1972 without making any recordings as far as is known. Their name was derived from the tarot card portraying five streams of water issuing from the hand of God.

Revolution (1968) [documentary]

Acker Bilk and His Paramount Jazz Band

Acker Bilk (Bernard Bilk, Pensford, England, 1929–)

If he were known for nothing else, Acker Bilk would still be world-famous for his hauntingly beautiful instrumental recording of "Stranger on the Shore." Aside from that he has been considered one of the world's great clarinetists since the late '50s. Usually billed as *Mr.* Acker Bilk (the nickname Acker derives from the British slang term for friend), he began playing in jazz orchestras before forming his own group about 1956.

With the British Invasion Bilk's brand of music — generally called trad jazz — became less saleable, but he continued to perform in cabarets and release albums, and had occasional recording successes like "Aria." He has referred to "Stranger on the Shore" as his "old age pension" and indeed it perseveres as one of the great melodies of all time.

It's Trad, Dad! (1962) * *It's All Over Town* (1963)

Acuff, Roy *see* Roy Acuff...

Airliners [unknown]

Junior Prom (1946)

Al Clauser and His Oklahoma Outlaws

Al Clauser (Henry Clauser, Manito, Illinois, 1911–1989); Curly Bray; Bud Roberts; Speed Foreman; Tex Hoeptner

Guitarist and songwriter Al Clauser may have been one of the first to popularize the term "western swing" in the late '20s. From the mid–1930s he and his string band (none of whom had ever previously been to Oklahoma despite their name) were staples on Midwestern and Oklahoma radio.

In the 1930s The Outlaws were carried on more than 230 stations. By the end of World War II the band had nine members and a very young singer named Clara Ann Fowler, later to be the famous Patti Page, who recorded her first song with them. The group disbanded in the 1950s; Clauser himself went to work on a television kiddie show.

Rootin' Tootin' Rhythm (1937)

Al Donahue and His Orchestra; Al Donahue's Orchestra

Al Donahue (1903–1983)

Nineteen twenty-five was the year in which the original orchestra of Al Donahue made its debut. They played everywhere from Boston to Florida and on steamships in between. So great became the demand from a particular hotel chain that he actually franchised his name so that there were numerous Donahue orchestras playing at any one time. Its (their) theme song was "Low Down Rhythm in a Top Hat."

By the 1940s Donahue's group became less of a hotel society band and more of a swing ensemble in order to compete with other big bands. He continued to tour extensively after relocating to the West Coast and ultimately became music director for a Bermuda-based steamship line.

Sweet Genevieve (1947)

Al Goodman and His Orchestra

Al Goodman (Alfred Goodman, Nikopol, Russia, 1890–1972)

In the mid–1930s Al Goodman's orchestra was the house band on radio's popular *Your Hit Parade*, and also appeared with Al Jolson and on the *Texaco Star Theater*. Later they worked on early television. Goodman also was a songwriter with such ditties as "Call of Love" and "Twilight" to his credit, and he contributed to Broadway musicals like the *Ziegfeld Follies* and *The Band Wagon*.

The Talk of Hollywood (1929)

Al Trace and His Silly Symphonists; Al Trace's Orchestra

Al Trace (Albert Trace, 1900–1993)

The very different songs "Mairzy Doats" and "You Call Everybody Darling" were the theme songs of Al Trace's orchestra. The latter, his own composition, was a number one hit in 1948. Although his band worked primarily in the Midwest, his 300-plus compositions, some written under pseudonyms like Clem Watts and Bob Hart, earned him a more national reputation. Among these were the novelty hit "If I'd Known You Were Comin' I'd Have Baked a Cake," "Monkey Doodle Doo" (sung in the Marx Brothers' first film *The Cocoanuts*) and "Wishin'." As the name Silly Symphonists implies, many of the songs performed by the band were comic ones, played with great Spike Jones–like gusto.

A drummer and sometime singer, Al Trace appeared with various groups and then formed his first band for the Chicago World's Fair in 1933. Thereafter they played at fashionable Chicago restaurants and hotels and on the radio. One of his ensembles was known as the Shuffle Rhythm band. He continued his musical activities up to 1975, and had also acted in some Charles Starrett westerns, even playing a sheriff in a few of them.

Rustlers of the Badlands (1945) * *Frontier Gun Law* (1946)

Albee Sisters [unknown]

Turn Off the Moon (1937)

Albert, Don *see* Don Albert and His Orchestra

Alice Cooper Band

Alice Cooper (Vincent Furnier, Detroit, Michigan, 1948–)

For a while Alice Cooper was the enfant terrible of the rock scene with his jet black hair, eye makeup and female drag costuming. He was notorious for supposedly biting the heads off chickens and thus was a pioneer of so-called "shock rock." Snakes were also a big part of the act, sometimes being used in most erotic ways. Other props seen in onstage were electric chairs, guillotines and gallows. He was also fond of misanthropically impaling female mannequins and smashing dolls.

Cooper first had a band called the Spiders, later to be the Nazz. He claims he got the professional name Alice Cooper when he asked a Ouija board whom he had been in a previous life. Such songs as "School's Out," "Only Women Bleed" and "I Never Cry" were popular, but it was his shtick that the public went for, and for a time in the early 1970s his was the hottest band in the world. He also appeared on his own in a few film roles.

Diary of a Mad Housewife (1970) "Ride with Me" * *Welcome to My Nightmare* (1975) [documentary]

All American Dance Band

Charlie Barnet; Benny Goodman; Harry James; Gene Krupa; Alvino Rey [and others]

The All American Dance Band was special indeed. It was made up of band leaders selected in a *Saturday Evening Post* poll and contained many of the great leaders of the day. Undoubtedly it was intended that they appear together in but one film.

Syncopation (1942)

All American Girl Band

The Joint Is Jumpin' (1949?)

All Girl Golden Slipper Band

Tall, Tan and Terrific (1946)

All-Stars *see* Teddy Buckner and His All-Stars; Tobin Mathews and the All Stars

Allen and Allen [unknown]

Beale Street Mama (1946?)

Allon Trio [unknown]

This Is the Army (1943)

Alvino Rey and His Orchestra

Alvino Rey (Alvin McBurney, Oakland, California, 1908–2004)

The so-called "King of the Guitar," Alvino Rey assumed his Spanish-sounding stage name at a time when Latin music was a hot commodity. He founded his dance orchestra in 1938 or '39 with four of the singing King Sisters, one of whom, Luise, he married. His opening theme song was the self-referential "Blue Rey"; the other was "Nighty Night."

A steel guitarist, Rey was a professional musician by age nineteen and had been a sideman with the Phil Spitalny, Russ Morgan and Horace Heidt orchestras. In the 1940s his own band had hits with the novelty tunes "Cement Mixer" and "Strip Polka," and with "Deep in the Heart of Texas."

Alvino Rey also is credited with developing several improvements to the guitar which led to the modern-day pedal guitar. In the 1960s he became a regular on the popular King Family television show; his last group was a jazz quartet that he formed in 1994 when he was well into his eighties.

Sing Your Worries Away (1942) * *Larceny with Music* (1943) * *Jam Session* (1944)

Amaral, Nestor *see* Nestor Amaral...

American G.I. Chorus

In their one film, which was baritone Nelson Eddy's final cinema outing, the American G.I. Chorus played prisoners.

Northwest Outpost (1947)

American Legion Band

Meet John Doe (1941)

American Revolution; Band Without a Name

The garage band American Revolution was previously called the Band Without a Name.

Thunder Alley (1967) "Thunder Alley" and "Time After Time" * *Born Wild* (1968) "Love Has Got Me Down"

American Rough Riders [unknown]

The Way of the West (1934)

Americans *see* Jay and the Americans

Ames, Ramsay *see* Ramsay Ames and Her Tropicanans

Andre Kostelanetz and His Orchestra

Andre Kostelanetz (St. Petersburg, Russia, 1901–1980)

Well-known for his great success in bringing so-called light classics to a mass public, Andre Kostelanetz sold a huge number of recordings, estimated to be in the fifty million range. His arrangements of popular music came to be called the "Kostelanetz sound," and he was both praised and criticized for stripping (some said bastardizing) classics down to their "essential" themes.

He also commissioned several new works from prominent American composers like Aaron Copland, Virgil Thompson, Ferde Grofe and Alan Hovhaness.

Kostelanetz had conducted opera companies in Europe prior to working at American radio networks starting in the late 1920s. He led the CBS Symphony Orchestra and was guest conductor for the New York Philharmonic for almost thirty years. One legendary concert he conducted in New York's Central Park in the 1960s was said to have attracted 200,000 people.

Artists and Models (1937) * *Music in My Heart* (1940)

Andrews Sisters

Laverne Andrews (Minneapolis, Minnesota, 1911–1967) (alto); Maxene Andrews (Minneapolis, Minnesota, 1916–1995) (2nd soprano); Patty Andrews (Patricia Andrews, Mound, Minnesota, 1918–) (soprano/lead vocals)

The three Andrews Sisters were perhaps the most iconic of all the sister acts. They were the very symbols of the home front during World War II with such standards as "Boogie Woogie Bugle Boy" and "Don't Sit Under the Apple Tree," and also had big hits with "Beer Barrel Polka," "Rum and Coca Cola," "Bei Mir Bist Du Schoen" (their first big success) and "Beat Me Daddy, Eight to the Bar."

The Andrews' numerous hit records, alone or with others such as Bing Crosby and Glenn Miller, ranged from patriotic to comic to romantic and suited almost every taste. They are credited with recording several hundred songs (of which nineteen garnered gold records) and selling some 90 million records.

Performing since about 1931, the Sisters toured on Midwest vaudeville circuits as admitted emulators of the then-popular Boswell Sisters. For the entire decade of the 1940s they remained at the top, but eventually the same changes that sent the big bands into decline affected their careers as well. In 1951 they more or less officially disbanded.

For a brief time both Patty and Maxene (considered the "pretty" one) tried to make it as solos but they re-teamed and continued performing, mainly in nightclubs, until Laverne's death. *Over There!*, a nostalgic stage musical based on their career, proved a smash hit and there was even a 1990s ballet, *Company B*, which used many of their hit records as its predominant musical score.

In movies the Andrews were sometimes top-billed and always played "themselves," with rubber-faced Patty getting the most attention. She had the majority of the lines and proved adept at comedy, more than holding her own with such veterans as Abbott and Costello. In later years she appeared solo in 1970's *The Phynx* and *The Gong Show Movie* (1980). Most often the Sisters were dressed exactly alike, as if they were triplets, because in its typical way Hollywood saw them as an inseparable ensemble, not individuals.

Argentine Nights (1940) * "Rhumboogie," "Oh He Loves Me," and "Hit the Road" * *Buck Privates* (1941) * "I'll Be with You in Apple Blossom Time," "Boogie Woogie Bugle Boy" and "You're a Lucky Fellow, Mr. Smith" * *In the*

The Andrews Sisters (from left, Maxene, Patty, La Verne) during World War II.

Navy (1941) * *Hold That Ghost* (1941) "Aurora" * *What's Cookin'?* (1942) * *Private Buckaroo* (1942) "Don't Sit Under the Apple Tree" and "Three Little Sisters" * *Give Out, Sisters* (1942) "Pennsylvania Polka" and "The New Generation" * *How's About It?* (1943) "Beer Barrel Polka" with new lyrics and re-titled "Here Comes the Navy," "East of the Rockies" and "Going Up" * *Swingtime Johnny* (1943) * *Always a Bridesmaid* (1943) "Thanks for the Buggy Ride," "That's My Affair" and "As Long As I Have You" * *Follow the Boys* (1944) * *Hollywood Canteen* (1944) * *Moonlight and Cactus* (1944) * *Her Lucky Night* (1945) "Straighten Up and Fly Right," "Is You Is or Is You Ain't My Baby?" and "The Polka Polka" * *Make Mine Music* (voices only) (1946) * "Johnny Fedora and Alice Bluebonnet" * *Road to Rio* (1947) * *Melody Time* (voices only) (1948)

Andy Iona and His Recording Hawaiians; Iona's Islanders

Andy Iona (Andy Long, Honolulu, Hawaii, 1902–1966)

A composer, songwriter and conductor, Andy Iona and his band the Islanders became the resident Hawaiian ensemble for Columbia Records. They played the kind of music that the haoles (tourists) considered "typical" Hawaiian music as well as more traditional native music and popular tunes.

In their 1930s heyday the Islanders were certainly one of the most famous Hawaiian bands in the world, performing at top hotels and clubs. They also recorded hundreds of tunes, many written by Iona himself, including "The Palm Trees Sing Aloha," "An Island Melody," "Pretty Red Hibiscus" and "On a Cocoanut Island."

Besides the couple of films in which he appeared onscreen, Andy Iona composed for pictures, toured with ice skating queen Sonia Henie for many years and recorded with another famous Hawaiian ensemble, the Sal Hoopii Trio. He was named to the Royal Hawaiian Steel Guitar Hall of Fame and Museum.

I Cover Chinatown (1936) * *Honolulu* (1939)

Andy Kirk and His Orchestra

Andy Kirk (Denver, Colorado or Newport, Kentucky, 1896/98–1992)

Saxophone player Andy Kirk played in various orchestras before establishing his own in 1929, an offshoot of the group called the Dark Clouds of Joy. He re-dubbed it Andy Kirk and the Twelve Clouds of Joy and it was active for almost twenty years, until 1948. One of their record hits was "Until the Real Thing Comes Along" which became their theme song.

Killer Diller (1948)

Andy Parker and the Plainsmen

Andy Parker (Mangum, Oklahoma, 1913–1977); Hank Caldwell (bassist); Charlie Morgan (guitar); George Bamby (accordion); Earl "Joaquin" Murphey (steel guitar); Harry Simms (fiddle); Paul "Clem" Smith (bassist); Leroy Kruble (accordion); Deuce Spriggins; Noel Boggs

A most popular western swing group, Andy Parker and his Plainsmen were familiar sights in radio and television, "B" oaters and even nightclubs. They also made numerous recordings, among them the hit "When It's Lamp Lighting Time in the Valley." Unlike most other country groups most of the members were not Southerners and they had had formal music training.

Parker had been an announcer and the voice of the "Singing Cowboy" on radio's *Death Valley Days* before the Plainsmen was formed in the mid–1940s. The group started out as a trio but soon expanded. The ensemble's longest association with any western movie star was the one with Eddie Dean for seven films beginning in 1947.

The Plainsmen also branched out with a Betty Grable "A" film. Andy Parker was a songwriter with hits to his credit like "Trail Dust," "A Calico Apron and a Gingham Gown," "Serenade to a Coyote" and the title song of the movie *Throw a Saddle on a Star*. He disbanded the group in the late 1950s; they were later inducted into the Western Music Hall of Fame.

Cowboy Blues (1946) * *Singing on the Trail* (1946) * *That Texas Jamboree* (1946) * *Shadow Valley* (1947) * *The Black Hills* (1947) * *Check Your Guns* (1948) * *The Hawk of Powder River* (1948) * *The Tioga Kid* (1948) * *The Westward Trail* (1948) * *Tornado Range* (1948) * *The Beautiful Blonde from Bashful Bend* (1949) * *River of No Return* (1954)

Anestos [unknown]

Minstrel Man (1944)

Animals

Eric Burdon (Walker-on-Tyne, England, 1941–) (vocals); Alan Price (keyboard); Charles Chandler (1939?–1996) (bassist); John Steel; Hilton Valentine; Dave Rowberry (1941?–2003) (keyboard)

One of the greatest bands to come to the shores of America in the wake of the British Invasion were the Animals whose recording of "The House of the Rising Sun" became an enduring classic. Other big hits were "We've Gotta Get Out of this Place" and "Don't Let Me Be Misunderstood."

They had begun as the Alan Price Combo and became the Animals about 1964 with the arrival of lead singer Eric Burdon. Hearing his passionately raw voice, seemingly almost untrained, was a powerful experience. Besides the films in which the Animals appeared together, Burdon played solo parts in the 1970s and '80s. After the Animals disbanded in 1966 he formed the bands Fire Department, War, and the Eric Burdon Band.

Get Yourself a College Girl (1964) * "Blue Feeling" and "Around and Around" * *Pop Gear* (1965) [documentary] "House of the Rising Sun" and "Don't Let Me Be Misunderstood" * *Go-Go Big Beat* (1965) [documentary] "Baby Let Me Take You Home" * *Go-Go Mania* (1965) * *It's a Bikini World* (1967) "We've Gotta Get Out of This Place" * *Tonite Let's All Make Love in London* (1967) [documentary] "When I Was Young" * *Monterey Pop* (1969) [documentary] "Paint It Black"

Anita Kerr Singers

Anita Kerr (Anita Grilli, Memphis, Tennessee, 1927–); Dottie Dillard (alto); Gil Wright (tenor); Louis Nunley (baritone)

Country singer Anita Kerr founded an ensemble that proved very popular as back-up singers for many country artists in the 1950s and '60s. It is estimated that they were heard on hundreds of recordings and they also appeared much on television, including the Arthur Godfrey and Smothers Brothers' shows. She also was a music arranger and composer of scores for television and movies.

When an entirely reconstituted group recorded with pop poet Rod McKuen they were dubbed the San Sebastian Strings and Singers. They also bore other names like Anita and the So and So's, under which handle they recorded the rock song "Joey Baby," and were known as the Little Dippers for "Forever."

At times the Anita Kerr Singers numbered as many as eight performers. Their own records were a mix of popular, gospel and "golden" classic tunes and they issued numerous albums, ultimately winning two Grammys. Kerr herself is credited with being one of the progenitors of the so-called Nashville Sound.

Country Music on Broadway (1964) [documentary]

Anson Weeks and His Orchestra

Anson Weeks (Oakland, California, 1896–1969)

"Come dancin' with Anson" was Anson Weeks' snappy tagline; his theme song, "I'm Writing You This Little Melody." He had formed his dance orchestra in 1924 and remained the house bandleader at San Francisco's fashionable Mark Hopkins Hotel for several years into the mid–1930s. The orchestra's shows there were

The Animals. Eric Burdon, second from right.

broadcast on local radio; it was not long before they got a national radio show as well.

Moving to New York sometime in the 1930s, the orchestra established itself at the tony St. Regis Hotel. After being injured in an accident, Weeks could only lead a band sporadically in the 1940s, mainly in San Francisco, and gave it up altogether in the post–War period.

Anson Weeks ultimately returned with smaller groups and was still working with a combo in the 1960s, albeit at venues far removed from those of his glory days. Among his alumni were several who later became famous in their own right: Dale Evans, Tony Martin, Bob Crosby and the inimitable Xavier Cugat.

Melody Parade (1943) * *The Big Show-Off* (1945) * *Rhythm Inn* (1951)

Anthony, Ray *see* **Ray Anthony...**

Ape Men *see* **Sam and the Ape Men**

Apollon, Dave *see* **Dave Apollon and His Orchestra**

Appel, Dave *see* **Dave Appel and the Applejacks**

Applejacks *see* **Dave Appel and the Applejacks**

Arcaraz, Luis *see* **Luis Arcaraz and His Orchestra**

Arias, Jose *see* **Jose Arias...**

Arizona Wranglers; Range Ranglers; Singing Constables; Wranglers

Hungry (Joe Ivins or Ivans) (mandolin); Iron Tail (Charles Hunter) (banjo); Dynamite (Len Dossey) (fiddle); Nubbins (J. E. Patterson) (guitar); Slicker (Laverne Costello) (banjo); Sleepy (Calvin Short) (harmonica); Loyal Underwood; Pee Wee (Glenn Strange, Weed, New Mexico, 1899–1973); Jack Kirk; Jack Jones; Chuck Baldra; Curtis McPeters; Ace Spriggins

The three men who were to form the Arizona Wranglers first came together as part of a band sponsored by the XXX Rootbeer Drive-in in Phoenix, Arizona. This rather unique beginning led to radio where the members assumed nicknames like Slicker, Hungry, Sleepy, Iron Tail, Nubbins and Dynamite.

Their real names were not publicized. Hulking Glenn Strange, who later became a character actor with such roles as Frankenstein's monster and a stint on television's *Gunsmoke* to his credit, was, not unexpectedly, dubbed Pee Wee.

The band had originally been known as "Sheriff" Loyal Underwood and His Arizona Wranglers during the late '20s and early '30s. With shifting membership, the Wranglers were also variously called the Range Ranglers, the Singing Constables, the Wranglers, the Radio Buckaroos and perhaps other names as well.

Stormy (1935) * *Cyclone of the Saddle* (1935) "Goin' Home," "The Old Wagon Train," "There's No Place Like Home" and "Range Riders" * *His Fighting Blood* (1935) * *The Law of 45's* (1935) * *Lawless Range* (1935) * *Westward Ho* (1935)

Armstrong, Louis *see* **Louis Armstrong...**

Arnall, Red *see* **Red Arnall and the Western Aces**

Arnaz, Desi *see* **Desi Arnaz and His Orchestra**

Arnheim, Gus *see* **Gus Arnheim...**

Art Davis and His Rhythm Riders

Art Davis (Audrey Davis, Texas, 1913–1987); Ace Dehne (guitar); Gene Haas; Rusty Cline (bassist); Tony Fiore (accordion)

Besides the feature film the Riders made a musical short, and Art Davis appeared as a solo performer in numerous "B" oaters.

The Texas Marshal (1941)

Art West and His Sunset Riders

Over the Santa Fe Trail (1947)

Artie Shaw and His Band

Artie Shaw (Arthur or Abraham Arshawsky, New York, New York, 1910–2004)

Clarinetist Artie Shaw was indisputably one of the greats of swing music. As a teenager he was already playing tenor sax in orchestras before switching to the clarinet, the instrument that made him a legend. In the mid–'30s he formed a string quartet that played his own compositions; the use of strings in a swing ensemble caused a sensation.

In 1936 he formed his first small band, then subsequently a big band that had its first major hit with "Begin the Beguine." This recording is among the biggest-selling of all time. Other hits were "Frenesi," "Indian Love Call," "'S'wonderful" and "What Is This Thing Called Love?"

In an era when bandleaders were expected to connect with their audiences, Shaw was touted as an intellectual and was considered something of an aloof snob. He openly disdained his fellow musicians for their lack of interests outside of music. "I'm cursed with serious-mindedness," he lamented. He also complained "I'm unhappy in the music business. Maybe I don't even belong in it ... for me the business part plain stinks."

Because of his dislike of being in the public gaze, Artie Shaw kept disbanding and re-starting bands, a pattern that went on into the 1980s. (At some point his theme song was the tellingly-titled "Nightmare.") His interest in classical music grew and he often appeared with symphony orchestras. He also satisfied his desire to be a writer, something that seemed to be his ultimate goal in life. (One of his works of fiction was entitled *I Love You, I Hate You, Drop Dead!*)

At times, Artie Shaw was as much publicized for his chaotic personal life (several non-lasting marriages with glamorous actresses like Ava Gardner, Evelyn Keyes and Lana Turner) and acerbic personality (he said his epitaph should read "Go away") as for his great musicianship. His celebrity always seemed a burden to him, but in spite of his efforts to escape it he never could. A 1985 documentary *Artie Shaw: Time Is All You've Got* was produced in Canada.

The Dancing Co-Ed (1939) * *Second Chorus* (1940) "Concerto for Clarinet" and "Frenesi"

Artie Sims and His Band
The Fight Never Ends (1948)

Ascencio Del Rio Trio
Ofelia Ascencio; Sara Ascencio; Emmy Del Rio
Tropic Holiday (1938) * *The Three Caballeros* (1944) (voices only?)

Astronauts
Rich Fifield (guitar); Bob Demmon (guitar); Dennis Lindsey (guitar); Jon Patterson (bassist); Jim Gallagher; Steve Douglas (Steve Kreisman) (saxophone)

Formed in the Boulder, Colorado area as the Stormtroopers about 1959, the Astronauts assumed their final name in 1962. They were a surf band in the style of the Beach Boys. Their only real hit was "Baja," but there were eight albums issued from 1963 to '65.

Surf Party (1964) * "Fire Water" and "Surf Party" * *Wild on the Beach* (1965) "Rock This World," "Little Speedy Gonzalez," "Snap It" and "Pyramid Stomp" * *Out of Sight* (1966) "Baby, Please Don't Go" * *Wild Wild Winter* (1966) "A Change of Heart"

Atkins, Tommy see Tommy Atkins Sextet

Atlanta Stone Mountain Choir
Stars and Stripes Forever (1952)

Avalon Boys
Chill Wills (1902–1978) (bass); Art Green; Walter Trask; Don Brookins

Led by deep-voiced Chill Wills, who went on to have a noted career as a character actor, the Avalon Boys were a popular quartet in the 1930s. They are without doubt best remembered for appearing with Laurel and Hardy in the classic western spoof *Way Out West*, in which the comedy duo did a charming dance to one of their tunes.

It's a Gift (1934) * *Bar 20 Rides Again* (1935) * *Anything Goes* (1936) * *Call of the Prairie* (1936) * *Nobody's Baby* (1937) * *Hideaway Girl* (1937) * *Way Out West* (1937)

Ayres, Mitch see Mitch Ayres and His Orchestra

Bachelors
Conleth Cluskey (1941–); Declan Cluskey (1942–); John Stokes (1940–)

In 1957 three young Irish lads founded the harmonica band the Harmonichords, later to become the Bachelors. They specialized in playing really old sentimental tunes with girls' names from the 1920s and '30s like "Ramona," "Marie," "Charmaine" and "Diane" and somewhat newer — but still sentimental — ones like "Chapel in the Moonlight" and "I Believe." Given their lovely sound, all were recording hits. The original group split in the 1980s and now there are two trios touring as the Bachelors.

It's All Over Town (1963) * *I've Gotta Horse* (1965) * *Disk-O-Tek Holiday* (1966) "Teenage Valentino," "The Fox" and "Low in the Valley"

Ball, Kenny *see* **Kenny Ball and His Jazzmen**

Ballew, Smith *see* **Smith Ballew and the Sons of the Sage**

Band Without a Name *see* **American Revolution**

Banda da Lua; Carmen Miranda Band

Itelio Jordao; Osvaldo Moraes Eboli; Aloysio Oliveira; Afonso Osorio; Stenio Osorio; Anibal Augusto Sardinha

The colorfully-garbed band that accompanied "Brazilian Bombshell" Carmen Miranda (1909–1955) to the United States in the late 1930s was alternatively known as the Banda da Lua and the Carmen Miranda Band. The latter name was undoubtedly used to capitalize on the somewhat meteoric American rise of the performer, who had been a major star in Brazil.

Miranda first appeared on Broadway before making her American film debut in *Down Argentine Way*. Her colorful (not to say garish) costumes, garbled English and spirited singing and dancing made her a much-imitated star in early 1940s 20th Century–Fox musicals. Her popularity — and therefore screen opportunities for the Banda da Lua — waned in the second half of the decade.

Down Argentine Way (1940) * *That Night in Rio* (1941) * *Springtime in the Rockies* (1942) * *The Gang's All Here* (1943) * *Greenwich Village* (1944) * *Something for the Boys* (1944) * *Nancy Goes to Rio* (1950)

Bangles
The Hooked Generation (1968)

Bantams
Mike Kirchner (1954?–); Jeff Kirchner (1956?–); Fritz Kirchner (1957?–)

Dubbed the "Kid Beatles," the Bantams released a mid–1960s album that featured cover versions of popular Beatles tunes. Signed by Warner Brothers to a five picture contract when the oldest brother was only twelve, they were billed as "three pre-teens with a rocking sound three times their size." In their second film they were billed as Mike, Jeff and Fritz Bantam.

The Cool Ones (1967) "I'm so Happy" * *You've Got to Be Smart* (1967)

Barbarians
Victor Moulton (drums)

A Cape Cod, Massachusetts, garage band, the Barbarians formed about 1963 and had a mild hit with "Are You a Boy or Are You a Girl?" They may have stood out from other such groups because their drummer had only one hand and a hook on the other. Their song "Moulty" memorialized him before the group disbanded about 1966.

The T.A.M.I. Show (1964) [documentary] "My Little Girl"

Barber, Chris *see* **Chris Barber...**

Barefield, Eddie *see* **Eddie Barefield's Trio**

Barnet, Charlie *see* **Charlie Barnet and His Orchestra**

Barra, Cappy *see* **Cappy Barra...**

Barrett, Curt *see* **Curt Barrett...**

Bar-Six Cowboys *see* **Ray Whitley and His Bar-Six Cowboys**

Basie, Count *see* **Count Basie...**

Basin Street Boys
Steve Gibson; Louis Dandridge; Joe Walls; Lloyd Mitchell; Pods Hollinsworth; George Thompson; Perry Anderson; Sam Hutcherson

There were two distinct groups called the

Basin Street Boys and the one formed in the 1940s was probably the more memorable. However, it was the earlier group which appeared in motion pictures. They were apparently given their name by a bandleader who thought that famous New Orleans landmark would give the group cachet, even if they had no known connection with that city.

Also previously known as the Four Dots and the Esquires, the Basin Street Boys began performing in the 1930s. They apparently issued only a single record (the racy "Come John Come") but were featured in some animated shorts like *Clean Pastures*, a parody of the famous *Green Pastures*. Steve Gibson went on to found the well-known Redcaps.

Top of the Town (1937) * *The Duke Is Tops* (1938)

Beach Boys

Brian Wilson (Hawthorne, California, 1942–); Dennis Wilson (Inglewood, California, 1944–1983); Carl Wilson (1946–1998); Mike Love (Los Angeles, California, 1941–); Al Jardine (Alan Jardine, Lima, Ohio, 1942–); Bruce Johnston; David Marks; Blondie Chaplin; Rick Fataar

Bands come and go with astonishing rapidity but the Beach Boys will undoubtedly remain one of the most iconic long after all the original members have passed from the scene. Their musical influence is still strong because they were able to evolve beyond their modest beginnings as a Southern California surf band. This is largely due to the troubled genius of Brian, the eldest Wilson brother and the driving force behind their success.

Formed in 1961 by the three Wilson brothers, their cousin and a friend, the Beach Boys began life as, variously, Kenny and the Cadets, Carl and the Passions and the Pendletones (after their clean cut image at the time). Early hits were typical surfing tunes like "Surfin' U.S.A." and "Surfin' Safari" that seemed to perfectly capture the fabled sun–drenched beach culture of the early and mid–1960s.

Songs such as "Little Deuce Coupe" and "Fun, Fun, Fun" continued to reflect the tastes of their largely teenage audiences. But the surf/beach movie craze was beginning to wane and the Beach Boys music widened its appeal. After roaring successes like "Help Me Rhonda" and "I Get Around" came one of the all-time greats, "Good Vibrations," a groundbreaking song that supposedly took Brian Wilson six months to perfect.

Eventually the successfully reinvented Beach Boys were touring and playing at venues like Carnegie Hall. From 1962 to 1981 they were only off the pop charts for two years and in the late '80s came additional hits. Their golden image survived years of struggle and continues to shine. A documentary about their career, *The Beach Boys: an American Band*, came out in 1985 and they were the subject of a made-for-television movie.

One Man's Challenge (1962) "Surfin' Safari" * *The T.A.M.I. Show* (1964) [documentary] "Surfin' U.S.A.," Surfer Girl" and other songs * *The Girls on the Beach* (1965) "The Girls on the Beach," "Lonely Sea" and "Little Honda" * *The Monkey's Uncle* (1965) "The Monkey's Uncle" * *Popcorn; an Audio/Visual Rock Thing* (1969) [documentary]

Bead Game

The People Next Door (1970) "Sweet Medusa" and "My Life in Review"

Beale Street Boys

Gus Cannon; Noah Lewis; Hosea Woods

Probably founded in the 1920s, the Beale Street Boys were a string/jug band that accompanied such greats as Fats Waller. One of the members wrote "Walk Right In," much later popularized by the Rooftop Singers during the folk music era. There apparently have been a few bands with this name, including the doo wop group that was popular in the late 1940s.

The Gift of Gab (1934)

Beatles

Paul McCartney (Liverpool, England, 1942–) (guitar); John Lennon (Liverpool, England, 1940–1980) (guitar); George Harrison (Liverpool, England, 1943–2001) (guitar); Ringo Starr (Richard Starkey, Liverpool, England, 1940–) (drums)

The group that started out as the Quarrymen and Johnny and the Moondogs, etc. was simply the biggest phenomenon in pop music history (although Elvis Presley fans might beg to differ).

They were a harbinger of the British Invasion, and are still considered one the greatest (as opposed to only the most popular) musical groups for their ever-maturing musicianship and, not incidentally, showmanship.

"Love Me Do" was only a minor hit on its introduction in England but a major one when it debuted in the U.S. in early 1964. From there it was immense fame and fortune for the so-called "mop tops" who dressed in tight Edwardian-style clothes and broadcast their insouciant opinions for all to hear. It did not hurt that John Lennon and Paul McCartney were master songwriters as well as performers. Early bubblegum-type hits like "I Want to Hold Your Hand" and "Can't Buy Me Love" were succeeded in the later years of their collaboration by numerous more musically complex compositions.

The Beatles' "Yesterday" is the most covered song in history, with more than 3,000 different recordings. It is estimated that sales of their music, including tapes, CDs and albums (e.g., *Sgt. Pepper's Lonely Hearts Club Band*, the *White Album* and *Revolver*) have sold more than one *billion* copies. Their final live performance came in 1969 and McCartney, Harrison and Lennon (murdered in 1980) went on to sterling careers of their own. Lennon often performed with his wife Yoko Ono, including in the Plastic Ono Band that appeared in the movie *Sweet Toronto* in 1970.

Their first movie *A Hard Day's Night*, directed by American Richard Lester, easily stands on its own as a most worthy comedy film, and is arguably the best movie made by any pop group. Drummer Ringo Starr, cast as the comedian of the Beatles, went on to an acting career of his own and appeared in several American films as a solo performer.

A Hard Day's Night (1964) "A Hard Day's Night," "Can't Buy Me Love" and several other songs * *What's Happening! The Beatles in the U.S.A.* (1964) [documentary] * *Pop Gear* (1965) [documentary] "She Loves You" and "Twist and Shout"* *Help!* (1965) "Help!," "Ticket to Ride" and several other songs * *Yellow Submarine* (voices only) (1969) "Eleanor Rigby," "Yellow Submarine," "When I'm Sixty-Four" and many other songs * *Let It Be* (1970) [documentary] * *The Day the Music Died* (1977) [documentary]

Beau Brummels

Sal Valentino (Sal Spampinato) (vocals); Ron Elliott (guitar); Ron Meagher (bassist); John Petersen (drummer); Declan Mulligan (guitar)

One of the first San Francisco–based groups to find national success, the Beau Brummels had a series of hits including "Laugh, Laugh," "You Tell Me Why" and "Just a Little." Many of their songs were written by guitarist Ron Elliott. Their name supposedly came about as a homage to British music.

Founded in 1964, the Beau Brummels disbanded about four years later and have briefly reunited a few times. They issued several albums and are considered a forerunner to the garage bands of today. Their "Laugh, Laugh" was chosen by the Rock and Roll Hall of Fame as one of the 500 greatest songs in R & R history.

The Village of the Giants (1965) "Woman, When It Comes to Your Love" * *Wild, Wild Winter* (1966) "Just Wait and See"

Bee Gees

Barry Gibb (Isle of Man, England, 1946–); Maurice Gibb (Isle of Man, England, 1949–2003); Robin Gibb (Isle of Man, England, 1949–)

The three brothers Gibb (Maurice and Robin were fraternal twins) were among the major voices of disco music in the 1970s with their driving, falsetto-enhanced hits such as "Stayin' Alive" and "You Should Be Dancing." They had been recording since the early 1960s and had hits in Australia before transferring some of their popularity to America with recordings like "I Started a Joke" and "Massachusetts."

It was the sound track of the 1977 John Travolta smash hit film *Saturday Night Fever* that made them household words. The sound track album from that movie remains one of the best-selling of all times with an estimated 40 million to date. Besides "Stayin' Alive," the singles "Night Fever" and "How Deep Is Your Love" rocketed to number one. They had an additional three more number one hits in short order. Younger brother Andy Gibb (1958–1988) also began a successful music career as a solo performer.

The Gibbs were so associated with the disco phenomenon that after its inevitable demise they found themselves unable to fully transfer their vast popularity into other kinds of music. When

Maurice died it was decided that they would not continue on as the Bee Gees, although the two remaining brothers have kept producing records. They were inducted into the Rock and Roll Hall of Fame in 1997 and the Vocal Music Hall of Fame in 2001.

Popcorn; an Audio/Visual Rock Thing (1969) [documentary]

Belew Twins

Bobby Belew; Benny Belew

Playing hillbilly-type music from an early age, the Belew Twins had their own television show that featured western music. They were somewhat imitative of the Everly Brothers.

Rock Baby, Rock It! (1957) "Hot Rock," "Lonesome" and "Love Me Baby"

Bell, Frankie *see* Frankie Bell and the Bellboys

Bell Boys *see* Jimmy Wakely...

Bell Sisters

Cynthia Strother (1935–); Kay Strother (1940–)

The Strother sisters were discovered on an early '50s television talent show when Cynthia was sixteen and Kay a mere eleven. They performed a song that Cynthia had written, titled "Bermuda," and both they and it became hits; the song sold more than one million copies. Adopting Bell, their mother's maiden name, for their act, the girls had follow-up hits that included "Wheel of Fortune" and "Hambone."

The winsome duo, who sometimes sang a cappella, appeared with many of the famous singers of the day (Perry Como, Rosemary Clooney, Bing Crosby, Mel Tormé and Frank Sinatra) on radio, and Bob Hope on television. They toured extensively; at age thirteen Kay was said to be youngest person ever to have gone on a USO tour (to Korea). Their careers peaked in the mid-'50s as they grew up but they continued to perform into the next decade.

Those Redheads from Seattle (1953) * *Cruisin' Down the River* (1953)

Bellboys *see* Frankie Bell and the Bellboys

Ben Bernie and Orchestra; Ben Bernie's Lads

Ben Bernie (Benjamin Anzelevitz, Bayonne, New Jersey, 1894–1943)

With his well-known catchword "yowsah," Ben Bernie was one of the few bandleaders with film roles big enough so that his characters had screen names other than his own. This was in part due to his expansive personality and gift for comedy. Known as the "Old Maestro," he had one of the top bands of the '20s and early 1930s with its theme songs "It's a Lonesome Old Town" and "Au Revoir, Pleasant Dreams."

Bernie had been in vaudeville in the 1910s before starting the band about 1922. It began as somewhat of a jazz ensemble and segued into the sweet band that enabled it to play at a posh New York hotel for a six year engagement. As a singer he was a proponent of the talk song: usually ⅞ talking and perhaps ⅛ singing. For publicity he and ex-vaudevillian columnist Walter Winchell engaged in a long-running "feud" which they carried into radio and the movies.

Shoot the Works (1934) * *Wake Up and Live* (1937) * *Love and Hisses* (1937)

Ben Carter Choir; Ben Carter's Colored Octette

Ben Carter (Benjamin Carter, Jr., Fairfield, Iowa, 1911–1946)

Originally a talent agent for African-American actors, Ben Carter found himself in demand for solo character roles in such 1930s–'40s films as *Little Old New York, Gone With the Wind, Maryland* and *Chad Hanna*.

Kentucky Blue Streak (1935) * *Mr. Big* (1943) * *Stars on Parade* (1944) * *Dixie Jamboree* (1944) * *This Is the Life* (1944)

Bender and Daum [unknown]

It All Came True (1940)

Benny Carter and His Band

Benny Carter (Bennett Carter, New York, New York, 1907–2003)

Equally at home on the trumpet, clarinet and saxophone, Benny Carter was one of the outstanding talents of the Big Band era. He was also the composer of such jazz standards as "When Lights Are Low" and "Blues in My Heart." As a teenager he had already been playing with some top African-American bands, including those of Earl Hines and Fletcher Henderson.

Carter formed his own big band in the early 1930s but disbanded it a couple of years later and then toured in Europe which welcomed him as a great exponent of the American jazz so loved over there. His enduringly successful band was started in 1938 and eventually contained sidemen like Miles Davis, before disbanding in 1946. "Melancholy Lullaby" was its theme song.

Some years later Benny Carter pared his orchestra down to a sextet and increasingly became involved in working for Hollywood studios, and later television, as a much in-demand arranger. He also worked for singers like Ella Fitzgerald, Billie Holiday and Louis Armstrong. He continued to tour, off and on, into the latter 1980s.

It was said of Benny Carter that "his playing is the rare combination of a ripened intellect and a complete musical soul." Dubbed "King" Carter by fellow musicians and still composing in his eighties, he was honored with many awards, including a Grammy Lifetime Achievement Award.

Thousands Cheer (1944)

Benny Goodman and His Band; Benny Goodman and His Orchestra; Benny Goodman Quartet

Benny Goodman (Benjamin Goodman, aka Beno Guttman, Chicago, Illinois, 1909–1986)

With the possible exception of Glenn Miller there simply was no more famous swing bandleader than Benny Goodman, the "King of Swing." His very name invokes that fabulous decade from the mid-1930s through the end of World War II: the Big Band Era. As a teenager, Benny Goodman and his clarinet were playing with the Ben Pollack orchestra and in the mid-1930s he formed his own band.

By 1935 the Goodman orchestra was nationally famous with literally thousands of young people jostling to get into their theater appearances. But the notoriously ambitious and demanding Benny Goodman was not wholly satisfied and in 1938 he was booked into Carnegie Hall for a landmark concert.

Goodman also formed a trio and then a quartet which was one of the first to feature African-American musicians (Lionel Hampton and Teddy Wilson) playing alongside their white colleagues. Although he can be credited with doing many positive things for band members, who included Bunny Berigan and Gene Krupa, he was also a martinet whose glare of dissatisfaction (dubbed the "Goodman ray") could inspire terror.

The band, whose theme songs included "Let's Dance" and "Don't Be That Way," continued to go from triumph to triumph with their popular radio show and a spate of hit recordings such as the legendary "Sing, Sing, Sing" and "Stompin' at the Savoy." Benny Goodman also turned with great success to classical music, recording several clarinet works by Mozart and Weber, as well as commissioning new works by Hindemith, Bartok, Stravinsky and Copland.

Never one to rest on his laurels and rarely satisfied, Goodman disbanded and re-formed his orchestra even when it was at the height of popularity. The 1955 film *The Benny Goodman Story*, starring Steve Allen, created new interest in the maestro and he got his own television show in the late 1950s. He continued to play into

Benny Goodman goes all out!

the 1980s. Besides the movies he made with his band he also played some solo roles (e.g., 1948's *A Song Is Born*), usually as "himself."

The Big Broadcast of 1937 (1936) * *Hollywood Hotel* (1938) * *The Powers Girl* (1943) * *The Gang's All Here* (1943) * *Stage Door Canteen* (1943) * *Sweet and Low-Down* (1944)

Bernard Brothers [unknown]
Panama Hattie (1942)

Bernie, Ben *see* Ben Bernie...

Bernie Lowe and His Orchestra
Bernie Lowe (Bernard Lowenthal, Philadelphia, Pennsylvania, 1917–1993)

Pianist Bernie Lowe had his own orchestra but was also a noted record producer who mentored several leading rock-and-roll groups including the Dovells.

Cha-Cha-Cha Boom (1956)

Betty and Beverly [unknown]
Casa Manana (1951)

Beverly Hill Billies
Elton Britt (James Baker, Marshall, Arkansas, 1913–1972) (harmonica and other instruments); Gabe Hemmingway (Curt Barrett); Mirandy (Martha Bauersfeld, Springfield, Missouri); Hank Skillet (Henry Blaeholder) (fiddle); Jad Scraggins (Ashley Dees) (guitar); Dave Donner (Stuart Hamblen); Lem H. Giles, H.D. [i.e., Horse Doctor] (Aleth Hansen, Wisconsin); Zeke Craddock (Leo Mannes, San Francisco, California) (accordion) Tom Murray (Chicago, Illinois(?)); Ezra Longnecker (Cyprian Paulette); Charlie Quirk (Charlie Slater, New York, New York); Rudy Sooter; Tall Feller (Glen Rice)

The establishment of the singing group the Beverly Hill Billies reads like something out of a Hollywood press agent's playbook, and could only have happened in that more naive age. In 1930 the ratings of a small radio station located near tony Beverly Hills, California needed a boost so one of the station executives claimed he had stumbled upon a lost village of hillbillies (complete with log cabins and a blacksmith) in the Malibu Mountains.

They supposedly had been out of touch with civilization for a century or more, but after much persuasion a few of them signed up with his station. The resulting Beverly Hill Billies became popular almost overnight and are considered the first Los Angeles–area country music group to have reached a wide audience. The act featured comedy, singing and yodeling, and they had such recording hits as "Red River Valley," "Cowboy Joe," "The Big Corral" and "When the Bloom Is on the Sage."

They were really a group of unaffiliated local musicians who had been playing for the movies, radio and area orchestras. After a couple of years with revolving membership, the group began drifting apart and at one point there were two groups claiming to be the "original" Hill Billies. One member founded his own band called, not unexpectedly, The *Hollywood* Hillbillies.

However, in one form or another they remained popular through the 1930s and proved to be influential with other western groups such as The Sons of the Pioneers.

Although they had a brief revival in the mid–1940s, an effort to bring them back in the next decade failed. They made the news a final time in 1963 when some of the former members sued the producers of the television hit *The Beverly Hillbillies* for infringement of their name—and won.

Frontier Justice (1935) * *Paradise Valley* (1936) * *The Big Show* (1936) * *Meet the Boyfriend* (1937) * *Tex Rides with the Boy Scouts* (1937) * *Rollin' Plains* (1938)

Big Brother and the Holding Company
Janis Joplin (Port Arthur, Texas, 1943–1970); Peter Albin (bassist); Travis Rivers; Sam Andrew

Aside from its singer Janis Joplin, Big Brother and the Holding Company was considered no more than a run-of-the-mill San Francisco Bay–area rock band. But she *was* its vocalist and her rawly passionate singing made them one of the hits of the now-legendary Monterey International Pop Festival in 1967. Her style was described as "cosmic."

The Company's big recordings included "Piece of My Heart" and "Ball and Chain." Joplin left the group in 1968 to form the Full Tilt Boogie Band and at her height of popularity was pulling down $50,000 a performance. She had the smash "Me and Bobby McGee" to her credit before her almost foreseeable early death from drug-related problems.

Petulia (1968) "Road Block" * *Monterey Pop* (1969) [documentary] "Ball and Chain"

Big Sid Catlett *see* Sid Catlett...

Bikini Sweethearts *see* Paul Hargett and His Bikini Sweethearts

Bilk, Acker *see* Acker Bilk and His Paramount Jazz Band

Bill Black's Combo

Bill Black (Tennessee, 1926–1965)

As an early exponent of rockabilly music, Bill Black teamed with guitarist Scotty Moore and an unknown named Elvis Presley to form a trio in the mid–1950s. They issued a few recordings before Presley soared to worldwide success; Black remained with him for a few more years.

He struck out on his own in 1959 with a rhythm-and-blues trio, the Bill Black Combo, and scored an almost immediate hit with "Smokie." Several more chart favorites followed: "White Silver Sands," "Josephine" and "Hearts of Stone." The Combo also toured with the Beatles on their very first American tour, but after the founder's death turned more to country music.

Teenage Millionaire (1961)

Bill Fleck and His Orchestra

Skybound (1935)

Bill Haley and His Comets

Bill Haley (William Haley, Highland Park, Michigan, 1925–1981); Frank Beecher; Joey D'Ambrosia (tenor sax); Greg Driscoll; John Grande (Philadelphia, Pennsylvania, 1930?–2006) (guitar); Dave Holly; Ralph Jones (drums); John Kay; Jim Lebak; Marshall Lytle (bassist); Steve Murray; Ray Parsons; Rudy Pompilli (tenor sax); Al Rex (bassist); Dick Richards, (drums); Pete Spencer; Jerry Tilley; Bill Williamson (guitar)

Now lauded as the "Father of Rock-and-Roll," guitarist Bill Haley was one of the first musicians to synthesize rhythm-and-blues, western swing, and hillbilly music into a sound that captured a white, teenage audience. One of his first groups was the Down Homers; another, the Four Aces of Western Swing, had a radio show in Pennsylvania. Haley also worked as a disc jockey at the station.

When a record producer thought of making the group a hillbilly band it was renamed Bill Haley and His Saddlemen (or Saddle Pals). They began recording cover versions of Black rhythm-and-blues songs and hit it big with "Rock the Joint." (He later claimed to have given rock-and-roll its name.) Bill Haley and the Comets then came into being with such hits as "Crazy, Man, Crazy," "Shake, Rattle and Roll," "Dim, Dim the Lights" and "Rock Around the Clock."

The latter song was used under the opening credits of the 1955 film *The Blackboard Jungle* and truly launched the rock-and-roll era. It subsequently sold more than twenty million records. For a brief time the group found fantastic success touring around the world, but soon others overshadowed Haley, the much more charismatic Elvis Presley being foremost among them.

Raspy-voiced Bill Haley, a rather homely, pudgy man, blind in one eye and with a trademark spit curl hairstyle was an unlikely candidate for film stardom. Although he did play "himself" in a few pictures, he could only find much work outside the U.S. in places like Mexico and England, and the majority of his pictures were made abroad. The group played together through the 1970s. It is estimated they had sold at least 60 million records. Haley, without the Comets, was inducted into the Rock and Roll Hall of Fame in 1997.

Rock Around the Clock (1956) * "Razzle Dazzle," "See You Later, Alligator," "Rudy's Rock," "Rock Around the Clock" and other songs * *Don't Knock the Rock* (1956) "Calling All Comets," "Hot Dog Buddy Buddy," "Rip It Up" and "Hook, Line and Sinker" * *Hier Bin Ich—Hier Bleib'ich* (Germany) (1958) * *Besito a Papa* (Mexico) (1960) * *Juventud Rebelde* (Mexico) (1961) * *A Ritmo de Twist* (Mexico) (1962) * *The London Rock and Roll Show* (1973) [documentary] * *Let the Good Times Roll* (1973) [documentary] * *Blue Suede Shoes* (1980) [documentary]

Bill Thompson Singers

The Big Beat (1958)

Billie and Blue [unknown]

Wild Wheels (1969)

Billy J. Kramer and the Dakotas

Billy J. Kramer (William Ashton, Liverpool, England, 1943–); Ray Jones; Tony Bookbinder; Mike Maxfield; Pete Maclaine; Robin MacDonald

With a string of hits in the mid–1960s, the British group Billy J. Kramer and the Dakotas was, for a brief while, one of the major bands in the British Invasion. The Dakotas had evolved via the names Billy Ford and the Phantoms and Billy Kramer and the Coasters. It no doubt helped immensely that most of their hits were written by Beatles John Lennon and Paul McCartney, generally songs that the Beatles did not themselves wish to record.

The Dakotas also covered some early Beatles' hits, but their most successful recordings included the catchy "Little Children," "Do You Want to Know a Secret?," "Bad to Me," "Planes and Boats and Trains" and "From a Window." By early 1966 the hits had stopped coming and the group disbanded within year or so. A new Dakotas re-formed in the 1980s.

The T.A.M.I. Show (1964) [documentary] "Little Children," "From a Window" and other songs * *Pop Gear* (1965) [documentary] "Little Children" * *Primitive London* (1965) [documentary]

Billy Lee's Band

Billy Lee (William Schlensker, Nelson, Indiana, 1929–1989)

A show business veteran at a very young age, Billy Lee had been on Chicago radio at the age of three. Trained at the ubiquitous Meglin Professional School for talented kids (or perhaps for children of hard-driving stage mothers), he was soon put into movies. After an appearance in an *Our Gang* short, he went into features in 1934 just in time to help put over the popular song "Wagon Wheels" in the western of the same name.

Lee had played the drums in a movie and in a later film he played with "his" band. It is possible that he did indeed have a viable band, but also possible that it was just a bunch of youngsters thrown together by the studio. Before he "retired" from the movies (i.e., grew up) in 1943, his best known role had been in *The Biscuit Eater* (1941).

Reg'lar Fellers (1941)

Billy May and Orchestra

Billy May (E. William May, Pittsburgh, Pennsylvania, 1916–2004)

Famous as an arranger, composer and conductor, Billy May did not have his own band until the 1950s, one of its hits being "In a Persian Market." Its theme song was the interestingly-named "Lean Baby." As early as 1938, he had played trumpet in Charlie Barnet's band and then appeared with Glenn Miller. His arrangement of the classic Ray Noble tune "Cherokee" is considered seminal, and he also arranged for such bandleaders as Ozzie Nelson and Phil Harris.

Among the May orchestra's musical signatures was the use of various trumpet mutes and the "slurping saxes," utilizing a glissando sound. He also worked with singers like Bing Crosby, Bobby Darin, Sammy Davis, Jr. and Ella Fitzgerald, produced some sixty albums for Columbia Records and wrote the scores for several Frank Sinatra films. Afterwards his work was heard on several television series, including *Naked City*.

Nightmare (1956)

Biltmore Quartet; Biltmore Trio

Eddie Bush; Paul Gibbons; Bill Seckler; Ches Kirkpartick

Hollywood Revue of 1929 (1929) * *Words and Music* (1929)

Bing Crosby and His Rhythm Boys

Bing Crosby (Harry Crosby, Tacoma, Washington, 1903–1977) (vocals); Al Rinker (1907–1982) (vocals); Harry Barris (1905–1962) (vocals/piano)

Bing Crosby and Al Rinker were in a college jazz band and vaudeville together before being teamed with Harry Barris when they joined Paul Whiteman's orchestra as vocalists. Barris was a talented songwriter who penned the standard "Mississippi Mud" among other tunes. The Rhythm Boys were largely a creation of Whiteman's for his film *King of Jazz*. Crosby, the ambitious crooner, soon became the dominant member of the group.

After being fired by Whiteman, probably because of Bing's drinking and devil-may-care attitude toward his work, the Rhythm Boys joined Gus Arnheim's band. It was not long before

Crosby began soloing more and more and released his first hit record "I Surrender Dear." He did not long remain a member of the Rhythm Boys, which soon broke up, and set out on a solo career that ultimately made him one of the world's most popular singers (the prototypical "crooner") and actors.

His movie career began in a low key with a series of Mack Sennett shorts, in one of which his theme song "When the Blue of the Night Meets the Gold of the Day" was featured. Barris also had a film career, mostly in bit roles in more than fifty movies, playing the piano in nightclub scenes. Rinker, as well, found a satisfying career as a solo performer.

King of Jazz (1930) * *Confessions of a Co-Ed* (1931)

Birdwatchers

Sammy Hall

The unprepossessingly-named Birdwatchers were a Miami-based pop band that was most active in the mid–1960s. They really never scored any big hits but had mild success with "I'm Gonna Love You Anyway" and "Girl I Got News for You."

The Wild Rebels (1967) "Can I Do It?"

Bit 'A Sweet

"Out of Sight, Out of Mind" was the one hit of the New York City garage band Bit 'A Sweet, and they did an album as well before themselves fading "out of sight."

Blonde on a Bum Trip (1968) "Is It on, Is It Off?" and "Out of Sight, Out of Mind"

Black, Bill *see* Bill Black's Combo

Black Knights

Ken Griffiths (guitar); Bill Kenny (bass guitar); Alan Shroeder (drums)

One of the many pop groups that briefly flourished in England at the time of the Beatles, the Black Knights' career was jump-started by their appearance in Gerry and the Pacemakers' *Ferry Cross the Mersey*. It led to a record contract — "I Gotta Woman" was their biggest success — and some touring in Europe but the band broke up within a short time.

Ferry Cross the Mersey (1965) "I Gotta Woman"

Blackwood Brothers

Doyle Blackwood (Ackerman, Mississippi, 1911–); James Blackwood (Ackerman, Mississippi, 1919–2002); R. W. Blackwood (Ackerman, Mississippi, 1921–1954); Roy Blackwood (Fentress, Mississippi, 1900–1971); Bill Shaw; Bill Lyles; Jackie Marshall; Cecil Blackwood; J. D. Sumner

Originally consisting of three brothers and one of their teenage sons, the Mississippi-born Blackwood Brothers began singing their gospel songs at the height of the Great Depression. In the next decade they were fixtures on the radio and recorded extensively, one of their successes being "Learning to Lean."

A favorite group of Elvis Presley's, the Blackwoods were frequent guest stars on the television shows of many country singers, as well as *Hee Haw* and *Grand Ole Opry*. They are said to have released some 200 albums, won several Grammy Awards and were inducted into the Gospel Music Hall of Fame in 1998. The Brothers also organized the first National Quartet Convention in the mid–1950s.

Sing a Song, for Heaven's Sake (1966) [documentary]

Blake, Eubie *see* Eubie Blake and His Orchestra

Blenders [unknown]

It Can't Last Forever (1937)

Blockbusters

Carnival Rock (1957) "Carnival Rock" * *Rock All Night* (1957)

Blue Caps *see* Gene Vincent and the Blue Caps

Blue Ridge Mountain Folks *see* Callahan Brothers and Their Blue Ridge Mountain Folks

Blue Ridge Quartet(te)

Elmo Fagg; Bill Crowe; Freddie Daniels; Burl Strevel; Ed Sprouse; Kenny Gates; George Younce

The Southern gospel ensemble Blue Ridge

Quartet had an impressive thirty plus–year run, recording from the mid-1940s to the '80s, during which time their tagline was the not-too-exaggerated "The Sweetest Sound This Side of Heaven." In later years they added country music to their repertoire and were said to have made more than 100 albums.

Sing a Song, for Heaven's Sake (1966) [documentary]

Bluettes [unknown]

Okay America (1932)

Bob Crosby and His Band; Bob Crosby and His Bobcats; Bob Crosby and His Orchestra; Bob Crosby's Orchestra

Bob Crosby (George Crosby, Spokane, Washington, 1913–1993)

A genial singer who was destined to often languish in the shadow of his older brother Bing, Bob Crosby was more a front man for his band than the actual leader. His first band, with many sidemen from New Orleans, played mostly Dixieland and helped to popularize it. Formed on the bones of the Ben Pollack orchestra about 1935, it was unobtrusively led by one of the saxophone players. Crosby had sung with Anson Weeks and the Dorsey brothers previously.

The band's vocal group the Bob-o-Links contained at one time or another such rising stars as Doris Day, Kay Starr and Gloria De Haven. Another of its subgroups was the Bobcats, an eight member ensemble. Hit recordings included "Muskrat Ramble," "Pagan Love Song," "South Rampart Street Parade" and "Big Noise from Winnetka." The standard "Summertime" was its theme song.

Although Bob Crosby described himself as the "only guy in show business who made it without talent," he did have a pleasant if not memorable singing voice. (A critic once said his voice had a tremolo wide enough to drive a Mack Truck through.) His personality, which resembled brother Bing's but was said to be more genuine, was certainly easy to take and by all accounts he was genuinely well-liked.

For a man "without talent" Crosby's career was a long and varied one. He fronted bands from 1935 to 1942 and then again sporadically from 1951 into the 1980s. He starred in the title role of the "B" programmer *The Singing Sheriff*,

Bob Crosby (with actress Janet Blair) about 1947.

as well as playing supporting roles, and worked in radio and television, including in Australia. The youngest of the five Crosby brothers did his family no discredit.

Let's Make Music (1941) * *Sis Hopkins* (1941) * *Reveille with Beverly* (1943) * *Presenting Lily Mars* (1943) * *Thousands Cheer* (1944) * *Pardon My Rhythm* (1944) * *When You're Smiling* (1950) * *Two Tickets to Broadway* (1951) * *Road to Bali* (1952) * *Senior Prom* (1958)

Bob Luman and the Shadows

Bob Luman (Nacogdoches or Black Jack, Texas, 1937–1978)

Country/rockabilly singer and guitarist Bob Luman was a regular on the *Louisiana Hayride* program but had little success with his recordings. In the late 1950s he even considered accepting a contract to play baseball with the Pittsburgh Pirates before finally getting on the country charts with "Let's Think About Living" and "The Great Snowman."

After joining the *Grand Ole Opry* in 1965, however, Luman did have a string of record hits and did much touring, apparently being the first country singer to play in Puerto Rico. He also had a solo role in at least one film, *The Nashville Sound*. His music seemed to be evolving closer to a rock style by the time of his early death.

Carnival Rock (1957) "This Is the Night" and "All Night Long"

Bob Mitchell Boys Choir; Robert B. Mitchell and His St. Brendan's Boys Choir; St. Brendan's Boys Choir

Robert Mitchell (1912–)

Robert Mitchell began playing the organ for silent movies in the mid–1920s and was still at it some eighty years later in movie revival houses. He had been a professional musician from age twelve. The choir for which he became famous was founded at St. Brendan's Catholic Church in Los Angeles in 1935 and began making films the next year under the name of the St. Brendan's Boys Choir.

The Choir's members were usually from ten to fifteen years of age and were seen in so many motion pictures, from musicals to westerns, that at times they seemed to be ubiquitous. Their most famous appearance was probably in *Going My Way*, the Academy Award–winning movie of 1944. A 1941 short in which they appeared, *40 Boys and a Song*, was nominated for its own Oscar.

As recently as 1994, the Choir was heard on the soundtrack for the remake of *Miracle on 34th Street*. During its long tenure the size of the group varied from five to twenty members, and among its alumni were boys who later became members of groups such as The Lettermen and The Sandpipers.

That Girl from Paris (1936) * *The Frontiersman* (1938) * *Carefree* (1938) * *College Swing* (1938) * *Everybody Sing* (1938) * *The Great Waltz* (1938) * *Love Affair* (1939) * *Blondie in Society* (1941) * *Meet John Doe* (1941) * *One Foot in Heaven* (1941) * *Tortilla Flat* (1942) * *Joan of Paris* (1942) * *Idaho* (1943) * *Good Luck, Mr. Yates* (1943) * *Sweet Rosie O'Grady* (1943) * *Christmas Holiday* (1944) * *Going My Way* (1944) * *Bells of Rosarita* (1945) * *Song of Arizona* (1946) * *The Jolson Story* (1947) * *The Babe Ruth Story* (1948) * *The Bishop's Wife* (1948) * *A Connecticut Yankee* (1948) * *Johnny Rocco* (1958)

Bob Scobey and His Band

Bob Scobey (Robert Scobey, Tucumcari, New Mexico, 1916–1963)

Trumpeter Bob Scobey played in many a dance band before establishing himself as a premier exponent of jazz and Dixieland. He formed his own group the Frisco Jazz Band in 1949 that was a driving force in the revival of Dixieland music.

Living Venus (1961)

Bob Wills and His Texas Playboys

Bob Wills (James or Jim Bob Wills, Kosse, Texas, 1905–1975) (fiddle/mandolin); Tommy Duncan (Hillsboro, Texas, 1911–1967) (lead singer); Alton Stricklin (piano); William McAuliffe (Houston, Texas, 1917–1988) (guitar); Johnny Lee Wills; June Whalin; Kermit Whalin; Everett Stover; O. W. Mayo (Mississippi, 1901–); Wayne Johnson; Harley Huggins; Joe Hilly; Jesse Ashlock; Luke Wills; Cotton Thompson; Eldon Shamblin (guitar)

After performing in a medicine/minstrel show (in blackface), Bob Wills formed his own fiddle band in 1930 and appeared on radio, eventually becoming a part of the western ensemble the Light Crust Doughboys, named for the show's sponsor the Burrus Light Crust Flour Company. Wills and Tommy Duncan, also a Doughboy, left in 1933 to establish the Playboys (later the Texas Playboys) in Oklahoma where they continued to broadcast for several years.

Bob Wills (dubbed the "Daddy of Western Swing") did not want his group to be another hillbilly band so he strove for a certain sophistication in their music and dress, which was their version of cowboy attire. He added a horn, drums and reed players to the group, something unusual in a western band. They supposedly had over 3,000 songs in their repertoire and had some record hits that included "San Antonio Rose" and "Bubbles in My Beer."

After Wills' Army discharge following World War II he re-formed the Playboys, which by now had as many as twenty-three members (later downsized). They performed at the *Grand Ole Opry* in the mid–1940s. Wills continued to tour into the 1960s and finally disbanded the group in 1965. In 1968 he was recognized as being one of the preeminent western performers by being voted into both the Country Music Hall of Fame in 1968 and the Cowboy Hall of Fame.

Go West, Young Lady (1941) * *The Lone Prairie* (1942) * *A Tornado in the Saddle* (1942) * *Riders of the Northwest Mounted* (1942) * *Saddles and Sagebrush* (1943) * *Silver City Raiders* (1943) *

The Vigilantes Ride (1944) * *Wyoming Hurricane* (1944) * *The Last Horseman* (1944) * *Blazing the Western Trail* (1945) * *Lawless Empire* (1945) * *Rhythm Round-Up* (1945)

Bobby Breen Quintet

It is uncertain whether the Bobby Breen Quintet is related to the Canadian boy soprano Bobby Breen (1927–) who was discovered by comedian Eddie Cantor and dubbed the "Boy Shirley Temple." The curly-haired singer made a series of popular programmers, many for RKO, before announcing his "retirement" in 1939 when his voice began to change. He made his final film in 1942 and attempted a nightclub comeback in the 1950s.

Curse of the Voodoo (1965)

Bobby Brooks Quartette; Bobby Brooks and the Cottonpicker Quartette

Top Man (1943) * *South of Dixie* (1944) * *This Is the Life* (1944)

Bobby Duncan Troupe [unknown]

Crime Without Passion (1934)

Bobby Fuller Four

Bobby Fuller (Baytown, Texas, 1942–1966); Randy Fuller; Jim Reese; DeWayne Quirico

The rollicking recording of "I Fought the Law" is the only long-lasting legacy of Bobby Fuller and his band mates because the leader was already dead by the age of twenty-three. Their music was a homage to that of rocker Buddy Holly and, in turn, the Fuller group was emulated by rock groups that succeeded them.

Before their one big hit, the Four's recording of "Love Made a Fool of You" had been a minor success but there were no others. The circumstances surrounding Bobby Fuller's death were very murky at the time and interest in the case lingered on, as demonstrated by the 1994 song "Who Killed Bobby Fuller?"

The Ghost in the Invisible Bikini (1966) "Sing-a-Ma-Thing" and "Make the Music Pretty"

Bobby Hargreaves Orchestra

Underworld (1937)

Bobby Harrison Trio

Varieties on Parade (1951)

Bobby Ramos and His Band; Bobby Ramos and His Rhumba Band; Bobby Ramos Band

Bobby Ramos was one of the first Latin American entertainers to have his own television show.

Suspense (1946) * *Hit Parade of 1951* (1950)

Bobby Sherwood and His Orchestra

Bobby Sherwood (Robert Sherwood, Indianapolis, Indiana, 1911–1981)

Bobby Sherwood was perhaps the only real-life bandleader who ever played a murderer in the movies, but this he did in the "B" film *Campus Sleuth*. He had begun his show business life as a banjo-playing child in his parent's vaudeville act before going to Hollywood to become a studio musician, arranger and composer. He also played piano, guitar, trumpet and trombone.

Sherwood was an arranger with the big bands of Tommy and Jimmy Dorsey and Artie Shaw, as well as an accompanist to Bing Crosby. With his own big band from 1942 to '49 Sherwood had hits like "The Elk's Parade" (his theme song) and "Moonlight Becomes You."

As the Big Band era wound down Bobby Sherwood parlayed his handsome looks and warm personality into acting, appearing as a solo performer in a Broadway show and the movie *Pal Joey*, as well as being a radio disc jockey. He was seen on the Milton Berle television show and made his final recordings in the mid–1950s.

Campus Sleuth (1948)

Bobby True Trio

Bobby True (Robert True, 1916?–1998)

The Bobby True Trio was formed following World War II and lasted until True co-founded the popular 1950s music/comedy group the Vagabonds. Somewhat of a prodigy, he had begun his career at the age of sixteen playing the guitar in the MGM studio orchestra.

Ladies of the Chorus (1948)

Bobcats *see* Bob Crosby and His Bobcats; Eddie Miller and His Bobcats

Bocheros

Los Bocheros were Basque singers.
Fiesta (1947)

Bombadiers

The Bombadiers were a vocal group.
Follow the Band (1943)

Bon-Aires *see* Don Coats and the Bon-Aires

Bond, Johnny *see* Johnny Bond and His Red River Valley Boys

Booker T. and the MG's

Booker T. Jones (1944–) (organ/piano); Steve Cropper (guitar); Donald Dunn (bassist); Lewie Steinberg (bassist); Al Jackson (d. 1975) (drums); Isaac Hayes; Carson Whitsett; Willie Hall

The soul band Booker T. and the MG's were initially a Memphis back-up band before they struck out on their own in 1962 with instrumental hits like "Green Onions." Their MG's name was adopted (or foisted upon them) at the time when car names were all the rage among rock groups.

As proponents of so-called "Southern soul," the MG's continued backing top singers including Otis Redding and Wilson Pickett while maintaining their own stardom. They appeared at major festivals like Monterey Pop and released successful albums and singles, including "Time Is Tight" and "Melting Pot."

Groups like the Beatles freely acknowledged the influence that Booker T. and the MG's had had on their music, but by the early '70s the band was faltering. However, they re-formed sporadically and continued to back artists like Bob Dylan, Stevie Wonder and Johnny Cash.

Booker T. and the MG's were inducted into the Rock and Roll Hall of Fame in 1992 and Booker was given a Grammy for lifetime achievement in 2007. The MG's still remain active to this day.
Monterey Pop (1969) [documentary]

Boot-Heel Boys *see* Meredith Neal and the Boot-Heel Boys

Borah Minevitch and His Gang; Borah Minevitch and His Harmonica Rascals; Borah Minevitch Rascals

Borah Minevitch (aka Borrah Minnevitch) (Kiev, Russia, 1902–1955); Jerry Murad (Jerry Muradian, Turkey, d. 1996); Johnny Puleo (1907–1983); Al Fiore (Al Fiorentino, 1923–1996); Richard Hayman; Leo Diamond

Dubbed "Little Boy Blew" for his expertise on the harmonica, the antic Borah Minevitch founded the comedy musical group the Harmonica Rascals in the latter 1920s. They were presumably the very first all-harmonica band, and featured the diminutive (about 4'6") but feisty Johnny Puleo as the mainspring of its on-stage anarchy. The Harmonica Rascals' success can be measured by the number of imitators that followed but never topped them.

Their physical shtick made the Harmonica Rascals a natural for the movies and they made several features and shorts. Eventually the group began to break up; Jerry Murad and Al Fiore departed the Rascals in the 1940s to found the Harmonicats. Puleo did a solo act before later taking over the group as leader. Minevitch himself moved to France in 1947 and became a film producer.

One in a Million (1937) * *Love Under Fire* (1938) * *Rascals* (1941) * *Hit Parade of 1941* (1941) * *Always in My Heart* (1942) * *Tramp, Tramp, Tramp* (1942) * *Top Man* (1943)

Boston Tea Party

Scream Free (1969)

Boswell Sisters

Connee Boswell (sometimes Connie) (Constance Boswell, New Orleans, Louisiana, 1907–1976); Martha Boswell (New Orleans, Louisiana, 1908–1958); Vet Boswell (Helvetia Boswell, New Orleans, Louisiana, 1909–1988)

Following the pioneering Brox Sisters and preceding the iconic Andrews Sisters were the Boswells, deservedly the most popular female trio of the 1930s. They performed with many of the leading bands and had some twenty hit recordings before they disbanded for marriage in 1936. Following this the wheelchair-bound Connee continued a successful solo career with recordings like "Bob White" and "Alexander's Ragtime Band."

28 Bowties

The Boswell Sisters with Bing Crosby, early 1930s.

The trio had begun recording in 1925, their smooth jazz-inflected voices contributing to such big hits as "Dinah," "Shout, Shout, Shout," "When I Take My Sugar to Tea," "The Object of My Affection" and "I'm Gonna Sit Right Down and Write Myself a Letter." They also did a little ditty called "Rock and Roll," proving that this phrase was around long before it gained its current meaning.

Trained as classical singers, Connee, Vet and Martha Boswell had gone into vaudeville as teenagers and began singing in the style for which they later became famous about the mid–1920s. Radio helped to cement their reputation which took a big leap about 1930. Besides the movies in which they appeared together, Connee, who continued to perform until 1975, played a solo role in 1959's *Senior Prom*. The Broadway show *Heebie Jeebies* was based on their lives.

The Big Broadcast (1932) "Crazy People" * *Meet the Baron* (1933)† * *Moulin Rouge* (1934) * *Transatlantic Merry-Go-Round* (1934)

†Their appearance has not been confirmed.

Bowties see Cirino and the Bowties

Boyd Triplets [unknown]
Hands Across the Border (1944) * *Smoky River Serenade* (1947) * *Midnight Frolics* (1949)

Boy's Choir of the St. Joseph's School
Rancho Grande (1940)

Boy's Town A Cappella Choir
Boy's Town (1938)

Brasil '66 see Sergio Mendes and Brasil '66

Brattle Street East
Feelin' Good (1966) "Don't Hurt Me Again," "The Way That I Need You," "Wicked Woman," "Watch Out Woman," "Ute, Ute," "It Isn't Right," "I Beg Your Pardon" and "Foolin' Around"

Brazilian Turunas [unknown]
Flying Down to Rio (1933)

Brazilians [unknown]
A Song Is Born (1948)

Breakaways see Joe Brown and the Breakaways

Breen, Bobby see Bobby Breen Quintet

Brewer Kids
The Brewer Kids were singers.
Rancho Grande (1940)

Brewster Twins
Barbara Brewster (Naomi Stevenson, Tucson, Arizona, 1918–2005); Gloria Brewster (Ruth Stevenson, Tucson, Arizona, 1918–1996)

With some help from studio publicity flacks, in the late 1930s the Brewsters were named the most beautiful twins in America. After their movie career ended Barbara went on to perform on the New York stage in the 1940s.

Wake Up and Live (1937) * *Wife, Doctor and Nurse* (1937) * *Life Begins in College* (1937)† * *Love and Hisses* (1937) * *Little Miss Broadway* (1938) * *Hold That Co-Ed* (1938) * *My Lucky Star* (1938) * *Thanks for Everything* (1938) * *Elsa Maxwell's Hotel for Women* (1939) * *20,000 Men a Year* (1939)

†Their appearance in this film has not been confirmed.

Brian Poole and the Tremeloes

Brian Poole (Barking, England, 1941–); Ricky West (guitar); Alan Blakely (guitar); Alan Howard (guitar); Dave Munden (drums)

The British group Brian Poole and the Tremeloes was formed in 1959. ("Tremeloes"— originally "Tremilos"— was their version of a synonym for the musical term "vibrato.") They were somewhat imitative of the Buddy Holly sound and entertained at U.S. bases in England. Early in the 1960s they bested an equally obscure band named the Beatles in a contest.

The Tremeloes' recordings were mainly covers of established hits like "Candy Man" and "Twist and Shout," as were their biggest U.K. successes "Do You Love Me?" and "Someone, Someone." Brian Poole departed for an unsuccessful solo career in 1966; the band continued on for a while longer and scored a number one hit with "Silence Is Golden."

Just for Fun (1963) "Keep on Dancin'" * *Go-Go Big Beat* (1965) [documentary] "Do You Love Me?" and "Someone"

Brian Sisters

Betty Brian (Rexburg, Idaho, 1923–); Doris Brian (Pocatello, Idaho, 1926–); Gwen Brian (Pocatello, Idaho, 1928–)

In the Shirley Temple era, when audiences were enthralled with cute child actors, the Brian Sisters and their stage mother were determined to make it in Hollywood. With their pleasant harmonizing ability the girls did succeed for a few years on radio, in nightclubs, personal appearances and in the movies.

Beginning with a 1936 "Our Gang" short they appeared in films until the start of the next decade (they later did soundtrack songs). The Brians also made musical shorts and soundies, and, when they inevitably began to grow up, found radio to be the medium that sustained their careers. Two of the sisters later sang with Jan Garber's orchestra.

Sing While You're Able (1937) * *New Faces of 1937* (1937) * *Thanks for Listening* (1937) * *Sally, Irene and Mary* (1938) * *Kentucky Moonshine* (1938) * *Little Miss Broadway* (1938) * *Second Fiddle* (1939) * *Love Affair* (1939) * *High School* (1940) * *Tin Pan Alley* (1940) * *Music in My Heart* (1940)

Bring, Lou see Lou Bring Orchestra

Britton, Frank and Milt see Frank and Milt Britton Band

Britton, Milt see Milt Britton and His Band

Bronco Busters see Buster Fite and His Bronco Busters; Merle Travis and His Bronco Busters

Brook Brothers

Ricky Brook (Winchester, England, 1943–); Geoffrey Brook (Winchester, England, 1940–)

In the 1950s and '60s the Brook Brothers found a modicum of success with covers of American songs, thus earning their reputation as the English Everly Brothers. They changed their professional name to the Brooks toward the end of their careers.

It's Trad, Dad! (1962) "Double Trouble"

Brooklyn Bridge

Johnny Maestro (lead singer); Fred Ferrara (baritone); Mike Gregorio (2nd tenor); Les Cauchi (1st tenor); Jim Macioce (guitar); Jim Rosica (bassist); Shelly Davis (trumpet); Joe Ruvio (saxophone); Artie Cantanzarita (drums)

Formed from a 1968 amalgamation of the groups the Del-Satins and the Rhythm Method, the Long Island–based Brooklyn Bridge had a hit with "The Worst That Could Happen." They had a somewhat different sound from their contemporaries that sprang from the combination of a pop band with a jazz ensemble.

Although the Brooklyn Bridge recorded only sporadically (and not at all for about ten years), they met with mild success playing in such venues as the Radio City Music Hall. It was enough to keep the brand name going into the 1990s with a couple of the original members.

It's Your Thing (1970) [documentary]

Brooks, Bobby see Bobby Brooks Quartette

Broome Brothers

Lee Broome; Ray Broome

The Broome Brothers trio, a vocal group, appeared on the radio and recorded during the

1950s, as well as making personal appearances with such luminaries as Gene Autry, Roy Rogers — and the Three Stooges.
Square Dance Jubilee (1949) * *Kentucky Jubilee* (1951)

Brothers Four
Bob Flick (bassist); John Paine (guitar); Mike Kirkland (guitar/banjo); Dick Foley (guitar)

Part of the wave of clean-cut folk singers to emerge in the 1950s, the Brothers Four were fraternity confreres who ultimately made more than fifty albums over a forty-plus year career. They found success both in intimate clubs and on the college circuit. Their poignant hit "Green Fields" remains an anthem of the folksong period and their "Green Leaves of Summer" was a hit in the next decade.
Hootenanny Hoot (1963)

Brown, James *see* James Brown and the Flames

Brown, Joe *see* Joe Brown...

Brown, Les *see* Les Brown and His Band

Brown Dots *see* Deek Watson and the Brown Dots

Brownies Trio [unknown]
The Loudspeaker (aka *The Loud Speaker*) (1934)

Brox Sisters
Bobbe Brox (aka Dagmar Brox) (Josephine Brock, Riverton, Iowa, 1901–1999); Lorayne Brox (Eunice Brock, Memphis, Tennessee, 1900–1993); Patricia Brox (Kathleen or Kathlyn Brock, Winchester, Kentucky, 1906–1988)

Perhaps somewhat (unfairly) overlooked today, the three Brox Sisters were probably the first great sister harmony trio, blazing the trail for those that followed with their jazz-inflected sound. The sisters appeared on Broadway several times, including various versions of the *Music Box Revue*, the *Ziegfeld Follies* and *The Cocoanuts*, a show with the Marx Brothers. They were said to be favorites of composer Irving Berlin.

In the all-star MGM film *Hollywood Revue of 1929* they (and Cliff "Ukulele Ike" Edwards) introduced the classic "Singin' in the Rain" to the movies. The Paul Whiteman feature *King of Jazz* saw them harmonizing with the Rhythm Boys featuring Bing Crosby. Besides their feature films, they also made a few musical short subjects. In one, *Hollywood Parade*, they imitated Marlene Dietrich singing "Falling in Love Again." They went their separate ways not too long thereafter.
Hollywood Revue of 1929 (1929) "Singin' in the Rain" * *Spring Is Here* (1930) * *King of Jazz* (1930)

Bruvvers *see* Joe Brown and the Bruvvers

Bryant, Jimmy *see* Jimmy Bryant and the Night Jumpers

Bryant, Marie *see* Marie Bryant Swing Band

Buccaneers
The Buccaneers were a group of eight singers.
Here Comes Cookie (1935)

Buck and Chickie Eddy; Buck, Chickie and Buck
Buck and Chickie Eddy were country/western musicians.
Cowboy Canteen (1944) * *Kentucky Jubilee* (1951)

Buckaroo Band
Ride 'Em Cowboy (1942)

Buckaroos *see also* Ken Maynard's Buckaroos
From Nashville with Music (1969) [documentary]

Buckner, Teddy *see* Teddy Buckner and His All-Stars

Buckner All-Stars *see* Teddy Buckner and His All-Stars

Buddy Defranco Quartet Combo

Buddy DeFranco (Boniface DeFranco, Camden, New Jersey, 1923–); Buddy Bregman; Teddy Buckner; Pete Jolly

Acclaimed as one of the leading jazz clarinetists of all time, Buddy DeFranco played with many big bands from a young age, including those of Gene Krupa, Ted Fio Rito and Tommy Dorsey. In the 1940s he helped to popularize the bebop style; in doing so he appeared with many famous Black musicians like Charlie Parker, Count Basie and Dizzy Gillespie.

DeFranco formed his own big band in the 1950s and then a jazz quartet that is considered to have been one of the finest such ensembles. He toured extensively and was still a creative force as a great jazz improviser into the new century.

The Wild Party (1956)

Buddy Rich and His Orchestra

Buddy Rich (Bernard Rich, Brooklyn, New York, 1917–1987)

Dubbed the "Fastest Drummer in the World," Buddy Rich had become a professional drummer by the age of nineteen, but he had been in vaudeville with his parents when he was a mere eighteen *months* old. As a small child he also appeared on Broadway; as "Baby Traps the Drum Wonder" Rich's ultimate career seemed to be foreordained.

In the early 1930s he was touted to be the second highest-paid child "star" in the country after the winsome Jackie Coogan. He supposedly had his own band when he was eleven, but it was as a sideman from 1937 that he played with such luminaries as Artie Shaw, Bunny Berigan and Tommy Dorsey. With some of these orchestras he appeared in film shorts and features.

At one time he was rumored to be the highest paid sideman of all time, pulling down at least $1,500 a week when that was real money. But his (over?)confidence in his abilities proved a constant source of tension. In the 1940s Buddy Rich formed his own (adult) band and was active in one group or another till the time of his death. A showcase of his drumming style was his theme song "Rain on the Roof."

Rich's talent was widely acknowledged — especially by him — and he received many awards, but his abrasiveness and arrogance were still very much a part of his personality. He was known to be quite the martinet with his band members, but it was his caustic — some would say cruel — wit that made him a popular guest star on television.

How's About It? (1943)

Buffalo Bills

Al Shea (lead); Vern Reed (tenor); Wayne Ward (baritone); Bill Spangenberg (bass) (d. 1963); Bill Delfield (tenor); Ross Davis (baritone); Ralph Bone (bass)

Integral to the success of the long-running Broadway musical and subsequent film *The Music Man* was a barbershop quartet, the Buffalo Bills. Their swoony rendition of "Lida Rose" was a high point of their roles as squabbling members of the school board in fabled River City, Iowa.

Since 1945 Al Shea had sung on a Buffalo, New York radio show as part of a quartet; a couple of years later he formed the group that would become the Bills. They had achieved some success touring military bases and in barbershop competitions when *Music Man* composer Meredith Willson heard them. The rest is (barbershop) history.

By the time the Buffalo Bills disbanded in 1967, after numerous personnel changes, they had racked up such mind-boggling statistics as more than 1,500 performances on Broadway, almost 700 radio programs, over 700 concerts and hundreds of nightclub, television, convention and state fair appearances. They also produced several albums of old favorites and were undoubtedly one of the famous barbershop groups of all time.

The Music Man (1962)

Burnette, Johnny *see* Johnny Burnette Trio

Burtnett, Earl *see* Earl Burtnett and Orchestra and Trio

Burton Sisters

The Burton Sisters were singers.

Monticello, Here We Come! (1950)

Busse, Henry *see* Henry Busse and His Orchestra

Buster Fite and His Bronco Busters; Buster Fite and His Saddle Tramps

Buster Fite; Jimmy Carroll (mandolin); Shorty Scott (fiddle); Hi Busse (accordion)

Buster Fite and the Saddle Tramps began recording about 1937, the year of their film appearance.

Roll Along Cowboy (1937)

Butera, Sam *see* Sam Butera and the Witnesses

Butterfield, Paul *see* Paul Butterfield Blues Band

Byrds

Roger McGuinn (Chicago, Illinois, 1942–) (guitar); Gene Clark (Harold Clark, Tipton, Missouri, 1944–1991) (guitar); David Crosby, Los Angeles, CA, 1941–) (guitar); Chris Hillman (Los Angeles or San Diego, California, 1944–) (bassist); Michael Clarke (Michael Dick, New York, New York, 1944–1994) (drums); Gram Parsons (Cecil Connor, Winterhaven, Florida, 1946–1973) (keyboard); Kevin Kelley (drums)

From 1964 to 1972 the Byrds were one of the most successful folk/rock bands in the world. They were leaders in playing such subgenres as space rock, raga rock, country rock and other "hyphenated" forms of rock-and-roll. Among their smash hits were "Mr. Tambourine Man" and "Turn! Turn! Turn!," both of which were virtual anthems of the hippie era.

Originally dubbed the Jet Set, a name hardly compatible with their image, they renamed themselves just in time for their first recording hit. Eventually they turned more to psychedelic music that included "Eight Miles High," supposedly a drug song (which they denied).

The Byrds' increasing musical emphasis on the druggie culture led to a diminishing of their popularity among more mainstream audiences but hit albums, eleven in all, kept coming. Two members, Gram Parsons and Chris Hillman, went on to the Flying Burrito Brothers.

The Big T.N.T. Show (1966) [documentary] "Mr. Tambourine Man," "Turn! Turn! Turn" and "The Bells of Rhymney" * *Stamping Ground* (1971) [documentary] "Old Blue"

Cab Calloway and His Band; Cab Calloway and His Orchestra

Cab Calloway (Cabel Calloway III, Rochester, New York, 1907–1994)

The immortalizer of "Minnie the Moocher" was the colorful, larger than life performer ("hi-de-hi, hi-de-ho") Cab Calloway. With his distinctive outfit of white (or yellow or powder blue) zoot suit–style tie and tails, and pomaded hair

The Byrds in their mop top days.

flying, he danced, scat sang and played the saxophone manically. (Sometimes he added a wide-brimmed hat to his ensemble.)

As a musician he perhaps was not always admired by his peers who did not consider him to be a jazz purist. But Calloway was more than the sum of his parts; he simply was a consummate entertainer who was rumored to have been the model for the character "Sportin' Life" in George Gershwin's *Porgy and Bess*.

And he certainly could put a song over; besides "Minnie" (his theme song) he popularized "St. James Infirmary," "Kicking the Gong Around" (a reference to drug addiction) and the drug anthem "Reefer Man." Calloway's first band was the Alabamians which he formed about 1929 and he led large groups until 1948 when he turned to smaller ensembles.

Cab Calloway was a fixture at Harlem's Cotton Club in the 1930s and his orchestra was the first to integrate several formerly all-white clubs. Besides film appearances with his band, he was seen over the decades as a character actor in movies like *The Cincinnati Kid* and *The Blues Brothers*. He also appeared much on television and wrote the *Hepster's Dictionary*.

The Big Broadcast (1932) * *International House* (1933) * *The Singing Kid* (1936) * *Manhattan Merry-Go-Round* (1937) * *Stormy Weather* (1943) * *Sensations of 1945* (1944) * *Hi-De-Ho* (1947)

Cabin Kids

Ruth (1924?–); Helen (1925?–); James (1926?–); Winifred (1929?–); Fred (1931?–)

The Cabin Kids was a very youthful singing group that appeared largely in comedy shorts, including the *Our Gang* series, musical shorts like *Gifts in Rhythm* and soundies (*Rhythm Saves the Day*).

Mississippi (1935) * *Hooray for Love* (1935) * *Round-Up Time in Texas* (1937) * *Git Along Little Dogies* (1937)

Cadillacs

Earl Carroll; Bobby Phillips; Lavern Drake; Johnny "Gus" Willingham; Earl Wade; James Clark; Charles Brooks; Cub Gaining

First known as the Carnations, the doo wop group that came to be the Cadillacs formed about 1953. They were one of the first rock groups to emphasize choreography, and were supposedly the first to be named after an automobile. During performances they were costumed in white jackets and black pants. Their first record was "Gloria," but they were basically a one-hit wonder.

That, however, was massive: 1955's "Speedoo," the nickname of group member Earl Carroll ("they often call me 'Speedoo,' but my real name is Mister Earl..."). At one point the Cadillacs tried for a more sophisticated sound, hoping to lure a wider audience. Finding little success (they even did a version of "Rudolph the Red-Nosed Reindeer") they reverted to their original style.

In 1957 the Cadillacs split into two groups but ultimately reunited only to divide again. "Peekaboo" (1959) was the original group's last success. None of its iterations had the modicum of fame they had had in earlier years but the Cadillacs continued on to ride the crest of rock nostalgia to the 1990s.

Go, Johnny, Go! (1959) "Please Mr. Johnson" and "Jay Walker"

Cal Shrum and His Rhythm Rangers; Cal Shrum's Gang; Cal Shrum's Rhythm Rangers; Cal Shrum's Rhythm Wranglers

Cal Shrum (Mountain Home, Arkansas, 1910–1996)

After his professional debut at a Denver radio station, Cal Shrum eventually migrated to Hollywood where he appeared in some fifty "B" westerns, mostly as a supporting solo performer. Some of the movies also featured his brother Walt and they made music together as well.

Shrum also made several pictures with his various musical groups and had a couple of mid–'40s starring roles in oaters (*Swing, Cowboy, Swing* and *Trouble at Melody Mesa*). He also established his own record label.

The Old Barn Dance (1938) * *Scatterbrain* (1940) * *Rollin' Home to Texas* (1940) * *Thunder Over the Prairie* (1941) * *The Rangers Take Over* (1942) * *Bad Men of Thunder Gap* (1943) * *Swing, Cowboy, Swing* (1946) * *Trouble at Melody Mesa* (1947)

Cal Tjader Band; Cal Tjader Quintet

Cal Tjader (Callen Tjader, Jr., St. Louis, Missouri, 1925–1982); Manuel Duran (piano); Carlos Duran (bassist); Bayardo Velarde (percussion); Edgardo Rosales (conga drum)

A master of many instruments, including the vibraphone, bongo drums and piano, Cal Tjader (the name is Swedish) was a highly-respected Latin and Afro-Cuban jazz musician. He was recognized in 1980 with a Grammy award for one of his many albums.

Tjader, a child of show business, began performing as a tap dancer at a young age and eventually hooked up with a Dixieland band. In the 1940s he was a member of Dave Brubeck's octet and then part of a trio with Brubeck. Before forming his own quintet he played with jazz pianist George Shearing and so had had experience with some of the leading jazz greats.

The mambo craze of the 1950s was a boon to Tjader's quintet and when it fizzled he formed several other small combos. His recording career hit its peak with the release of the album "Soul Sauce" that sold more than 100,000 copies in the mid–'60s, considered his greatest period. He is still looked on as one of the leading lights of his field.

The Big Beat (1958) * *For Singles Only* (1968)

Caldwell, Hank see Hank Caldwell and His Saddle Kings

California Collegians; Original California Collegians

Fred MacMurray (Kankakee, Illinois, 1908–1991)

Veterans of vaudeville, the musicians and singers of the California Collegians appeared on Broadway in several 1930s musicals, including *Roberta* and *Fifty Million Frenchmen*. One of their claims to fame now is that a young Fred MacMurray, one day to be a major movie star, was among their members.

It seems that they were neither really Californians nor college students, nor could any of them read music after the one group member who did know how departed. The Californians drafted unknown saxophone player MacMurray to help them learn melodies by ear and to be a vocalist. He joined the ensemble for a while and then went on to Hollywood and fame.

To Beat the Band (1935) * *College Holiday* (1936) * *Champagne Waltz* (1937) * *Top Of the Town* (1937)

California Junior Symphony Orchestra see Peter Meremblum Junior California Symphony Orchestra

Californians see Abe Lyman and His Californians; Rudy Sooter and His Californians

Callahan Brothers and Their Blue Ridge Mountain Folks

Joe Callahan (Walter Callahan, Laurel, North Carolina); Bill Callahan (Homer Callahan, Laurel, North Carolina, 1912–1971)

The Callahans were a brother act that performed blues and ballads in the 1930s and '40s. Yodeling was part of their musical repertoire, one of their hits being a double yodel version of "St. Louis Blues." They were professionally inactive after 1951.

Springtime in Texas (1945)

Calloway, Cab see Cab Calloway...

Calloway Sisters

Liz Calloway; Ann Calloway

Music City, U.S.A. (1966) [documentary]

Calypsomaniacs see Herb Jeffries' Calypsomaniacs

Calypsonians see Lord Flea Calypsonians...; Mac Niles and the Calypsonians

Cameo Girls [unknown]

Linda, Be Good (1947)

Canned Heat

Alan Wilson (d. 1970) (harmonica); Bob Hite (d. 1981) (harmonica); Henry Vestine (d. 1997) (guitar); Larry Taylor (bassist); Adolfo de la Parra (drums); Frank Cook (drums)

Founded about 1965 or '66, Canned Heat (the name derived from a 1920s recording of "Canned Heat Blues") made a popular hit at the 1967 Monterey Pop Festival and then fabled Woodstock. They played an eclectic combination of boogie, rock and blues. Among their top recordings were "On the Road Again," "Goin' Up the Country" and "Fried Hockey Boogie."

Canned Heat survives to this day, having made almost forty albums and playing at international festivals. In so doing, they have brought many forgotten or unrecognized blues men out of obscurity to play with them, and their music is often heard on movie soundtracks and television commercials

Monterey Pop (1969) [documentary] " Rollin' and Tumblin'" * *The Naked Zoo* (1970) "One Kind Favor" * *Woodstock* (1970) [documentary] * *Stamping Ground* (1971) [documentary] "Human Condition"

Canova Family

Judy Canova (Juliette Canova, Starke or Waldo, Florida, 1913–1983); Zeke Canova (Leon Canova, Florida, 1898–1980); Anne Canova (Diane Canova, Florida, 1909–1994); Pete Canova (Harry Canova, Florida, 1904–1947)

In real life the Canovas were musically trained and thus a far cry from their stage personas as raucous hillbillies. It was an act that brought them a measure of fame. The youngest, Juliette, professionally known as Judy, later broke out to a very successful solo career in radio and the movies.

The Canovas first appeared on local Florida radio and in the early '30s took their yokel act to New York as the Three Georgia Crickets. Zeke played the guitar and ukulele, while sisters Judy and Anne (known as the Happiness Girls) warbled nasally in their outfits of gingham dresses and pigtails.

Soon Judy, who was now the Canova standout, and family were heard on prestigious radio shows and performed in Broadway shows. Brother Harry (aka Pete) briefly joined them but 1939 was to mark the end of the Canovas as a family act.

A solo turn in another Broadway show that year brought Judy back to the attention of Hollywood, and Republic cast her in a popular series of low-budget movies beginning with *Scatterbrain* in 1940 and ending in 1955. In all she appeared in some seventeen starring films.

Judy Canova's long running radio show (1943 to '53) proved to be successful, and she recorded into the 1950s as well. Her persona continued to be that of a man-chasing, English-mangling but goodhearted yokel whose catchphrase was "You're telling I." The Canova Family re-teamed briefly for a television appearance in the early 1950s.

In Caliente (1935) * *Broadway Gondolier* (1935) * *Artists and Models* (1937) * *Thrill of a Lifetime* (1937)

Canteen Vocalaires

Hi' Ya, Sailor (1943)

Cappy Barra Boys; Cappy Barra's Harmonica Ensemble

Maurice Duke; Charles Leighton; George Fields; Sam Scheckter; Don Ripps; Phil King; Sam Sperling; Nat Bergman; Phil Solomon; Alan Greene; Leon Lafell (Leon Lehrfeld, 1913–); Joe Mullendore; Pro Robbins (Irving Rubenstein)

If it seems that the name Cappy Barra sounds familiar, it does — the harmonica ensemble was (oddly) named for the large South American rodent, the capybara. The group was formed in the mid–1930s and played in vaudeville and theaters and on the radio.

The Cappy Barra Boys always had a non-musician as front man and spokesman for their group, the first one being founder Maurice Duke. Their specialty was playing harmonica music that imitated big band instruments and arrangements. The original group disbanded in 1944 and subsequently was reconstituted with new members.

Mad About Music (1938) * *Rockin' in the Rockies* (1945) * *Radio Stars on Parade* (1945) * *Smart Politics* (1948)

Carl Hoff and the Hit Parade Orchestra

Carl Hoff (1905?–1965)

With his theme song of "I Could Use a Dream" Carl Hoff had his own orchestra from the early 1940s. He had previously led the band on the *Lucky Strike Hit Parade* radio program where his outgoing personality was popular. A violinist and sax player, he was also the music director for several radio and television stars, among them Perry Como, Martha Raye and Patti Page.

The Hit Parade (1937)

Carle, Frankie *see* Frankie Carle...

Carlos Molina and His Music of the Americas; Carlos Molina and His Orchestra; Carlos Molina and Orchestra

Club Havana (1945) * *Belle of Old New Mexico* (1950) * *With a Song in My Heart* (1952) * *Meet Danny Wilson* (1952)

Carmen Cavallaro and Orchestra

Carmen Cavallaro (New York, New York, 1913–1989)

The "Poet of the Piano" was the name bestowed upon Carmen Cavallaro, one of the showiest pianists of his time. He was somewhat of a young prodigy who played with a variety of big bands before establishing his own in 1939. He and his group, which grew to as many as fourteen members, played in most of the top hotels and swank nightclubs throughout the country. Their theme song was "My Sentimental Heart."

Cavallaro was sort of a precursor to, and an acknowledged influence on, Liberace in that his piano arrangements were extremely lush and featured classical themes in popular settings. In turn he had been influenced by society pianist Eddy Duchin so, fittingly, it was his hands seen playing the piano for Tyrone Power in *The Eddy Duchin Story*.

In the 1940s he appeared in a few films (e.g. *Diamond Horseshoe*) without his band, playing the piano with brio. During the 1950s and '60s Carmen Cavallaro led smaller, more jazz-oriented ensembles and in 1963 had one of his few chart hits with "Sukiyaki." His band released almost twenty albums over the years.

Hollywood Canteen (1944) * *The Time, the Place and the Girl* (1946)

Carmen Miranda Band *see* Banda da Lua

Carole Lombard Singers

Carole Lombard; Gwen Johnson; Jackie Ward; Marjorie Crawford

Viva Las Vegas (1963) "What'd I Say" * *Fireball 500* (1966)

Carpenter, Ike *see* Ike Carpenter...

Carroll, Johnny *see* Johnny Carroll and His Hot Rocks

Carroll Brothers

Pete Carroll

Founded about 1957 the Carroll Brothers made a few singles and an album entitled "College Twist Party."

Don't Knock the Twist (1962) "Bo Diddley"

Carter, Ben *see* Ben Carter...

Carter, Benny *see* Benny Carter and His Band

Carter Family *see* Mother Maybelle and the Carter Family

Casa Loma Orchestra *see* Glen Gray and His Casa Loma Orchestra

Cascades

John Gummoe (guitar); Lenny Green (guitar); Dave Wilson (drums); Eddie Snyder (guitar); Dave Szabo (keyboard); Dave Stevens (bassist)

The San Diego–based band that became the Cascades began life as the interestingly-named Thundernotes in the late 1950s. Their new name supposedly came from the brand of dishwasher soap. They had released some unsuccessful songs before recording the song that leader John Gummoe had written when in the Navy.

That turned out to be "Rhythm of the Rain" (written during a storm at sea and featuring a celesta) and it propelled them to the very top of the pop charts in 1962, particularly in some Asian countries. The song marked their pinnacle; subsequent recordings like "The Last Leaf" scored a minor blip before the group disbanded.

Catalina Caper (1967) "There's a New World"

Cass County Boys; Cass County Trio

Fred Martin (Linden, Texas, 1916–) (lead singer/accordion); Bert Dodson (1915–1994) (tenor/bassist); Jerry Scroggins (Mt. Pleasant, Texas, 1911–2004) (baritone/guitar)

Best-known for their appearances in Gene Autry and Charles Starrett movies and on Autry's radio and television shows, the Cass County Boys formed in 1935 or '36 at a radio station where they were staff musicians. They had all been performing on the radio in the Southwest;

The Cass County Boys (outside of cell) in *The Last Days of Boot Hill* (with Smiley Burnette in jail).

Bert Dodson sang with the famous Light Crust Doughboys.

Originally called the Early Birds, their later name was taken from the Texas county in which Fred Martin was born. The Cass County Boys continued performing together into the 1950s, and when Gene Autry phased out his performing career they did too. In 1996 they were inducted into the Western Music Association Hall of Fame.

Sioux City Sue (1946) * *Trail to San Antone* (1947) * *Twilight on the Rio Grande* (1947) * *Buckaroo from Powder River* (1947) * *The Last Days of Boot Hill* (1947) * *Saddle Pals* (1947) * *Robin Hood of Texas* (1947) * *Trail to Laredo* (1948) * *Loaded Pistols* (1949) * *Tucson* (1949) * *Riders of the Whistling Pines* (1949) * *Holiday Rhythm* (1950) * *The Kid from Amarillo* (1951) * *Blue Canadian Rockies* (1952) * *Apache Country* (1952) * *Wagon Team* (1952) * *On Top of Old Smoky* (1953)

Castaways

James Donna (keyboard); Robert Folschow (guitar); Roy Hensley (d. 2005) (bassist); Dennis Craswell (drums)

There were (and are) a few bands bearing the name of the Castaways; the one that made the single film and had a single big hit record is a Minnesota-based garage band. Founded in the early 1960s, their hit "Liar Liar" came in 1965 and they have continued performing to the current day.

It's a Bikini World (1967) "Liar Liar"

Catalinas

One of the many bands playing so-called beach music, the North Carolina–based Catalinas formed in 1957. Among their records were "Summertime's Calling Me," "Hey Little Girl" and "Facts of Love." They are still active today.

Moonshine Mountain (1964)

Catlett, Sid see Sid Catlett...

Cats and the Fiddle

Austin Powell (guitar); Jimmie Henderson (d. 1940) (1st tenor/guitar); Chuck Barksdale (d. 1941) (bass/bassist); Ernie Price (2nd tenor/tipple); Herbie Miles; Lloyd Grimes; George Steinbeck; Mifflin Branford; Hank Haslett; Shirley Moore

"I Miss You So" was the biggest hit for the jazz/gospel/vocal/instrumental quintet called the Cats and the Fiddle. Formed in Chicago in 1937, they mostly played at clubs catering to an African-American audience. Other successful recordings included "That's My Desire" and "I'll Never Let You Go."

Among the Cats' unusual accompaniment was the tipple, a ten-stringed instrument that sounded like a ukulele. The group disbanded about 1950 but re-formed a few years later with different members.

Two Gun Man from Harlem (1938) * *The Duke Is Tops* (1938) * *Goin' Places* (1939) "Jeepers Creepers"

Cavallaro, Carmen see Carmen Cavallaro and Orchestra

Cavallo, Jimmy see Jimmy Cavallo and the House Rockers

Cavanaugh, Page *see* Page Cavanaugh Trio

Cavell, Andy *see* Andy Cavell and the Saints

CBS-KMBC Texas Rangers *see* Texas Rangers

C.C. Ryders *see* Wayne Cochran and the C.C. Ryders

Cecil Stewart and His Royal Rogues
Cecil Stewart (1899–1960)
　Besides the film he made with his ensemble, Cecil Stewart had many a movie bit playing the piano or organ.
　Always Leave Them Laughing (1949)

Ceepee Johnson and His Orchestra
Mystery in Swing (1940)

Cell Block Seven
Wearing the trademark black and white striped outfits illustrative of their name, the Cell Block Seven was a Dixieland band that was primarily Texas-based. They opened for Bob Hope when he performed in that state and also played Las Vegas, but the major television exposure they hoped for was not forthcoming. Their planned performance on the Ed Sullivan Show was cut because the show ran too long.
　Rock Baby, Rock It! (1957) "The Saints Come Rockin' In"

Charioteers
Billy Williams (1911–1972) (lead tenor); Eddie Jackson (2nd tenor); Howard Daniel (bass); Ira Williams (baritone); James Sherman (piano)
　Formed in 1930 as the gospel group the Harmony Four at Wilberforce University in Ohio, the Charioteers were named the best quartet in Ohio in 1931, leading to many radio performances. Some ten years later they converted to close-harmony popular music a la the Ink Spots.
　Although never rivaling that iconic ensemble, they did produce several successful recordings including "So Long," "Open the Door Richard" and "A Kiss and a Rose," their biggest hit in 1949.
　Regulars on the Bing Crosby radio show in the 1940s, the Charioteers also backed such singers as Frank Sinatra, Pearl Bailey, and Buddy Clark on his hit rendition of "Now Is the Hour." Founder Billy Williams departed to appear on Sid Caesar's television show (with his new Billy Williams Quartet) and his former group disbanded in 1957.
　Road Show (1941)

Charles, Ray *see* Ray Charles Orchestra

Charles and Gabrielle [unknown]
Midnight Frolics (1949)

Charlie
Steve White; Tom Eppolito; Bob Compton; Ray Barry; Tony Sorci
　Charlie was a Chicago-based garage band.
　Blast Off Girls (1967) "Bad Day" and "Good Night Ladies"

Charlie Barnet and His Orchestra
Charlie Barnet (New York, New York, 1913–1991)
　Born wealthy with a silver spoon (or perhaps baton) in his mouth, saxophone player Charlie Barnet had led an orchestra by the age of seventeen on a trans–Atlantic liner. He was a foe of segregated orchestras and hired Black musicians two years before the more publicized Benny Goodman did so (Lena Horne was a vocalist), and also played the Apollo Theater in Harlem.
　Admittedly patterning himself after Duke Ellington, Barnet had a big band called the "blackest white band of all." His first orchestra was formed in 1932 or '33 and it introduced the vocal group the Modernaires. Among his hit recordings were "Cherokee" (their theme song) and "Skyliner"; in all he composed more than twenty-five Billboard charters from 1936 to '46.
　Charlie Barnet's original band was disbanded in the late 1940s but he returned with groups in the 1960s and '70s. His private life almost succeeded in overshadowing his musical one: he was wed eleven times but airily dismissed five because they had been quickly annulled.
　Juke Box Jenny (1942) * *Jamboree* (1944) * *Jam Session* (1944) * *Music in Manhattan* (1944) * *Idea Girl* (1946) * *Freddie Steps Out* (1946)

Charlie Louvin and His Band

Charlie Louvin (Charles Loudermilk, Rainesville, Alabama, 1927–)

Better known as part of the close-harmony duo the Louvin Brothers, Charlie Louvin and his brother Ira (né Lonnie Loudermilk, 1924–1965) were a well-known mandolin/guitar country music act.

Their recordings ran from rockabilly to gospel and they were noted songwriters as well. The Louvins had several recording hits in the 1950s and early '60s, including "When I Stop Dreaming," before they each went solo in 1963.

Baritone Charlie continued to turn out hits like "Think I'll Go Somewhere and Cry Myself to Sleep" and "I Don't Love You Anymore," and had some thirty singles that hit the charts. But it was as one of a pair that he found his greatest success, a teaming that influenced brother acts to follow, notably Phil and Don Everly.

Music City U.S.A. (1966) [documentary]

Charlie Spivak and His Orchestra

Charlie Spivak (Kiev, Ukraine or New Haven, Connecticut, 1905/07–1982)

Trumpeter "Cheery, Chubby" Charlie Spivak was a sideman with many orchestras in the 1920s and '30s, including Bob Crosby, the Dorsey brothers and Glenn Miller, before striking out on his own in 1939. With his easy-listening, suitable for dancing music his orchestra met with continuing success through the 1950s. Thereafter he led smaller ensembles sporadically to the 1970s.

Among the group's hit recordings were "Let's Go Home," "Autumn Nocturne" and "Star Dreams," their theme song. His sidemen included bandleaders-to-be Nelson Riddle and Les Elgart, as well as vocalist June Hutton. With suitable modesty Spivak was dubbed "the man who plays the sweetest trumpet in the world."

Pin Up Girl (1943)

Charmers [unknown]

South of Dixie (1944)

Cheatin' Hearts

Second Fiddle to a Steel Guitar (1965)

Checkerboard Band

Sid Sherman, George Thall; Art Wenzel

The Checkerboard Band picked a good film for their one cinema appearance in features. Gene Autry's *South of the Border* was a huge success and is considered one of his best.

South of the Border (1939)

Chelito and Gabriel [unknown]

With Love and Kisses (1936)

Chellette Sisters

Mary Jo Chellette; Judy Chellette; Carolyn Chellette

The young (sub-teen) Chellette Sisters sang on the radio in Texas and made recordings.

Country Western Hoedown (1967)

Chicagoans *see* Pete Daily and His Chicagoans

Chickie and Buck *see* Buck, Chickie and Buck

Chico Hamilton Quintet

Chico Hamilton (Forestorn Hamilton, Los Angeles, California, 1921–) (clarinet/drums); Buddy Collette (saxophone and other instruments); Jim Hall (guitar); Fred Katz (cello); Carson Smith (bass)

The Chico Hamilton Quintet, which was active mainly in the 1950s, has been called a chamber-jazz group. They featured contrapuntal music in which each instrument contributed its own line and improvised interplay between instruments. Hamilton had previously played with such jazz greats as Gerry Mulligan, Lionel Hampton and Count Basie.

Compared to similar groups the Chico Hamilton Quintet played more softly and with more subtle tonal shadings. Their first album was released in 1955 and they did a series of live radio broadcasts. By the early 1960s their sound had evolved into more of a "bop" style and in mid-decade Hamilton disbanded the Quintet to concentrate on composing and scoring for movies and television. He did lead other groups thereafter from time to time.

The Sweet Smell of Success (1957) * *Jazz on a Summer's Day* (1960) [documentary]

Chiffons

Judy Craig (1946–); Patricia Bennett (1947–); Barbara Lee (1944–1992); Sylvia Peterson (1946–)

The original Chiffons were a young teen trio when they formed in The Bronx, New York, in 1960. They had their first minor success with "Tonight's the Night," but another girl group, the Shirelles, had a bigger hit with it. By the time they added a fourth member they were ready to record their huge number one blockbuster "He's So Fine" (with its catchy first line "Doo lang, doo lang, doo lang").

The Chiffons never topped that song, which has become one of the most played songs of the golden oldie era. Later records like "One Fine Day," "I Have a Boyfriend" (the Wobble was danced to it) and "A Love So Fine" met with some plaudits as well. They also simultaneously recorded under the name of the Four Pennies and found mild success with "My Block."

The quartet was one of the Beatles' opening acts for their first American tour and they continued to produce hit recordings like "Sailor Boy" and especially "Sweet Talkin' Guy" into the late 1960s. The Chiffons continue to perform today in local venues as more or less a nostalgia group.

Disk-O-Tek Holiday (1966) "Nobody Knows What's Goin' on"

Child, Lario *see* Lario Child Orchestra

Chiquita Hernandez Orchestra

Lawless Land (1936)

Chocolate Watch Band

Mark Loomis (guitar/keyboard); Gary Andrijasevich (drums); Sean Tolby (guitar); Bill Flores (bassist); Dave Aguilar (vocals/harmonica)

The San Jose, California–based Chocolate Watch Band formed in 1965. They were a psychedelic rock band that had a short career — initially disbanding in 1968 — but were influential nevertheless. After re-forming, the group continued to release albums into the next century.

Riot on Sunset Strip (1967) * "Sitting There Standing" and "Don't Need Your Lovin'" * *The Love-Ins* (1967) "Are You Gonna Be There at the Love-In?"

Chords [unknown]

Stars on Parade (1944)

Chris Barber's Jazz Band; Chris Barber's Jazz Band with Ottilie Patterson

Chris Barber (Donald Barber, Welwyn Garden City, England, 1930–); Monty Sunshine (clarinet)

Jazz trombone player Chris Barber formed his first band in 1949 and throughout the following decades was very successful touring in European concert halls. He modeled his ensembles after those of great New Orleans jazz artists like King Oliver, eventually forming the Chris Barber Jazz and Blues Band. The group's one substantial hit was "Petite Fleur."

He was most influential in popularizing blues music in Britain by encouraging native artists, including blues singer Ottilie Patterson. By the turn of the 21st century it is estimated that Barber had performed more than 10,000 concerts and made thousands of recordings. He has since grown his band into the BIG Chris Barber Band.

Look Back in Anger (1958) * *It's Trad, Dad!* (1962)

Christian, Tommy *see* Tommy Christian and His Band

Christopher Columbus and His Swing Crew

Christopher Columbus (Joseph Morris, Atlantic City, New Jersey, 1903–)

Moon Over Harlem (1939)

Chuck Faulkner Band

Song of the Open Road (1944)

Chuck Wagon Gang

Sing a Song, for Heaven's Sake (1966) [documentary]

Chuckles

Tommy Romano (guitar); Tommy (later Russ) Gilberto (bassist); Phil Benti (accordion); Teddy Randazzo

Named for the Chuckles candy bar, the Brooklyn-based Chuckles began as a comedy team about 1949, and when they switched to music retained many of their former antics such as tossing cream pies. This shtick made them a natural for television and they guest-starred on several major programs.

The Chuckles' big hit was 1954's "Runaround," a million seller, and there was a later, less rousing, success with "And the Angels Sing." Teddy Randazzo, who had replaced original member Phil Benti, had a minor acting and solo singing career (the lead of *Rock, Rock, Rock* and the hit record "The Way of a Clown").

The Girl Can't Help It (1956)

Chuy Reyes and His Mambo Orchestra; Chuy Reyes and His Orchestra; Chuy Reyes and Orchestra

Holiday Rhythm (1950) * *Everybody's Dancin'* (1950)

Cimini Male Chorus *see* Raymond Maurel and the Cimini Male Chorus

Cirino and the Bowties

Cirino Colacrai (Brooklyn, New York)

A musician since childhood and a songwriter of some talent, Cirino Colacrai had several of his songs performed by the Three Chuckles, a pop group to which he belonged. In the mid–1950s he struck out on his own with the Bowties and had mild hits with "Rosemarie" and "Anytime."

Cirino and the Bowties were part of the rock shows presented in New York theaters, did lounge shows, and got the star treatment from legendary disc jockey Alan Freed. However there was really nothing to differentiate them from other such acts and they faded into obscurity.

Rock, Rock, Rock (1956) "Ever Since I Can Remember" and "Rock, Pretty Baby"

City Slickers *see* Spike Jones and the City Slickers

Clara Ward Singers

Clara Ward (Philadelphia, Pennsylvania, 1924–1973); Marion Williams; Henrietta Waddy (alto); Frances Steadman; Kitty Parham

Singing in her Baptist church from the age of five, Clara Ward began touring as a young girl with her mother Gertrude and older sister Willa, but it was her powerful voice that was the standout. Later, her ensemble the Famous Ward Singers became the number one female gospel group in the United States in the 1950s. She was also credited with having written some 500 gospel songs.

They began recording in 1948 and their hit records included "Surely, Our God Is Able" and "How I Got Over." They also toured extensively in the Middle and Far East. The Singers were not without controversy since they dressed in expensive gowns, wigs and jewelry rather than the somber robes some in their audiences might have preferred. And they also appeared in commercial venues like nightclubs where alcohol was served.

The original group disbanded in 1958 but a few years later Ward established another gospel group that continued to find success, even performing at Presidential inaugurations. Singers like Aretha Franklin freely acknowledged their debt to Clara Ward.

Spree (1967) [documentary] * *It's Your Thing* (1970) [documentary]

Clarence Muse Singers

Clarence Muse (Baltimore, Maryland, 1889–1979)

The holder of a law degree, Clarence Muse appeared in some 200 films culminating with *The Black Stallion* in the year he died. A veteran of vaudeville and the Negro theater in New York and Chicago, and also a trained opera singer, he entered films in 1929.

Muse was known for his dignified image on-screen, although like most Black actors of the time he sometimes had to portray a stereotypical Stepin Fetchit–like character. Among his pictures were *Hearts in Dixie*, *Arrowsmith*, *Porgy and Bess*, *Huckleberry Finn* and *Night and Day*.

He was also the composer of the song standard "Sleepy Time Down South" and had written music for movies. Muse also did much television work. Very fittingly, the beloved actor was inducted into the Black Filmmakers Hall of Fame.

Gentleman from Dixie (1941)

Clark, Dave *see* Dave Clark Five

Clark, Judy *see* Judy Clark and Her Rhythm Cowgirls

Clark Brothers
The Clark Brothers were multi-talented. They both tap danced and did a mean imitation of the close harmony masters the Ink Spots.
Killer Diller (1948)

Clauser, Al *see* Al Clauser and His Oklahoma Outlaws

Clear Light
Bob Seal (guitar); Robbie Robison (guitar); Michael Ney; Dallas Taylor; Doug Lubahn

The intriguing Brain Train was the original name of the acid rock group that came to be known as Clear Light. Founded about 1966, their first recording came in the following year and they also produced a few albums.
The President's Analyst (1967) "She's Ready to Be Free"

Clements, Curly *see* Curly Clements and His Rodeo Rangers

Cletro, Eddie *see* Eddie Cletro and His Roundup Boys

Clovers
Harold Lucas; Matthew McQuarter (tenor); Harold Winley (bass); John Bailey (lead); Bill Harris (guitar); Thomas Woods (tenor); Billy Shelton (bass)

The Clovers were formed in 1949 as the Four Clovers. Famous record mogul Ahmet Ertegun took an interest in them and even wrote many of their early songs. A couple of them, "Don't You Know I Love You?" and "Fool, Fool, Fool," became substantial hits.

Originally a group very much in the close-harmony style of the Ink Spots, by the early 1950s the Clovers had migrated to a more blues-oriented style. Their song "Hey Miss Fannie" is considered by some to be one of the very earliest rock-and-roll recordings.

Follow-up recordings such as "Devil or Angel," "One Mint Julep," "Ting-A-Ling" and "In the Middle of the Night" also became hits. Their biggest, coming in 1959 after a period of declining popularity, was "Love Potion Number Nine."

Ultimately the Clovers had more than twenty chart records before their breakup in 1961 and are considered to have been one of 1950s' most successful rhythm-and-blues groups. They reformed and continued to play well into the 1980s.
Harlem Jazz Festival (1955) [documentary] * *Rhythm-and-Blues Revue* (1955) [documentary] "Your Cash Ain't Nothing But Trash" * *Rock 'n' Roll Revue* (1955/56) [documentary]

Clyde Valley Stompers
The Clyde Valley Stompers were one of the top jazz bands in Scotland.
It's All Happening (1963)

Coats, Don *see* Don Coats and the Bon-Aires

Cochran, Nick *see* Nick Cochran's Musical Cowhands

Cochran, Wayne *see* Wayne Cochran and the C.C. Ryders

Cocker, Joe *see* Joe Cocker and the Grease Band

Cockneys
Befitting their name, the Cockneys were a 1960s English group whose colorful onstage costumes were the pearl button-covered outfits of that famous London breed. Their recordings were few, "After Tomorrow" being the most successful, and their performing life relatively short.
Go-Go Big Beat! (1965) [documentary]

Cocoanut Grove Ambassadors *see* Gus Arnheim and His Cocoanut Grove Ambassadors

Cole, King *see* King Cole Trio

Collins Sisters [unknown]
Country Western Hoedown (1967)

Colorado Cowboys *see* Walt Shrum and His Colorado Cowboys

Colorado Hillbillies *see* **Walt Shrum and His Colorado Hillbillies**

Colorado Rangers *see* **Ozie Waters and His Colorado Rangers**

Columbus, Christopher *see* **Christopher Columbus and His Swing Crew**

Comets *see* **Bill Haley and His Comets**

Comfortable Chair
Bernie Schwartz (vocals); Barbara Wallace (vocals); Gene Earfin (guitar); Gary Davis (bassist); Greg Leroy (drums); Ted Baczek (keyboard)

The California-based psychedelic group the Comfortable Chair was formed in the late 1960s and disappeared almost without trace following the release of their self-titled album.

How to Commit Marriage (1969) "Be Me"

Committee
Petulia (1968)

Coney Island Kids [unknown]
Rock, Rock, Rock (1956)

Congo Choir *see* **Prince Modupe's Congo Choir**

Conlon, Jud *see* **Judd Conlon Group**

Connecticut Yankees
Rudy Vallee (Hubert Vallee, Island Pond, Vermont, 1901–1986)

Although he went on to great fame on the radio, Broadway, and movies, the iconic image of Rudy Vallee is that of him projecting his nasal voice through a megaphone. This was presumably to be better heard at public appearances but also smacks of good publicity.

He began his musical career playing the saxophone in theaters and hotels and did radio broadcasts in England where he was appearing at the time. It was at a club appearance that he unveiled his signature greeting "Heigh-ho everybody."

The band he formed in the mid-1920s, the Connecticut Yankees (he was a Yale man), consisted of violins, saxophones and a piano (no brass), with Vallee singing in various languages through his longish nose. Among their record hits were "The Stein Song" (from the University of Maine) and "Vieni Vieni." Their theme song was "My Time Is Your Time."

Though Vallee was one of the first matinee idol singers he was an unlikely one, with his downward slanting eyes, frizzed hair and frankly not a great singing voice. He later became a gifted comic actor but in his first film, 1929's *The Vagabond Lover*, he gave an embarrassingly amateurish performance. (It was rumored that every time he tried to deliver a line, the director would shout for him to sing.)

His band mates also had some lines and all gave more credible performances than did their leader. It was on the radio that Vallee began to find more justified fame with his very significant guest stars and burgeoning comic talent. This ability he later was to use so well in numerous movies such *The Palm Beach Story, Gentlemen Marry Brunettes* and *How to Succeed in Business Without Really Trying*.

The Vagabond Lover (1929) * *Sweet Music* (1935)

Cooke and Browne [unknown]
52nd Street (1937)

Cooley, Spade *see* **Spade Cooley and His Orchestra**

Cooper, Alice *see* **Alice Cooper Band**

Copelands [unknown]
Sensations of 1945 (1944)

Coral Islanders *see* **Hubert Smith and His Coral Islanders**

Corn Colonel and His Band; Freddie Fisher and His Schnickelfritz Band; Schnickelfritz Band
Freddie Fisher (Lourdes, Iowa, 1904–1967)

The leader of the Schnickelfritz Band (the name means something like "scamp" in German), Freddie Fisher was also known as Colonel Corn of Dixieland. Based in Minnesota, and founded about 1934, the band was discovered by crooner Rudy Vallee in 1937 and put on the radio.

As its name might suggest, the Schnickelfritz ensemble was heavily into comedy antics in the manner of Spike Jones, who came along a few years later. During the acme of Fisher's career in the 1930s and '40s he was said to have made about 200 recordings.

Gold Diggers in Paris (1938) * *The Sultan's Daughter* (1944) * *Seven Days Ashore* (1944) * *Jamboree* (1944) * *That's My Baby* (1944) * *Make Mine Laughs* (1949)

Corps De Ballet and Glee Club
Bitter Sweet (1940)

Cotton, Darlene *see* Darlene Cotton Quartet

Cotton and Chick Watts [unknown]
Yes Sir, Mr. Bones (1951)

Cotton Club Orchestra
There were Cotton Club Orchestras in both New York's Harlem and in Los Angeles. It is possible that both appeared in films.

Check and Double Check (1930) * *Taxi!* (1932) * *Bargain with Bullets* (1937)

Cottonpicker Quartette *see* Bobby Brooks and the Cottonpicker Quartette

Count Basie and His Octet; Count Basie and His Orchestra; Count Basie and Orchestra; Count Basie Septet
Count Basie (William Basie, Red Bank, New Jersey, 1904–1984).

Although he was not considered a great instrumental virtuoso or an innovator in composition, Count Basie was noted for organizing outstanding jazz bands with the best sidemen, and vocalists like Billie Holiday. As a performer it was said that he could produce more music with two fingers on the piano than most people with all ten. He also played the organ.

Basie led integrated bands from 1935 to 1950

A natty Count Basie.

and smaller groups, including a sextet, until about 1983, but he occasionally re-formed larger ensembles. Known for the yachting cap he always wore onstage, he was the composer of the famous 1937 tune "One o'Clock Jump," his theme song.

His band's recordings included "April in Paris" and "Swingin' the Blues." Basie was undoubtedly one of jazz's most beloved figures and was recognized by Kennedy Center Honors in 1981. His had been one of the first bands to play a Royal Command Performance before Queen Elizabeth II.

Policy Man (1938) * *Reveille with Beverly* (1943) * *Top Man* (1943) * *Crazy House* (1943) * *Hit Parade of 1943* (1943) * *Harlem Jazz Festival* (1955) [documentary] * *Jamboree* (1957) "Jamboree" and One O'Clock Jump" * *Sex and the Single Girl* (1964) * *Made in Paris* (1966)

Country Boys *see* Len Nash and His Country Boys

Country Gentlemen
The Country Gentlemen were a vocal ensemble.
The Big Hangover (1950)

Country Joe and the Fish

Joe McDonald; Barry Melton (guitar); Chicken Hirsch

"Country" Joe McDonald and Barry "The Fish" Melton were the core of their self-named psychedelic band. They appeared at prominent festivals (Monterey Pop and Woodstock) and with most of the major bands of the mid–1960s and early '70s. Consistent with the mood of those times they were vocal opponents of the war in Vietnam.

Revolution (1968) [documentary] * "Fixin' to Die Rag" * *Monterey Pop* (1969) [documentary] "Section 43" * *G-as-s-s-s* (1968; released 1970) "World That We All Dreamed of" * *Woodstock* (1970) [documentary] "Rockin' Soul Music" * *Zachariah* (1971) "We're the Crackers," "All I Need" and "Poor But Honest Crackers" * *More American Graffiti* (1979) "I-Feel-Like-I'm Fixin'-to-Die-Rag"

Country Junction Boys

Country Music Jamboree (1970)

Counts [unknown]

The Biggest Bundle of Them All (1968)

Cow, Minnie *see* Minnie Cow and His Orchestra

Cowtown Wranglers *see* Hobie Shepp and the Cowtown Wranglers

Cream

Eric Clapton (guitar); Ginger Baker (drums); Jack Bruce (bassist)

Before they formed Cream, one of the most celebrated British rock bands of the later 1960s, the trio of musicians had been veterans of other groups. Eric Clapton particularly was feted as one of the premier guitarists of his time.

Cream produced many hits including "Sunshine of Your Love," "I Feel Free" and "Crossroads." It was not long, however, before the members' clashing egos led to a breakup in 1968. Despite its brief time in the limelight the band's reputation remains intact and there have been rapturously-received reunions.

Cream's Farewell Concert (1968) [documentary] "I'm So Glad," "Sunshine of Your Love" and other songs

Creole Chorus

Spirit of Youth (1938)

Crew Chiefs [unknown]

Swing the Western Way (1947)

Crickets

Buddy Holly (Charles Holley, Texas, 1936–1959); Niki Sullivan (South Gate, California) (guitar); Joe Mauldin (bassist); Jerry Allison (drums); Larry Wellborn (bassist); Sonny Curtis (Meadow, Texas, 1937–); Jerry Naylor (aka Jackie Garrard) (Stephenville, Texas, 1939–)

Inevitably, the Crickets are associated with pop singer Buddy Holly whose great talent and early death made him an enduring legend. The Crickets were formed in 1957, the year they recorded the smash hit "That'll Be the Day." Afterwards the group was considered Holly's backup and their recordings were sometimes credited to Buddy Holly and the Crickets or only to him.

Originally based in Lubbock, Texas, the Crickets had hit after hit, including "Peggy Sue" (the name of Jerry Allison's wife). Buddy Holly earned increasing fame and went on to a solo career in New York before his 1959 death in a plane crash. The Crickets continued performing and were still releasing albums into the 21st century.

Just for Fun (1963) "My Little Girl" and "Teardrops Fall Like Rain" * *The Girls on the Beach* (1965) ("They Call Her) La Bamba"

Crinoline Choir

Ivie Anderson

A Day at the Races (1937) * *Broadway Melody of 1938* (1937)

Crosby, Bing *see* Bing Crosby and His Rhythm Boys

Crosby, Bob *see* Bob Crosby...

Crosby, Stills, Nash and Young

David Crosby (1941–); Stephen Stills (Dallas, Texas, 1945–) (lead guitar); Graham Nash (1942–); Neil Young (Toronto, Canada, 1945–)

The three-man core of the famous harmony group were David Crosby, Stephen Stills and Graham Nash who joined forces in 1969 playing country-rock. As a trio they quickly gained a reputation for both their smooth singing and songwriting abilities. Individually they had previously performed with top rock groups like the Byrds, Buffalo Springfield and the Hollies.

The threesome's fame increased following their appearance at the Woodstock festival and composition of such popular pieces as "Suite: Judy Blue Eyes" and "Long Time Gone." Their first hit was "Marrakesh Express" in 1969. Graham Nash wrote the popular "Just a Song Before I Go."

Neil Young was added to make up the quartet of Crosby, Stills, Nash and Young and their music took on a more political tone. The group's success on recordings and in live concerts did not prevent internal dissension and they disbanded in 1971, only to have periodic reunions thereafter.

They continued to regroup as trios and duos in various combinations and their influence on other musicians remains strong to this day. David Crosby acted in several films including *Hook* and *Backdraft*. His volatile personality had caused him to be fired from the Byrds and he continued to make headlines with arrests for drug and firearms violations.

Woodstock (1970) [documentary] "Suite: Judy Blue Eyes" * *Celebration at Big Sur* (1971) [documentary] * *No Nukes* (1980) [documentary]

Cubanos [unknown]
Bop Girl Goes Calypso (1957)

Cugat, Xavier *see* Xavier Cugat and His Orchestra

Cullen and Pauline [unknown]
A Day at the Races (1937)

Curly Clements and His Rodeo Rangers
Six-Gun Law (1948)

Curly Williams and His Georgia Peach Pickers
Curly (sometimes Curley) Williams (Dock Williams, 1913–1970) (fiddle); Joseph Williams (guitar); Sanford Williams (bassist); Clyde Harris (guitar); Joe Pope (piano); Jimmy Selph (guitar)

Originally known as the Santa Fe Trail Riders, the Georgia Peach Pickers played on radio in the South, including on the Grand Ole Opry. They were considered one of the better western/hillbilly swing bands in the 1940s and '50s with recordings like "Georgia Boogie," "Good Old Alabam'" and "Texas Swing." Leader Curly Williams was also a songwriter.

Riders of the Lone Star (1947) "Oh Monah" and "Let Me By"

Curt Barrett and the Trailsmen; Curt Barrett's Trailsmen
Curt Barrett (Gerald Barrett, Morehouse, Missouri, 1906–1989) (guitar); Harry Duncan (fiddle); Stanley Ellison (accordion); Clarence Dooley (bassist)

Besides his film appearances with the Trailsmen, Barrett appeared solo in almost thirty movies and on 1950s television. He had begun performing western music when he was a teenager on the rodeo circuit.

Song of the Prairie (1945) * *Gunning for Vengeance* (1946) * *Drifting Along* (1946) * *The Gentleman from Texas* (1946) * *Raiders of the South* (1947) * *Mask of the Dragon* (1951)

Curtis Mosby and His Orchestra
Curtis Mosby (Kansas City, Missouri)

Drummer and sometime violinist Curtis Mosby played for the jazz ensembles the Tennessee Ten and the Blue Blowers from the 1920s. Late in that decade he scored music for the pioneering Black talkie *Hallelujah* and also appeared in it. Later he operated nightclubs in Los Angeles.

Hallelujah! (1929) * *Broken Strings* (1940)

Cyrkle
Don Dannermann (guitar); Tom Dawes (guitar); Earl Pickens (keyboard); Marty Fried (drums)

The rock band the Cyrkle had a wild ride from an obscure college band known as the Rhondells to being managed by Beatles' manager Brian Epstein. They are best-known for their 1966 hit "Red Rubber Ball" and "Turn-Down Day."

In 1966 the Cyrkle was chosen to open for a Beatles' tour on which they played to as many as 70,000 people. But with their mentor Brian Epstein's death in 1967 the band lost momentum and soon broke up. However, they were a talented group and much more than just a flash in the pan.

The Minx (1967, released 1969) "Murray the Why"

Dahl, Ted *see* Ted Dahl and His Orchestra

Daily, Pete *see* Pete Daily and His Chicagoans

Dakotas *see* Billy J. Kramer and the Dakotas

Dale, Dick *see* Dick Dale and the Del Tones

Daley, Jimmy *see* Jimmy Daley...

Dandridge Girls Trio; Dandridge Sisters

Dorothy Dandridge (Cleveland, Ohio, 1922–1965); Vivian Dandridge (d. 1991); Etta Jones

Since her early death the beautiful Dorothy Dandridge has been the fascinating subject of numerous books and television programs. The daughter of actress Ruby Dandridge, she and her older sister Vivian started in show business as the multi-talented Wonder Children who sang, danced and even performed acrobatics.

The elder Dandridge, a fierce stage mother, eventually teamed her children with Etta Jones, dubbing them the Dandridge Sisters. After they moved to Southern California both the "sisters" and mother embarked on a screen career. Usually playing sassy maids, Ruby was the more successful in films but the girls also got small roles. They also scored an engagement at the Cotton Club.

The "sister" act disbanded in the mid-1940s when Dorothy married dancer Harold Nicholas. She grew to be a legendary beauty and embarked on her own solo career singing with the Jimmy Lunceford band. Her screen career as a leading lady took off in the 1950s, but she had played small parts since the 1930s and appeared in about twenty-five pictures.

Dandridge found success in such films as *Carmen Jones* (with an Oscar nomination), *Bright Road*, *Island in the Sun* and *Porgy and Bess*. But her own personal demons and the implicit racism of the day doomed her career and, ultimately, her as well. She and Vivian had had a falling-out in the 1950s and never met again. In 1999 Halle Berry portrayed her in a made-for-television film.

The Big Broadcast of 1936 * *Easy to Take* (1936) * *It Can't Last Forever* (1937)

Danny and the Juniors

Frank Maffei (2nd tenor); Danny Rapp (d. 1983); Joe Terry (Joe Terranova) (baritone); Dave White (David Tricker) (1st tenor); Billy Carlucci

The irresistible "At the Hop" (originally titled "Do the Bop"), a veritable anthem of the golden age of rock and roll, was written by a band member of Danny and the Juniors and performed by them. They were one of the first groups to reinterpret Black rhythm-and-blues music for a white audience.

Starting out as the Philadelphia-based Juvenaires in the mid–1950s, the quartet never again topped that massive two-and-a-half million seller but did have modest successes with "Rock and Roll Is Here to Stay," "Back to the Hop" and "Twistin' U.S.A."

The Philadelphia-based Juniors were voted the best new group of 1957 and toured with some of the great rock artists of the 1950s, as well as making numerous television appearances. They officially broke up in 1964 but have made sporadic reunions.

More than fifty years later some of the original Juniors are still playing under the name of Danny and the Juniors, Featuring Joe Terry and continuing to remind audiences of that great bygone age of rock.

Let's Rock! (1958) "At the Hop" * *Let the Good Times Roll* (1973) [documentary] "At the Hop"

Darby, Ken *see* Ken Darby...

Darlene Cotton Quartet
Sugar Daddy (1968)

Darling Sisters

Polly Darling (Pauline Goebel, Houston, Texas, 1928–); Maryellen Darling (Maryellen Goebel, Houston, Texas, 1924–2004)

48 D'Artega

The young western singers known as the Darling Sisters toured U.S. military bases during World War II and had their own television show in the early 1950s. They also made history of sorts by being among the opening acts of gangster Bugsy Siegel's new Flamingo Hotel in Las Vegas just after the war.

Varieties on Parade (1951)

D'Artega and His All-Girl Orchestra

Alfonso D'Artega (Mexico?, 1907–1998)

A songwriter, conductor and arranger, Alfonso D'Artega had conducted many symphony orchestras and had bona fides as a serious musician. The all-girl orchestra he fronted in one film was thus a novelty sideline to the major part of his career. His best known composition was the pretty "In the Blue of Evening." He also (improbably) played Tchaikovsky in the movie *Carnegie Hall*.

You Can't Ration Love (1944)

Dave Apollon and His Orchestra

Dave Apollon (Kiev, Russia, 1897–1972)

Modestly billed as the "World's Greatest Mandolin Virtuoso," Dave Apollon made his first mark in the United States in vaudeville. He was a man of many parts, being a nightclub entrepreneur, appearing on Broadway and in numerous musical film shorts, and making recordings with a group of musicians from the Philippines.

Some of Apollon's earlier records featured an intriguing combination of gypsy, Latin and ragtime music. He wound up his career as a long-time Las Vegas attraction and released several albums of his music.

Merry-Go-Round of 1938 (1937)

Dave Appell and the Applejacks

Dave Appell (Philadelphia, Pennsylvania, 1922–)

Starting out as an arranger for several dance bands and as a record producer, Dave Appell wrote a jazzed-up version of the Mexican hat dance called "The Mexican Hat Rock." This was the Applejacks' biggest hit; they later had a lesser success with "Rocka-Conga."

Don't Knock the Rock (1956) * *Go-Go Big Beat* (1965) [documentary] "Like Dreamers Do" * *Disk-O-Tek Holiday* (1966) "Tell Me When"

Dave Clark Five

Denis Payton (Walthamstow, England, 1943?–2006) (saxophone/guitar/harmonica); Dave Clark (London, England, 1942–) (percussion); Mike Smith (London, England, 1943–2008) (piano/organ); Rick Huxley (Dartford, England, 1944–) (bass); Lenny Davidson (Enfield, England, 1944–) (guitar)

At one point early in the British Invasion the Dave Clark Five rivaled the mighty Beatles in hit records and fan mania with their so-called "Tottenham Sound" (the London area where Clark was born). The group had originally been formed to raise money to send a youth soccer team abroad.

The Five's U.S. tours were sell-outs and they had more than twenty chart songs. The late 1963 release "Glad All Over" was their first big hit and was followed by the equally large "Bits and Pieces," both selling more than two million copies.

Such venues as the Ed Sullivan television show and even Carnegie Hall showcased them. However, unlike the Beatles, the individual members

The Dave Clark Five.

of the Dave Clark Five did not develop the public personas that would distinguish them from each other.

Although further hits like "Over and Over," "Because" and "I Like It Like That" came along they had no top charters after 1967, and by the early 1970s they had disbanded. Their starring movie *Having a Wild Weekend*, in which they played movie stuntmen, marked the directorial debut of John Boorman.

Get Yourself a College Girl (1964) * "Whenever You're Around" and "Thinking of You Baby" * *Having a Wild Weekend* (1965) "Catch Us If You Can," "I Can't Stand It," "Sweet Memories" and several other songs * *American Music—from Folk to Jazz to Pop* (1967) [documentary]

Dave Miller and His New York French Casino Band
Meet John Doe (1941)

Davis, Art *see* Art Davis and His Rhythm Riders

Davis, Jimmie *see* Jimmie Davis...

Davis, Johnny *see* Johnny "Scat" Davis and His Orchestra

Davis, Meyer *see* Meyer Davis and His Orchestra

Davis, Spencer *see* Spencer Davis Group

Davis and Johnson [unknown]
Casa Manana (1951)

Dawson, Ted *see* Ted Dawson and Orchestra

Day, Dawn and Dusk
Bob Carver (piano); Eddie Coleman; Gus Simmons

The instrumental trio calling themselves Day, Dawn and Dusk probably began their professional careers in the 1940s. They played an eclectic mix of musical styles and released their first recordings late in the decade, continuing on through the late 1950s. Among their records were "The Kiss That Broke My Heart," "Let the Tears Fall" and "Anytime."

Dancing in Manhattan (1944)

Dean, Eddie *see* Eddie Dean Trio

Dean, Jimmy *see* Jimmy Dean and His Trail Riders

Debonairs [unknown]
Priorities on Parade (1942)

Debutantes; Debutantes Quartet
The Debutantes were a trio who sang with the orchestra of Ted Fio Rito in the mid-1930s. In *The Wizard of Oz* they were heard as the voices of the Lullaby League.

The Wizard of Oz (1939) (voices only) * *Babes on Broadway* (1942)

De Castro Sisters
Peggy De Castro (Marguerita De Castro, Dominican Republic, 1921–2004); Babette De Castro (d. 1993); Cherie De Castro

Beginning in the 1940s as a Latin music act in nightclubs, and dubbing themselves the "Cuban Bombshells" (they were also called the Cuban

The very glamorous De Castro Sisters.

Andrews Sisters), the three De Castros were protégées of Brazilian star Carmen Miranda.

The De Castros profitably turned to pop in the next decade. It was in this period that their big hit "Teach Me Tonight" was recorded and the 1950s proved to be their most popular time. When Babette left the act in 1958 she was replaced by their cousin Olgita (1936?–2000).

The extremely glamorous sisters did several novelty tunes like "Boom Boom Boomerang," "Biddle-Dee Bop" and "Rockin' and Rollin' in Hawaii" as well as more standard ballads, so they could never be pigeonholed.

Rhythm Round-Up (1945) * *Stairway for a Star* (1946?) * *Over the Santa Fe Trail* (1947) * *Copacabana* (1947)

Dee, Joey *see* Joey Dee and the Starliters

Deek Watson and the Brown Dots

Deek Watson (Ivory Watson, Washington, D.C., 1909–1969) (2nd tenor); Joe King (lead tenor) (soon replaced by Jimmie Nabbie); Jimmy Gordon (bass); William "Pat" Best (baritone/guitar)

Deek Watson began singing in groups with names like the Percolating Puppies and the Four Ruff Brothers that finally transmogrified into the beloved Ink Spots. He departed that group acrimoniously in 1944 and attempted to establish an offshoot with the same name. When he was stopped by a lawsuit, he founded the Brown Dots, obviously hoping to recreate the magic of his former group.

However, the Brown Dots were more into swing tunes, while the Ink Spots favored sweeter sounds. They played mostly in theaters and also had two fifteen minute radio shows, recording their first song "(For) Sentimental Reasons" in 1945, which became a hit for several other artists,

Unfortunately, Watson was a pugnacious man (as he had been with the Ink Spots) and he and his new group did not get along too well. By late 1946 the other Brown Dots had left to form the Sentimentalists and eventually became the Four Tunes. As such they went on to become a major pop group in the 1950s.

In the meantime, Deek Watson formed another group called the Brown Dots that made some recordings, and then he reinvented himself yet again as Deek Watson and the Four Dots.

He never recaptured the glory days of the original Ink Spots, but at some point he got legal permission to head a new Ink Spots group in which he performed nearly to the time of his death.

Boy! What a Girl (1946) * "Satchelmouth Baby" and "Just in Case You Change Your Mind" * *Sepia Cinderella* (1946) "Long Legged Lizzie" and "Is It Right?" * *Harlem Follies* (1950)

Deep River Boys

Harry Douglas (baritone); Jimmy Lundy; Edward Ware (bass); Vernon Gardner (1st tenor); George Lawson (2nd tenor); Leroy Wayman; Rhett Butler

Despite their Biblical-sounding name the Deep River Boys were not primarily a gospel group. Formed in Virginia in the mid–1930s and winners of a Major Bowes radio amateur contest, they toured military bases during World War II and had some success on Broadway and in appearances with early television stars like Milton Berle and Kate Smith.

Finding as much success in Canada and Europe as they did in their native country, the Boys recorded such tunes as "By the Light of the Silvery Moon," "Solid as a Rock" and "Tuxedo Junction." They had long engagements at such venues as the London Palladium.

In the 1950s the Deep River Boys became a trio that toured Europe for half of each year and produced recordings the rest of the time. With the last original member Harry Douglas they remained active into the 1980s.

Tales of Manhattan (1942)†

†Their appearance in the film has not been verified.

Defranco, Buddy *see* Buddy Defranco Quartet Combo

Del-Aires

Ronnie Linares (guitar); Gary Jones (bassist); Bobby Osborne (saxophone); John Becker (drums)

From the late 1950s the Del-Aires were a New Jersey band playing clubs in the New York area, and they issued a few minor records like "Elaine," "Arlene" and "I'm Your Baby." During a 1963 gig in a New Jersey nightspot two police officers were shot to death. The group broke up shortly thereafter.

The Horror of Party Beach (1964) "Joyride" "The Zombie Stomp" "You Are Not a Summer Love" "Just Wigglin' and Wobblin'" "Elaine" and "Gotcha Where I Want You"

Del Rio *see* Ascencio Del Rio Trio

Del Tones *see* Dick Dale and the Del Tones

Del-Vikings (aka Dell-Vikings)

David Lerchey (1938–2005); Norman Wright; Clarence Quick (bass); Kripp Johnson (Corinthian Johnson, 1933–1990) (tenor); Donald "Gus" Backus; Don Jackson (baritone); Samuel Patterson (tenor); Bernard Robertson (2nd tenor)

One of the few racially mixed rock groups of its time, the Del-Vikings (sometimes spelled Dell-Vikings with and without a hyphen) formed about 1955 as a group of Air Force buddies. Part of their unusual name came from the Vikings, a baseball team.

Eventually they produced several big hits; one of them "Come Go with Me" landed in the top ten, supposedly the first top ten song to be performed by an ethnically-mixed group. The song had originally been sung in an Air Force talent show in which the Del-Vikings bested 700 competitors.

For complicated contractual reasons, the Del-Vikings split up into two groups and one assumed the name Dell-Vikings. The lilting "Whispering Bells" followed and with "Cool Shake" the groups had three hits on the charts simultaneously.

The two Vikings groups re-formed and broke apart with some regularity until the Dell-Vikings (also known as the Versatiles) disbanded. Their brother ensemble also broke up in 1965 only to re-team briefly a few years later.

The Big Beat (1958) "Can't Wait"

Dell Vikings *see* Del-Vikings

Delta Rhythm Boys

Lee Gaines (d. 1987) (bass); Carl Jones; Kelsey Pharr; Traverse Crawford (2nd tenor); Elmaurice Miller (1st tenor); Essie Atkins (baritone); Clinton Holland; Buddy Collette; A. Grant; Chico Hamilton; Red Mack

Aside from the recordings "Dry Bones" and "Just A-Sittin' and A-Rockin'" the Delta Rhythm Boys found little success in that medium during the dozen years following their formation in the mid–1930s at Oklahoma's Langston University. While there they were known as the Frederick Hall Quartet, after their musical mentor.

Despite the dearth of recording hits, they had done many live performances and appeared on radio and in Broadway shows like *The Hot Mikado* and *Hellzapoppin'*. They also were under contract to Universal Studio and made many films.

What finally brought them recording popularity was the first of their tours to Europe in 1949, during which they made some records that included Swedish and Finnish folk tunes. They actually had made their first professional appearances abroad as well, on Buenos Aires radio and then touring South America.

Among their records were "Sentimental Journey," "Don't Ask Me Why" and "I'll Never Get Out of This World Alive." Their popularity abroad, especially in France, led to the Delta Rhythm Boys establishing a home base there and probably prolonging their careers by some fifty years.

You'll Never Get Rich (1941) * *Crazy House* (1943) * *Hi'Ya, Sailor* (1943) * *So's Your Uncle* (1943) * *Week-End Pass* (1944) * *The Reckless Age* (1944) * *Hi, Good Lookin'* (1944) * *Follow the Boys* (1944) * *Night Club Girl* (1945) * *Easy to Look at* (1945) * *Rock 'n' Roll Revue* (1955/56) [documentary] * *Rhythm and Blues Revue* (1955) [documentary]

De Lugg, Milton *see* Milton De Lugg and His Swing Wing

De Marco Sisters

Ann De Marco (Rome, New York); Joan De Marco (Rome, New York); Gloria De Marco (Rome, New York); Terry De Marco (Rome, New York); Arlene De Marco (Rome, New York)

The five De Marco Sisters hit their acme in the ten years from 1945 to 1955 with their infectious harmony, although some of them had begun performing as early as 1937. They were

The De Marco Sisters on a radio show (1945).

popular on radio (the *Fred Allen Show*) and television, and toured with some of the top singers of the day, including Frank Sinatra, Dean Martin and Nat Cole.

The De Marcos' recordings were numerous and popular, including "It's Been a Long, Long Time," "Under the Bamboo Tree," "This Love of Mine" and "I'm Through with Love."

Skirts Ahoy! (1952)

Denny, Jack *see* Jack Denny and His Orchestra

Desi Arnaz and His Orchestra

Desi Arnaz (Desiderio Arnaz y De Acha III, Santiago, Cuba, 1917–1986)

Very little that Desi Arnaz did as an orchestra leader or actor in early 1940s films (*Too Many Girls, Bataan,* etc.) was destined to match his later worldwide fame as the often-beleaguered "Ricky Ricardo" in the beloved 1950s television series *I Love Lucy*. He played the harried husband of ditsy redhead Lucy (Lucille Ball) and this is his inevitable legacy. His band was often featured on the show.

Although he played the guitar and drums and sang a wide variety of songs, the raucous, conga drum-accompanied "Babalu" seemed to be his theme song. Despite its ubiquity, however, his orchestra's theme song actually was "Cuban Pete." He toured widely with his band and made theater appearances at a time when Latin-American music was very popular.

Desi Arnaz was not considered a great musician; however, he *was* great as the "straight man" to his wife. In reality he was more than that, having impeccable timing and wonderfully comedic line delivery. He was a lot more than the mere bongo player some had dismissively thought him to be.

Cuban Pete (1946)

Deuce Spriggins and His Band

Deuce Spriggins (bassist); Carolina Cotton (Helen Hagstrom, Cash, Arkansas, 1925–1997) (vocals); Hank Caldwell

Formerly members of the Spade Cooley orchestra, married couple Deuce Spriggins and Carolina Cotton founded their own western swing group in 1945. She had appeared in many westerns and was a well-known singer and yodeler.

The short-lived band, which also featured Andy Parker and the Plainsmen, played mainly in Southern California venues and made very few recordings before disbanding about a year later.

Song of the Prairie (1945) * *That Texas Jamboree* (1946) * *Cowboy Blues* (1946) * *Singing on the Trail* (1946)

Diamond, Leo *see* **Leo Diamond...**

Diamond Brothers *see* **Leo Diamond...**

Diamonds

Stan Fisher (lead); Dave Somerville (lead); Ted Kowalski (tenor); Phil Levitt (baritone); Bill Reed (bass); John Felton (d. 1982)

Not to be confused with the New York–based African-American group of the same name, the Canadian-based Diamonds had numerous hits between 1956 and 1961, many of them cover records of Black artists. These included "Why Do Fools Fall in Love?" and "Love, Love, Love."

The Diamonds' first major success was "Little Darlin'" (a five million seller, complete with cowbells and castanets), followed by "Church Bells May Ring" and "The Stroll," one of their few original songs, which became a dance craze.

At one time the most successful white pop group of the 1950s, by 1961 there were no original members left but they reunited briefly in 1974. By then at least two or maybe more groups were performing under the Diamonds' name. In one iteration or another, they are still performing today.

The Big Beat (1958) "Where Mary Goes" and "Little Darlin'"

Dick and Dee Dee

Dick St. John (Richard Gosting, 1940–2003); Dee Dee (Mary Sperling)

In the late 1950s the youngsters who were to become Dick and Dee Dee first met in junior high school. It was not until they were in college that they began their nine-year collaboration, a teaming that included the smash "The Mountain's High." Together they were to have five top thirty hits, with the duo's signature combination of doo wop, soul and rhythm-and-blues music.

Dick, who was also a songwriter, and Dee Dee were semi-regulars on the popular 1960s television show *Shindig* before Dee Dee departed the act. She was replaced by Dick's wife Sandy. In the meantime such recordings as "Young and in Love," "Turn Around" and "Thou Shalt Not Steal" were heard on the airwaves.

Wild Wild Winter (1966) "Heartbeats"

Dick Dale and the Del-Tones

Dick Dale (Richard Monsour, Quincy or Boston, Massachusetts, 1937–)

"King of the Surf Guitar" was the name given to Dick Dale who is often credited with popularizing surf music. The first hit in that genre was said to be his "Let's Go Trippin'" in 1961 which paved the way for the Beach Boys and others who followed.

Although in the early days Dale mainly confined himself to Southern California venues, his powerful reverberating guitar style was very influential throughout the country. With the Del-Tones he produced other hits including "Miserlou," "Surf Beat" and "Scavenger." He staged a comeback in the 1980s when he undertook his first national tour.

Multi-talented Dick Dale played several instruments including the trumpet, drums, piano, saxophone and most famously his right-handed guitar which he played with his left hand without reversing the strings.

Beach Party (1963) "Secret Surfin' Spot" and "Surfin' and a-Swingin'" * *A Swingin' Affair* (1963) "A Swingin' Affair" * *Rebel in the Ring* (1963) "Miserlou" * *Muscle Beach Party* (1965) "Muscle Beach Party," "Surfin' Woodie" and "My First Love"

Dick Stabile and His Band

Dick Stabile (Newark, New Jersey, 1909–1980)

The favorite bandleader of the comedy team of Dean Martin and Jerry Lewis, Dick Stabile got his start playing saxophone in Broadway theater orchestras of the 1920s. For several years thereafter the orchestra of Ben Bernie was his home before he assembled his own group in 1935 or '36. During the War he led a Coast Guard band.

Stabile's orchestra, whose theme song was the pretty "Blue Nocturne," made many recordings without having a breakout hit. Their biggest success proved to be at the New York World's Fair of 1939–'40, leading to gigs at some of the top hotels. His was also the house band at the Slapsie Maxie's club in Hollywood.

His association with Martin and Lewis, which was to persevere with one or the other after their breakup in 1956, lasted until his death. Their association had begun in 1949 at Ciro's nightclub in Los Angeles. Stabile worked with them on television, radio, recordings and in the movies, in which he played an occasional solo acting role, as in *At War with the Army*.

My Friend Irma Goes West (1950) * *Sailor Beware* (1951) * *The Caddy* (1953)

Dick Winslow and His Orchestra

Winter Carnival (1939)

Dingalings *see* Jimmy Daley and the Dingalings

Dinning Sisters

Lou Dinning (Ella Dinning, Kentucky, 1922–) (alto); Ginger Dinning (Virginia Dinning, Oklahoma, 1924–) (lead vocals); Jean Dinning (Eugenia Dinning, Oklahoma, 1924–) (soprano); Jayne Bundesen; Tootsie Dinning (Dolores Dinning)

Although perhaps less known today than they deserve, the three Dinning Sisters (the younger two were twins) were very popular in their day. Blessed with perfect pitch, they started their careers with the orchestra of their brother Ace, sang close harmony on their own radio show while in their teens, appeared in local nightclubs, and toured with the Herbie Holmes Orchestra.

After signing with NBC in 1939 for their own radio program, they launched a successful career in important nightclubs and on major radio shows, including the National Barn Dance. Some of the cast of that program, including the Dinnings, made a few mid-'40s movies. An earlier engagement in Hollywood had led to an appearance in a wartime musical film.

Among the Sisters' popular recordings together were "My Adobe Hacienda," "I Wonder Who's Kissing Her Now" and their big success the million seller "Buttons and Bows." They also did novelty tunes like "The Iggity Song" and "Down in the Diving Bell."

Eldest sister Lou Dinning went solo in the 1940s and was eventually replaced by younger sister Tootsie. She recorded such songs as "The Little White Cloud That Cried" and "Nobody Else but Me."

Their popularity waned in the mid–1950s and the Dinning Sisters retired from the scene in the 1960s. But musical talent ran in the family; younger brother Mark had a hit rock-and-roll record "Teen Angel" a few years later.

Strictly in the Groove (1942) * *The National Barn Dance* (1944) * *Rhythm Round-Up* (1945) * *That Texas Jamboree* (1946) * *Throw a Saddle on a Star* (1946) * *Fun and Fancy Free* (1947) (voices only) * *Melody Time* (1948) (voices only)

Dino, Desi and Billy

Dino (Dean Paul Martin, Santa Monica, California, 1951–1987); Desi (also known as Desi Arnaz, Jr.) (Desiderio Arnaz IV, 1953–); Billy (William Hinsche, Philippines, 1951–)

When you want to break into show business it does not hurt to be the scions of celebrity. This describes two members of the pop trio Dino, Desi and Billy, the former two teenagers being the sons of stars Dean Martin and Desi Arnaz respectively. The elder Martin's pal Frank Sinatra was the one who gave them their start on his record label and their one major film starred Dean Martin.

The trio found brief celebrity in the mid–1960s with tunes such as "I'm a Fool" and "Not the Lovin' Kind." They did not play instruments on their

The Dinning Sisters (at left) in *That Texas Jamboree*.

recordings and were not great singers, but they did open for such superior acts as the Beach Boys.

Their fame did not outlive their teen years and by 1970 Dino, Desi and Billy had gone their separate ways. Desi turned into a not too bad juvenile actor and appeared with his mother Lucille Ball on one of her television series. Young Dean also gave acting a shot before his early accidental death.

Murderers' Row (1966) "If You're Thinking What I'm Thinking" * *Follow Me* (1969)

Dixie Jubilee Singers; Jubilee Singers

Hallelujah! (1929) "Let My People Go," "Swing Low, Sweet Chariot" and "Gimme Dat Old Time Religion" * *Show Boat* (1929) (voices only) * *Swanee River* (1931)

Don Albert and His Orchestra

Don Albert (Albert Dominique, New Orleans, Louisiana, 1908/09–1980)

Trumpeter Don Albert formed his own band about 1932 after he had played throughout the South with another band from the age of seventeen. Although his orchestra recorded few tunes, their "Sheik of Araby" and "Liza" made a minor splash. The ensemble disbanded but he continued working with other orchestras to the late 1960s. If true, one of his claims to fame was that he invented the term "swing band."

Beale Street Mama (1946?)

Don Coats and the Bon-Aires

Rock Baby, Rock It! (1957) "China Star," "Love Never Forgets" and other songs

Don Cossack Chorus

Serge Jaroff, conductor
Maytime (1937) * *Hotel Imperial* (1939)

Don Heywood and His Band

The Exile (1931)

Don Randi Trio Plus One

Don Randi (New York, New York, 1937–)

A music arranger and composer for various Hollywood studios, Don Randi also led the jazz group Quest and has recorded many albums.

Fireball 500 (1966) "Country Carnival"

Dona Drake and Her Girl Band

Dona Drake (aka Rita Rio, Rita Shaw, Una Vilon and Rita Ray) (Rita Novella, Mexico City, Mexico, 1914–1989)

From 1935 to the '50s Dona Drake mainly acted in "B" films with an occasional more expensively-produced opus like *The Road to Morocco* and *Star-Spangled Rhythm*. She had previously been a band vocalist and was a band leader from 1936 to 1940 under one of her several names, Rita Rio. That ensemble made at least one musical short, but it was probably an entirely different group that made the feature.

Salute for Three (1943)

Donahue, Al *see* Al Donahue...

Doors

Jim Morrison (1943–1971) (vocals); Robby Krieger (1946?–) (guitar); Ray Manzarek (1939?–) (organ/keyboard); John Densmore (1945?–) (drums)

The legendary rock group the Doors was founded by two UCLA film school students Jim Morrison and Ray Manzarek in 1965, and it has lasted in one form or another to the current time. The charismatic and classically handsome (and often arrested) Jim Morrison became a separate legend in himself as their young, doomed leader.

The Doors' name supposedly came from the William Blake poem about the "doors of perception." By 1966 the group had secured a reputation both positive and infamous, due to the often-drunken or coked-up obscene outbursts of Morrison. Although they were often fired because of this it naturally served to increase their fame.

Many of their songs, such as "The End" and "Light My Fire," were practically production numbers since they lasted much longer than the standard length of rock tunes. These numbers and "Hello, I Love You" made the Doors one of the top bands in the country during the latter 1960s, during which time they released seven gold albums.

In 1969 Morrison was accused of exposing himself during a concert in Miami and this incident, together with his consuming addictions, led to the slow decline of the band. The last appearance of the original members came in 1970. The best seller *No One Gets Out of Here Alive* was written about the band, and the film *The Doors* starred Val Kilmer as Jim Morrison.

The Doors Are Open (1968) [documentary] "When the Music's Over," "Five to One" and several other songs * *Feast of Friends* (1970) [documentary] "Strange Days," "Wild Child" and several other songs * *The Day the Music Died* (1977) [documentary]

Dorene Sisters

He's My Guy (1943) "Boogie Woogie Bugle Man"

Doris Eaton and the Radio Pictures Beauty Chorus [unknown]

Doris Eaton (Norfolk, Virginia, 1904–)

Still going strong at the time of this writing (2008), centenarian former Ziegfeld Follies girl Doris Eaton was in silent movies by the early 1920s. Primarily a dancer, she was in several Broadway shows prior to retiring from show business and then operating several dance studios. She made her first film appearance in many decades in Jim Carrey's *Man on the Moon* in 1999.

Street Girl (1929)

Dorothy Mccarthy and the Three Dots [unknown]

Mama Steps Out (1937)

Dorris *see* Uncle Dave Macon and His Son, Dorris

Dorr's St. Luke's Choristers

Ripley Dorr, director

Although perhaps little known today, the St. Luke's Choristers, a young male ensemble, may have made the most film appearances of any similar group, such as the Robert (Bob) Mitchell Boys Choir. Many of the Choristers' pictures were very prestigious MGM productions.

A Tale of Two Cities (1935) * *Rainbow on the River* (1936) * *San Francisco* (1936) * *The Firefly* (1937) * *The Green Light* (1937) * *Make a Wish* (1937) * *The Prince and the Pauper* (1937) * *Song of the City* (1937) * *Boys Town* (1938) * *A Christmas Carol* (1938) * *Marie Antoinette* (1938) * *The Girl of the Golden West* (1938) * *Three Comrades* (1938) * *Fisherman's Wharf* (1939) * *The Big Store* (1941) * *Men of Boys Town* (1941) * *New Wine* (1941) * *Sundown* (1941) * *Babes on Broadway* (1942) * *Mrs. Miniver* (1942) * *Random Harvest* (1942) * *Tish* (1942) * *Marriage Is a Private Affair* (1944) * *Mrs. Parkington* (1944) * *The Cheaters* (1945) * *The Corn Is Green* (1945) * *Mexicana* (1945) * *Yolanda and the Thief* (1945) * *Out California Way* (1946) * *Walk Softly Stranger* (1950) * *The Great Caruso* (1951)

Dorsey, Jimmy *see* Jimmy Dorsey and His Orchestra

Dorsey, Tommy *see* Tommy Dorsey and His Orchestra

Douglas, Milton *see* Milton Douglas and Orchestra

Dovells

Jerry Summers (Jerry Gross) (lead tenor); Len Barry (Len Borisoff) (tenor); Mike Dennis (Mike Freda) (2nd tenor); Arnie Satin (Arnie Silver) (baritone); Danny Brooks (Jim Mealey) (bass); Mark Stevens (Mark Gordesky) (tenor)

The Philadelphia-based Brooktones did not find much success until the name Deauvilles (after the Miami hotel) was suggested to them. They liked the sound of it but not the spelling—and so another pop band got its roundabout naming. The band's members also adopted new names for themselves.

However the Dovells' name was finally spelled, it spelled s-u-c-c-e-s-s after the rollicking "The Bristol Stomp" was released. They seemed to specialize in short-lived dance fads with records like "Do the New Continental," "Bristol Twistin' Annie," "Hully Gully Baby" and "The Jitterbug." Their biggest hit, after "Bristol Stomp," came with "You Can't Sit Down" in 1963.

They frequently appeared in normally Black venues with African-American bands and also played back-up for pop soloists like Fabian, Jackie Wilson and Chubby Checker, in one of whose films they appeared.

With many new members the Dovells performed in Las Vegas toward the end of their time together and by the 1970s changing musical tastes led to their demise. In 1991, with golden oldie nostalgia going strong, an album of their "greatest hits" was issued.

Don't Knock the Twist (1962) "The Bristol Stomp" and "Doin' the New Continental" * *A Swingin' Summer* (1965)

Downey Sisters [unknown]
Gift of Gab (1934) * *High Hat* (1937)

Doye O'Dell and the Radio Rangers
Doye O'Dell (Allen O'Dell, Plainview or Gustine, Texas, 1912–2001)

Fiddle and guitar player Doye O'Dell (he adopted his middle name for performing) was on the radio in Texas about 1931 before he made his way to New York where he formed Doye O'Dell and the Radio Rangers.

After relocating to the West Coast he had a big success with "Old Shep" and recorded many other novelty songs, including the country hit "Diesel Smoke, Dangerous Curves." O'Dell claimed to have been groomed to take over for Roy Rogers in case Republic's "King of the Cowboys" had been drafted during World War II.

This did not happen but he did appear without his band in a slew of films with Charles Starrett and some postwar Rogers' movies like *Under California Stars* and *Along the Navajo Trail*. He also had his own shows on television, including one for children that won two Emmys, and he had briefly been part of the Sons of the Pioneers.

The Pioneers (1941) * *Fugitive Valley* (1941) * *Man from Rainbow Valley* (1946) * *Heldorado* (1946) * *Last Frontier Uprising* (1947) * *Whirlwind Raiders* (1948) * *Home in San Antone* (1949) * *Son of a Badman* (1949)

Drake, Dona *see* Dona Drake and Her Girl Band

Dreamers *see* The Four Dreamers; Freddie and the Dreamers

Dry Creek Road
Groupies (1970) [documentary] "Mr. Sun"

Duane Eddy and the Rebel Rousers
Duane Eddy (Corning, New York, 1938–); Steve Douglas (saxophone)

Guitarist Duane Eddy found fame playing his trademark "twangy" sound on his electric guitar's bass strings. From 1958 to 1963 he had about fifteen Top Forty records, "Rebel Rouser" being his best known. Others included "Forty Miles of Bad Road," the theme from the television show *Peter Gunn* and "Cannonball."

Although Eddy himself lost some popularity in the 1960s he was an undoubted influence on such famous musicians as the Beatles' George Harrison. He continued to issue albums and had minor hits with tunes like "Guitar Man" and the theme from the television show *Have Gun, Will Travel*.

In succeeding decades Duane Eddy played the occasional movie role and had a record hit in England as well as some success with country music. He resumed live performing in the 1980s and was inducted into the Rock and Roll Hall of Fame in 1994.

Because They're Young (1960) "Shazam"

Duchin, Eddie *see* Eddie Duchin...

Duke Ellington and His Band; Duke Ellington and His Orchestra
Duke Ellington (Edward Ellington, Washington, D. C., 1899–1974)

Considered one of the great figures of 20th century music, pianist Edward "Duke" Ellington defied categorization. He essayed all types of music from jazz to the many sophisticated melodies he wrote and/or made famous. From the 1920s, when he was a fixture at Harlem's Cotton Club and had a radio program, he was enormously popular. He had formed his first ensemble, a small jazz band, in 1924.

A measure of Ellington's cachet was that his band members tended to remain with him for most of their careers, some over forty years. The 1940s are viewed as his epitome, coincident with the tenure of Billy Strayhorn, the (sometimes unheralded) creator of many of his most famous pieces. Among the band's big recordings were "Mood Indigo," "Take the "A" Train" (their theme song) and "Sophisticated Lady."

Among Duke Ellington's accomplishments were longer tone poem–like pieces such as "The Far East Suite," "Black, Brown and Beige," "Creole Rhapsody" and "Diminuendo and Crescendo in Blue." He kept producing innovative music up to the end of his life, even essaying sacred music, and was nominated for a Pulitzer

Prize in 1965. The Broadway musical *Sophisticated Ladies*, consisting solely of his compositions, debuted in 1981.

As a performer, handsome Duke Ellington was the very embodiment of suavity. He was always impeccably outfitted, often with top hat and tails, as he sat at the piano. Considered both a national and international treasure, he was awarded the Presidential Medal of Freedom and France's Legion of Honor.

Check and Double Check (1930) * *This Is the Night* (1932)†* *Belle of the Nineties* (1934) * *Murder at the Vanities* (1934) * *The Hit Parade* (1937) * *Cabin in the Sky* (1943) * *Jazz Festival* (1955) [documentary] * *Rhythm-and-Blues Revue* (1955) [documentary] **Rock 'n' Roll Revue* (1955/56) [documentary]

†Their participation in this film is uncertain.

Duke Ellington (at piano) and band in *Rock 'n' Roll Revue*.

Dukes of Dixieland

Frank Assunto (New Orleans, Louisiana, 1922–1974) (trumpet); Fred Assunto (Jennings, Louisiana, 1929–1966) (trombone); Jac Assunto; Pete Fountain

The Assunto brothers were part of bandleader Horace Heidt's Youth Opportunity Program about the late 1940s, and they then became respected new faces on the New Orleans Dixieland scene. Their father Jac was an early member of the ensemble that was variously known as the Basin Street Four, Five or Six and the Junior Dixie Band.

The Dukes achieved national popularity in the late 1950s, the peak of their fame probably coming early in the following decade. They recorded at least a dozen successful albums and toured until the untimely death of Fred Assunto, at which time the group disbanded.

It's Trad, Dad! (1962)

Duncan, Bobby *see* Bobby Duncan Troupe

Duncan, Tommy *see* Tommy Duncan and His Western All Stars

Duncan's Beauty Show Girls [unknown]

Juke Joint (1947)

Dunham, Sonny *see* Sonny Dunham and His Orchestra

Durant, Eddie *see* Eddie Durant and His Rhumba Orchestra

Earl Burtnett and His Orchestra and Trio

Earl Burtnett (Harrisburg, Pennsylvania, 1899–1936)

In 1918 young Earl Burtnett joined the Art Hickman band, a San Francisco ensemble, and some time after appearing in the *Ziegfeld Follies* with the band he was asked to take over as front man. Since they were based on the West Coast they had the chance to appear in early talking pictures.

Beginning in the early 1930s Burtnett had a band that played in Texas and Chicago for lengthy engagements. He was also the writer of such songs as "Down Honolulu Way," "Sleep" and "Leave Me with a Smile."

The Flying Fool (1929) * *Party Girl* (1930)

Earl Grant Trio

Earl Grant (1931?–1970)

Jazz organist Earl Grant recorded almost fifty albums and some 100 singles, with hits like "Ebb Tide" and "At the End of the Rainbow." The former high school teacher also worked extensively in clubs and appeared on television.

Juke Box Rhythm (1959) "I Feel It Right Here" and "Last Night"

Easy Riders

Terry Gilkyson (Hamilton Gilkyson, Phoenixville, Pennsylvania, 1916–1999); Rich Dehr; Frank Miller

Although the folk music trio the Easy Riders had some success performing songs they had written they also provided other singers with substantial hits: Dean Martin ("Memories Are Made of This") and Frankie Laine ("Cry of the Wild Goose"). The Riders made out well too with their million seller "Marianne" and "C. C. Rider."

In the 1960s founder Terry Gilkyson departed the Easy Riders for a career composing music for films and was nominated for an Academy Award. But other groups continued to benefit from the Riders' songwriting skills. The poignant "Green Fields" and "Sloop John B." became great successes for the Brothers Four and the Beach Boys respectively.

Calypso Joe (1957)

Eberle, Ray *see* Ray Eberle and His Orchestra

Ebony Trio

The film in which the Ebony Trio appeared may have been a compilation of previously released musical shorts and/or soundies.

Harlem on Parade (1946?)

Ed Young Fife and Drum Corps

The Corps specialized in playing African-American folk music.

Festival (1967) [documentary]

Eddie Barefield's Trio

Eddie Barefield (sometimes Barfield) (Edward Barefield, Scandia, New York, 1909–1991)

A clarinetist and saxophonist, Eddie Barefield played with various African-American bands including those of Fletcher Henderson, Ella Fitzgerald and Cab Calloway. Although he never reached the top rungs of fame he managed to sustain a lengthy career as a sideman and also arranged for some of the most prominent big bands (Glenn Miller, Jimmy Dorsey, etc.).

Barefield was still going strong into the 1980s playing with the Ringling Brothers Barnum and Bailey circus band. He had also worked as an ABC staff musician and done stints in Broadway orchestras. In other words, he was the prototype of the sometimes anonymous working musician who helped make others shine — and he did so for well over fifty years.

Bargain with Bullets (1937)

Eddie Cletro and His Roundup Boys

Eddie Cletro (Eddie O'Clethero, Trenton, New Jersey, 1917–) (rhythm guitar); Tommy Sargent (steel guitar); Clem Atwater (drums); Joe Bardelli (piano); Bill Flynn (bassist); Eddie Carver (accordion); Joe DeRose (fiddle); John Stout (fiddle); Ernie Ball (steel guitar)

New Jersey "cowboy" Eddie Cletro was leading his own band at age fourteen and playing the guitar and ukulele. By the early 1940s he was in Los Angeles — and not being too successful — until his orchestra switched to western swing from the hotel music they had been playing. Among the Playboys' recordings were "Rock 'n' Roll Cowboy," "Sittin' and A-Rockin'" and "Springtime in the Rockies."

After going into western swing Cletro went whole hog, even claiming his hometown was in Oklahoma. He changed the instrumentation of his group, adding fiddles and an accordion and shortened his name. For a while he also worked with one of Spade Cooley's bands and had a television show in the 1950s.

Trail of the Rustlers (1950)

Eddie Dean Trio

Eddie Dean (Edgar Glosup, Posey, Texas, 1907–1999)

Appearing in Hollywood bit parts from 1936, Eddie Dean (called the "Golden Cowboy") graduated to his own series of singing westerns from 1945 to 1948, although he was definitely a far better singer than an actor. He was supposedly the first "B" singing oater star to appear in color films. Previously he had appeared with such stalwarts as Gene Autry, Bill (Hopalong Cassidy) Boyd and Roy Rogers.

Dean's theme song was "On the Banks of the Sunny San Juan." With his brother Jimmy Dean (not the later sausage king) he appeared on the *Melody Ranch* radio show and was also heard on Judy Canova's program. As a composer he wrote popular songs like "I Dreamed of a Hillbilly Heaven" and "One Has My Name, the Other Has My Heart."

Fighting Bill Fargo (1942)

Eddie Duchin and His Central Park Casino Dance Orchestra; Eddie Duchin and His Orchestra

Eddie (sometimes Eddy) Duchin (Cambridge, Massachusetts, 1910–1951)

Although acknowledged to be somewhat lacking in his musicianship, pianist Eddie Duchin was a handsome, suave and popular heartthrob. Those attributes were enough to get him work with top society orchestras, like those of Nat Brandwynne and Leo Reisman, whose ensemble he "inherited" in 1931. As a leader, with his theme song the swoony "My Twilight Dream," he continued playing in swank venues like the Plaza Hotel and Cocoanut Grove.

Duchin's numerous radio appearances and tours increased his popularity and he worked to improve his orchestra's sound; his own, however, continued to be problematic. One of his sidemen lamented, perhaps with comic exasperation, that he could make thirty-two mistakes in a thirty-two bar solo and still get an ovation.

Eddie Duchin's postwar orchestra was considered to be his best but like many a romantic hero he died very young. It was more the image than the reality that lived on after him when he was portrayed by Tyrone Power in the film *The Eddy Duchin Story*.

Mr. Broadway (1933) * *Coronado* (1935) * *The Hit Parade* (1937)

Eddie Durant and His Rhumba Orchestra

I'll Sell My Life (1941) * *Time Out for Rhythm* (1941) * *Flying with Music* (1942)

Eddie Heywood and His Orchestra

Eddie Heywood (Atlanta, Georgia, 1915–1989)

After having played with orchestras from the early 1930s, jazz pianist Eddie Heywood formed his own band about 1940 and then later a trio and a sextet. Their World War II–era recording of "Begin the Beguine" was a hit, as was "The More I See You," and the group flourished for the next few years.

However in 1947 Heywood was struck with temporary partial paralysis of his hands and it was not until the 1950s that he could again perform. Although a second attack of paralysis came some years later he managed to stay active into the 1980s. He also wrote the music for at least two classic songs: "Canadian Sunset" and "Soft Summer Breeze."

Junior Prom (1946) * *The Dark Corner* (1946)

Eddie Lebaron and Orchestra

Eddie LeBaron (Eduardo Gastine, Venezuela, 1907?–1983)

Eddie Duchin (at left) in a Vitaphone short (1933).

Besides leading a band at Hollywood's Cocoanut Grove, Eddie LeBaron produced some Spanish language films made in Hollywood. One of them, *Castillos en el Aire (Castles in the Air)*, was said to be the very first of its type filmed there. At one time he was co-owner of the famed Trocadero nightclub.

Harvest Melody (1943) * *She's for Me* (1943) * *Lady, Let's Dance!* (1944) * *Trocadero* (1944) * *Perilous Holiday* (1946) * *Casa Manana* (1951)

Eddie Miller and His Bobcats

Eddie Miller (New Orleans, Louisiana, 1911–1991)

A well-regarded saxophone and clarinet player, Eddie Miller worked with Ben Pollack and Bob Crosby in the pre-war era and formed his own band in 1944. The Bobcats had been associated with Bob Crosby in the 1930s so how Miller got to use the name is unknown. The band was a short-lived ensemble that existed for about three years, its theme song being ("Love's Got Me in a) Lazy Mood."

Mr. Big (1943)

Eddie Rio and Brothers see Rio Brothers

Eddy, Buck and Chickie see Buck and Chicky Eddy

Eddy, Duane see Duane Eddy and the Rebel Rousers

Eddy Duchin and His Orchestra see Eddie Duchin and His Orchestra

Edwards, J.C. see J.C. Edwards and Band

Edwin Hawkins Singers

Edwin Hawkins (Oakland or San Francisco, California, 1943–)

The great 1969 gospel song "Oh Happy Day" is probably the one for which the Edwin Hawkins Singers will be best remembered. It has supposedly sold more than seven million copies and was awarded a Grammy, one of four that its leader has won. He has passed his gift to younger generations of musicians by his annual Edwin Hawkins Music and Arts Seminar.

Hawkins was a part of his family's gospel choir at a very young age and he has continued making music for more than fifty years, both as part of his Singers and as a solo after 1980. He is credited with developing a new style of contemporary gospel music (sometimes fused with classical motifs) and has also occasionally branched out into rhythm-and-blues.

It's Your Thing (1970) [documentary] * *Celebration at Big Sur* (1971) [documentary]

Eight Black Streaks

Delrose Summers

The Eight Black Streaks was an African-American band.

Swanee Showboat (1947?)

Eight Buckaroos

Twilight on the Prairie (1944)

8 Rhythmeers [unknown]

Slightly Terrific (1945)

Elder Lovelies

Mabel Hart; Mabel Butterworth; Ivanetta Gardner

Originally a nonprofessional group that did community singing in Southern California, the ten women were taken up by comedian/entrepreneur Ken Murray as a novelty. He named them the Elder Lovelies (sometimes known as Ken Murray's Elder Lovelies) and they appeared in his *Blackouts*, a long running Los Angeles stage phenomenon.

A few of the Lovelies had been in vaudeville and at the time of their "discovery" were all in their sixties and seventies. When they appeared in their first movie their combined age was almost 725 years. One member joked that wolves still whistled at them, but not through their own teeth!

Isn't It Romantic? (1948) * *Square Dance Jubilee* (1949)

Elderbloom Chorus

It All Came True (1940)

Electric Flag

Mike Bloomfield (d. 1981) (guitar); Buddy Miles (drums); Barry Goldberg (keyboard); Harvey Brooks (guitar); Paul Beaver (synthesizer); Marcus Doubleday (trumpet/flugelhorn); Bobby Notkoff (violin); Peter Strazza (saxophone); Nick Gravenites (vocals)

The blues/psychedelic band Electric Flag was formed in 1967 and broke up some two years later. Its members were all seasoned musicians whose albums later proved influential even if not particularly successful at the time. Although they appeared at the Monterey Pop Festival they were not included in the documentary film of that legendary event.

You Are What You Eat (1968) [documentary]

Elgart, Les *see* Les Elgart and His Orchestra

Elk Chanters

As their name indicated, the Elk Chanters were affiliated with a Los Angeles Elks Lodge and had won the title of Elks Club National Champion Singers.

General Spanky (1936)

Ellington, Duke *see* Duke Ellington...

Emcees

Scream of the Butterfly (1965)

Enemies

Cory Wells

Harper (1966) * *Riot on Sunset Strip* (1967)

"Jolene" and "I'm Leaving You"

Ennis, Skinnay *see* Skinnay Ennis and His Band

Enric Madriguera and His Orchestra

Enric Madriguera (Barcelona, Spain, 1904–1973)

Considered a pioneer of Latin-American music in the United States, Enric Madriguera formed his first band in the late '20s. He had previously been the music director for Columbia Records in South America. His music, popularized during club dates, hotel gigs and on the radio, carried the orchestra into the early 1950s with its theme song "Adios." Madriguera had an outgoing personality that attracted crowds, as well as his fellow Latin musicians on whom he had a considerable influence musically. He was also a composer among whose songs were "Forbidden Love," "The Language of Love" and "Flowers of Spain."

The Thrill of Brazil (1946)

Eric Burdon and the Animals *see* Animals

Ernest Tubb and His Texas Troubadors

Ernest Tubb (near Crisp, Texas, 1914–1984); Jimmy Short (guitar); Tommy Paige (guitar); Billy Byrd (William Byrd, Tennessee, 1917–2001) (guitar); Red Herron; Jack Drake; Leon Short

One of the shining lights of country music, guitarist Ernest (Ernie) Tubb had a long, distinguished career as a singer-songwriter and was a stalwart of the *Grand Ole Opry* from 1943 on. Beginning in the late 1930s he had begun recording and appeared on local radio shows. "Blue Eyed Elaine" proved to be his first successful recording.

He was an acknowledged imitator of Jimmie Rodgers early in his career before finding his own significant voice in the early '40s. The Texas Troubadors, with whom Tubb appeared in "B" oaters, was his first band in 1943. Dubbed the "Gold Chain Troubador," he continued to turn out solo country hits like "Waltz Across Texas," "Blue Christmas," "Soldier's Last Letter" and "Tomorrow Never Comes" and also recorded with the likes of the Andrews Sisters, Red Foley and Loretta Lynn.

He was also honored as a selfless booster of stars-to-be like Lynn, Johnny Cash, Patsy Cline and Hank Snow. Ernest Tubb had a gold record for 1941's "Walking the Floor Over You" and in 1965 he was one of the first to be elected to the Country Music Hall of Fame. In the 1960s the Texas Troubadors was converted into a dance band with whom Tubb toured extensively for some fifteen years, doing as many as 200 shows annually.

The Fighting Buckaroo (1943) * *Riding West* (1944) * *Jamboree* (1944) * *Hollywood Barn Dance* (1947)

Ernesto Lecuona and the Palan Brothers Cuban Orchestra; Lecuona Cuban Boys

Ernesto Lecuona (Guanabacoa, Cuba, 1895–1963)

The famous Cuban pianist and composer Ernesto Lecuona did much for his native country by helping to establish such music ensembles as the Havana Symphony. His fame as a composer spread far beyond his own country and eventually Hollywood came calling.

The "Andalucia Suite" (from which the American standard "The Breeze and I" was "borrowed") is one Lecuona's most played pieces. Altogether he wrote more than 175 pieces for solo piano and over 400 songs, including the classics "Malaguena" and "Siboney." The prodigious composer also produced operas and zarzuelas, ballets and theater pieces.

In Hollywood, working for several studios, he was nominated for an Oscar for a film that produced one of his best-known songs "Siempre en Mi Corazon" ("Always in My Heart"). For his versatility and musicianship Lecuona earned his nickname of the "Cuban [George] Gershwin."

The Palan Brothers Cuban Orchestra was one of the first Latin orchestras to play in the United States. It was later renamed the Lecuona Cuban Boys and continued on for many years thereafter.

Cuban Love Song (1931) * *Carnival in Costa Rica* (1947)

Ernie Freeman Combo

Ernie Freeman (1923?–1981)

A Grammy winning arranger for numerous singers from Bing Crosby and Frank Sinatra to Paul Simon and Art Garfunkel, Ernie Freeman started out playing piano for such stars as Dinah Washington and Dorothy Dandridge. Besides his two Grammys his accomplishments include arranging the music for thirty-five gold albums and 140 gold singles, among them "Strangers in the Night" and "Everybody Loves Somebody."

Rock Around the Clock (1956)

Eslava, Jose see Jose Eslava's Orchestra

Esquire Trio

The Tunnel of Love (1958)

Esquires see Four Esquires

Esy Morales and His Rhumba Band

Esy Morales (Puerto Rico, 1917–1950)

Flutist Esy Morales's band was usually known as the Latin Rhythms Orchestra but in their one film appearance it was dubbed Esy Morales and His Rhumba Band. Before he led his own orchestra Morales had played with Xavier Cugat.

Criss Cross (1949)

Eton Boys; Four Eton Boys

Jack Day (baritone); Earl Smith (1st tenor); Art Gentry (2nd tenor); Charles Day (bass)

The Eton Boys were a popular singing quartet in the 1930s who appeared on bandleader Ray Bloch's radio show. They also made many movie musical shorts and recordings.

Moonlight and Pretzels (1933)

Etude Ethiopian Chorus

In Laurel and Hardy's first talking feature *Pardon Us* the Etude Ethiopian Chorus played sharecroppers and accompanied Oliver Hardy in singing the delightful "Lazy Moon," as well as providing the musical background for Stan Laurel's eccentric dance.

Pardon Us (1931) * *Hell's Highway* (1932) †

†Their appearance in this film is not confirmed.

E-Types

Blonde on a Bum Trip (1968) "Put the Clock Back on the Wall"

Eubie Blake and His Orchestra

Eubie Blake (James Blake, Baltimore, Maryland, 1883–1983)

In his long career and 100 years of existence Eubie Blake became a most revered figure. He played the organ and piano (reportedly in a brothel when he was a teenager) with his exceptionally long, thin fingers which were said to cover twelve piano keys.

He appeared in vaudeville, led an orchestra and wrote songs for Broadway musicals. His fabled teaming with Noble Sissle (1889–1975) produced the "Dixie Duo" in vaudeville and fruitful musical collaboration for many years thereafter.

With Sissle and other Black performers Blake brought forth *Shuffle Along*, the first successful African-American musical produced on the Great White Way. Its hits included "I'm Just Wild About Harry" and "Love Will Find a Way." Other Blake/Sissle all–Black shows followed. In all he is credited with writing some 300 songs, including "You Were Meant for Me."

The two men were among the pioneers of early talking film as well. In 1923 they appeared in a Lee De Forest Phonofilm experimental short in which Sissle sang to Eubie Blake's piano accompaniment. They performed together until 1927. In the early 1930s Blake formed his own orchestra. He continued to make public appearances well into old age, collaborating on an album with Sissle entitled "86 Years of Eubie Blake."

The Broadway show *Eubie!* honored his life and he performed in one way or another until he was ninety-nine years young. At ninety it was said he was as "robust as a rooster ... a lively, volatile, adamant and noisy character." Blake, the son of freed slaves, was awarded the Medal of Freedom in 1981.

Harlem Is Heaven (1932)

Everett Hoagland and Band

Future bandleaders Stan Kenton and Spike Jones were sidemen in clarinetist Everett Hoagland's orchestras which dated back to the 1920s. He was an early exponent of swing and jazz but in the 1930s opted for "society" music which perhaps was more lucrative at the time.

Among the recordings of Hoagland's post-jazz bands were "I'm Too Romantic," "The Moon and the Willow Tree" and "Drifting Down the River of Dreams." He had also been the chief musical arranger for the RKO studio.

Okay, America! (1932)

Exciters Band

Bobby Fry (bassist); Don Hargrave (Don Hardgrave, 1939–1999); Jim Rector (drums); Jack Merrill (guitar); Larry Ogden (saxophone); Candy Johnson

Starting out as the Igniters in the early 1960s, the Exciters Band (not to be confused with the girl group the Exciters) played the Las Vegas lounges. At some point the group began featuring the frenetic dancing of blonde Candy Johnson who went on to make her mark in the beach/surfing films so popular in the mid–1960s.

Her wild terpsichorean gyrations were a memorable highlight of that short-lived genre; publicists dubbed her "Miss Perpetual Motion." Johnson's "specialty" may have been what got the Exciters noticed in the first place but it was their music that the musicians wanted to be known for, not gimmickry.

This tension caused a split between her and the band and both careers suffered. By the end of the decade that had brought them both fleeting fame they were little heard of again.

Bikini Beach (1964) "Gotcha Where I Want You"

Eyes of Blue

Ritchie Francis (guitar); Gary Hopkins (vocals); Wyndam Rees (vocals); Phil Ryan (keyboard); Ray Williams (bassist); R. Bennett (bassist); John Weathers (drums)

They began as a soul-based group but the English band Eyes of Blue later broadened its repertoire to rock, jazz, rhythm-and-blues and even classical music. Among their recordings were "Love Is the Law" and "Crossroads of Time."

Connecting Rooms (1969)

Faded Blue

The Faded Blue was a Chicago-based garage band.

Blast-Off Girls (1967) "The Next Time," "You Got Me Where You Want Me" and several other songs

Falkner Orchestra

Johnny Doughboy (1942)

Fallen Angels

Jack Bryant (bassist); Wally Cook (guitar); Howard Danchik (keyboard); Jack Lauritsen (multi-instruments); John Molloy (drums)

The Washington D.C.–based Fallen Angels seemed headed for big things after their 1965 formation. Their much-admired music was a fusion of various styles, including jazz and classical, and their stage presence was arresting. Sometimes the entire stage was dark except for bright strobe lights. In the end the band did not live up to its promise.

The Revolution Is in Your Head (1970) [documentary]

Family Dog
You Are What You Eat (1968) [documentary]

Famous Shaw Negro Choir *see* Freita Shaw...

Fantasy
Musical Mutiny (1970) "Understand"

Farmer Sisters [unknown]
John Lair's Renfro Valley Barn Dance (1966)

Father Machias Lani's Chorus; Father Lani's Chorus
The Girl of the Golden West (1938) * *Marie Antoinette* (1938)

Faulkner, Chuck *see* Chuck Faulkner Band

Feder Sisters [unknown]
Miriam Feder; Sylvia Feder
Catskill Honeymoon (1950)

Felix and His Martinques [unknown]
Havana Rose (1951)

Fenton, Shane *see* Shane Fenton and the Fentones

Fields, Shep *see* Shep Fields and His Orchestra

Fifth Dimension
Billy Davis, Jr.; Marilyn McCoo; Florence LaRue; Lamonte McLemore; Ron Townson (d. 2001)

For a while in the late 1960s and '70s the Fifth Dimension was a popular vocal group with smash renditions of "Up, Up and Away" (the winner of several Grammy Awards) and "Aquarius/Let the Sun Shine in" from the musical *Hair*. They had formed as the Versatiles about 1966 and changed names when they began to record.

"Go Where You Wanna Go" was their first chart recording.

The group went from strength to strength with more hits including "Wedding Bell Blues," "Never My Love" and ("Last Night) I Didn't Get to Sleep at All." When attractive married couple Marilyn McCoo and Billy Davis left the group to launch their own careers in 1975 the Fifth Dimension continued on but never did match their previous glories. A few reunions followed and the group was inducted into the Vocal Music Hall of Fame in 2002.

Popcorn: an Audio/Visual Rock Thing (1969) [documentary]

Finks
Jake Cavaliere (organ); Dave Klein (percussion); Gregg Hunt (guitar)

Playing an early version of surfing music, the Finks produced but a single album before splitting up.

The Big Cube (1969)

Fio Rito, Ted *see* Ted Fio Rito and His Band

Firehouse Five Plus Two
Danny Alguire (trumpet); Harper Goff (banjo); Ward Kimball (trombone); Clark Mallery (clarinet); Monte Mountjoy (drums); Ed Penner (tuba); Frank Thomas (piano)

All members of the Disney Studios animation department, the Dixieland jazz band Firehouse Five Plus Two began playing together as an amateur group in the late 1940s. As they gained in popularity from the mid–1950s to 1970 they recorded more than a dozen albums.

In keeping with their name the band sported firemen's uniforms and traveled around in a 1914 vintage fire truck. Their music often featured the sounds of sirens and large doses of humor.

Hit Parade of 1951 (1950) * *Grounds for Marriage* (1950)

Fite, Buster *see* Buster Fite...

Five Hertzogs [unknown]
Crazy House (1943)

Five Jones Boys; Jones Quintette

Jimmy Springs (tenor); William Bartley; Herman Wood; Louis Wood; Charles Hopkins

Based in Los Angeles from the mid–1930s, the Five Jones Boys originally hailed from Illinois. They were specialists in emulating musical instruments with their voices, a talent known as a human orchestra. The Boys subsequently joined together with the Four Blackbirds to form a larger group known as the Jones Boys Sing Band.

The Big Show (1936) * *Racing Blood* (1936) * *Can This Be Dixie?* (1937)

Five Miller Sisters

Rockin' the Blues (1956) [documentary] "Everybody's Havin' a Ball" and "Do You Wanna Blow?"

Five Music Maids *see* Music Maids

Five Pennies *see* Red Nichols and His Five Pennies

Five Radio Buckaroos

Five Bad Men (1935)

Five Satins; Fred Parris and His Satins

Fred Parris (1936–) (lead vocals); Stanley Dortch (tenor); Wes Forbes; Lewis Peeples (tenor); Rich Freeman; Sy Hopkins; Bill Baker (vocals); Eddie Martin (baritone); Jim Freeman (bass); Al Denby; Jessie Murphy (piano)

Once lead singer of the doo-wop group the Scarlets (or Scarletts), Fred Parris supposedly composed the rock classic "In the Still of the Night (sometimes rendered as "Nite") while on Army guard duty in 1956. He had formed the Four Satins in 1953 and it was apparently these four who recorded the iconic melody. They subsequently became the Five Satins.

By the time their next recording, and only other chart song, "To the Aisle" became a hit, Parris was still in the military, and the Satins had different membership. It was this group that scored mildly with "Shadows" and also had a minor success with "I'll Be Seeing You."

They disbanded in the early 1960s but Parris cashed in on the "oldies" craze and the reconstituted Satins were active into the 1980s, even having a few more records on the charts. In the meantime "In the Still of the Night" has gone on to sell millions of copies.

The Sweet Beat (1959) * *The Amorous Sex* (1962) "In the Still of the Nite" * *Been Down So Long It Looks Like Up to Me* (1970) * *Let the Good Times Roll* (1973) [documentary]

Five Stairsteps; Five Stairsteps and Cubie

Clarence Burke, Jr. (lead vocalist); Alohe Burke (contralto); James Burke (1st tenor); Kenneth Burke (2nd tenor); Dennis Burke (baritone); Cubie Burke

The "First Family of Soul" (a name later assumed by the Jackson 5) was the soubriquet of the Five Stairsteps, best known for the 1970 hit "O-o-h Child," and so named because of their comparative heights. The siblings' recording days began in their teens after they won first prize in a Chicago talent contest in the mid–1960s. When little brother Cubie was added to the ensemble he was a mere two years old, surely making him the youngest member of any such group.

Other charters for the Five Stairsteps included "World of Fantasy," "From Us to You" and "You Waited Too Long." All told, seventeen of their recordings hit the rhythm-and-blues charts; twelve made the pop charts.

Eventually, with the departure of some family members, they shortened their name to just the Stairsteps and continued on until the mid–1970s. The four male members formed the Invisible Man's Band in 1980 and brother Kenneth later went on to a fairly distinguished solo career.

Soul to Soul (1970) [documentary] * *It's Your Thing* (1970) [documentary]

Five Stars

The Five Stars recorded "Ooh Shucks" which was written by Berry Gordy, founder of Motown Records.

Rock Baby, Rock It! (1957) "Hey Juanita" and "Your Love Is All I Need"

Flames *see* James Brown and the Famous Flames

Flamingos

Jacob Carey (d. 1996) (bass); Ezikial Carey (d. 2001) (tenor); Paul Wilson (baritone); Johnny

Carter (tenor); Earl Lewis (lead); Nate Nelson; Tommy Hunt; Sollie McElroy (lead)

The Swallows, the Five Flamingos and the El Flamingos were the names this rock quintet went by before they simplified it to just the Flamingos in the early 1950s. In mid-decade they recorded a few minor hit rhythm-and-blues numbers like "A Kiss from Your Lips" and "The Vow" but real success came with the sweet harmonies of the 1930s classic "I Only Have Eyes for You."

In 1957 the Flamingos became a quartet. Swooningly romantic songs continued to be the their forte in such recordings as "Love Walked in," "Golden Teardrops," "Mio Amore" and "Lovers Never Say Goodbye." The period from 1959 to 1961 is regarded as their most prolific, and their last charter was in 1970.

The group split into two (one being called the *Modern* Flamingos) in the early '60s; the "original" quintet kept performing into the new century. They have been inducted into the Vocal Group Hall of Fame and the Rock and Roll Hall of Fame.

Rock, Rock, Rock (1956) "Would I Be Crying?" * *Go, Johnny, Go!* (1958) "Jump Children"

Fleck, Bill *see* Bill Fleck and His Orchestra

Flennoy Trio

Lorenzo Flennoy (piano); Gene Phillips (guitar); Winston Williams (bass)

Mr. Ace (1946) "Now and Then"

Flores Brothers

Pepe Guizar

The Flores Brothers were Latin musicians.

Down Argentine Way (1940) * *That Night in Rio* (1941) * *Rio Rita* (1942) * *Mexican Hayride* (1948)

Fly-By-Nytes

Robert Lewis (guitar)

The Fly-By-Nytes were a Chicago garage band whose sole picture appearances might be due to the fact that band member Robert Lewis was the son of the director. For their appearance in director H. G. Lewis's film *Gruesome Twosome* they were called the Beach-side Band.

The Girl, the Body and the Pill (1967) * *Gruesome Twosome* (1967)

Flying Burrito Brothers

Pete Kleinow (South Bend, Indiana, 1934–2007) (steel guitar); Gram Parsons (Cecil Connor III, Winterhaven, Florida, 1946–1973); Chris Hillman (Los Angeles or San Diego, California, 1944–) (guitar/mandolin); Chris Ethridge (piano/bassist); Jon Corneal

There have actually been two bands called the Flying Burrito Brothers; the second "borrowed" the name about 1968 and became famous. The original one eventually styled themselves the Flying Burrito Brothers East. The new West Coast group's initial country rock album "The Gilded Palace of Sin" was not a great seller, but had the "legs" to make it most influential over the years.

The Brothers, with their gaudy version of western outfits, gained a kind of cult following and were much admired by famous musicians, among whom were Bob Dylan and the Rolling Stones. One of their bigger singles "White Line Fever" came before they shortened their name to the Burrito Brothers.

Although the Burrito Brothers was supposedly disbanded at the end of the 20th century, it has continued to perform in various incarnations (e.g., Burrito Deluxe) until the present day.

Gimme Shelter (1970) [documentary] "Six Days on the Road" * *Celebration at Big Sur* (1971) [documentary]

Flying "L" Ranch Quartet(te)

Bill Palmer; Harry Hall; George McCaslin; Fred Graves

The barbershop/close harmony group that was to become the Flying "L" Ranch Quartet(te) was formed from members of various other groups that performed in amateur contests in the Middle West. They fortuitously came together in the early 1940s when competing in one such contest.

Temporarily calling themselves the Mystic Four and then the Mainstreeters, the quartet got a local radio show and while performing in a club were discovered by the governor of Oklahoma. They began making recordings like "Beau Blanc Visage" and "Hereford Heaven."

It was at that point that the Flying "L" Ranch Quartet(te) assumed their final name and became mainstays at numerous Oklahoma official functions. Before disbanding in the late 1950s

they performed at state and national inaugurals, including that of Harry Truman.
Home in Oklahoma (1946)

Foley, Red *see* **Red Foley and His Saddle Pals**

Fontane Sisters
Marge Rosse (New Milford, New Jersey); Geri Rosse (New Milford, New Jersey); Bea Rosse (New Milford, New Jersey)

"Hearts Made of Stone," with its catchy refrain of "no, no, no, no," etc. was the Fontane Sisters' number one gold smash in 1954. Like their other hits it was a cover of earlier recordings made mainly by Black groups. They had been previously known as the Three Sisters and had performed as crooner Perry Como's backup group.

Although never having another such big hit, the Sisters succeeded again with covers of "Eddie My Love," "Rollin' Stone" and "I'm Stickin' with You." They also recorded many novelty numbers like "If I Knew You Were Comin', I'd've Baked a Cake" and country tunes. Ultimately their dearth of original songs caused their popularity to decline following their last charter "Chanson D'Amour."
(Abbott and Costello) In Society (1944)

Ford, Harris and Jones Trio
The Trio was probably a singing group.
Thank Your Lucky Stars (1943)

Forte Four
John Schaeffer II (Los Angeles, CA, 1946–); Guy Watson; Dan Anthony; Ernie Earnshaw (Spencer Earnshaw)

The Forte Four were musicians led by John Schaeffer who originally had a surf band.
Viva Las Vegas (1964) "The Climb" * *The Cool Ones* (1967)

Four Aces
Al Alberts (Al Albertini, Philadelphia, Pennsylvania) (lead); Dave Mahoney; Louis Silvestri (drums); Rosario Vaccaro (trumpet); Fred Diodati

The Pennsylvania-based Four Aces had a million seller with ("It's No) Sin" and went on to even greater glory with a string of big hits including "Stranger in Paradise," "It's a Woman's World" "Three Coins in the Fountain," "Tell Me Why," "Heart of My Heart" and "Heart and Soul." They may be best remembered for their swooningly romantic "Love Is a Many-Splendored Thing."

The close harmony group had had its genesis just after World War II with Al Alberts and Dave Mahoney as a duo. Their greatest success lay in the 1950s; between 1951 and 1956 they had at least one record a year in the top twenty. They continued on until the 1970s when they split in two, one successor being the Original Four Aces which performed into the 1980s. They were inducted into the Vocal Group Hall of Fame in 2001.
The Big Beat (1958) "Nobody Else But Me"

Four Amigos
The Four Amigos often served as background vocalists for Elvis Presley.
Fun in Acapulco (1963)

Four Chicks and Chuck
Chuck Goldstein

Originally a member of the famous harmony quintet the Modernaires, Chuck Goldstein departed that group to form the Four Chicks and Chuck.
Singing on the Trail (1946)

Four Coins
George Mahramas; Michael Mahramas (tenor); George Mantalis (tenor); James Gregorakis (baritone)

Starting out as the Four Keys, the Four Coins renamed themselves following the success of the then-current film *Three Coins in the Fountain*. Most of them had been band instrumentalists. Their first recording hit was 1955's "Memories of You" and they had no others until their only million seller "Shangri-La" two years later.

After "My Sin" the Coins' pop music efforts declined in popularity but they turned their Greek-American heritage to good advantage with an album of Greek songs. When they disbanded, a new group called the Original Three Coins was formed but it did not endure.
Jamboree (1957) "A Broken Promise"

Four Dreamers

The Four Dreamers were a vocal group.
The Big Store (1941) * *Carolina Blues* (1944)

Four Esquires

The Four Esquires were a musical group.
It's a Great Life! (1935) * *All-American Sweetheart* (1937) * *Can This Be Dixie?* (1937) * *Rosalie* (1937) * *Saratoga* (1937) * *Top of the Town* (1937)

Four Eton Boys *see* Eton Boys

Four Freshmen; Four Freshmen Quartette

Ken Albers (John Albers, Woodbury, New Jersey, 1924–2007); Ross Barbour (1928–); Don Barbour (Columbus, Indiana, 1927–1961); Bob Flanigan (1926–) (lead); Hal Kratzsch (d. 1970); Ken Errair (1928–); Marvin Pruitt

After having experimented with such names as the Toppers and Hal's Harmonizers (or Harmonaires) the vocal/instrumental quartet chose the Four Freshmen as their soon-to-be famous name. Formed by brothers Don and Ross Barbour about 1947 or '48, their mellifluous voices were first heard when they were indeed college students in Indiana. They toured throughout the Midwest before being discovered by jazz great Stan Kenton.

The close-harmony group excelled in mellow standards like "Mood Indigo" and "Moonglow," as well as more modern tunes such as "It's a Blue World" and "Graduation Day," their biggest hit. By the mid–1950s the Freshmen were mixing a generous dollop of jazz-flavored tunes into the repertoire and ultimately released more than forty albums. One of them resided on the charts for over eight months, setting a record for a modern jazz ensemble.

In 1953 they won the *Down Beat Magazine* poll as the best jazz vocal group. Into the 1960s the much-emulated original Freshmen remained popular and with new lineups of talent they still perform and have been an acknowledged influence on groups such as the Beach Boys. In 2000, more than fifty years after its founding, the group again won a *Down Beat Magazine* poll, this time for Vocal Group of the Year.

Rich, Young and Pretty (1951) "How Do You Like Your Eggs in the Morning?" * *Lucy Gallant* (1955) "How Can I Tell Her?"

Four Ink Spots *see* Ink Spots

Four Lads

Corrado Codarini (bass); John Toorish (lead singer); James Arnold (2nd tenor); Frank Busseri (baritone)

Toronto-based former choir boys, the Four Lads brought their pleasing close harmony to venues all over the world and appeared much on television. Before they had a hit record of their own they were the back-up group to professional "sobber" Johnnie Ray on two of his million sellers: "Cry" and "The Little White Cloud That Cried."

Formed about 1950, they originally had dubbed themselves the Four Dukes. Three years later their hit novelty tune "Istanbul (Not Constantinople)" garnered them a hit of their own and they also scored with "Skokiaan" and "Down By the Riverside."

In 1955 the nostalgic "Moments to Remember" proved their biggest success. The Lads' lively version of "Standin' on the Corner" was their final pop hit but throughout the 1950s they continued to release singles and albums and are still active to this day. They were inducted into the Vocal Group Hall of Fame in 2003.

Enchanted Island (1958)

Four Mills Brothers *see* Mills Brothers

Four Night Hawks

Call of the Rockies (1931)

Four Playboys

The Four Playboys were a musical group that performed on orchestra leader Ben Bernie's radio show in the 1930s.

New Faces of 1937 (1937) * *You're a Sweetheart* (1937) * *College Swing* (1938)

Four Preps

Bruce Belland (Chicago, Illinois, 1936–) (lead tenor); Ed Cobb (1938?–1999) (bass); Marv Ingram (Marvin Inabnett, d. 1999) (2nd tenor); Glen Larson (1937–) (1st tenor); David Somerville

The song "26 Miles (Santa Catalina)" sung by the Four Preps became one of the veritable anthems of the California lifestyle. Although more than a dozen of their recordings reached the pop charts beginning in 1956 they never topped that hit.

Other Four Preps songs included "Big Man" and the folk-flavored "Down By the Station." Formed as a high school group in the mid–1950s doing parodies of other groups, the Preps were active for almost a dozen years thereafter. During that time they appeared often on major television shows.

The Preps were hailed as the most promising vocal group of 1958 by the influential *Cash Box Magazine*. They broke up in 1967 but regrouped with some of the original members in the 1980s and are still performing today.

Gidget (1959) "Cinderella"

Four Seasons
Frankie Valli (Francis Castelluccio, Newark or Belleville, New Jersey, 1937–); Nick De Vito; Bob Gaudio; Hank Majewski; Tommy De Vito; Nick Massi (Nicholas Macioci, Newark, New Jersey, 1927?–2000)

The smash hit Tony-winning 2005 Broadway musical *Jersey Boys* brought Frankie Valli and the Four Seasons back into public consciousness in a big way. The travails and triumphs of that uber-popular rock group seemed to make it a natural for theatrical treatment. The many 1950s and '60s tunes featured in the production added to the nostalgic experience.

Possibly most remembered for Valli's falsetto on hits like "Sherry," "Walk Like a Man," "Big Girls Don't Cry" and "Candy Girl," the Four Seasons had begun around 1954 as the Varietones and then the Four Lovers. In '56 they had scored a mild hit with "You Are the Apple of My Eye" but then languished for several years thereafter. The name under which they attained world fame was adopted in 1961.

Nineteen sixty-two proved to be the Seasons' breakout year and the group even flourished during the British Invasion years with more hits like "Dawn (Go Away)," "Let's Hang On," "Can't Take My Eyes Off You" and "Rag Doll." But inevitably the hits stopped coming and by the latter 1960s internal (largely financial) troubles began to take their toll.

Frankie Valli embarked on a solo career and had successful singles like "Oh, What a Night" and "My Eyes Adored You." With forty-six chart records and some 85 million records sold, the group is still a great draw at rock-and-roll revival venues and they have been inducted into both the Rock and Roll Hall of Fame (1990) and the Vocal Group Hall of Fame.

Beach Ball (1965) "Dawn (Go Away)"

Four Singing Notables *see* **Notables**

Four Singing Tramps
Swing It, Professor (1937)

Four Society Girls [unknown]
Sing a Jingle (1944)

Four Spirits of Rhythm
The Four Spirits of Rhythm was a vocal group.
Sweetheart of the Campus (1941)

Four Squires [unknown]
Swing It, Professor (1937)

Four Teens [unknown]
Hit the Ice (1943)

Four Tones *see* **Herb Jeffries and the Four Tones**

Four Toppers *see* **Steve Gibson's Red Caps**

Four Tunes
Lawless Valley (1938)

Four V's [unknown]
I Love a Bandleader (1945)

Four Williams Brothers *see* **Williams Brothers**

Fourmations *see* **T.J. and the Fourmations**

Fourmost
Brian O'Hara (Liverpool, England, 1942–1999) (guitar); Mike Millward (Bromborough, England, 1942–1966) (guitar); Billy Hatton (Liverpool,

England, 1941–); Dave Lovelady (Liverpool, England, 1942–); Joey Bower

After being signed by Beatles' manager Brian Epstein, the British band Fourmost was given songs composed by John Lennon and Paul McCartney that the Beatles did not perform. These included "Hello, Little Girl" and "I'm in Love." They only issued a single album and had one modest hit "A Little Lovin'." The band, which included some rather lame comedy along with their songs, stopped recording in the 1960s but did continue to tour thereafter.

Pop Gear (1965) [documentary] "A Little Lovin'" * *Ferry Cross the Mersey* (1965)

Foursome

Gil Mershon; Ray Johnson; Del Porter; Dwight Snyder

Stolen Heaven (1931) * *Go West, Young Lady* (1941)

Fox and Walters [unknown]

The Big Broadcast of 1936 (1935)

Foy Willing and the Riders of the Purple Sage

Foy Willing (Foy Willingham, Texas, 1914–1978) (baritone); Al Sloey (Iowa, 1912–1975) (tenor); Dick Reinhart (lead vocals); Jimmy Dean (James Glosup, 1903–1970); Darol Rice (clarinet); Charlie Morgan; Scotty Harrell; Johnny Paul (John Girardi) (fiddle); Bud Sievert (Burton Sievert) (accordion); Jerry Vaughn (rhythm guitar); Billy Liebert; Paul Sellers; Neely Plumb (clarinet); Freddy Traveres (accordion)

Foy Willing began his career on local radio and then did a stint in the mid–1930s on a New York radio program. He and pal Al Sloey came to Hollywood in the early 1940s, fortuitously hooking up with another western swinger, Jimmy Wakely.

The busy Wakely decided to turn his own band over to Willing, thus giving birth to Foy Willing and the Riders of the Purple Sage. They were not the original Riders of the Purple Sage, who dated back to 1933; in fact they were probably third in line with the name.

The Riders began their screen career with oater hero Charles Starrett, but were not always billed that way in their earlier films with him. Willing also performed some acting roles on his own. They sang on the *Hollywood Barn Dance* and other radio programs, and had their first hit "Texas Blues" in 1944.

They also began making films with cowboy star Monte Hale, but it was their 1948 teaming with Republic star Roy Rogers (in *Grand Canyon Trail*) that brought the Riders of the Purple Sage into their own in movies. They replaced his longtime cohorts the Sons of the Pioneers, after a contract dispute, and remained with him through *Heart of the Rockies*, when they were in turn replaced by the Roy Rogers Riders.

They also sang on Rogers' radio program. In 1952, with the "B" movie western itself riding into the sunset, the Riders of the Purple Sage did the same. However, there were a few reunions, one being with a Gene Autry tour and others to make recordings.

In terms of the sheer number of films they made, the group was certainly one of the most prolific. They also had record hits like "Cool Water," "Ghost Riders in the Sky" and "No One to Cry to," and in 1991 they were inducted into the Western Music Association Hall of Fame.

Twilight on the Prairie (1944) * *Sing Me a Song of Texas* (1945) * *Saddle Serenade* (1945) * *Throw a Saddle on a Star* (1946) * *Out California Way* (1946) * *The Last Frontier Uprising* (1947) * *Along the Oregon Trail* (1947) * *Under Colorado Skies* (1947) * *California Firebrand* (1948) * *The Timber Trail* (1948) * *Grand Canyon Trail* (1948) * *The Far Frontier* (1948) * *Susanna Pass* (1949) * *Down Dakota Way* (1949) * *The Golden Stallion* (1949) * *Bells of Coronado* (1950) * *Twilight in the Sierras* (1950) * *Trigger, Jr.* (1950) * *Sunset in the West* (1950) * *North of the Great Divide* (1950) * *Trail of Robin Hood* (1950) * *Heart of the Rockies* (1951) * *Disc Jockey* (1951)

Frank, J. L. *see* J. L. Frank's Golden West Cowboys

Frank and Milt Britton Band

Comedy was the hallmark of the Frank and Milt Britton band which had begun in vaudeville. The wacky hi-jinks extended to smashing instruments over the players' heads. Milt later had his own ensemble.

Moonlight and Pretzels (1933) * *Sweet Music* (1935)

Frank Newman and His Band

The Shadow of Silk Lennox (1935)

Frankie Carle and Orchestra; Frankie Carle and His Orchestra

Frankie Carle (Francis Carlone, Providence, Rhode Island, 1903–2001)

In show business from about 1918, pianist Frankie Carle played with the Horace Heidt and Mal Hallett bands in the 1930s and formed his own group in 1944. Much heard on radio, the orchestra's theme song was Carle's "Sunrise Serenade." Other recordings included "Lover's Lullaby" and "Dream Lullaby," prior to the band's disbanding in the 1950s.

Carle won the magazine *Orchestra World*'s "Nation's Outstanding Musician" award in both 1942 and '43. In a few films he appeared without his orchestra as a pianist, sometimes billed as "Frankie Carle and His Piano." He continued performing into the 1980s, frequently with an all-girl quartet called Frankie Carle and His Girl Friends.

Riverboat Rhythm (1946) * *Sweetheart of Sigma Chi* (1946) * *Variety Time* (1948) * *Make Mine Laughs* (1949) * *Footlight Varieties* (1951)

Frankie Lymon and the Teenagers

Frankie Lymon (Franklin Lymon, New York, New York, 1942–1968); Joe Negroni (baritone); Herman Santiago (1st tenor) (d. 1978); Jimmy Merchant (2nd tenor); Sherman Garnes (bass) (d. 1977)

Once upon a time a racially-mixed group (African-American and Puerto Rican) variously called the Coupe de Villes, Ermines and Premiers had a song called "Why Do Birds Sing So Gay?" They needed a high tenor to put it over and found thirteen-year-old Frankie Lymon to fill the bill. The fairy tale was complete when they changed the song title to "Why Do Fools Fall in Love?" and became known as the Teenagers. It was an overwhelming smash hit in early 1956.

Like many fairy tales this one even had a princess in it: the Teenagers played a command performance before Princess Margaret of Britain. But also like many fairy tales this one was to have a dark ending. Before that happened the group with the clean-cut image scored many television and theater appearances and had a few other fairly successful recordings like "The ABCs of Love," "I Want You to Be My Girl" and "I'm Not a Juvenile Delinquent."

Since the falsetto voice of Frankie Lymon was the signature of the Teenagers, he was soon persuaded to go out as a solo act. Inevitably, his voice began to deepen and by the age of fifteen he was pretty much of a has-been. Tragically, drug abuse led to an early death at age twenty-five.

Before that his marital tangles had made headlines and in 1998 he was the subject of a movie called — inevitably — *Why Do Fools Fall in Love?* Despite all of the later troubles, Frankie Lymon and the Teenagers had been a strong influence on many groups that followed. In 1993 they were inducted into the Rock and Roll Hall of Fame and the Vocal Group Hall of Fame in 2000.

Rock Rock Rock (1956) "Baby Baby" and "I'm Not a Juvenile Delinquent" * *Don't Knock the Rock* (1956) * *Mr. Rock 'n' Roll* (1957) "Fortunate Fella" and "Love Put Me Out of My Head"

Frankie Valli and the Four Seasons *see* Four Seasons

Fraternity Brothers

World By Night (1961) [documentary]

Fraunfelder Family

Reinhardt Fraunfelder, Sr.; Reinhardt Fraunfelder, Jr.; William Fraunfelder; Betty Fraunfelder; Ruth Fraunfelder

When you hear yodeling in the Disney classic *Snow White and the Seven Dwarfs* it is courtesy of the Fraunfelder family who, being Swiss, came by their talents naturally. Later, they even taught yodeling in California public schools and still later were affiliated with the Schlitz Brewing Company, becoming known as the Schlitz Family Fraunfelder.

Snow White and the Seven Dwarfs (1937) (voices only) * *The Great Waltz* (1938) * *Paradise for Three* (1938)

Fred Palmer's Orchestra

The Notorious Elinor Lee (1940)

Fred Parris and His Satins *see* Five Satins

Fred Waring and His Pennsylvanians

Fred Waring (Tyrone, Pennsylvania, 1900–1984)

Dubbed "The Man Who Taught America to Sing," Fred Waring was a man of "firsts." To him and His Pennsylvanians belongs the (possible) honor of being the very first orchestra to appear in a sound feature film, *Syncopation*, in early 1929. His performing career was to continue for some fifty years more, culminating in an appearance at Ronald Reagan's first inaugural in 1981. The President awarded him a Congressional Gold Medal.

His first band, a six-man string group, bore the odd name of Waring's Banjazztra in which he played the violin and banjo. To his credit it was later rechristened The Pennsylvanians and their first recording "Sleep" was a major hit, becoming the band's theme song. Originally a jazz-influenced band, they were supposedly the first to record a George Gershwin song, the first to record with a chorus, and the first to make an electronic recording (in 1925).

The Pennsylvanians supposedly made more than 2,000 recordings and also had their own radio show in the early '20s. They later evolved from a jazz-oriented group into more of a dance band that played strictly middle-of-the-road melodies.

Because of a royalties dispute the ensemble did not make any records in the 1930s, but were heard on Waring's radio show and in live appearances. They were quite popular on college campuses and also were seen in Broadway shows.

Choral music continued to be spotlighted in his performances and some members of the Waring Glee Club went on to respectable careers, including Hollywood leading ladies (and sisters) Rosemary, Priscilla and Lola Lane, as well as vocalist, later bandleader, Johnny "Scat" Davis. Among the Glee Club's directors were entertainer/author Kay Thompson and the inimitable Robert Shaw who later established his own famous chorale.

Other Fred Waring recordings that made it big included "Love for Sale," "The Whiffenpoof Song," "Button Up Your Overcoat" and "Way Back Home." From the late 1940s to the mid–'50s Fred Waring had his own television show and — yes — may have been the first bandleader to do so.

Although these days he is not numbered among the great orchestra leaders, his name does live on in one of his inventions, the Waring Blender. He had other inventions to his credit as well, and was considered a shrewd entrepreneur.

Syncopation (1929) * *Varsity Show* (1937) * *Melody Time* (1948) (music only?)

Freddie and the Dreamers

Freddie Garrity (Manchester, England, 1936–2006)

The 1965 recording of "I'm Telling You Now" was Freddie and the Dreamers' biggest success in both the U.S. and Europe, and for a time the British band was favorably compared with the Beatles. Leader Freddie Garrity was also known for his wild stage antics that led to the dance known as the Freddie, which in turn led to the record "Do the Freddie."

Other Dreamers' successes included "You Were Made for Me" and "Over You." The group disbanded in 1969 but re-formed in 1976 and continued to tour for the next twenty-five years.

What a Crazy World (1963) * *Cuckoo Patrol* (1965) * *Seaside Swingers* (1965) "What's Cooking?" and "Don't Do That to Me" * *Out of Sight* (1966) "Funny Over You" and "A Love Like You" * *Disk-O-Tek Holiday* (1966) "You Were Made for Me" and "Just for You"

Freddie Bell and the Bellboys

Freddie Bell (Philadelphia, Pennsylvania)

Probably as well-known from their European tours as in the U.S., Freddie Bell and the Bell Boys had "Giddy-Up-A-Ding-Dong" to their credit in the mid–'50s. In America they did television and club appearances, especially in Las Vegas, and are still touring today.

Rock Around the Clock (1956) "I'm Gonna Teach You How to Rock" and "Giddy-Up-A-Ding-Dong" * *Rumble on the Docks* (1956) "Get the First Train Out of Town" * *Get Yourself a College Girl* (1964) "Talkin' About Love"

Freddie Fisher and His Schnicklefritz Band *see* Corn Colonel and His Band

Freddie Martin and Orchestra

Freddie (sometimes Freddy) Martin (Cleveland, Ohio, 1906–1983)

A leading tenor saxophonist, Freddie Martin led one of the pre-eminent "sweet" bands during the Big Band era. The first of his successful groups dates to the mid–1930s, and although his fame peaked during World War II he continued to play "Music in the Martin Manner" into the 1970s. He also had his own television program in the early 1950s

Martin's theme song, "borrowed" from a Tchaikovsky piano concerto, was the evocative and very successful "Tonight We Love." Another "borrowing" was "Flight of the Bumblebee"; yet another was "I Look at Heaven" from an Edvard Grieg concerto.

Among Freddie Martin's famous sidemen were bandleaders-to-be Claude Thornhill, Alvino Rey and Russ Morgan (who shamelessly filched Martin's tagline, changing it to "Music in the *Morgan* Manner").

Seven Days Leave (1942) * *Hit Parade of 1943* (1943) * *What's Buzzin' Cousin?* (1943) * *Stage Door Canteen* (1943) * *Senior Prom* (1958) * *The Big Beat* (1958)

Freddie Rich and His Orchestra

Freddie Rich (Warsaw, Poland, 1898–1956)

Both a pianist and composer, Freddie Rich led an orchestra at the posh Waldorf-Astoria Hotel in New York and also worked for the Hollywood studios. He had also been musical director for several radio stations. Along the way his sidemen included the Dorsey brothers and Benny Goodman. Among his compositions were "Penthouse Serenade" and "On the Riviera."

A WAVE, a WAC and a Marine (1944)

Freddie Slack and His Orchestra

Freddie Slack (Frederick Slack, Westby or La Crosse, Wisconsin, 1910–1965)

Before constituting his own West Coast group in 1942, Freddie Slack was a sideman on drums, then switching to the piano, with many bandleaders including Earl Burtnett, Lenny Hayton, Ben Pollack and the great Jimmy Dorsey. With his own band (which featured instruments outlined in neon lights) Slack had a hit with "Cow Cow Boogie," one of the most remembered of the boogie-woogie tunes that were sweeping the country then.

Other Slack hits included "Mister Five by Five," "Kitten on the Keys" and "Beat Me Daddy, Eight to the Bar." His theme song was "Strange Cargo" and he wrote songs himself, the most notable being the enduring "The House of Blue Lights"

After the boogie craze passed, Freddie Slack did not change much professionally with the times and his orchestra disbanded in the early 1950s, but he did remain musically active for another decade. Among his well-known band members had been the famous swing singer Ella Mae Morse and saxophonist/arranger Les Baxter.

The Sky's the Limit (1943) * *Reveille with Beverly* (1943) * *Hat Check Honey* (1944) * *Seven Days Ashore* (1944) * *Take It Big* (1944) * *Babes on Swing Street* (1944) * *Follow the Boys* (1944) * *High School Hero* (1946)

Freddy Martin see Freddie Martin and Orchestra

Freedom Singers

Cordell Reagon; Bernice Johnson; Charles Neblett; Rutha Harris; Matt Jones

Founded in 1962 to raise money for the Student Non-Violent Coordinating Committee (SNCC), the Freedom Singers were literally a strong voice in the civil rights movement of the 1960s. They enlarged their scope by performing at venues like the Newport Jazz Festival before re-forming as an all-male quartet in 1964.

Festival (1967) [documentary] "Freedom" and "We Shall Overcome"

Freeman, Ernie see Ernie Freeman Combo

Freewheelers

Once Upon a Coffeehouse (1965)

Freita Shaw Singers; Freita Shaw's Etudes; Famous Shaw Negro Choir

Harmony Lane (1935) * *General Spanky* (1937) * *High Hat* (1937)

Frey and Bragiotti

Frey and Bragiotti played dual pianos.

Social Register (1934)

Frost, Larry see Larry Frost and the Hollywood Chamber Jazz Group

Fugs

Ed Sanders; Tuli Kupferberg; Ken Weaver (drums); Peter Stampfel; Steve Weber

Toward the beginning of the Vietnam War in 1965 a group calling itself by a euphemism of a familiar four-letter word was formed. This was the Fugs who proceeded to forcefully sing and speak out against the war. Their anti-establishment songs which freely mentioned drug-taking and the current political situation brought them both praise and condemnation.

The Fugs released albums, the second of which made the charts, and played in New York clubs where they indulged in controversial acts like mock flag burning, thus drawing the F.B.I.'s attention.

The F.B.I. report referred to the Fugs as "beatniks" but cleared them of wrongdoing and they proceeded, relatively unmolested, to perform until 1969 when they played a final concert. The group briefly reunited in the 1980s and again about twenty years later.

Chappaqua (1966) [documentary] "I Couldn't Get High" * *Diaries, Notes and Sketches* (1969) * *The Revolution Is in Your Head* (1970) [documentary]

Fuller, Bobby *see* Bobby Fuller Four

Fuller, Walter *see* Walter Fuller...

Futuras

The Futuras were a garage band, possibly from Ohio.

Rat Fink (1965)

G-Men

The G-Men were Elvis Presley's back-up group in one of his films.

Double Trouble (1966)

Gaillard, Slim *see* Slim and Slam

Galli Sisters

Norma Galli

The Galli Sisters sang with the Art Mooney band in the late 1940s.

Down in "Arkansaw" (1938)

Garber, Jan *see* Jan Garber...

Gardner, Poison *see* Poison Gardner Trio

Gary Lewis and the Playboys

Gary Lewis (1946–) (drums); David Walker (guitar); Al Ramsay (guitar); David Costell (lead guitar); John West (keyboard); Tom Tripplehorn; Carl Radle; Jimmy Karstein

Although he is the oldest son of antic comedian Jerry Lewis, Gary Lewis and his band were supposedly hired at Disneyland incognito. By the time their first hit "This Diamond Ring" came along in 1964 his antecedents were undoubtedly well-known. He even played his father as a youth in *Rock-a-Bye Baby*.

That is not to say the Playboys did not deserve their success; their recordings were indeed very lively. However they did not actually play their instruments on "This Diamond Ring" (studio musicians dubbed them) and Lewis's voice was also partly overdubbed.

Other hits like "Count Me In," "Sure Gonna Miss Her," "She's Just My Style" and "Everybody Loves a Clown" followed. In 1965 Lewis won the *Cash Box Magazine* award as Best Male Vocalist. The band made many television appearances, including the *Ed Sullivan Show*.

When Gary Lewis was drafted into the military in 1966 the steam went out of the Playboys, never to be recaptured. Their time at the top had been brief but they did earn eight gold records, four gold albums and had seventeen Top Forty hits. Lewis still tours with a group of that name.

The Nutty Professor (1963)† * *A Swingin' Summer* (1965) "Nitro" and "Out to Lunch" * *The Family Jewels* (1965) "Little Miss Go-Go" and "This Diamond Ring" * *Out of Sight* (1966) "Malibu Run"

†This may have been a solo appearance by Gary.

Gateway Trio

Jerry Waller (banjo); Betty Man (guitar); Milt Chapman (bassist)

From the demise of the folk music group the Gateway Singers sprung the Gateway Trio in the early 1960s. Their first albums were in the tradition of the folk music revival then popular but as that genre waned in popularity they turned more to a folk rock sound. They also released singles like "Soldiers Who Want to Be Heroes." Their

time in the limelight was short, lasting only about three years to 1965.
Hootenanny Hoot (1963)

Gay Land and the Thunderbirds

Although its name makes it sound more like a rock group, Gay Land and the Thunderbirds was a hillbilly music ensemble.
Moonshine Mountain (1964)

Gene Krupa and His Band; Gene Krupa and His Orchestra; Gene Krupa Orchestra

Gene Krupa (Chicago, Illinois, 1909–1973)

Handsome and charismatic, Gene Krupa could fairly be called the first of the star drummers. Besides his unforgettably flamboyant playing, he is also credited with upgrading the role of drummers in orchestras and encouraging the development of a more modern drum set. He also pounded on a set of steampipes!

Krupa played in the pit for Broadway shows but made his reputation with many of the great bandleaders of his day, including Red Nichols and especially Benny Goodman. With that demanding taskmaster Krupa played the drums on the classic recording of "Sing Sing Sing," considered the first extended jazz drum solo. He had made his first recordings as early as 1927.

Possibly because of Krupa's scene-stealing playing, his mouth busily chewing gum and hair flipping, he split with Goodman and formed his own orchestra in 1939. With its theme song "Starburst," it met with initial success. At times it was a huge ensemble featuring a string section with more than thirty members. "Drum Boogie" was a big hit for them.

With a marijuana arrest and jail sentence of almost three months during World War II, Gene Krupa temporarily lost his band but ultimately restarted and performed with it into the early 1950s. Following that he essayed smaller ensembles that he led off and on for the next twenty years. He also played a few film roles (like *The Benny Goodman Story*) without his band.

In 1959 Gene Krupa was the subject — or victim — of the ill-received movie biography *The Gene Krupa Story*, starring Sal Mineo. Like most of these spurious biopics it played somewhat fast and loose with the true facts of his life. One of its advertising taglines blared "He hammered out the savage tempo of the Jazz Era!"

Some Like It Hot (1939) * *Ball of Fire* (1941) * *George White's Scandals* (1945) * *Beat the Band* (1947) * *Glamour Girl* (1948) * *Smart Politics* (1948)

Gene Vincent and His Blue Caps; Gene Vincent and the Blue Caps

Gene Vincent (Vincent Craddock, Norfolk, Virginia, 1935–1971); Jack Neal (bassist); Willie Williams (guitar); Cliff Gallup (guitar); Johnny Meeks (guitar); Dickie Harrell (drums)

In collaboration with a local disc jockey, rockabilly singer Gene Vincent wrote the novelty pop tune "Be-Bop-a-Lula" and parlayed it into a Top Ten hit in 1956. His group called themselves Gene Vincent and the (or His) Blue Caps and were supposedly named after the blue golfing hat worn by then–President Dwight Eisenhower.

After a couple of other modestly successful records, "Wear My Ring," "Lotta Lovin'" and "Dance to the Bop," the group disbanded in 1958. This was at least partly caused by Vincent's alcohol addiction, presumably a result of the many injuries he had suffered over the years.

Gene Vincent thereupon moved to England where he proved a wildly popular attraction in live shows and on television, assuming the persona of a black leather–jacketed tough guy with a duck-tail haircut. He also made a couple of films there. The Blue Caps had always been greeted rapturously in both Europe and Japan.

The Girl Can't Help It (1956) "Be-Bop-a-Lula" * *Hot Rod Gang* (1958) "Baby Blue," "Dance in the Street," "Lovely Loretta" and "Dance to the Bop."

Genteels

The Genteels were best known for their 1962 recording of "Take It Off."
One Man's Challenge (1962) "The Hitchhiker"

Gentrys

Larry Raspberry; Jimmy Hart

The infectious sound of "Keep on Dancing" proved to be the Gentrys' only rock hit, but that one was a million seller. The Memphis-based garage band consisting of seven members was formed in 1963, disbanded three years later, and was briefly revived in the 1970s.

It's a Bikini World (1967) "Spread It on Thick"

George Lawson and His Band
The Joint Is Jumpin' (1949)

George Mitchell and His Swing Orchestra
It's a Wonderful Day (1949)

George Olsen and His Orchestra
George Olsen (Portland, Oregon, 1893–1971)

The 1926 recording of "Who" was a million-seller for George Olsen and his orchestra. They played in vaudeville houses and also found success in several major 1920s Broadway shows, including *Whoopee*, *Good News* and *Sunny*.

Olsen was a drummer who led an orchestra for some thirty years, finally disbanding it in 1950. His theme song was "Beyond the Blue Horizon," in which can be heard the numerous sound effects (the chugging of a train, etc.) for which his ensemble was noted.

Happy Days (1930) * *Whoopee!* (1930)

George Shearing Quintet
George Shearing (London, England, 1919–); Cal Tjader; Margie Hyams; Denzil Best; Israel Crosby; Joe Pass; Gary Burton; Chuck Wayne; John Levy

Born blind, George Shearing nonetheless became a celebrated jazz pianist, first in England and then in the United States where he established residency. In the 1930s he appeared in London hotels and clubs before joining a dance band and also playing on BBC radio. His style of playing was known as the "locked hands" technique.

For a brief time Shearing had a big band but he found fame with a quintet, consisting of piano, guitar, bass, drums and vibraphone. They produced many hit recordings including "September in the Rain" and the famous "Lullaby of Birdland," his own composition. In latter years he led groups of various sizes and played as a solo.

George Shearing's career underwent somewhat of a renaissance in the 1970s and he found himself in demand for festivals and new recordings. He collaborated frequently with Mel Tormé, Peggy Lee and other well-known singers and was still active into the new century.

Disc Jockey (1951)† * *The Big Beat* (1958)
†Shearing may have appeared solo.

Georgia Crackers *see* Hank Newman and His Georgia Crackers

Georgia Peach Pickers *see* Curly Williams and His Georgia Peach Pickers

Georgia Sea Island Singers
The Gullah dialect and traditions of the Sea Islands off Georgia are in the good hands of the Georgia Sea Island Singers, an ensemble that dates back to 1920 or so. Originally dubbed the Spiritual Singers Society of Coastal Georgia, they were brought to the attention of a wider audience by folklorist Alan Lomax almost fifty years ago.

The Singers now travel the world with their songs and stories about the rich heritage of the Gullahs, whose ancestors were slaves. They have performed for Presidents, at the Olympic Games and at major world festivals, as well as releasing albums of their folk music.

Festival (1967) [documentary]

Gerry and the Pacemakers
Gerry Marsden (Gerard Marsden, Liverpool, England, 1942–); Freddy Marsden (Liverpool, England, 1940–); Les Maguire (Woolsey, England, 1941–); Les Chadwick (John Chadwick, 1943–)

For a brief time at the onset of the British Invasion, the rock group Gerry and the Pacemakers rivaled the Beatles in popularity. They had some basic similarities with the Fab Four in that they were also managed by Brian Epstein and had performed in Hamburg, Germany at the beginning of their careers.

The Pacemakers was founded by Gerry Marsden, out of Liverpool's skittle music scene, when he was seventeen and in the mid-'60s they scored with their plaintive hit "Ferry Cross the Mersey." They also recorded the sobby "Don't Let the Sun Catch You Crying" and "How Do You Do It?"

But the group failed to delineate the distinct personalities of individual group members, as the Beatles did, and so fell back into the pack and disbanded in 1967. They re-formed in the mid–70s.

The T.A.M.I. Show (1964) [documentary]
"Maybelline," "Don't Let the Sun Catch You

Crying" and other songs * *Ferry Cross the Mersey* (1965) "Ferry 'Cross the Mersey," "This Thing Called Love" and several other songs

Gibson, Steve see **Steve Gibson's Redcaps**

Girlfriend Trio [unknown]
Moonlight and Pretzels (1933)

Girls In Cellophane [unknown]
International House (1933)

Glamourette Quartet [unknown]
Olga San Juan (Brooklyn, New York, 1927–); Nancy Porter; Carol Deere; Audrey Young
Out of This World (1945)

Glaser Brothers
Jim Glaser (James Glaser, Spaulding, Nebraska, 1937–); Tompall Glaser (Thomas Glaser, Spaulding, Nebraska, 1933–); Chuck Glaser (Charles Glaser, Spaulding, Nebraska, 1936–)

It was in the 1950s that the trio began their careers as the country singers Tompall (for *Thomas Paul* Glaser) and the Glaser Brothers. They recorded on their own ("California Girl," "Through the Eyes of Love" and "Rings") as well as backing prominent country singers like Marty Robbins on his hit "El Paso."

The brothers had multiple talents besides singing: writing songs for themselves and others, producing records, and opening a recording studio and encouraging future stars like Willie Nelson to perform for them. They officially broke up the act in 1973 but continued solo careers. In the 1970s they were voted Vocal Group of the Decade and ultimately won nearly every country music award.
Country Boy (1966)

Glass Bottle
The People Next Door (1970) "Mama, Don't You Wait Up for Me"

Glen Gray and His Casa Loma Orchestra
Glen Gray (Glen Knoblauch or Knoblaugh), Metamora or Roanoke, Illinois, 1906–1963)

Although it was by no means the greatest of

Glen Gray (1941).

the big bands, the Casa Loma Orchestra is one that somehow evokes that period in the minds of aficionados. Called the Orange Blossoms from its founding in the mid–1920s until 1929, it took its permanent name from a Toronto hotel.

The group was a cooperative band, one of the first, in which members shared in the profits. Tenor saxophonist Glen Gray was little more than a front man from the mid–1930s on. They were one of the earlier white jazz bands and seemed particularly successful with college students.

Among Casa Loma's to-be famous musicians were Bix Biederbecke, Ray Eberle and Pee Wee Hunt. Their popular theme song was "Smoke Rings," with other recordings including "No Name Jive," "For You," "Stompin' Around" and "Malady in F."

By the 1940s the Casa Loma Orchestra was losing its popularity to more adventuresome bands and it disbanded about 1945. Glen Gray himself continued to record with studio bands and released several albums of big band music.
Time Out for Rhythm (1941) * *Gals, Incorporated* (1943) * *Jam Session* (1944)

Glenn Miller and His Orchestra; Glenn Miller Singers
Glenn Miller (Alton Glenn Miller, Clarinda, Iowa, 1904–1944)

Glenn Miller (center), with Cesar Romero (left) from *Orchestra Wives*.

When Major Glenn Miller disappeared over the English Channel in 1944 he became a legend, instead of just a highly successful bandleader who might have faded as did his contemporaries. Before he reached the pinnacle in the Big Band era he had been a trombone sideman for Benny Goodman, Ben Pollack, Red Nichols and the Dorsey brothers, among others.

By 1937 Miller had formed the orchestra that rapidly became famous for the "Miller sound." One aspect of that was a gradual fading of the music only to have it come blaring back with the previous segment repeated. In his relations with band members, he was a dour, sometimes ruthless disciplinarian and a sharp businessman.

With vocalists like Marion Hutton, the Modernaires and Ray Eberle the band turned out such massive hits as "Elmer's Tune," "American Patrol," "Chattanooga Choo Choo," "String of Pearls," "In the Mood," "Moonlight Cocktail," "Kalamazoo" and their theme song "Moonlight Serenade."

In his two starring films Miller acquitted himself well and revealed at least some minimal acting chops. In the second he played Gene Morrison, a struggling bandleader in the Midwest, a role that perhaps had some resonance to his own pre-fame life. In the 1953 biopic *The Glenn Miller Story* he was portrayed by the somewhat miscast Jimmy Stewart.

Although he probably could have avoided the draft, Glenn Miller chose to enlist in 1942 and form a military orchestra. After his mysterious and not definitively-solved vanishing, the band was taken over by Miller sideman and singer Tex Beneke. It toured successfully for decades thereafter and even now the name of Glenn Miller evokes a golden age in American swing music.

Sun Valley Serenade (1941) * *Orchestra Wives* (1942) * *Crazy House* (1943)

Glory Roads

Hot Thrills and Warm Chills (1967)

GoldeBriars

Dottie Holmberg (Los Angeles, California); Sheri Holmberg; Curt Boettcher (guitar); Ron Neilson (guitar/banjo); Ron Edgar (drums)

Sailing on the popular tide of the 1960s folk music revival were the GoldeBriars. They recorded three albums (the unreleased last of which veered more into folk-rock) before breaking up about 1965. They had performed together for less than three years.

Once Upon a Coffeehouse (1965)

Golden Gate Four; Golden Gate Quartet

Willie Johnson (d. 1998) (baritone); William Langford (2nd tenor); Orlandus Wilson (Chesapeake, Virginia, 1917?–1999) (bass); A. C. Griffin; Robert Ford; Henry Owens (1st tenor); Clyde Riddick

Styling their gospel music "jubilee" singing, the Norfolk, Virginia–based Golden Gate Quartet (originally the Golden Gate Jubilee Quartet) began performing about 1934 and were recording a few years later. Among their spirituals were the standards "Ezekiel Saw the Wheel," "Swing Low, Sweet Chariot" and "Down By the Riverside," which they infused with jazz styling.

They were so well-received that they branched out into pop music following the lead of such greats as the Mills Brothers. Like them they imitated musical instruments. Among career highlights was their 1938 "From Spirituals to Swing"

Carnegie Hall appearance. They were frequently heard on radio and also sang at Franklin Roosevelt's 1941 inaugural.

During the war years the Quartet's music took on a patriotic hue with such recordings as the novelty "Stalin Wasn't Stallin'" and "Comin' in on a Wing and a Prayer." Later in the 1940s they even experimented with a rhythm-and-blues sound but that was not their métier. In 1947 they scored a success with "Shadrach."

Ultimately the group did a tour of Europe and then resettled in France where African-American performers were wildly appreciated. They did not perform in the U.S. again until 1994. Over the years the Golden Gate Quartet has earned a reputation as the foremost practitioner of their jubilee style and was inducted into the Vocal Group Hall of Fame in 1998.

Star Spangled Rhythm (1943) * *Hit Parade of 1943* (1943) * *Hollywood Canteen* (1944) "The General Jumped At Dawn" * *A Song Is Born* (1948)

Golden West Cowboys *see* J. L. Frank's Golden West Cowboys; Pee Wee King and His Golden West Cowboys

Golden Westerners
Gentleman from Arizona (1939) * *Gauchos of El Dorado* (1941) "Way Out There"

Goodman, Al *see* Al Goodman and His Orchestra

Goodman, Benny *see* Benny Goodman...

Goofers
Bop Girl Goes Calypso (1957) "Wow, I'm Gonna Rock and Roll 'Til I Die"

Gordian Knot
The Young Runaways (1968) "Ophelia's Dream"

Gordon, Rosco *see* Rosco Gordon and the Red Tops

Gospel Chorale Singers
Sing a Song, for Heaven's Sake (1966) [documentary]

Gospel Echoes
Sing a Song, for Heaven's Sake (1966) [documentary]

Gould, Morton *see* Morton Gould and His Orchestra

Gould, Satch *see* Satch Gould and His Boys

Gourmet's Delight
Gas-s-s-s (1970)

Gracia Granada's Orchestra
Law and Lawless (1932)

Granada, Gracia *see* Gracia Granada's Orchestra

Grant, Earl *see* Earl Grant Trio

Grant, Kirby *see* Kirby Grant and Orchestra

Grass Roots
Warren Entner (Boston, Massachusetts, 1944–) (guitar/keyboard); Creed Bratton (Los Angeles, California, 1943–) (guitar); Rob Grill (Los Angeles, California, 1944–) (bassist); Rick Coonce (Eric Coonce, Los Angeles, California, 1946–) (drums); Dennis Provisor (Los Angeles, California, 1950–) (keyboard); Terry Furlong (London, England, 1942–) (guitar)

Although they became a very successful folk-rock group the Grass Roots were initially manufactured by a couple of songwriters to cash in on that genre's popularity. In the mid–1960s a random group of musicians made a record and were dubbed the Grass Roots although such a band did not really exist.

Eventually the Los Angeles–based band the 13th Floor assumed the Grass Roots name and began recording. Their first effort "Let's Live for Today" charted in the Top Ten and was followed by other hits like "Midnight Confessions," "Two Divided By Love" and "Temptation Eyes."

By the time it initially disbanded in 1975 the Grass Roots, which had evolved from a quartet into a quintet, had sold many millions of records and had been on *Billboard* charts for more than 300 consecutive weeks. Two of their albums had gone platinum and several others gold.

In 1982 the Grass Roots was revived and held a July Fourth concert that attracted an audience of over a half million fans. In spite of its origins as the band that "never was" it acquitted itself very well and has continued to perform to this day.

With Six You Get Eggroll (1968) "Feelings"

Grateful Dead

Jerry Garcia (Jerome Garcia, San Francisco, California, 1942–1995) (vocals/guitar); Bob Weir (guitar); Ron McKernan (d. 1973) (keyboard/harmonica/percussion); Phil Lesh (guitar); Bill Kreutzmann (drums); Keith Godchaux (1948?–1980); Brent Mydland (1953?–1980); Vince Welnick (Phoenix, Arizona, 1955?–2006); Mickey Hart

Some members of the Grateful Dead began their careers in the jug band Mother McCree's Uptown Jug Champions, and then reconstituted themselves as the Warlocks. When they dropped that name in favor of their memorable new one, they found lasting fame and became veritable symbols of the 1960s LSD counterculture. Their live appearances were invariably tumultuous.

There is more than one story about the origin of the Grateful Dead's name, including borrowing it from the *Tibetan Book of the Dead* or a British ballad. In any case, the band embraced psychedelic electronic music, frequently melding several musical genres together: bluegrass, blues, country, folk rock, rhythm-and-blues.

The Dead's early albums did not garner much notice but by 1970 they had hit their stride with their charismatic, troubled leader Jerry Garcia. They had but one Top Ten hit, "Touch of Grey," and other well-received singles including "Casey Jones" and "Truckin'." But their later albums were smash hits courtesy of their fans (the "Deadheads") who followed them from venue to venue.

In 1977 there was a self-titled documentary (or so-called "rockumentary") made about the group. In 1996, shortly after Garcia's death, the Grateful Dead disbanded but reunited as just the Dead in 2003. To this day the band remains enormously influential and even legendary. Garcia himself gained the inestimable honor of having an ice cream flavor named for him: Cherry Garcia.

Petulia (1968) "Viola Lee Blues" * *Fillmore* (1972) [documentary]

Gray, Glen *see* Glen Gray and His Casa Loma Orchestra

Grayson, Hal *see* Hal Grayson's Orchestra

Grease Band *see* Joe Cocker and the Grease Band

Great Lakes Naval Station Choir
The Navy Way (1944)

Green, Jimmie *see* Jimmie Green's Orchestra

Green, Johnny *see* Johnny Green and His Orchestra

Grier, Jimmy *see* Jimmie Grier and His Orchestra

Grit
Musical Mutiny (1970)

Groove
Popcorn: an Audio/Visual Rock Thing (1969) [documentary]

Groove Boys *see* Skinnay Ennis and the Groove Boys

Gross, Leon *see* Leon Gross' Orchestra

Group
Mondo Mod (1967) "Feel a Whole Lot Better" and "Follow Me"

Guadalahara Boys; Guadalajara Trio
Jesus Castillon; Lamberto Leyva; Mario Santos

The Guadalajara Trio (aka the Guadalahara Boys) exemplified Hollywood's stereotypical idea of what Mexican musicians should look like.

Dressed in gaudy outfits and always smiling happily, they graced many a Hollywood musical and western. They also played with orchestras, including that of Desi Arnaz, and were sometimes seen on his *I Love Lucy* television show.

Boss of Bullion City (1941) * *Fiesta* (1941) * *The Masked Rider* (1941) * *Rio Rita* (1942) * *Allergic to Love* (1944) * *Bathing Beauty* (1944) * *Broadway Rhythm* (1944) * *That's My Baby* (1944) * *Hands Across the Border* (1944) * *South of the Rio Grande* (1945) * *Masquerade in Mexico* (1946) * *Slightly Scandalous* (1946) * *Trail to Mexico* (1946) * *Fiesta* (1947) * *That's My Gal* (1947)

Guardsmen; Guardsmen Quartet

William Brandt; Earl Hunsaker; Henry Iblings; Dudley Kuzzell

We're Not Dressing (1934) * *The Parson of Panamint* (1941) * *Playmates* (1941) * *Riders of the Timberline* (1941) * *Cairo* (1942) * *Ship Ahoy* (1942) * *Stagecoach Buckaroo* (1942) * *Hail the Conquering Hero* (1944)

Gus Arnheim and His Cocoanut Grove Ambassadors; Gus Arnheim and His Orchestra

Gus Arnheim (Philadelphia, Pennsylvania, 1897/99–1955)

From the latter days of the 1920s Jazz Age Gus Arnheim had a very popular West Coast orchestra, performing at the Cocoanut Grove nightclub in Hollywood and touring extensively. Being a local boy, so to speak, his ensemble was also one of the earliest to appear in sound films; the orchestra performed in musical shorts as early as 1928.

Among those who had worked in the band were crooners Bing Crosby (when he was part of the Rhythm Boys) and Russ Columbo, Stan Kenton, Woody Herman and Fred MacMurray. Arnheim himself had made his professional debut as the pianist with the Syncopated Five.

Gus Arnheim was also a noted songwriter among whose standards were "I Surrender Dear" (Crosby's first big hit), "Mandalay," "I Cried for You" and "Sweet and Lovely," his theme song. Over the years his orchestra evolved its sound to keep up with changing musical tastes and so he was able to be active into the 1950s with smaller combos.

Broadway (1929) * *Half Marriage* (1929) * *Street Girl* (1929) * *Flying High* (1931) * *Scarface* (1932) * *Gift of Gab* (1934) * *Palooka* (1934)

Guy Lombardo and His Orchestra; Guy Lombardo and His Royal Canadians

Guy Lombardo (Gaetano Lombardo, London, Ontario, 1902–1977); Carmen Lombardo (London, Ontario, 1903–1971); Lebert Lombardo (1905–1993); Victor Lombardo (1911–1994)

"The Sweetest Music This Side of Heaven" issued forth from the band of Guy Lombardo starting in 1924. There had previously been a Lombardo quartet with his brothers Victor, Lebert and Carmen. With them he formed the Royal Canadians and added sister Rosemarie as a vocalist.

The orchestra is estimated to have sold an astounding 300 million recordings, more than any other dance band. Among their numerous hits were "Winter Wonderland," "Humoresque," "The Third Man Theme," "Seems Like Old Times," "Little White Lies," "September in the Rain" and "Easter Parade."

The band was very big on the radio and was the house orchestra at New York's Roosevelt Hotel for some thirty years. They were such a fixture on New Year's Eve broadcasts that "Auld Lang Syne" practically became *their* song. All the Lombardos were talented musicians: Guy, violin; Lebert, drums and trumpet; Carmen flute and saxophone, and Victor clarinet and saxophone.

Guy Lombardo's smooth personality and the dance music of the Royal Canadians made them very popular, and both Lebert and Carmen provided some of the vocals. Some critics thought the orchestra musically unvarying, hence uninteresting — even squaresville; however this did not prevent them from being a force well into the 1970s.

It was perhaps this traditional quality that enabled the Canadians to perform at many Presidential inaugurations and World Series openings. Not too long after Guy's death the orchestra disbanded but was briefly resurrected in the late 1980s.

Many Happy Returns (1934) * *Stage Door Canteen* (1943) * *No Leave, No Love* (1946)

Habanera Sextette (aka Sextetto Habanero)

Hell Harbor (1930)

Hacker Duo [unknown]
David Hacker; June Hacker
Hi'Ya, Sailor (1943)

Hairston, Jester *see* Jester Hairston Choir

Hal Grayson's Orchestra
Hal Grayson (Harold Grayson, Los Angeles, California, 1908–1959)

Betty Grable and "Liltin'" Martha Tilton were two of Hal Grayson's vocalists and helped to make his sweet band popular from the 1930s through the end of World War II. Unfortunately his later publicity came largely for his headline-making arrests for public inebriation and schizophrenia.

Night World (1932)

Hal Kemp and His Orchestra
Hal Kemp (James Kemp, Marion, Alabama, 1904–1940)

Although he started out with a jazz group, in the 1930s Hal Kemp led one of the most popular sweet bands in the country. Its theme songs were "Got a Date with an Angel" and "When Summer Is Gone." Among his vocalists was bandleader-to-be Skinnay Ennis who had recording hits with "You're the Top" and "It's Easy to Remember."

Kemp's ensemble was dubbed the "typewriter band" for its clipped sound. Ultimately he opted for a more swing-oriented style and the ensemble began losing some of its edge with audiences. His early death in an automobile accident soon put an end to his orchestra as well.

Radio City Revels (1938)

Hal Mcintyre and His Orchestra; Hal Mcintyre's Orchestra
Hal McIntyre (Harold McIntyre, Cromwell, Connecticut, 1914/19–1959)

A sideman for Benny Goodman and Glenn Miller, alto saxophonist/clarinetist Hal McIntyre formed his own band about 1941. With its theme songs the pretty "Moon Mist" and "Ecstasy," it was grandly billed as the "Band That America Loves." It proved popular during the War and played top venues across the country, but thereafter declined in popularity and disbanded in the 1950s.

Hey, Rookie! (1944) * *Eadie Was a Lady* (1945) * *Sing Me a Song of Texas* (1945)

Haley, Bill *see* Bill Haley and His Comets

Hall, Juanita *see* Juanita Hall...

Hall Johnson Choir
Hall Johnson (Francis Johnson, Athens, Georgia, 1888–1970)

One of the most revered African-American musicologists, violinist Hall Johnson played in orchestras, including those of Broadway shows, and taught music before founding his famous choir in 1925. It went by the name of the Harlem Jubilee Singers until the original eight members persuaded their founder to name it for himself. At times it grew to as many as sixty members.

The Choir performed on Broadway in such shows as *Green Pastures*, as well as in Johnson's own folk opera *Run Little Chillun*. By the mid-1930s Hollywood had beckoned and their mellifluous voices were heard in many films. Even if they were presented in stereotypical fashion, at least they were enjoyed by a wider audience than they had reached before.

Hall Johnson continued to compose and he was a leading champion of preserving authentic Black spirituals dating from the days of slavery. Dubbed the "Black Stokowski," he was heaped with honors over the years. He also taught and influenced such famous singers as Shirley Verrett, Marian Anderson and Harry Belafonte.

The Green Pastures (1936) * *Follow Your Heart* (1936) * *Dimples* (1936) * *Hearts Divided* (1936) * *Banjo on My Knee* (1936) * *Rainbow on the River* (1936) * *My Old Kentucky Home* (1938) * *Saint Louis Blues* (1939) * *Way Down South* (1939) * *Zenobia* (1939) * *Swanee River* (1940) * *In Old Missouri* (1940) * *Meet John Doe* (1941) * *Road to Zanzibar* (1941) * *Heart of the Golden West* (1942) * *Lady for a Night* (1942) * *Tales of Manhattan* (1942) * *Syncopation* (1942) * *Cabin in the Sky* (1943) * *The Peanut Man* (1947)

Hamilton, Chico *see* Chico Hamilton Quintet

Hampton, Lionel *see* Lionel Hampton...

Hampton University Choral Choir

Located in Hampton, Virginia, in the southeastern part of the state, Hampton University is a historically black school.

Hits and Bits of 1938 (1938)

Hank Caldwell and His Saddle Kings

Hank Caldwell (Vernal, Utah) (fiddle); Bud Smith (Utah) (accordion); Jimmy Widner (Alabama) (guitar); Hal Metzger (Kansas) (fiddle)

Having worked with a variety of performers including Roy Rogers, Jimmy Wakely and Deuce Spriggins, Hank Caldwell formed the Saddle Kings, which was active in the 1950s.

He was also a songwriter, one of which was "Throw a Saddle on a Star" the title song of a movie. The western in which the Saddle Kings appeared is considered to be just about the final one in the string of "B" oater second features stretching back to the silent days.

The Lawless Rider (1954)

Hank Newman and His Georgia Crackers

Hank Newman (Hawkinsville, Georgia?, 1905–1978) (guitar); Slim Newman (Hawkinsville, Georgia?); Bob Newman (Hawkinsville, Georgia?, 1915–) (bassist); Hal Snyder (Harold Snyder, Columbus, Ohio) (guitar); Winnie Waters (Kentucky, 1919–) (fiddle); Johnny Sipes (accordion)

Popular on Midwestern radio stations for their western swing music and rural comedy, the three Newman brothers, Hank, Slim and Bob, were the nucleus of the Georgia Crackers. Among their recordings were "Rats in My Closet," "Horses, Women and Wine" and "Broken Doll."

The Fighting Frontiersman (1946) * *South of the Chisholm Trail* (1947) * *Desert Vigilante* (1948)

Hank Penny and His Plantation Boys

Hank Penny (Herbert Penny, Birmingham, Alabama, 1918–1992); Carl Stewart (fiddle); Louis Innes (guitar/bassist); Roy Langham (guitar); Slim Duncan; Frank Buckley; Bob Morgan

Somewhat a jack-of-all-trades, Hank Penny was a comic, disc jockey, singer and bandleader (even briefly fronting an all-girl band) during his colorful career. He had been performing on radio by the age of fifteen and formed the Radio Cowboys in the late 1930s.

The Plantation Boys, a western swing product of the mid–1940s, appeared on Cincinnati radio, playing with, among others, the young singer Doris Day and guitarist Merle Travis. On the West Coast, Penny stooged for Spade Cooley on the latter's television show as "The Plain Ol' Country Boy"

Hank Penny led many groups in his career, including the Penny Serenaders, the Painted Post Rangers and a Las Vegas casino orchestra before winding down his career. His bands had had a few western swing hits including "Steel Guitar Stomp," "Bloodshot Eyes" and "Get Yourself a Redhead." He also wrote "Won't You Ride My Little Red Wagon."

Heading West (1946) * *The Blazing Trail* (1949) * *Frontier Outpost* (1950)

Hargett, Paul see Paul Hargett and the Bikini Sweethearts

Hargreaves, Bobby see Bobby Hargreaves Orchestra

Harlemania Orchestra

The Duke Is Tops (1938)

Harlem's Apache Chorus

Underworld (1937)

Harmon, Manny see Manny Harmon and His Orchestra

Harmonaires see Leo Diamond and His Harmonaires

Harmonettes [unknown]

Secret Sinners (1933)

Harmonicats see Jerry Murad and His Harmonicats

Harmony Four Quartette

On with the Show (1929)

Harold and Lola [unknown]

Pan-Americana (1945) * *Variety Time* (1948)

Harper's Bizarre

Ted Templeman (drums/guitar); Dick Scoppettone (guitar/bassist); Eddie James (guitar); Dick Yount (bassist); John Petersen (drums)

The rock group the Tikis evolved into the Harper's Bizarre about the time they released the hit song "Feelin' Groovy" (aka "The 59th Street Bridge Song") in 1967. They experimented with a variety of sounds, but in general their music was on the easy-listening side with recordings of classic tunes like "Chattanooga Choo Choo" and "Anything Goes." The band broke up in 1969.

You Are What You Eat (1968) [documentary]

Harps O'Swing

Carolina Blues (1944)

Harptones

Willie Winfield (lead); Nicky Clark (2nd lead/1st tenor); Jimmy Winfield; Clyde Winfield; Bill Galloway (baritone); Johnny Bronson; Raoul Cita (tenor); Curtis Cherebin; William Dempsey (2nd tenor); Bill Brown (bass); Fred Taylor

In spite of the fact that the Harptones did not have a Top Forty record nor did they make the rhythm-and-blues charts, they are still considered to have been one of the great doo-wop groups. The smooth "A Sunday Kind of Love," "Since I Fell for You" and the haunting "The Shrine of Saint Cecelia" are among their best-remembered recordings. "Why Should I Love You?" did at least make the pop charts.

The Harptones had started out as the intriguingly named 115th Street Tin Can Band, became the Skylarks, and then the Harps, but changed that when they learned about a similarly-named ensemble. They began recording in 1953 and performed in cream-colored suits.

Their latter-day appearances were mostly at nostalgia-based concerts into the 1990s. In 2002 the group was inducted into the Vocal Group Hall of Fame. The movie in which they appeared is considered to be among the first rhythm-and-blues movies.

Rockin' the Blues (1956) [documentary] "First Last and Only Girl," "Hot Rod Baby" and other songs

Harris, Jet *see* Jet Harris and the Jet Blacks

Harris, Phil *see* Phil Harris and His Orchestra

Harris and Scott [unknown]

Souls of Sin (1949)

Harrison, Bobby *see* Bobby Harrison Trio

Harry James and His Band; Harry James and His Music Makers

Harry James (Albany, Georgia, 1916–1983)

A child of circus performers and leader of a circus band himself, Harry James went up in the world as a drummer, then a trumpeter, with dance bands from the age of thirteen. Among them were the Ben Pollack and Benny Goodman orchestras. His virtuoso style of playing was frequently featured in solo performances, and by his early twenties he had formed his own organization.

Harry James and band *Springtime in the Rockies.*

James is credited with "discovering" Frank Sinatra in a small club in 1939 and hired "Old Blue Eyes" as a vocalist. Other of his band singers included Dick Haymes, Connie Haines, Helen Forrest and Kitty Kallen. It was not too long before the band was rated among the best in the country with recordings like "I've Heard That Song Before," "Flight of the Bumblebee," "All or Nothing at All," "You Made Me Love You" and their theme song "Ciribiribin."

In its personal appearances James' band drew sell-out, sometimes delirious, crowds but with the post-war decrease in big band popularity he disbanded the group. Eventually he re-started it, with a smaller string section, and toured into the 1980s. His was probably the last really popular big band to survive changing musical tastes.

Harry James' popularity was certainly helped by his affable public persona and his much publicized marriage to movie musical queen Betty Grable. Besides the many films in which he appeared with his band, he played a straight role in the western *Outlaw Queen*. His was the horn playing dubbed in the film *Young Man with a Horn*.

Private Buckaroo (1942) * *Springtime in the Rockies* (1942) * *Best Foot Forward* (1943) * *Bathing Beauty* (1944) * *Two Girls and a Sailor* (1944) * *If I'm Lucky* (1946) * *Do You Love Me?* (1946) * *I'll Get By* (1950) * *The Benny Goodman Story* (1956) * *The Opposite Sex* (1956) * *Loving You* (1957) * *The Big Beat* (1958) * *The Ladies Man* (1961)

Harry Owens and His Royal Hawaiians

Harry Owens (O'Neill, Nebraska, 1902–1986)

The classic "Sweet Leilani" was written by bandleader Harry Owens who had formed his first ensemble in 1926. The song was composed upon his daughter's birth and popularized by Bing Crosby in the film *Waikiki Wedding*. It won the Academy Award for Best Song and has sold some 20 million copies to date. Naturally, it was the group's theme song as well.

Owens and his orchestra the Royal Hawaiians, named for their base the Royal Hawaiian Hotel, were heard on the popular radio program *Hawaii Calls* and later had a television show. They symbolized Hawaii for millions of listeners and were indeed credited for boosting tourism to that then–U.S. territory.

He had founded the band in 1934 and begun broadcasting from Honolulu two years later. A booster of everything Hawaiian, Harry Owens used steel guitars to enhance his orchestra's sound and native singer Hilo Hattie added to the appeal of the ensemble. (It was still basically the Hawaiian Islands as homogenized for the non–Hawaiian, however.) His music has been described as "sweet, rhythmic and danceable."

It's a Date (1940) * *Song of the Islands* (1942) * *Hat Check Honey* (1944) * *Lake Placid Serenade* (1944)

Havana Casino Orchestra

Don Azpiazu (piano)

The Havana Casino Orchestra was instrumental in introducing the Cuban rumba-like dance music known as "son" to American audiences in the late 1920s. They also were probably the first authentic Cuban dance band to perform on Broadway. The orchestra popularized "The Peanut Vendor" ("Manicero"), which became somewhat of a national craze, and "Green Eyes."

Stolen Heaven (1931)

Hawaiians *see* Lani Mcintyre and His Hawaiians

Hawkins, Edwin *see* Edwin Hawkins Singers

Hayes, Tubby *see* Tubby Hayes Quintet

Heavenly Choir

Go Down, Death! (1944/46)

Heaven's Devils

Starlet (1969)

Hedgehoppers Anonymous

Run with the Wind (1966)

Heidt, Horace *see* Horace Heidt and His Orchestra

Hell's Bells

My Tale Is Hot (1964)

Henri Woode and His Sextet

Henri Woode (William Woode, Omaha, Nebraska, 1909–1994)

That Man of Mine (1946)

Henry Busse and His Orchestra

Henry Busse (Holland or Magdeburg, Germany, 1894–1955)

Trumpeter Henry Busse performed in a "jass" band and played for silent movies before joining Paul Whiteman during World War One. He also co-composed some of Whiteman's popular tunes, including "Wang Wang Blues." He was supposedly the first dance band member to use a mute in his trumpet.

In the late 1920s he established his own dance orchestra, purveying a "sweet sound" with recordings like "When Day Is Done," one of their theme songs. He became known as "Hot Lips" after the orchestra's other theme song. They were based in Chicago in the 1930s and later at one of New York's tonier hotels.

During the Second World War Busse's orchestra, also known as the Shuffle Rhythm Band after their style of playing, became more of a swing group. They remained successful until the Big Band era drew to a close and he remained in harness until the time of his sudden death, ironically at an undertaker's convention in Memphis.

Lady Let's Dance (1944) * *Rhapsody in Blue* (1945) * *The Fabulous Dorseys* (1947)

Henry King and His Orchestra; Henry King's Orchestra

Henry King (1903/06–1974)

Pianist Henry King led a successful society dance orchestra in the 1930s which played at top hotels, and whose theme song was "A Blues Serenade." For a time he also appeared on the George Burns–Gracie Allen radio program. Later in the decade he switched to featuring Latin American music and remained active into the 1950s.

The Sunset Murder Case (1941) * *The Yanks Are Coming* (1942) * *Spotlight Scandals* (1943) * *Sweethearts of the U.S.A.* (1944) * *Out of This World* (1945)

Herb Jeffries and the Four Tones; Herb Jeffries' Calypsomaniacs

Herb Jeffries (sometimes Herbert Jeffreys or Jeffrey), Detroit, Michigan, 1911/12–); Lucius Brooks; Leon Buck; Rudolph Hunter; John Porter; Ira Hardin

Singer and jazz musician Herb Jeffries' career took a most unusual turn in the late 1930s when he starred in four singing westerns. This would not have been noteworthy except that they had all–Black casts, in which he played hero Bob Blake. (He supposedly had his face darkened so he would look more "Black.") Noted character actors like Charlie Chan's Mantan Moreland and Amos and Andy's Spencer Williams played in support, as did the vocal group the Four Tones.

Nicknamed the "Bronze Buckaroo," the title of one of his movies, the tall, handsome crooner was well-known to the African-American community but much less so to other audiences despite his striking good looks and talent. This changed when his smooth baritone made big hits of "Satin Doll," "Angel Eyes" and especially "Flamingo."

Jeffries appeared with the orchestras of Earl Hines and Duke Ellington, being the last surviving member of the latter band. His career has enjoyed longevity — he was still recording well into his eighties — and during the short-lived calypso craze, he did a film with his later group the Calypsomaniacs. Still later he made several appearances as an actor on television shows.

Harlem on the Prairie (1937) * *Two Gun Man from Harlem* (1938) * *Harlem Rides the Range* (1939) * *The Bronze Buckaroo* (1939) * *One Dark Night* (1939) * *Calypso Joe* (1957)

Herb Miller and His Orchestra

Herb Miller (John Miller, North Platte, Nebraska, 1915–1987)

As the much younger brother of legendary bandmeister Glenn Miller, trumpeter Herb Miller had a lot to live up to, particularly since he established his first short-lived band at the height of Glenn's fame. By the late 1950s Herb's reconstituted group was still playing in hotels but he never really emerged from his big brother's shadow in America.

Miller eventually relocated to England in the late 1960s where his physical similarity to Glenn — as well as the similarity of his orchestra to the elder Miller's — led to a modicum of success. His son John took over leadership after Herb's death and as the John Miller Orchestra it is still active.

Spotlight Scandals (1943)

Herman, Woody see Woody Herman and His Orchestra

Herman's Hermits

Peter Noone (aka Peter Novack) (Manchester, England, 1947–); Derek Leckenby (1943?–1994) (guitar); Karl Green (bassist); Barry Whitwam (Jan Whitwam, Prestbury, England, 1946–) (drums); Keith Hopwood (guitar); Alan Wrigley (guitar); Steve Titterington (drums)

Originally known as the Heartbeats, the popular British Invasion band Herman's Hermits (once and future actor Peter Noone was "Herman") sold over fifty million recordings. They included "Mrs. Brown, You've Got a Lovely Daughter," "Can't You Hear My Heartbeat?," "Henry the Eighth" and their first hit "I'm on to Something Good."

The Hermits were a clean-cut group of young men and front man Noone exuded boyish charm with his bright smile and winsomely crooked teeth. He had been an experienced actor from childhood in Britain and after moving permanently to America continued his show biz career mainly on television, including daytime serials.

The group was together from about 1963 to the time Peter Noone departed in 1971. Their last big hit record was 1967's "There's a Kind of Hush." The band, now in more than one version, has continued to be popular in concerts and on tour up to today.

Pop Gear (1965) [documentary] "I'm in to Something Good" * *When the Boys Meet the Girls* (1965) "Bidin' My Time" and "Listen People" * *Hold On!* (1966) "Hold on," "Got a Feeling," "Make Me Happy" and several other songs * *Mrs. Brown, You've Got a Lovely Daughter* (1968) "Lemon and Lime," "The World Is for the Young" and several other songs

Herman's Mountaineers

Herman's Mountaineers were western swing musicians.

Heart of the Rockies (1937)

Hernandez, Chiquita see Chiquita Hernandez Orchestra

Heroes of Cranberry Farm

The Heroes of Cranberry Farm was a Miami, Florida–based band.

Devil Rider! (1970) "The Wind"

Herrera, Humberto see Humberto Herrera and His Orchestra

Herrera Sisters

The Herrera Sisters were singers.

Down Mexico Way (1941) "La Cachita," "Guadalajara" and "Down Mexico Way"

Herth, Milt see Milt Herth Trio

Heywood, Don see Don Heywood and His Band

Heywood, Eddie see Eddie Heywood and His Orchestra

Hi-Lo Jack and the Dame

Don Elliott (Donald Helfman, Somerville, New Jersey, 1926–1984); Jimmy Farmer; Maury Laws; Fran Carroll; Jack Steinharter

The singing group Hi-Lo Jack and the Dame were perhaps best

Herman (Peter Noone, center) with the Hermits.

known for the timeless song "Would You Rather Be a Colonel with an Eagle on Your Shoulder, or a Private with a Chicken on Your Knee?"
Hey, Rookie! (1944)

Hi-Lo's
Gene Puerling (Milwaukee, Wisconsin, 1929–2008) (bass-baritone); Bob Strasen (baritone); Bob Morse (Pasadena, California, 1927–2001) (baritone); Clark Burroughs (Los Angeles, California, 1930–) (tenor); Don Shelton (Tyler, Texas, 1934–) (tenor)

Named for their wide vocal range, and perhaps for the noticeable differences in their heights, the Hi-Lo's were a close harmony a cappella quartet. They undoubtedly were the inspiration for succeeding groups like the Manhattan Transfer. Originally formed in 1953, they disbanded during the British Invasion only to rebound in the 1970s to renewed popularity, appearing at the Monterey Jazz Festival.

With their great technical expertise, mellow sound and occasional essays into comic patter, the Hi Lo's soon became much admired, appearing on television with the likes of Rosemary Clooney (almost forty appearances on her show alone), Nat Cole, Judy Garland, Peggy Lee and Frank Sinatra.

With such exposure, their albums sold well, although they only had a single charter, "My Baby Just Cares for Me" in 1954. They even recorded advertising jingles for TV shows. The Hi Lo's also toured successfully, singing at venues like Madison Square Garden, the Hollywood Bowl and London's Royal Albert Hall.

Calypso Heat Wave (1957) * *Everything's Ducky* (1961) * *Good Neighbor Sam* (1964)

Hip Paraders [unknown]
Harlem Follies (1949?)

Hit Parade Orchestra *see* Carl Hoff and the Hit Parade Orchestra

Hite, Les *see* Les Hite and His Orchestra; *see also* Cotton Club Orchestra

Hoagland, Everett *see* Everett Hoagland and Band

Hobie Shepp and the Cowtown Wranglers
Corn's-A-Poppin' (1956?)

Hobnobbers [unknown]
Yes Sir, Mr. Bones (1951)

Hoff, Carl *see* Carl Hoff and the Hit Parade Orchestra

Hollies
Allan Clarke (lead vocals); Graham Nash (guitar); Terry Sylvester; Eric Haydock (bassist); Tony Hicks (guitar); Bernie Colvert; Donald Rathbone (drums)

The original members of the pop band the Hollies were based in and around Manchester, England. Among their greatest harmonic influences were such groups as the Everly Brothers and the Beach Boys. In Europe, at least, their fame came to rival that of their musical mentors.

The recording of "Just One Look" was the Hollies' earliest success in the mid–1960s, and "Bus Stop" proved another big winner for them. The band flirted with a psychedelic sound later in the decade, issuing records like "He Ain't Heavy, He's My Brother."

During the 1970s the Hollies' popularity began to decline somewhat but they still had such hits as "Long Cool Woman" and "The Air That I Breathe," and they have continued to tour to this day. Probably their most famous alumnus is Graham Nash, a founding member of Crosby, Nash and Stills.

It's All Over Town (1963) * *Go-Go Big Beat!* (1965) [documentary] "Here I Go Again" and "Baby That's All" * *After the Fox* (1966)

Hollywood Canteen Kids
Warne Marsh (1927–1987); Billy Byers; Karl Kiffle

Mainly performing during World War II, the Hollywood Canteen Kids was a band consisting of young musicians led by Karl Kiffle.

Song of the Open Road (1944)

Hollywood Rock 'N' Rollers [unknown]
Untamed Youth (1957)

Hollywood Symphony Orchestra

Concert Magic (1948) [documentary]

Homer and Jethro

Homer (Henry Haynes, Knoxville, Tennessee, 1918/20–1971) (guitar); Jethro (Kenneth Burns, Knoxville, Tennessee, 1920/23–1989) (mandolin); Ken Eidson (guitar)

It was supposedly a radio program mis-introduction that turned Junior and Dude (pronounced Dudee) into Homer and Jethro. In any event it was the name they continued to use throughout their subsequent career from the 1930s to the '60s. They had first teamed in 1932.

Their shtick ranged from extreme hillbilly versions of popular songs to writing parodies of hit tunes like "Baby It's Cold Outside" and "How Much Is That Doggie in the Window?" However, they were also serious musicians who released several albums, including some jazz, and the duo backed up other country artists.

"The Battle of Kookamonga," the Homer and Jethro parody of the smash hit "The Battle of New Orleans," won them a Grammy in 1959. By then they had expanded their audiences via Las Vegas and television appearances and their jazz music. Following Homer's death Jethro had a successful solo career and they were both elected to the Country Music Hall of Fame.

Second Fiddle to a Steel Guitar (1965)

Hondells

Ritchie Burns; Glen Campbell (Delight, Arkansas, 1936–); Curt Boettcher; Chuck Girard; Joe Kelly

The surf rock group the Hondells did not even really exist when their hit record "Little Honda" hit the charts in 1964. Assorted musicians and singers had been assembled by the record producer just for that one song, and when it became a success an actual group needed to be formed. Among the "hired guns" was country star-to-be Glen Campbell.

It got stranger still. The Hondells' first album was so hastily produced that its cover pictured two people who were not actually in the group at all. Ritchie Burns, a backup singer on "Little Honda" was hired to front the ensemble which went on to appear in beach movies, make television appearances and issue further, mostly unsuccessful, records.

Only two Hondells singles made the charts after their initial hit: "My Buddy Seat" and a cover of "Younger Girl." With such a shaky beginning the makeshift group had disbanded by the end of the 1960s.

Ski Party (1965) * "The Gasser" and "Ski Party" * *Beach Ball* (1965) "My Buddy Seat" * *Beach Blanket Bingo* (1965) "The Cycle Set"

Honeycombs

Dennis D'Ell (London, England, 1943–); Honey Lantree (Hayes, England, 1943–); John Lantree (Newbury, England, 1941–); Alan Ward (Nottingham, England, 1945–); Martin Murray (London, England, 1939–)

The Honeycombs were an English pop group of the mid–1960s who were somewhat unusual in that they had a female drummer. Their one major success was "Have I the Right?," with a couple of pale follow-ups like "Is It Because?" and "Something Better Beginning."

Pop Gear (1965) [documentary] "Have I the Right" and "Eyes"

Hoopii, Sal *see* Sal Hoopii and His Hawaiian Band

Hoosier Hot Shots

Kenneth Trietsch (Arcadia, Indiana, 1903–1987) (banjo/guitar); Hezzie (Paul Trietsch, Arcadia, Indiana, 1905–1979) (washboard/drums); Gabrielle Hawkins (Charles Ward, Knightstown, Indiana, 1904–1992) (clarinet); Frank Kettering (Monmouth, Illinois, 1909–1973) (banjo/flute); Gil Taylor (1914–1981) (brass)

The multi-talented Hoosier Hot Shots did everything except play the kitchen sink, but they *were* champions on "instruments" like the washboard and auto horn. The group's founders, the Trietsch brothers, had gotten their start in a family vaudeville act known as Ezra Buzzington's Rustic Revelers. It was on the radio from 1935 that they first found fame.

The Hot Shots' act was a zany one; one of the members stated that what they had to sell was a "product called stupid." It proved a most successful product with songs like "I Like Bananas Because They Have No Bones" and "From the Andes to the Indies in His Undies," as well as more traditional ditties like "Take Me Out to the Ballgame." These were among about 300 recordings.

The trademark of the Hoosier Hot Shots was the phrase "Are you ready, Hezzie?" directed at Paul Trietsch by his brother Ken. Their radio success inevitably brought them to Hollywood for a long series of films, including many "B" singing westerns. During World War II, with their ubiquitous films and U.S.O. tours, the Hot Shots were so successful that a bomber was named after them.

They were top-billed in at least three films (*Hoosier Holiday*, *Swing the Western Way* and *Over the Santa Fe Trail*). The popularity of the Hoosier Hot Shots had declined considerably by the end of the 1950s; however, they had influenced many ensembles that "murdered" music as they did. Foremost among their disciples was Spike Jones. The Hoosiers themselves soldiered on in one form or another into the '70s.

In Old Monterey (1939) * *Hoosier Holiday* (1943) * *The National Barn Dance* (1944) * *Swing in the Saddle* (1944) * *Rhythm Round-Up* (1945) * *Sing Me a Song of Texas* (1945) * *Rockin' in the Rockies* (1945) * *Song of the Prairie* (1945) * *Cowboy Blues* (1946) * *Lone Star Moonlight* (1946) * *Singing on the Trail* (1946) * *That Texas Jamboree* (1946) * *Throw a Saddle on a Star* (1946) * *Over the Santa Fe Trail* (1947) * *Rose of Santa Rosa* (1947) * *Smoky River Serenade* (1947) * *Swing the Western Way* (1947) * *The Arkansas Swing* (1947) * *Singin' Spurs* (1948) * *Song of Idaho* (1948) * *Hollywood Varieties* (1950)

Horace Heidt and His Orchestra

Horace Heidt (Alameda, California, 1901–1986)

Perhaps many bandleaders were more musically talented than Horace Heidt, and indeed he was criticized for being more about flash than substance. He was also described as conducting himself a bit like President Richard Nixon: stiff and self-conscious with an insincere smile. But very few had his shrewd acumen when it came to a successful and most profitable career.

Heidt had formed his first orchestra, the Californians, about 1923 and his second, the Brigadiers, almost ten years later. Their most famous moniker came to be Horace Heidt and His Musical Knights. They were featured on a very popular radio show called *Pot O' Gold* which gave away cash to its listeners. The band also went in for spectacle, one reviewer stating that

Horace Heidt.

"any minute you expect one of them to come swooping down at you from the ceiling on a flying trapeze."

Heidt did hire some notable music makers, including the King Sisters, Alvino Rey, Tex Beneke and Bobby Hackett. Among his vocal groups was Donna and Her Don Juans, which featured both movie singer Gordon MacRae and later Oscar winner Art Carney.

The band's popular recordings included "Ti-Pi-Tin," "Deep in the Heart of Texas," "I Don't Want to Set the World on Fire," and "The Man with the Mandolin." "I'll Love You in My Dreams" was its theme song.

Both during and after his orchestra days, which ended in the mid–1950s, Horace Heidt became very wealthy in Southern California real estate. His contemporaries may have figuratively laughed at him when he was leading his orchestra, but in golden retirement he definitely had the last laugh.

Pot O' Gold (1941)

Hot Rocks *see* Johnny Carroll and His Hot Rocks

Hot Shots [unknown]

Thumbs Up (1943)

House Rockers *see* **Jimmy Cavallo and the House Rockers**

Houston and Dorsey
Houston and Dorsey were comedy singers.
Daytona Beach Weekend (1965) "Wreck of the John B." and "Hootenanny Annie"

Hubba Hubba Girls [unknown]
Jivin' in Be-Bop (1947)

Hubert Smith and His Coral Islanders
Lost Lagoon (1958)

Hudson Wonders [unknown]
See My Lawyer (1945)

Hughes Kiddies [unknown]
Dancing Lady (1933)

Humberto Herrera and His Orchestra
Too Many Blondes (1941)

Hundred Hollywood Honies [unknown]
Sitting Pretty (1933)

Hurricanes
Rockin' the Blues (1956) [documentary] "You Put Me Out of My Misery" and "That Army Life"

Hutton, Ina Ray *see* **Ina Ray Hutton...**

Ike and Tina Turner
Ike Turner (Clarksdale, Mississippi, 1931–2007); Tina Turner (Anna Mae Bullock, Brownsville, Tennessee, 1939?–)

Arguably, there is no singer who can match the dynamism of Tina Turner when it comes to delivering a song. Her sheer talent, physicality and showmanship is simply unparalleled in the field of rhythm-and-blues, but such raw talent needed shaping and that is what her then-husband Ike Turner provided for her. Their *Ike and Tina Turner Revue* was — before it became a victim of their tempestuous relationship — one of the great ensembles in rock history. It featured the sexy all-girl background singer-dancers, the Ikettes.

Ike displayed his musicality at a very young age as a pianist and accompanist, eventually becoming a radio disc jockey and then member of the Kings of Rhythm, an R & B group. He also began playing on guitar as well, backing many of the era's great performers. In 1951 he recorded "Rocket 88," which some believe was the first true rock-and-roll record.

In the late 1950s he met young Anna Mae Bullock (soon to be Tina Turner) and their teaming became the stuff of legend. Hit records like "A Fool in Love" and "It's Gonna Work Out Fine" shortly followed. She was soon to be known as the "Queen of Rock and Roll" and was ultimately to win seven Grammy Awards.

Over the next ten years many smash Ike and Tina Turner recordings followed: "River Deep, Mountain High," "The Midnight Special" and the classic "Proud Mary." They went their separate ways in 1975 and Tina brought her raw onstage persona into film acting (*The Who's Tommy*, *Mad Max Beyond Thunderdome*).

Tina continued to make rapturously-received personal appearances and hit recordings. The fame — or notoriety — of the Turners' years together was sealed with the release of the major 1993 biopic *What's Love Got to Do With It?* During the 1990s she was still releasing albums that sold well into the millions. Ike also had a strong resurgence in the 1990s and won a Grammy in 2006 for best blues album. They had been inducted into the Rock and Roll Hall of Fame in 1991.

The Big T.N.T. Show (1966) [documentary] "Shake!," "It's Gonna Work Out Fine," "Please Please Please" and "Goodbye, So Long" * *Gimme Shelter* (1970) [documentary] "I've Been Loving You Too Long" * *It's Your Thing* (1970) [documentary] * *Soul to Soul* (1971) [documentary] "River Deep Mountain High," "Soul to Soul" and other songs * *Taking Off* (1971) "Goodbye, So Long"

Ike Carpenter and Orchestra; Ike Carpenter and His Orchestra
Ike Carpenter (Durham, North Carolina, 1923–)

If the band of piano player Ike Carpenter sounded somewhat like that of Duke Ellington it was probably no coincidence. It issued cover recordings of several of his hits, including "Take the A Train." However, their major hit "Pachuco

Hop," which came in 1953, seemed to be theirs alone. The band thrived for about a decade from the mid-1940s.

Holiday Rhythm (1950)

Ikettes

Delores Johnson (aka Flora Williams); Eloise Hester; Josephine "Joshie" Armstead; Vanetta Fields; Jessie Smith; Robbie Montgomery

Although they were the well-known back-up group for Ike (from whom they got their name) and Tina Turner, the Ikettes were successful in their own right with such 1960s hits as "I'm So Thankful," "I'm Blue," "Fine Fine Fine" and "Peaches and Cream."

They were one of the most famous back-up groups, not only for their spirited singing but their sexy dance moves as well. The members of the Ikettes changed somewhat frequently since Ike Turner was well known for his "thriftiness" in paying his performers and granting them royalties. At one point, Turner created two groups of Ikettes, one to tour and one to remain with his revue.

The frustrated original group left to go out on their own but Ike legally prevented them from using the name the New Ikettes, as he did when they tried performing as the Mirettes, Formerly the Ikettes. Finally they adopted the Mirettes name, under which they were never as successful.

The Big T.N.T. Show (1966) [documentary] * *Soul To Soul* (1971) [documentary]

Imperials

Armond Morales (bass); Jake Hess (lead singer); Gary McSpadden (baritone); Henry Slaughter (piano); Sherrill Neilsen (tenor)

More than forty albums and forty years later the Imperials (not to be confused with other groups of that name, e.g., Little Anthony and the Imperials) are still going strong. Originally a gospel group, they switched to a harder techno-pop sound in the 1980s but are still considered to be one of the great Christian music bands.

The Imperials have had some number one records, have been awarded four Grammy awards and were one of the gospel groups backing Elvis Presley. They have also received over a dozen Dove awards, given by the Gospel Music Association for best gospel and Christian music.

Sing a Song, for Heaven's Sake (1966) [documentary] * *Elvis—That's the Way It is* (1970) [documentary]

In Group

At the time they appeared in their movie the In Group was a teenage band.

Where Angels Go, Trouble Follows (1968) "Where Angels Go, Trouble Follows"

Ina Ray Hutton and Her Orchestra; Ina Ray Hutton and Her Melodears

Ina Ray Hutton (Odessa Cowan?, Chicago, Illinois, 1916–1984)

The "Blonde Bombshell of Rhythm" was one of the sobriquets by which bandleader Ina Ray Hutton was known. (She was supposedly the half sister of singer June Hutton.) Probably the most

A bit past her prime, but Ina Ray Hutton still swings a mean baton.

famous of the female bandleaders, she was basically not a musician herself but made a fetching front (wo)man with her attractive figure and vivacious personality.

A child performer in vaudeville and later a Broadway chorine (including the *Ziegfeld Follies*), Hutton began fronting her all-girl band in the mid–1930s. Rather than actually conducting it she just kind of pranced fetchingly around the stage. Despite her lack of musical chops the band, with its theme song of "Gotta Have Your Love," was enough of a novelty to be successful.

By the end of the decade Ina Ray had switched to an all-male band but that new novelty wore off before too many years and in the mid–'40s she was back with the all-female version. She was much seen on television in the 1950s, and may well have been the model for the character of the blonde bandleader "Sweet Sue" in Billy Wilder's *Some Like It Hot*.

The Big Broadcast of 1936 (1935) * *Ever Since Venus* (1944)

Ink Spots

Jerry Daniels (Indianapolis, Indiana, 1915–1995) (1st tenor); Orville Jones (Chicago, Illinois, 1902–1944) (bass); Charles Fuqua (New Haven, Connecticut, 1910–1971) (2nd tenor/baritone); Bill Kenny (Philadelphia, Pennsylvania, 1914–1978) (tenor); Ivory "Deek" Watson (Washington, D.C., 1909–1969)

Would the Ink Spots have been so famous if they had been called the Percolating Puppies — or the Riff Brothers? Those were just two of the names they tried before settling in 1932 on the one by which they attained worldwide fame. They also experimented with the Swingin' Gate Brothers and King, Jack and Jester.

An Indianapolis-based quartet dating from the late 1920s, they hit the big time a decade later with the iconic and much-imitated "If I Didn't Care." The addition of Bill Kenny and his quavering high tenor to the group in 1936 was just what they needed to really break out. They were among the first Black groups to cross over to formerly all-white venues like the Waldorf-Astoria Hotel.

Throughout the 1940s the mellifluous Ink Spots remained one of the pre-eminent Black vocal groups with such hits as "It's a Sin to Tell a Lie," "My Prayer," "When the Swallows Come Back to Capistrano," "Whispering Grass," "I Don't Want to Set the World on Fire" and "To Each His Own."

Many of their estimated 250 recordings sold in the millions and more than forty-five were bona fide hits. Although the rock-and-roll phenomenon spelled the end of their reign at the top, their sweetly haunting melodies continued to influence those who followed.

The Ink Spots were acknowledged to be one of very best groups of its kind and more than one group of its name is still touring today. (At one time there were alleged to be some *forty* groups using their name because it had not been copyrighted.) They were inducted into the Grammy Hall of Fame, the Rock and Roll Hall of Fame and the Vocal Group Hall of Fame.

The Great American Broadcast (1941) * *Pardon My Sarong* (1942)

Inspirations *see* Sam the Soul and the Inspirations

International Hotel Orchestra

Joe Guercio, leader

The International Hotel Orchestra was a thirty-five piece ensemble.

Elvis—That's the Way It Is (1970) [documentary]

International Sweethearts of Rhythm

Anna Mae Winburn, leader

An interracial, though largely Black, all-girl swing band, the International Sweethearts of Rhythm was formed about 1937 with pupils of a Mississippi school for poor children. Later they became independent of the school and hired some professional musicians. In order for them to perform in the then-segregated Southern states the white members actually had to blacken their faces.

The Sweethearts played in clubs and theaters and performed in Army camps during the War, the period of their greatest success. They initially disbanded in 1948 but were re-formed and lasted in their new iteration to the mid-1950s.

That Man of Mine (1946)

Iona, Andy *see* Andy Iona and His Recording Hawaiians

Iona's Islanders *see* **Andy Iona and His Recording Hawaiians**

Iris and Pierre [unknown]
Club Havana (1945)

Iron Butterfly
Doug Ingle (keyboard); Ron Bushy (drums); Jerry Penrod; Darryl DeLoach; Danny Weis; Lee Dorman (guitar); Erik Brann (also Braunn) (Pekin, Illinois, 1950–2003) (guitar)

The hard rock/heavy metal/psychedelic/acid band Iron Butterfly prospered from 1966 to 1971 and is probably best known today for the 1968 platinum album and single "In-A-Gadda-Da-Vida." (Unsubstantiated legend has it that this is a drug-slurred pronunciation of "In the Garden of Eden.")

That seventeen minute-long piece sold many millions of copies and has been heard on movie sound tracks and even *The Simpsons* television show. Before disbanding in 1971 Iron Butterfly issued several more albums. On the strength of those early successes it was able to regroup a few years later and in one form or another continues to perform today.

Musical Mutiny (1970) "In A-Gadda-Da-Vida," "Soul Experience" and "In the Time of Our Lives"

Isham Jones and His Orchestra
Isham Jones (Coalton, Ohio, 1894–1956)

The leader of what has been described as the "greatest sweet ensemble of all times" and "one of the finest all-around dance bands in the history of music," Isham Jones was also a prolific composer ("It Had to Be You," "I'll See You in My Dreams," "The One I Love Belongs to Somebody Else.")

His most popular band was one he had begun in the 1920s and disbanded in the '30s; among its hits was "Stardust." Its theme song was "You're Just a Dream Come True." Some of the members of that band became the nucleus of the first Woody Herman organization.

Jones himself started up a new orchestra early in the 1940s. In spite of the encomiums showered on his orchestra and his own musicianship, he was possessed of an off-putting somber personality, not a formula for long-term audience popularity.

Mr. Broadway (1933) * *Convention Girl* (1935)

Isley Brothers
O'Kelly Isley (Cincinnati, Ohio, 1937–1986); Rudolph Isley (Cincinnati, Ohio, 1939–); Ronald Isley (Cincinnati, Ohio, 1941–); Vernon Isley (d. 1955); Ernie Isley (1952–); Marvin Isley

For over fifty years the Isley Brothers and their descendants have made music in many genres including gospel, rock, soul and doo wop. Among their influential hits have been the self-penned million seller "Shout!" and "Twist and Shout." Originally a quartet they became a trio upon the death of brother Vernon in the mid–1950s and since then have performed in various configurations.

In the 1960s other successes like "It's Your Thing" and "This Old Heart of Mine" followed for the Isleys. In the 1970s and early '80s, as they added brothers Ernie and Marvin, there were hit albums and their songs appeared more than twenty-five times on the rhythm-and-blues charts and twelve slots on the pop charts.

Although the very topmost rung of stardom eluded them their influence on other groups has been considerable and their motto could well be "Steady and Enduring." The Isley Brothers were inducted into the Rock and Roll Hall of Fame in 1992 and the Vocal Group Hall of Fame eleven years later.

It's Your Thing (1970) [documentary]

Israelite Spiritual Church Choir of New Orleans
Pete Kelly's Blues (1955)

Ivie Anderson and the Crinoline Choir *see* **Crinoline Choir**

Jack and Mack [unknown]
Around the World (1944)

Jack Denny and His Orchestra
Jack Denny (Indiana, 1895–1950)

Jack Denny's ensemble was a hotel band that played the finer establishments in the U.S. and Canada. The dance orchestra probably reached the height of its popularity in the early 1930s and was notable for having no brass section, just saxophones, clarinets and strings. It also occasionally utilized three pianos.

Moonlight and Pretzels (1933)

Jack McVea and Orchestra

Jack McVea (John McVea, Los Angeles, 1914–2000)

As the co-writer of the novelty tune "Open the Door, Richard" (based on an old vaudeville routine), Jack McVea carved himself a small corner of immortality. Primarily a tenor saxophonist, he played with Lionel Hampton's band and others before forming his own group, sometimes called the Door Openers.

The 1940s seemed to be McVea's greatest period of popularity, when he played music that was somewhat of a transition between jazz and rhythm-and-blues. From the 1960s to the '90s he worked at Disneyland as a clarinetist in the theme park's strolling Dixieland band. He had also worked at MGM.

Sarge Goes to College (1947) "Open the Door, Richard"

Jack Teagarden and His Orchestra

Jack Teagarden (Weldon Teagarden, Vernon, Texas, 1905–1964)

Famous from the late 1920s as a jazz trombonist, orchestra leader and singer (a baritone-tenor), Jack Teagarden played with top names like Ben Pollack, Paul Whiteman, Louis Armstrong and Red Nichols. He had his own big band from 1939 to 1946, with which he occasionally sang, and in the 1950s played in Louis Armstrong's Dixieland sextet as well as leading his own sextet.

Although never matching the financial success of the top bandleaders, Teagarden was widely admired by his peers and was an influence on those who came after. He is considered among the greatest of the jazz musicians of his day as well as a formidable jazz singer.

Jack Teagarden's theme song was "I Gotta Right to Sing the Blues"; among his record hits was "The Sheik of Araby." He appeared in a few films, like *Thanks a Million* and *Birth of the Blues*, before making the screen appearances with his band and also did a few movies in the 1950s.

So's Your Uncle (1943) * *Hi, Good Lookin'* (1944) * *Twilight on the Prairie* (1944)

Jackie and Gayle

Jackie Miller; Gayle Caldwell

Jackie and Gayle were a singing duo.

Wild on the Beach (1965) "Winter Nocturne"

* *Wild Wild Winter* (1966) "Our Love's Gonna Snowball"

Jackie Moran's Band

Jackie Moran (John Moran, Chicago, Illinois, 1922–1990)

Discovered by "America's Sweetheart" Mary Pickford about 1936, Moran was a winsome, and for a time very sought-after, child actor. The highlight of his career probably was 1938's *The Adventures of Tom Sawyer*. His band-leading may well have been little more than a publicity gimmick.

Over an eleven year span, Moran appeared in at least thirty movies which included *Valiant Is the Word for Carrie*, *Gone with the Wind*, *Mad About Music* and his last, *Betty Co-Ed*, in 1947. Like many former child actors he was a troubled adult and had numerous run-ins with the law in the late '40s and early '50s, resulting in a prison sentence.

Let's Go Collegiate (1941)

Jackson Brothers [unknown]

It Can't Last Forever (1937)

James, Harry *see* Harry James...

James Brown and the Famous Flames

James Brown (Barnwell, South Carolina, 1933–2006)

It is said that no single performer influenced Black music the way James Brown did. Called the "Godfather of Soul and "Mr. Dynamite," his hits included "Papa's Got a Brand New Bag," "It's a Man's World," "Night Train" "I Got You (I Feel Good"), among many others. His album "Live at the Apollo" is considered a milestone of modern music; the Library of Congress named it number twenty-four on their list of the top 500 albums of all time.

Despite his highly publicized personal life, that included a prison term and numerous brushes with the law, he was one of the first to be inducted into the Rock and Roll Hall of Fame with other icons like Elvis Presley and Chuck Berry. He had almost 100 songs in the rhythm-and-blues top forty charts.

The Famous Flames were an outgrowth of a gospel group called the Gospel Starlighters, their first hit being "Please, Please, Please" in 1955.

Brown's time with the Flames did not do much to showcase his prodigious talent and he ultimately made his career as a solo performer. During that time his trademark manic energy onstage seemingly never flagged. He made solo film performances in *The Blues Brothers* (as a preacher) and other movies that spotlighted his over-the-top persona.

Although James Brown's legal problems continued until shortly before his death, the honors continued as well. He received the Kennedy Center Honors in 2003 and some eleven years earlier had been given the Grammy Lifetime Achievement Award. His raw talent was recognized, imitated and acknowledged by many rock and roll greats including Mick Jagger of the Rolling Stones.

The T.A.M.I. Show (1964) [documentary] "Out of Sight," "Prisoner of Love" and other songs * *Ski Party* (1965) "I Got You (I Feel Good)"

Jan and Dean

Jan Berry (William Berry, Los Angeles, California, 1941–2004); Dean Torrence (Los Angeles, California, 1940–)

Along with the Beach Boys, high school friends Jan and Dean were the iconic face of Southern California's surfing culture. Jan Berry found success first, partnering with Arnie Ginsburg as Jan and Arnie, with the rollicking "Jennie Lee."

With Dean Torrence (and sometimes Brian Wilson) Jan was the creative force behind such smash hits of the 1960s as "Surf City," "The Little Old Lady from Pasadena," "Honolulu Lulu," "Drag City" and "Dead Man's Curve."

The latter song, about a fatal crash on Sunset Boulevard, was unfortunately prophetic in that Jan's career was later cut short by a near-fatal crash. This occurred in 1966 when they just been signed for their first starring movie to be called *Easy Come, Easy Go*.

The film was cancelled and Berry's resulting brain damage led to a break-up of the team. It kept him out of the public eye during a long and painful recovery during which he had to re-learn walking and talking.

However, in the late 1970s a made-for-television movie called *Dead Man's Curve*, containing many of their greatest hits, put the duo back into the spotlight at a time when rock nostalgia was growing. They began touring again in the 1980s, including concerts in China, and performed into the 1990s.

The T.A.M.I. Show (1964) [documentary] "Here They Come," "The Little Old Lady from Pasadena" and "Sidewalk Surfin'"

Jan Garber and His Orchestra; Jan Garber and His Band

Jan Garber (Indianapolis, Indiana, 1894–1977)

The long-lived Jan Garber band changed its focus over the decades from "hot" in the 1920s, "sweet" in the '30s, to "swing" in the next decade, and finally back to "sweet" in 1945. A band director for the armed forces during World War I, Garber launched his first orchestra just after the war.

He ultimately re-formed a band by taking over another leader's entire ensemble. The group, whose theme songs were "My Dear" and "Mexicali Rose," became very popular in the 1930s. This was not only through its music but by comedy skits as well, no doubt honed by their appearances on the Burns and Allen radio show.

The leader himself was called the "Idol of the Air Lanes" when the band was on the radio in Chicago, and then had to live up to the tongue-twisting rubric "Mighty Little Maestro of Modern Melody."

During his more than fifty years on the bandstand Jan Garber became known for the number of one-night stands his orchestra played in the nation's smartest clubs and other venues. Latterly, they performed in Las Vegas and even at horse shows. In the 1970s his daughter took over the band until it was disbanded in 1973.

So's Your Uncle (1943) * *Here Comes Elmer* (1943) * *Sweethearts of the U.S.A.* (1944) * *Jam Session* (1944)

Jan Rubini Orchestra

Jan Rubini (Sweden?, 1904–1989)

Jan Rubini was a violinist who essayed several solo movie roles as — not surprisingly — a violinist in café scenes and such. Among these films were *The Merry Widow* and *Bal Tabarin*.

Café Metropole (1937)

Jan Savitt and His Orchestra; Jan Savitt and His Top Hatters

Jan Savitt (Jacob Savetnick, Shumsk or Leningrad, Russia, 1907/13–1948)

Classically trained violinist Jan Savitt was somewhat of a child prodigy and was playing with the Philadelphia Symphony by the age of nineteen, supposedly the youngest ever to do so. He had already organized a string quartet in the 1920s and was a musical director for a radio station before forming his own band, the Top Hatters, in 1937.

The orchestra was known for the musical sound called "shuffle rhythm," built around a pianist playing in double time. It proved to be quite successful. His was supposedly one of the first white orchestras to engage an African-American vocalist.

The band's theme songs were "From Out of Space" and "Quaker City Jazz" and among its record hits were "720 in the Books" and "It's a Wonderful World." Savitt is credited with composing such standards as "Now and Forever," "Moonrise" and "It Must Be Love."

Betty Co-Ed (1946) * *High School Hero* (1946) * *That's My Gal* (1947)

Jay and the Americans

Kenny Vance (Kenneth Rosenberg, 1943–); Sandy Deane (Sandy Yaguda, 1943–); Sidell Sherman; Howard Kane (Howard Kirschenbaum); John Traynor (lead); David Black (later Jay Black) (David Blatt (1938–); Marty Sanders (1941–)

As the Harbor Lights (or Lites), their original moniker, the doo wop ensemble found little success from their inception on Long Island, New York in 1959. As Jay and the Americans they hit the rock-and-roll big time. The name derived from member John Traynor's nickname (although they had first been dubbed the risible Blinky Jones and the Americans).

"She Cried," their second single, rose to number five on the pop charts. Others included "Only in America," "Come a Little Bit Closer" and the smash "Cara Mia." At this point the Americans began successfully reviving golden oldies like "Some Enchanted Evening," "Hushabye" and "This Magic Moment."

Jay and the Americans disbanded in 1971 but with some original members did nostalgia shows into the 1980s and occasionally thereafter. With their mellow vocals, they were undoubtedly one of the leading soft rock groups of their time and Jay Black continues to tour with his group Jay Black and the Americans.

Wild Wild Winter (1966) "Two of a Kind"

Jazzmen *see* **Kenny Ball and the Jazzmen; Mike Cotton and His Jazzmen**

J.B. and the Playboys

Bill Hill; Andy Kaye; Allan Nicholls; Doug West; Louis Yachnin

The Canadian-based teenagers J. B. and the Playboys were active from 1962 to '65 and then changed their name to the Jaybees to avoid confusion with Gary Lewis's Playboys. Subsequently they became the Carnival Connection. Among their recordings were "My Delight," "I'm Not Satisfied" and "Tears of Woe."

The Playgirl Killer (1966) "Leave My Woman Alone," "If You Don't Wanna, You Don't Hafta" and "Do the Waterbug"

J.C. Edwards and Band

Dancing Feet (1935)

Jefferson Airplane

Grace Slick (Grace Wing, Palo Alto, California, 1939?–); Jorma Kaukonen (guitar); Marty Balin; Paul Kantner; Spencer Dryden (1938?–2005) (drums); Bob Harvey (bassist); John Creach (1917–1994); Skip Spence (Alexander Spence, 1947?–1999)

The origin of the name Jefferson Airplane is obscure (legend has it the slang for a roach clip for marijuana cigarettes) but it was the distinctive name of a famous psychedelic band. Founded in 1965 they made memorable appearances at the Monterey Pop and Woodstock festivals.

With its LSD–inspired songs like "White Rabbit" and "Somebody to Love" and the album "Surrealistic Pillow," the group became a symbol of the 1960s drug culture. (Grace Slick was known as the "Acid Queen.") Their last album under the Jefferson Airplane name came in 1974 and some of the members then formed the Jefferson Starship.

Because of legal action the band abbreviated its name to just Starship in the mid–1980s and had a few number one hits, including "Nothing's Gonna Stop Us Now" and "Sara." By 1990 the long-lived band finally disbanded.

But the fame of the band lingered on and at least two versions of the Jefferson Starship, including one dubbed "the Next Generation," continue to tour to the present day. Jefferson Airplane came to represent a legendary era when San Francisco–based musical groups all but dominated the American music scene. They were inducted into the Rock and Roll Hall of Fame in 1996.

Monterey Pop (1969) [documentary] "High Flying Bird" and "Today" * *Gimme Shelter* (1970) [documentary] "The Other Side of This Life" * *Stamping Ground* (1971) [documentary] "White Rabbit" * *Fillmore* (1972) [documentary]

Jeffries, Herb *see* **Herb Jeffries...**

Jenkins, Polly *see* **Polly Jenkins and Her Plowboys**

Jerry Murad and His Harmonicats

Jerry Murad (Jerry Muradian, Turkey, d. 1996); Al Fiore (Al Fiorentino, 1923–1996); Don Les (Dominic Leshinski, 1914/15–1994)

The Harmonicats trio was founded when Jerry Murad and Al Fiore departed Borah Minevitch's Harmonica Rascals in the mid–1940s. Like that group, the Harmonicats helped to popularize their instruments with the smash 1947 recording of "Peg O' My Heart."

Playing the chromatic (diatonic), chord and bass harmonicas the trio recorded through the latter 1960s, releasing popular albums like "What's New, Harmonicats?" Murad continued to perform with various versions of the ensemble until his death.

Footlight Varieties (1951)

Jerry Wald and His Orchestra

Jerry Wald (Jervis Wald, Newark, New Jersey, 1918/19–1973)

A clarinetist who apparently modeled himself after Artie Shaw (but waxed irritable at the comparison), Jerry Wald went so far as to man his orchestra with many of Shaw's ex-sidemen. Perhaps he placed himself too much in Shaw's shadow — even playing in his style — because he never established much of a reputation of his own.

Wald, who had formed his band in the early 1940s, was not even identified with one theme song, instead trying out such tunes as "Laura," The Moon's on Fire" and a ditty entitled "Clarinet High Jinx." He later had a smaller combo and also was one of the bandleaders on the Jackie Gleason television show.

Little Miss Broadway (1947) * *Swing the Western Way* (1947) * *Vacation Days* (1947)

Jesse and James [unknown]

The appearance in this film of Jesse and James was shot for, and deleted from, an earlier film.

Variety Time (1948)

Jesse Stafford and His Orchestra

The Jesse Stafford orchestra had first been led by bandleader Rudy Wiedoeft before he was killed in an auto accident. Stafford, who was his trombonist, then took it over and it flourished for the nine years from 1928 to 1937.

Close Harmony (1929)

Jester Hairston Singers

Jester Hairston (Belews Creek, North Carolina, 1901–2000)

In later life a respected character actor well-known to television audiences in series such as *Amen* and *That's My Mama*, Jester Hairston was a highly-educated musician. He came to Hollywood in 1935 as the assistant director of the famed Hall Johnson Choir and went on to conduct and arrange choral music for film soundtracks with composers like Dmitri Tiomkin.

As an actor Hairston had been on the *Amos 'n' Andy* radio show for many years, but music appeared to be his primary love. He was a composer of note with numerous gospel tunes to his credit. As a solo actor he appeared in such movies as *The Alamo*, *Tarzan's Hidden Jungle* and *To Kill a Mockingbird*, and it was he who dubbed Sidney Poitier's singing voice in the Oscar-winning *Lilies of the Field*.

Yes Sir, Mr. Bones (1951)

Jesters

Guy Bonham; Wamp Carlson; Red Latham

The Jesters were western swing musicians.

The Badlands of Dakota (1941) * *Cowboy in the Clouds* (1943) * *Both Barrels Blazing* (1945) * *The Cisco Kid in Old New Mexico* (1945) * *The Return of the Durango Kid* (1945)

Jet Blacks *see* **Jet Harris and the Jet Blacks**

Jet Harris and the Jet Blacks

Jet Harris (Kingsbury, England, 1939–)

The major contribution of Jet Harris to music was that he popularized the bass guitar in the United Kingdom. In recognition of his work with that instrument he was awarded a prestigious Fender Lifetime Achievement Award.

Just For Fun (1963) "Man from Nowhere"

Jim, Jake and Joan

Jake Holmes; Joan Rivers (Joan Molinsky, Brooklyn, New York, 1933–); Jim Connell

Before she was the acerbic comedienne of "Can we talk?," celebrity interviews and plastic surgery fame, Joan Rivers was the "Joan" of the folk singing/comedy trio Jim, Jake and Joan. Jake Holmes had a solid reputation as a singer/songwriter who composed "Dazed and Confused" and "Be All You Can Be," which was adopted for military recruitment.

The three were brought together by a club manager who hoped to replicate the success of such groups as the Revuers and even Peter, Paul and Mary. Rivers could not sing particularly well but with large doses of topical comedy thrown in they managed to thrive for a while. However, clashing temperaments brought finis to the act.

Once Upon a Coffeehouse (1965)

Jim Kweskin Jug Band

Jim Kweskin (Stamford, Connecticut, 1940–) (guitar); Geoff Muldaur; Fritz Richmond (John Richmond) (jug/washtub bass); Mel Lyman (banjo/harmonica); Bill Keith (banjo); Maria D'Amato (later Muldaur) (fiddle)

A very popular folk music band during its fairly brief existence, the Jim Kweskin Jug Band was founded in 1963 in Cambridge, Massachusetts. Their music tended toward jazzy and blues tunes of 1920s vintage; among their recordings were "Over Seas Stomp" and "Viola Lee Blues." They also issued several albums.

Via stints in clubs and on television, the band was seemingly gaining nationwide success when Kweskin broke it up and joined a hippie commune run by ex-band member Mel Lyman. In the 1980s he formed a new band.

Festival (1967) [documentary] "Improvised Rag"

Jimmie Davis and His Rainbow Ramblers; Jimmie Davis and His Singing Buckaroos; Jimmie Davis and His Sunshine Band

Jimmie Davis (Quitman or Beech Springs, Louisiana, 1899/1903–2000)

To Jimmie Davis goes the distinction of not only having been a western swing notable but also twice governor of Louisiana (in non-consecutive terms). It was said of him "he served two terms as governor and was never indicted. That's a genuine achievement." His singing career preceded — and immeasurably helped — his political one. On radio he was known as the "Dixie Blue Yodeler."

His professional and political lives inevitably merged. During his first run for office his opponents played some of the raunchy blues songs he had recorded in an effort to impugn his morality but it had the opposite effect. He won the race but absented himself from his official duties often so he could appear in films.

If former schoolteacher Jimmie Davis is to be remembered at all outside of his political career, it will be for penning the enduring classic "You Are My Sunshine." He also wrote such deathless ditties as "Bed Bug Blues" and "High-Powered Mama, Get Yourself in Gear."

The 1947 film *Louisiana* was based on Davis's life. He continued to make personal appearances singing at festivals and other venues well into his latter nineties and was elected to the Country Music Hall Of Fame in 1972.

The Singing Buckaroo (1937) * *Strictly in the Groove* (1942) * *Riding Through Nevada* (1942) * *Frontier Fury* (1943) * *Cyclone Prairie Rangers* (1944) * *Mississippi Rhythm* (1949) * *Square Dance Katy* (1950)

Jimmie Green's Orchestra

Go Down, Death! (1946?)

Jimmie Grier and His Orchestra

Jimmie (sometimes Jimmy) Grier (Pittsburgh, Pennsylvania, 1902–1959)

Multi-instrumentalist (clarinet, saxophone, violin, etc.) Jimmie Grier had been an arranger for Gus Arnheim's Cocoanut Grove Orchestra and took over the "room" about 1930 when the latter moved on. His theme song was "Music in the Moonlight" and one of his big record hits "The Object of My Affection." Vocalists included the then very popular Donald Novis and Harry Barris, formerly of Bing Crosby's Rhythm Boys.

The Cohens and the Kellys in Hollywood (1932) * *Transatlantic Merry-Go-Round* (1934) * *Broadway Melody of 1936* (1935) †* *Times Square Lady* (1935) * *Nobody's Baby* (1937) * *Hollywood Bound* (1946)

†Their appearance in this film has not been confirmed.

Jimmie Lewis and His Texas Cowboys *see* Texas Jim Lewis...

Jimmie Lunceford and His Band *see* Jimmy Lunceford and His Band

Jimmie Noone and His Band

Jimmie (sometimes Jimmy) Noone (Cut Off, Louisiana, 1895–1944)

By 1912 clarinetist Jimmie Noone was already playing professionally in New Orleans and then Chicago with greats like King Oliver and Kid Ory. Starting in 1926 he led his own jazz ensembles until the 1940s. "Sweet Lorraine" was his theme song.

Among those of his sidemen who went on to considerable careers were Earl "Fatha" Hines and Teddy Wilson. Although lesser known than some of his contemporaries, Noone is considered to have been one the great clarinetists and was a considerable influence on those who followed.

Block Busters (1944)

Jimmy Bryant and the Night Jumpers

Jimmy Bryant (1925?–1980)

The Skydivers (1963) "Ha-So," "Tobacco Worm" and "Stratosphere Boogie"

Jimmy Cavallo and the House Rockers

Jimmy Cavallo (1927–)

Considered to be one of the first white groups to play what was historically Black rhythm-and-blues music, the Jimmy Cavallo band played at East Coast clubs in the late 1940s. They also produced a few recordings in the early '50s like "Rock the Joint" and "Ha Ha Ha Blues."

After his original band disbanded in the mid–1950s Cavallo took over an existing one and renamed it the House Rockers. They began receiving national attention, appearing in major theaters and publicized by famed disc jockey Alan Freed who invariably pronounced Jimmy Cavallo's name as *Cavello*.

The House Rockers were supposedly the first white rock group to appear at Harlem's Apollo Theater. Although they never had a big hit record they did tour with some of the major performers of the day and Jimmy Cavallo's original band is credited with being one of the first rock-and-roll bands, even before that term had been invented.

Rock, Rock, Rock (1956) "Rock, Rock, Rock" and "The Big Beat" * *Go, Johnny, Go!* (1959)

Jimmy Daley and the Dingalings; Jimmy Daley's Dingalings

Among the late 1950s recordings of Jimmy Daley and the Dingalings were "Bongo Rock" and "Red Lips and Green Eyes."

Rock, Pretty Baby (1956) "Can I Steal a Little Love?," "Rock, Pretty Baby" and other songs * *Summer Lovers* (1958)

Jimmy Dean and His Trail Riders

Jimmy Dean (James Glosup)

Jimmy Dean was the brother of singing cowboy Eddie Dean — and no relation to the television sausage purveyor.

I'll Tell the World (1945)

Jimmy Dorsey and His Orchestra

Jimmy Dorsey (James Dorsey, Shenandoah, Pennsylvania, 1904–1957)

Although he was known as the "quiet" and more amiable Dorsey brother (Tommy was the other), Jimmy Dorsey had a quick temper and could hold up his end very well in the many scraps the brothers got into. Early in their careers they had had a band together, with sidemen like Glenn Miller and Bob Crosby.

They went their own ways in 1935 to pursue their own extremely successful solo careers. Prior to that Dorsey played clarinet and alto sax with such greats as Vincent Lopez, Red Nichols and Paul Whiteman, and had been part of his father's brass band at the age of eight.

Jimmy Dorsey was considered to have one of the greatest swing bands, no small credit going to vocalists Bob Eberly and Helen O'Connell who produced enormously popular recordings like "Tangerine" "Green Eyes" and "Amapola." "Contrasts" was the orchestra's theme song, "So Rare" was its last major hit. By about 1943 it had reached its zenith.

Jimmy's screen presence in both features and musical shorts was less charismatic than that of his brother. As an actor he was quite dull, even when he played "himself" in the film *The Fabulous Dorseys*. In 1953 the Dorsey brothers once again reunited to co-lead a band.

The Fleet's in (1942) * *I Dood It* (1943) * *Lost in a Harem* (1944) * *Hollywood Canteen* (1944) * *Four Jills in a Jeep* (1944) * *The Fabulous Dorseys* (1947) * *Music Man* (1948)

Jimmy Grier and His Orchestra *see* Jimmie Grier and His Orchestra

Jimmy Le Fevre and His Saddle Pals; Jimmy's Saddle Pals

Springtime in the Rockies (1937) * *Frontier Town* (1938)

Jimmy Lunceford and His Band

Jimmy (sometimes Jimmie) Lunceford (Fulton, Missouri, 1902–1947)

Swing bandleader Jimmy Lunceford was credited with developing his own sound, the "Lunceford two-beat." While most bands of the era played a four-beat rhythm his ensemble used a two-beat rhythm. The saxophone/ vibraphone player formed a showy band in the late 1920s and hit the big time in the mid-'30s while playing at the Cotton Club and other top venues.

Many consider his group, sometimes dubbed the "Harlem Express," to have been one of the most exciting African-American swing bands. With the famous trumpeter Sy Oliver as a sideman and arranger, the Lunceford band produced exuberant recordings like "Margie," "Organ Grinders Swing," "'Taint What You Do," "For Dancers Only" and "Monotony in Four Flats."

With their theme song of "Uptown Blues" they continued on through World War II, but Jimmy Lunceford's parsimony caused dissension and his musicians began to desert him. After his death during a road tour the group soldiered on for another couple of years and then disbanded.

Blues in the Night (1941)

Jimmy Noone and His Band *see* Jimmie Noone and His Band

Jimmy Smith and His Orchestra

The Devil's Playground (1937)

Jimmy Smith Trio

Jimmy Smith (James Smith, Norristown, Pennsylvania, 1925–2005); Donald Bailey; Quentin Warren

A noted jazz organist from 1954, Jimmy Smith made numerous well-received recordings. He won a radio talent contest at the age of nine and had played with small ensembles before forming his own trio (organ, guitar, drums) in the 1950s. He was still producing albums in the 1990s and along the way appeared at such venues as New York's Birdland and the Newport Jazz Festival.

Get Yourself a College Girl (1964) "The Sermon" and "Comin' Home Johnny"

Jimmy Wakely and His Cowboy Band; Jimmy Wakely and His Oklahoma Cowboys; Jimmy Wakely and His Rough Riders; Jimmy Wakely and His Saddle Pals; Jimmy Wakely Trio; Bell Boys

Jimmy Wakely (James Wakely, Mineola, Arkansas, 1914–1982); Johnny Bond (Cyrus Bond, Enville, Oklahoma, 1915–1978); Scotty Harrell; Dick Reinhart (Tishomingo, Oklahoma, 1907–1948); Eddie Snyder

Cowboy great Gene Autry was instrumental in bringing Jimmy Wakely to Hollywood after seeing his group The Bell Boys perform. They were named after their radio show sponsor the Bell Clothing Stores but had originally called themselves the Singing Cowboys Trio.

Other members of the trio, which had been formed about 1937, were Johnny Bond and Scotty Harrell. They joined Autry's popular radio show *Melody Ranch* and made their first film, Roy Rogers' *Saga of Death Valley*, in 1939. Under various names Wakely's western bands supported many "B" cowboys of the day, including Charles Starrett, Johnny Mack Brown, Tex Ritter and the Range Busters.

Jimmy Wakely and group in *Swing in the Saddle* (1944).

Although he was no great actor, Wakely was prized for his singing and earned his own Monogram Studio series beginning with *Song of the Range* (1944). He made almost thirty low-budget starring films through 1949's *Lawless Code*. That was the year he was voted the number one western singer.

The year previous he had been named the fourth most popular western film actor. But Jimmy Wakely was probably better known for his later radio, television and recording work. He had the ability to sell records to pop music audiences as well as country/western fans and was credited with some fifteen million sales.

Among his hit records were "Beautiful Brown Eyes," "Slipping Around," "One Has My Name," "I Love You So Much It Hurts" and "Silver Bells." He also composed songs, among them the title song of his film *Song of the Sierras*. He remained active in show business through the mid–1970s. A fervent believer in preserving the heritage of western swing, he established an archive at a Los Angeles–area university.

Springtime in the Rockies (1937) * *Saga of Death Valley* (1939) * *Trailing Double Trouble* (1940) * *Texas Terrors* (1940) * *The Tulsa Kid* (1940) * *Stick to Your Guns* (1941) * *Bury Me Not on the Lone Prairie* (1941) * *Twilight on the Trail* (1941) * *Deep in the Heart of Texas* (1942) * *Heart of the Rio Grande* (1942) * *Little Joe, the Wrangler* (1942) * *The Old Chisholm Trail* (1942) * *Strictly in the Groove* (1942) * *Cowboy from Lonesome River* (1943) * *Cheyenne Roundup* (1943) * *Robin Hood of the Range* (1943) * *The Lone Star Trail* (1943) * *Riders of San Joaquin* (1943) * *Tenting Tonight on the Old Camp Ground* (1943) * *Swing in the Saddle* (1944)

Jimmy's Saddle Pals see Jimmy Le Fevre and His Saddle Pals

J. L. Frank's Golden West Cowboys

The Golden West Cowboys made several recordings with singing cowboy Gene Autry and appeared with him in their one film.

Goldmine in the Sky (1938)

Joe and Eddie

Joe Gilbert (tenor); Eddie Brown (baritone)

The folk singing/gospel duo of Joe and Eddie could sing sweet ballads like "The First Time Ever I Saw Your Face" and also perform a rousing "Tsena Tsena," but they are probably best known for the knee-slapper "There's a Meetin' Here Tonight." During their career they issued numerous albums.

Hootenanny Hoot (1963)

Joe Brown and the Breakaways; Joe Brown and the Bruvvers

An early British rocker — the pre-fame Beatles opened shows for *him*— Joe Brown accompanied American stars like Johnny Cash and Eddie Cochran when they toured in England. His groups recorded extensively and into the twenty-first century he was still doing live shows.

Just For Fun (1963) "Let Her Go" and "What's the Name of the Game?" * *What a Crazy World* (1963) "Layabout's Lament," "Bruvvers" and other songs

Joe Cocker and the Grease Band

Joe Cocker (John Cocker, Sheffield, England, 1944–)

One of those rockers who has persevered with his music through many ups and downs, Joe Cocker started out covering Beatles records like "With a Little Help from My Friends." With his trademark onstage physicality at such venues as the Woodstock Festival, he was a most watchable showman.

The raspy-voiced Cocker found some considerable success touring the United States and also with records like "Cry Me a River," "The Letter" and "Feelin' Alright," many of them being covers of other artists' songs. Some of his albums were big hits, scoring platinum-level sales.

Cocker's first hit was 1984's "I'll Cry Instead." His biggest single proved to be the haunting "Up Where We Belong" in the 1980s and he had another success with "You Are So Beautiful."

Groupies (1970) [documentary] "Delta Lady" * *Mad Dogs and Englishmen* (1971) [documentary]

Joe Johnson and His Orchestra

Free, White and 21 (1962) "The Hobo Twist"

Joe Reichman and His Orchestra

Joe Reichman (St. Louis, Missouri, 1898?–1970)

A bandleader with an exuberant, smiling personality, but known — perhaps affectionately, perhaps unflatteringly — as "the old piano pounder," Joe Reichman led a society band that played mainly in hotels. The group, with their theme song of "Variations in G," made several recordings in the 1930s and early '40s.

Out of This World (1945)

Joey Dee and the Starliters

Joey Dee (Joseph DiNicola, Passaic, New Jersey, 1940–); Don Martin (drums); John Yanick (guitar); Vinnie Correo (guitar); Ralph Fazio (accordion); Dave McLean (guitar); Oresti Intorella (piano); Willie Davis; Carlton Lattimore (organ)

Joey Dee fortuitously became linked with a dance craze that would make his group the Starliters famous when they were hired to play at an obscure New York nightspot. The dance was the twist and the club at which they were signed to appear (and become the house band) was the Peppermint Lounge.

The twist mania drew many celebrities to the small Manhattan club that rapidly became the flavor of the month. Dee and the Starliters released "The Peppermint Twist," which took off rapidly and hit number one on the pop charts, and they also did albums.

"What Kind of Love Is This?" was another hit but in an entirely different vein. After the twist craze ended Joey Dee formed the group Everyday People. In his second film he was top-billed as an actor.

Hey, Let's Twist! (1961) "Roly Poly," "Peppermint Twist" and other songs * *Two Tickets to Paris* (1962) "Willy Willy" and "Twistin' on a Liner"

John J. Luther's Cowboy Band; John J. Luther's Ranch Boys

Rough Riding Ranger (1935) * *Pals of the Range* (1935) * *The Fighting Buckaroo* (1943)

John Kirby and Band; John Kirby and Orchestra; John Kirby's Band

John Kirby (Baltimore, Maryland, 1908–1952)

From 1930 bassist John Kirby worked with prominent African-American bands like those of Lucky Millinder, Fletcher Henderson and Chick Webb before establishing his own groups. One of them, perhaps the sextet he organized in 1937, was dubbed "The Biggest Little Band in the World." He played in posh hotels like the Waldorf-Astoria, had his own radio program, and gave a concert at Carnegie Hall in 1950.

Sepia Cinderella (1947) * *Harlem Follies* (1950)

John La Salle Jazz Combo

The Courtship of Eddie's Father (1963)

John Scott Trotter [and His Orchestra?]

John Scott Trotter (Charlotte, North Carolina, 1908–1975)

Rotund John Scott Trotter was an acclaimed music arranger/director for bandleader Hal Kemp and such giants as Bing Crosby. Indeed, he was somewhat of a jolly giant himself— at a weight of about 300 pounds. He had been the music director for Crosby from 1937 to 1954, one of his sidemen being the inimitable Spike Jones.

In the 1950s the affable Trotter was a fixture on the popular George Gobel television show on which his rotundity was the object of ribbing from the diminutive comedian. He then rejoined Bing for the crooner's mid–1960s television series. Trotter also arranged the music for several motion pictures, including Crosby's *Pennies from Heaven* and *Rhythm on the River*.

Rhythm on the River (1940) † * *Kiss the Boys Goodbye* (1941) †

†It is uncertain whether Trotter appeared with his orchestra.

Johnny and the Tornadoes

Gas-s-s-s (1970)

Johnny Bond and His Red River Valley Boys

Johnny Bond (Cyrus Bond, Enville, Oklahoma, 1910–1978); Jimmy Dean; Wesley Tuttle; Paul Sells

Johnny Bond is credited with writing more than 500 songs, including "Hot Rod Lincoln," "Cimarron" and "Gone and Left Me Blues." He had once been part of Jimmy Wakely's musical ensembles. After his movie career ended he was seen on Los Angeles television.

Arizona Trail (1943) * *Frontier Law* (1943) * *Marshal of Gunsmoke* (1944) * *Oklahoma Raiders* (1944) * *Song of the Range* (1944)

Johnny Bond.

Johnny Burnette Trio

Johnny Burnette (Memphis, Tennessee, 1934–1964); Paul Burlison (Brownsville, Tennessee, 1929–); Dorsey Burnette (Memphis, Tennessee, 1932–1979); Johnny Black

After knocking around the fringes of the music business, the Burnette brothers and Paul Burlison formed the Johnny Burnette Trio in 1953. They found no notable success even after winning on *Ted Mack's Amateur Hour*, a popular television show, and recording such tunes as "Train Kept A-Rollin'." The trio broke up about 1957.

However, the Burnettes were songwriters, among whose tunes was "It's Late," a hit recorded by Rick Nelson. By the 1960s the brothers had begun recording again themselves and Johnny finally found substantial success with "Dreamin'" and "You're Sixteen."

Rock, Rock, Rock (1956) "Lonesome Train on a Lonesome Track"

Johnny Carroll and His Hot Rocks

Johnny Carroll (John Carrell, d. 1995)

Rockabilly was the style of singer Johnny Carroll; his hits included Crazy, Crazy Lovin'," "Wild, Wild Women" and "Hot Rocks."

Rock Baby, Rock It (1957) "Crazy, Crazy Lovin'," "Rockin' Maybelle" and other songs

Johnny Green and His Orchestra

Johnny Green (John Green, New York, New York, 1908–1989)

A prominent songwriter as well as orchestra leader, Johnny (later John) Green wrote such hits as "Hello, My Lover, Goodbye" (his theme song), "Body and Soul" and "I Cover the Waterfront." He had started at a young age as an arranger for Guy Lombardo and accompanied such performers as Ethel Merman and opera singer James Melton.

Conducting and composing work followed and he found himself in demand at movie studios as well as on radio. He led his own hotel band from the 1930s. It was at MGM that John Green found a lengthy career from the mid–1940s leading the MGM Orchestra for many of the studio's most famous musical pictures.

Green conducted the orchestra in several musical short subjects, usually popular classical pieces

like overtures. One of them won an Academy Award, and he also won Oscars for his musical direction on *Easter Parade*, *An American in Paris*, *West Side Story* and *Oliver!* He had been nominated fourteen times. In 1973 he was elected to the Songwriters Hall of Fame.
Start Cheering (1938)

Johnny Long and His Orchestra

Johnny Long (Newell, North Carolina, 1915–1972)

A left-handed violinist, Johnny Long had a college band called the Duke Collegians that metamorphosed into a professional orchestra whose theme song was "The White Star of Sigma Nu." The band played at some of the big hotels and ballrooms and recorded World War II–era songs like "No Love, No Nothin'," "Just a Shanty in Old Shanty Town" and "My Dreams Are Getting Better All the Time."

In the Bud Abbott/Lou Costello film *Hit the Ice*, Long played "himself," displaying minimal acting ability and a bland personality. But he did get the girl so in that sense was a romantic lead, however briefly. Although leading a popular enough orchestra, Johnny Long was never rated among the swing bands' pantheon but nevertheless continued on into the 1960s.

Hit the Ice (1943) * *Follies Girl* (1943)

Johnny Luther's Cowboy Band *see* John J. Luther's Cowboy Band

Johnny Luther's Ranch Boys *see* John J. Luther's Cowboy Band

Johnny Olenn and His Group

Johnny Olenn (Johnny McCord, San Antonio, Texas, 1936–)

Steel guitarist Johnny Olenn started his career with a band in Texas (as one of the Ah Ha Boys) then formed his own group the Jokers in the mid–1950s. They began recording about the same time ("Candy Kisses," "The Magic Touch," "Born Reckless") and enjoyed a very long engagement playing in Las Vegas lounges. In the 1980s the group toured extensively in Europe.

The Girl Can't Help It (1956) "My Idea of Love" and "Ain't Gonna Cry No More" * *Born Reckless* (1959) "You, Lovable You"

Johnny "Scat" Davis and His Orchestra

Johnny Davis (Brazil, Indiana, 1910?–1983)

The best-remembered cinema image of red-headed Johnny "Scat" Davis was his peppy rendition of "Hooray for Hollywood" (from 1937's *Hollywood Hotel*) sung while marching jauntily down a studio back lot city street. He played a supporting role in that film as he did in several others.

A cornet player, and former sideman and vocalist for Fred Waring's orchestra, he had formed his own band in 1939. He had also worked with Red Nichols and Smith Ballew and in latter days played at Ronald Reagan's inaugural ball.

Sarong Girl (1943)

Johnson, Ceepee *see* Ceepee Johnson and His Orchestra

Johnson, Hall *see* Hall Johnson Choir

Johnson, Joe *see* Joe Johnson and His Orchestra

Jones, Isham *see* Isham Jones and His Orchestra

Jones, Spike *see* Spike Jones...

Jones Boys *see* Five Jones Boys

Jones Quintette *see* Five Jones Boys

Joni Lyman and the Reflections *see* Reflections

Jordan, Louis *see* Louis Jordan...

Jordanaires

Hugh Jarrett (bass); Bob Hubbard (1928–) (2nd tenor); Bill Matthews (1923–2003) (1st tenor); Monty Matthews (1927–2005) (baritone); Neil (Neal?) Matthews (1930?–2000) (2nd tenor); Culley Holt (1925–1980) (bass); Bob Money (1929–2005) (piano); Gordon Stokes (1924–) (1st tenor); Hoyt Hawkins (1927–1982) (2nd tenor/baritone); Ray Walker

Formed as a male barbershop quartet in

Springfield, Missouri in 1948, the Jordanaires (named for the Jordan River) were probably best known as one of Elvis Presley's favorite back-up groups ("All Shook Up," "Are You Lonesome Tonight?," "It's Now or Never"). They even were dubbed the "sound behind the King," with whom they appeared until 1970.

The Jordanaires also gave their vocal support to many another country and pop singer as well, including such disparate performers as Rick Nelson, Julie Andrews, Marty Robbins and Connie Francis. The total number of recordings on which they sung probably number into the thousands.

They also recorded albums of their own, for one of which they received a Grammy Award, and had a hit single with "Sugaree" in 1956. They were also regulars on the *Grand Ole Opry* show. The group remained together into the 1990s and in 1998 they were voted into the Gospel Music Hall of Fame.

Jailhouse Rock (1957) * *Loving You* (1957) * *Country Music Holiday* (1958) * *King Creole* (1958) * *G. I. Blues* (1960) * *Blue Hawaii* (1961) * *Buffalo Gun* (1961) * *It Happened at the World's Fair* (1963) * *Kissin' Cousins* (1964) * *Country Music Caravan* (1964) [documentary] * *Roustabout* (1964) * *Tennessee Jamboree* (1964) * *Girl Happy* (1965) * *Stay Away, Joe* (1968) * *From Nashville with Music* (1969) [documentary]

Jose Arias and His Mexican Tipica Orchestra; Jose Arias Spanish Orchestra
Fiesta (1941) * *Song of Mexico* (1945)

Jose Eslava's Orchestra
Gaucho Serenade (1940)

Jose Pacheco and His Continental Orchestra
Song of the Gringo (1936)

Juanita Hall Choir; Juanita Hall Singers
Juanita Hall (1901–1968)

Probably best-known for her role as Bloody Mary in the landmark 1948 musical *South Pacific*, Juanita Hall was an African-American actress and singer who played sometimes played "exotic" ethnicities in movies and on Broadway. She had been the first Black woman to win a Tony Award (for *South Pacific*) but for some reason her voice was dubbed in the film version.

Earlier Hall had appeared with the Hall Johnson Choir and had formed her own choir in the 1930s as one of the Works Progress Administration's cultural programs. A later Broadway role was in *Flower Drum Song* in which she played a Chinese woman and she also reprised this role on film.

Paradise in Harlem (1940) * *Miracle in Harlem* (1948)

Jubalaires; Jubilaires
Caleb Ginyard Jr.; Ted Brooks; George McFadden; John Jennings; Bill Johnson (guitar)

Primarily a gospel music group, the Jubalaires, also known as the Jubilaires, appeared on radio in the 1940s, including stints with Arthur Godfrey and Phil Harris. Among their recordings were "I Know," "Before This Time Another Year" and "It Ain't What You Want That Does You Good."

Dubbed the "best quartet on the air east of the Pacific," the Jubilaires temporarily split into two groups in the mid-'40s, one of which did the radio broadcasts while the other toured. They recorded into the early part of the next decade.

The Joint Is Jumpin' (1949) * *Duchess of Idaho* (1950) * *Hit the Deck* (1955)

Jubilaires *see* Jubalaires

Jubilee Four
Bill Johnson; George McFadden; Jimmy Adams; Ted Brooks

Viva Las Vegas (1964) "What'd I Say?"

Jubilee Singers *see* Dixie Jubilee Singers

Judd Conlon Group; Jud Conlon Singers; Jud Conlon Rhythmaires
Jud Conlon (aka Judd Conlon) (Cuba City, Wisconsin, 1910?–1966)

Cha-Cha-Cha Boom (1956)

Judy Clark and Her Rhythm Cowgirls; Judy Clark and the Six Solid Senders
Judy Clark had been part of the singing act the Sentimentalists with her three sisters. She also

performed acting roles in many movies besides the ones in which she appeared with her musical groups.

Hey, Rookie! (1944) * *Lone Star Moonlight* (1946)

Juniors *see* Danny and the Juniors

Kaleidoscope

Solomon Feldthouse; David Lindley (guitar); Chris Darrow; Chester Crill; John Vidican

Between 1967 and 1970 the Los Angeles–based Kaleidoscope band recorded a few albums and some singles. They were primarily a psychedelic band but were eclectic, even including some folk and Middle East music, as well as Duke Ellington and Cab Calloway tunes.

Among their recordings, on which they utilized a wide range of stringed instruments, were "Egyptian Gardens" and "Pulsating Dream." Although not overly successful in their active years, the band has gained retroactive respect for their musical versatility.

Revolution (1968) [documentary] * *Captain Milkshake* (1969) "Lie to Me"

Kay Kyser and His Orchestra; Kay Kyser's Band

Kay Kyser (James Kyser, Rocky Mount, North Carolina, 1905–1985); Harry Babbitt (1914?–2004); Ish Kabibble (Merwyn Bogue, Erie, Pennsylvania, 1908–1994)

To Kay Kyser belongs the honor of being one of the most effectively utilized bandleaders in the movies. Whereas most of his confrèères just stood stiffly in front of their bands with a pasted-on smile, his rather nerdy looks and persona made him a natural to play reluctant Bob Hope–type "heroes" in a few comedy thrillers.

The films were specifically tailored to his modest acting talents and in them he usually played "himself." In reality he was far from the meek person he portrayed, being a shrewd and demanding businessman and taskmaster. In movies he was often surrounded by star talent, including John Barrymore who was in his self-parodying phase.

Kyser did have a natural gift for comedy, differentiating his swing band from most others with his very popular radio program *Kay Kyser's Kollege of Musical Knowledge* that began in 1938. In keeping with the theme he and the band members wore academic caps and gowns. It was a musical quiz show that popularized the "ol' perfesser's" catchphrases such as "That's right, you're wrong," which became the title of his first film.

The band had musical chops as well, with more than ten number one records, including the novelty "Three Little Fishes," "Slow Boat to China" and "Praise the Lord and Pass the Ammunition." (Their theme song was "Thinking of You.") Among Kyser's associates were band singers like Ginny Simms, Harry Babbitt, beauteous Georgia Carroll (whom he wed), and comic trumpet player "Ish Kabibble," with his sugar bowl haircut.

He maintained the orchestra until about 1950 following the transfer of his radio show to television. Because of his comedic talents his orchestra's musicianship has probably been overlooked, and it is not counted among the great big swing bands. (Kay Kyser himself could neither read

Kay Kyser and the band with Ish Kabibble (Merwyn Bogue).

music nor play an instrument.) In retirement he kept his hand in show business as the head of the Christian Science Church's film and broadcast division.

That's Right— You're Wrong (1939) * *You'll Find Out* (1940) * *Playmates* (1941) * *My Favorite Spy* (1942) * *Stage Door Canteen* (1943) * *Thousands Cheer* (1944) * *Swing Fever* (1944) * *Around the World* (1944) * *Carolina Blues* (1944)

Kay Thompson and Her Radio Choir

Kay Thompson (Katherine Fink, St. Louis, Missouri, 1903/09–1998); Bea Wain; Al Rinker; Ken Lane; John Smedberg

Multi-talented Kay Thompson was a band singer, music arranger, actress, choral director, vocal coach and author. It was singing that first brought her to public attention in the 1930s and in the 1940s she worked at MGM coaching talent the likes of Judy Garland and Frank Sinatra. She had previously worked with many radio personalities and also on Broadway shows.

In the late 1940s Thompson hit the nightclub circuit with crooner Andy Williams and his three older brothers in a sophisticated act that played many of the top nightspots. This undoubtedly earned her the Eve Arden–like role in the 1957 Fred Astaire film *Funny Face* that featured her witty repartee and singing. She also had a role in 1970's *Tell Me That You Love Me, Junie Moon*.

If she is remembered now it could well be for creating Eloise, a precocious little girl who lived at New York's Plaza Hotel (as did Thompson herself) and had a variety of amusing adventures portrayed in a series of four popular books and in television movies.

Kay Thompson was the kind of performer rarely seen now, a sophisticated master of many arts. A critic once said she was "more than an act; she is an experience." Her radio choir, which was established in the mid–1930s was called the Rhythm Singers and had as many as sixteen members. Many accompanied her to Hollywood for the one film in which they appeared.

Manhattan Merry-Go-Round (1937)

Kaye, Mary *see* Mary Kaye Trio

Kaye, Sammy *see* Sammy Kaye and His Orchestra

Keith, "Shootsie" *see* "Shootsie" Keith and the Savannah Club Chorus

Kemp, Hal *see* Hal Kemp and His Orchestra

Ken Darby Chorus; Ken Darby's Octet

Ken Darby (Hebron, Nebraska, 1909–1992)

A performer on the esoteric nose flute, Ken Darby began playing the organ in silent film days and wound up winning three Academy Awards for film scores and best musical adaptation. Besides leadership of his own musical groups, he had been a member of the Kings Men. Perhaps his most enduring accomplishment is the composition of the Elvis Presley classic "Love Me Tender."

Broadway Serenade (1939) * *Make Mine Music* (1946)

Ken Maynard's Buckaroos

Chuck Baldra; Bob Card; Al Haskell; Jack Jones

Although cowboy star Ken Maynard (1895–1973) was credited as being one of the very first singing cowboys in 1930, it is very likely that his voice was dubbed most of the time. His 1933 oater *Strawberry Roan* is considered to have been the first "real" singing western, and it was in one of his movies, *Old Santa Fe*, that Gene Autry made his own debut.

Maynard had been in movies since the mid–1920s and his career was to last for another twenty years. It is very probable that Ken Maynard's Buckaroos was not a formal group but was composed of pick-up singers who may have primarily sung in other western ensembles. At any rate they were not even credited in their one known film appearance.

Smoking Guns (1934)

Kenny Ball and His Jazzmen

Kenny Ball (Ilford, England, 1930–)

With hit recordings like "Samantha" and "Midnight in Moscow" Kenny Ball and His Jazzmen have been one of the leading jazz bands since 1958. The group has scored on record charts more than a dozen times and continues to tour today.

It's Trad, Dad! (1962) * *Live It Up!* (1963) "Rondo" and "Hand Me Down My Walking Shoes"

Kenton, Stan *see* **Stan Kenton and His Orchestra**

Kentucky Colonels
Clarence White (Madawaska, Maine, 1944–1973) (guitar); Roland White (mandolin); Eric White, Jr. (banjo/bassist); Billy Ray Lathum; Roger Bush; Leroy Mack (Leroy MacNees)

Starting out in the 1950s as a band playing country and French-Canadian music, the White Brothers soon switched to bluegrass and dubbed themselves the Country Boys. Based in Southern California, they were regulars on local radio and television.

At the time of recording their first album in 1962 they became the Kentucky Colonels. Their albums were sometimes vocal and instrumental, at other times all-instrumental. In the early '60s they appeared at the Newport Folk Festival and enjoyed success in folk music venues around the country with their progressive bluegrass.

The British Invasion of the mid–1960s brought at least a temporary end to the folk phenomenon that had been so popular since the Weavers' days, and by mid-decade the Kentucky Colonels had disbanded.

The Farmer's Other Daughter (1965)

Kerr, Anita *see* **Anita Kerr Singers**

Kim Loo Sisters
The Kim Loo Sisters were a Chinese-American vocal trio singing with the Ina Ray Hutton orchestra in the 1940s.

Meet Miss Bobby Sox (1944)

King, Henry *see* **Henry King...**

King, Pee Wee *see* **Pee Wee King and His Golden West Cowboys**

King Cole Trio
Nat "King" Cole (Nathaniel Coles, Montgomery, Alabama, 1917–1965) (piano); Oscar Moore (guitar); Wesley Prince (bassist); Johnny Miller (bassist)

Simply one of the greatest singer/musicians, velvety-voiced Nat King Cole had a band in his teenage years before forming the King Cole Trio in the late 1930s. They had their first modicum of success with "Sweet Lorraine" in 1940 and were later so popular that Capitol Records was dubbed the "house that Nat built."

Another hit was "Straighten Up and Fly Right." They were also the first Black combo to have a sponsored radio show. A small group like the Trio was somewhat of a novelty in the Big Band era and was a beacon for many such ensembles that followed.

While continuing to perform with his group, Cole made many solo recordings that appealed more to mainstream audiences. Such massive sellers as "Mona Lisa," "Nature Boy," "Unforgettable" and "The Christmas Song" may not have pleased jazz purists but they remain much-beloved classics today.

Although his career seemed to be settling into the more pop song realm Nat Cole did continue to issue jazz albums and he even experimented with foreign language material. Into the 1960s hits poured from his dulcet voice: "Those Hazy, Lazy Days of Summer" and "That Sunday, That Summer."

Nat King Cole also became a competent actor, appearing in many movies, including the lead role in a biopic about the composer W. C. Handy. He was also one of the very first Black artists to have a coast-to-coast television show.

He was still near the peak of his talent when he died, his final film *Cat Ballou* being released posthumously. In the 1990s he was poignantly heard again when, by the grace of recording technology, his daughter Natalie accompanied him on a re-released version of his "Unforgettable."

Here Comes Elmer (1943) * *See My Lawyer* (1945) * *Breakfast in Hollywood* (1946) * *Killer Diller* (1948) * *Rhythm-and-Blues Revue* (1955) [documentary]

King Sisters
Alyce King (Alyce Driggs, Salt Lake City or Payson, Utah, 1916–1996); Donna King (Donna Driggs, Sanford, Colorado, 1918–2007); Luise King (Luise Driggs, Salt Lake City or Payson, Utah, 1914?–1997); Yvonne King (Yvonne Driggs, Salt Lake City, Utah); Maxine King (Maxine Driggs); Marilyn King (Marilyn Driggs)

The several King Sisters combined in various configurations in their performances. There were usually no fewer than four sisters, and sometimes six of them warbled together. The added two

A passel of King Sisters.

Always a family "corporation," in later years a veritable swarm of Kings joined the act and the King Cousins came into being as a group. The Sisters' recordings were legion and included "I'll Get By," "Cielito Lindo" "You Made Me Love You," "Pagan Love Song" and "Jersey Bounce."

Crash Donovan (1936) * *Sing Your Worries Away* (1942) * *Follow the Band* (1943) * *Larceny with Music* (1943) * *Meet the People* (1944) * *Thrill Of a Romance* (1945) * *The Great Morgan* (1945) * *On Stage Everybody* (1945) * *Cuban Pete* (1946)

Kingsmen

The Kingsmen were a rock group whose great claim to fame is their version of the old, racy — and much Bowdlerized — standard "Louie Louie" and its often incomprehensible lyrics.

How to Stuff a Wild Bikini (1965) "Give Her Lovin'"

King's Men; King's Men Octet

were often their mother and a family friend or sister Maxine.

Although they were no threat to the reputations of fabled sister acts like the Andrews Sisters, the Kings' drive and show biz smarts propelled them to success. Following on the heels of the Boswell Sisters, they sang with Horace Heidt's orchestra in the 1930s and subsequently were featured by bandleader Alvino Rey, who was married to Luise King.

The King Sisters remained a significant presence through the '60s with their high-rated television show. Their popularity had declined in the post-war period, after their stint with Kay Kyser, but television proved a boon to returning them to a wider public. By this time sister Marilyn had joined them.

They harmonized in a slew of movies, but the King's Men's lasting film fame will be that they were the voices of the pugnacious Lollipop Guild in *The Wizard of Oz*. In most of their western movies they were seen backing up the sonorous-voiced but non-singing William Boyd, aka Hopalong Cassidy.

Going Hollywood (1933) * *We're Not Dressing* (1934) * *Alexander's Ragtime Band* (1938) * *Vacation from Love* (1938) * *Honolulu* (1939) * *The Wizard of Oz* (1939) (voices only) * *The Renegade Trail* (1939) * *Law of the Pampas* (1939) * *Saint Louis Blues* (1939) * *Knights of the Range* (1940) * *The Showdown* (1940) * *Stagecoach War* (1940) * *The Roundup* (1941) * *Puddin' Head* (1941)† * *The Man from Montana* (1941) * *Two-Faced Woman* (1941) * *Juke Box Jenny* (1942) *

Cairo (1942) * *Call Out the Marines* (1942) * *For Me and My Gal* (1942) * *Follow the Boys* (1943) * *Girl Crazy* (1943) * *Hi, Buddy* (1943) * *The Kansan* (1943) * *You're a Lucky Fellow, Mr. Smith* (1943) * *Heavenly Days* (1944) * *Sing a Jingle* (1944) * *Make Mine Music* (voices only) (1946) * *Fun and Fancy Free* (voices only) (1947) * *It Happened on Fifth Avenue* (1947) * *The Babe Ruth Story* (1948) * *Love That Brute* (1950)

†Their appearance in this film is not confirmed.

Kirby, John *see* John Kirby...

Kirby Grant and Orchestra

Kirby Grant (aka Robert Stanton) (Kirby Hoon, Jr., Butte, Montana, 1911–1985)

With his bland good looks Kirby Grant was a natural for the "B" films, including many westerns, in which he invariably was cast from the 1930s. But he was somewhat of a dark horse; he had studied classical violin, had an excellent singing voice, and from time to time conducted a dance band. In his early career he assumed the stage name of Robert Stanton, later to be used by Dick Haymes' brother.

Although he had some fifty acting roles in films, he was seen with his band in only a couple of movies and rarely was given a chance to sing. Grant's best-remembered role was as *Sky King* in the 1950s television show of the same name in which he played a pilot. His residual fame from that show later led to appearances in a touring circus.

Blondie Goes Latin (1941) * *Ghost Catchers* (1944)

Kirk, Andy *see* Andy Kirk and His Orchestra

Knickerbockers

Buddy Randell (William Crandall, d. 1998) (saxophone); Jimmy Walker (drums); Beau Charles (Robert Cecchino) (guitar); John Charles (John Cecchino) (bassist)

The New Jersey–based rock group the Knickerbockers lasted only about three years in the mid–1960s. Their one top twenty hit "Lies" in 1966 appeared to be an imitation of the Beatles, perhaps the reason for its success. Some fans even thought it actually was a "lost" Beatles side.

"One Track Mind" was their only other mild hit and they were semi-regulars on a Dick Clark television show. The Knickerbockers re-formed a couple of times after their 1968 dissolution, but their own style remained undistinguished and their imitative music did nothing to sustain success.

Out of Sight (1966) "It's Not Unusual"

Kostelanetz, Andre *see* Andre Kostelanetz and His Orchestra

Kramer, Billy J. *see* Billy J. Kramer and the Dakotas

Krupa, Gene *see* Gene Krupa...

Kweskin, Jim *see* Jim Kweskin Jug Band

Kyser, Kay *see* Kay Kyser...

La Dell Sisters [unknown]
Country Music Holiday (1958)

Lady Birds

The Lady Birds was perhaps one of the most unusual of all musical groups in that it was composed of four *topless* ladies. The guitarists were by all accounts competent enough musicians even though they were "requested" to depart from their home base in New Jersey. They subsequently found a home in the more welcoming environs of Las Vegas.

The Wild, Wild World of Jayne Mansfield (1968) [documentary] "I Just Can't Stand It"

Lady Killer Quartette
It All Came True (1940) * *Atlantic City* (1944)

La Mare, Nappy *see* Nappy La Mare and His Dixieland Band

Lancers [unknown]
The Big Beat (1958)

Land, Gay *see* Gay Land and the Thunderbirds

Lani, Machias *see* Father Machias Lani...

Lario Child Orchestra
Behind the Mike (1937)

Larks
Don Julian (lead vocals); Ronald Barrett (tenor); Earl Jones (baritone); Randy Jones (d. 2002) (bass)

The Larks were a trio founded by Don Julian in 1953, the novelty tune "The Jerk" being their one major success. Follow-up efforts such as "Jerk Once More" and "Keep Jerkin'" did not prove to be hits.

Harlem Jazz Festival (1955) [documentary]

Larry Frost and the Hollywood Chamber Jazz Orchestra
Larry Frost; Bob Drasnin; Ollie Mitchell; Dick Houlgate; Phil Gray; Gene Estes; Mel Pollan; Ritchie Frost; Rubin Leon

Stakeout on Dope Street (1958)†

†Although Larry Frost played a small role in this film it is not certain his orchestra appeared onscreen.

La Salle, John *see* John La Salle's Jazz Combo

Lavert, Paul *see* Paul Lavert and His Singing Cavemen

Lawson, George *see* George Lawson and His Band

Layson Brothers [unknown]
Crazy House (1943) * *Carolina Blues* (1944)

Leaves
Jim Pons (bassist); John Beck (vocals); Bill Rinehart (lead guitar); Tom Ray; Robert Reiner; Bobby Arlin (guitar)

The rollicking "Hey Joe" was the Leaves' contribution to the charts in 1966. They had originally been a bunch of Los Angeles fraternity brothers calling themselves the Rockwells when they got together to perform in 1963. Fortuitously, crooner Pat Boone heard them sing at a local club and arranged a record contract for them.

The Leaves had one other minor local success with "Too Many People" and produced a couple of albums before disbanding in 1967. They also appeared on obligatory television shows like *American Bandstand* and *Shivaree*. Although they remained obscure, their big hit was covered by many others and is considered a rock-and-roll standard.

The Cool Ones (1967) "In the House of Dr. Stone"

Lebaron, Eddie *see* Eddie Lebaron and Orchestra

Lecuona, Ernesto *see* Ernesto Lecuona and the Palan Brothers Cuban Orchestra

Lecuona Cuban Boys *see* Ernesto Lecuona...

Lee, Billy *see* Billy Lee's Band

Lee Norman Trio; Lee Norman's Orchestra
Keep Punching (1939) * *Boarding House Blues* (1948?)

Lee Sisters
Miriam Lee; Jean Lee; Maree Lee; Virginia Halcombe

The Lee Sisters, three actual siblings and a "ringer," were primarily known for singing with the band of Vaughn Monroe in the 1940s.

Varieties on Parade (1951)

Leighton Noble and His Orchestra
Leighton Noble (Faye Jepsen, Pasadena, California, 1912–1994)

A vocalist and bandleader who segued successfully into acting in the 1940s, handsome Leighton Noble rather lived up to his aristocratic-sounding (but assumed) name. He led his orchestra in upscale venues from New York's posh Waldorf-Astoria to the Cocoanut Grove nightclub in Hollywood.

The band, whose theme song was "I'll See You in My Dreams," featured an electronic instrument called the novachord. Noble, who had previously appeared with several orchestras as a singer, moved his "sweet" orchestra to the West Coast in 1940. While there his acting career included films like *Gift of Gab*, *It Ain't Hay* and *White Christmas*.

He later resumed his first vocation, becoming a musical director at a hotel in Lake Tahoe before retiring in 1965. Leighton Noble had a television show during the 1950s and is credited with introducing Liberace and the comedy team of Rowan and Martin (*Laugh-In*) to a wider public.

Crazy House (1943)

Len Nash and His Country Boys

From 1929 to '33 the Los Angeles–based music group Len Nash and His Country Boys had a popular radio show. Their records included "On the Road to California" and "Kelly Blues."

Mountain Justice (1930)

Leo Diamond and His Harmonaires; Leo Diamond and His Solidaires; Leo Diamond Quartet; Diamond Brothers; Three Diamond Brothers

Leo Diamond (New York, New York, 1915–1966); Abe Diamond; Dick Hayman, Harry Roller; Pete Maggio; Jerry Geller; Maurice Fineman; Buddy Raye

In his time one of a handful of famous harmonica players, Leo Diamond began his career with Borah Minevitch's Harmonica Rascals. He then established his own ensembles before striking out as a solo in the 1950s. Besides appearing in nightclubs, he made recordings that combined harmonica music (he played all the parts) with various colorful sound effects.

Somewhat of a musical innovator, Diamond was also an arranger and songwriter of such ditties as "The Girls of Brazil," "Skin Diver's Suite" and "Off Shore." The latter became a hit for him, as did the recording of his "Melody of Love" in the mid–'50s.

Freshman Year (1937) * *Strictly in the Groove* (1942) * *He's My Guy* (1943) * *Coney Island* (1943) * *Hi'Ya, Sailor* (1943) * *Sweet Rosie O'Grady* (1943) * *Week-End Pass* (1944) * *Forever Yours* (1945) * *Swing Out, Sister* (1945) * *One Too Many* (1950)

Leo Reisman and His Band

Leo Reisman (Boston, Massachusetts, 1897–1961)

Violinist and pianist Leo Reisman was a popular bandleader in the 1920s and '30s. He had played professionally from the age of twelve and had been a member of the Baltimore Symphony Orchestra. With its theme song "What Is This Thing Called Love?" his band dated from the late 1910s and was ensconced for many years at top hotels in New York and Boston.

Dubbed the "String Quartet of Dance Bands" by no less a personage than composer Jerome Kern, Reisman's orchestra featured such notables as Eddie Duchin, Fred Astaire and Harold Arlen before they found fame elsewhere. By the early 1940s, with swing music in the ascendancy, Reisman's smooth sound was not in favor and his orchestra eventually disbanded.

Harlem on Parade (1946?)

Leon Gross' Orchestra

God's Step Children (1938) * *Swing!* (1938)

Leonardo and Zola [unknown]

Sepia Cinderella (1947)

Leopold Stokowski and His Symphony Orchestra

Leopold Stokowski (Antoni Stokowski, London, England, 1882–1977)

Despite the rumors over the years that he was actually named Leo Stokes, Leopold Stokowski apparently was the scion of a genuinely Polish family. There are still mysteries about him, however; for instance, the origin of his somewhat Middle European accent. As a young organist he played with many church choirs before starting a professional career about 1905 as an organist and conductor.

At first with the Cincinnati Symphony, Leopold Stokowski found his niche in 1912 at the Philadelphia Orchestra with whom he gained worldwide fame and fortune in an almost thirty year tenure. There he established a rather eccentric persona with his long, flowing hair, and flamboyant conducting with bare hands, rather than a baton.

Given his outsized personality, his showmanship sometimes seemed to be the focus of attention instead of the music. His highly publicized personal life, involving such women as Gloria Vanderbilt and Greta Garbo, also made headlines.

The romantic gaze of Leopold Stokowski.

Apparently his white mane and ascetic face were irresistible to women.

In later years Stokowski fostered the concept of youth concerts and became conductor of the NBC Symphony, the New York City Symphony and the Hollywood Bowl Orchestra. He was also involved with many other ensembles, made numerous recordings, and was active in music almost to the time of his death at ninety-five. In 1941 he was awarded a special Oscar for "unique achievement in creating a new form of visualized music in Walt Disney's *Fantasia*."

The Big Broadcast of 1937 (1936) * *One Hundred Men and a Girl* (1937) * *Fantasia* (1940)

Les Brown and His Band

Les Brown (Reinerton, Pennsylvania, 1912–2001)

According to the venerable *Guinness Book of Records* Les Brown was the leader of the longest lasting musical group in pop music history. His orchestra, famously called "Les Brown and His Band of Renown," was formed in 1938 and was still touring close to the time of his death.

The band produced numerous hit records including "I've Got My Love to Keep Me Warm," "Joltin' Joe DiMaggio," "My Dreams Are Getting Better All the Time," "Sentimental Journey" (their theme song, popularized by vocalist Doris Day) and "Ramona."

It was probably most known for its association with Bob Hope. Les Brown accompanied Hope on eighteen of his Christmas tours and traded barbs with him on the radio. He also was on the Dean Martin television show from 1965 to 1974.

Seven Days Leave (1942) * *The Nutty Professor* (1963) * *Bob Hope Vietnam Christmas Show* (1966)†

†Although this was originally made for television, scenes were added for a theatrical release.

Les Elgart and His Orchestra

Les Elgart (New Haven, Connecticut, 1918–1995)

Trumpeter Les Elgart was a sideman in the orchestras of Raymond Scott, Harry James, Bunny Berigan and Charlie Spivak prior to forming a band with his brother about 1945. The Les and Larry Elgart Orchestra (known for the so-called "Elgart sound") thrived for only a short while until disagreements between the siblings caused it to disband.

The brothers' orchestra was re-formed in the early '50s, mainly finding its niche on the college circuit, and they also put out many albums. Though Les was not considered to be the musician that his brother Larry was, he had led his own band. By the end of the 1950s he had more or less stopped performing.

Senior Prom (1958)

Les Hite and His Orchestra

Les Hite (DuQuoin, Illinois, 1903–1962)

Among the instruments bandleader Les Hite played were the piano, alto saxophone and xylophone. In 1930 he had taken over the Quality Serenaders orchestra which he later "loaned" to Louis Armstrong for gigs in the early '30s. The band's theme song was "It Must Have Been a Dream" and among its members were Lionel Hampton and Dizzy Gillespie.

As the Sebastian's Cotton Club Orchestra, Hite's group was based at Los Angeles's Cotton Club for several years in the 1930s. They played for many film sound tracks, but made only a few commercial recordings, among them "Jersey Bounce" and "T-Bone Blues" in the early 1940s. The orchestra disbanded in 1945.

Bargain with Bullets (1937) * *Fools for Scandal* (1938)

Les Paul Trio
Les Paul (Lester Polfuss [also Polfus], Waukesha, Wisconsin, 1915/16–)

Famed as the father of the electric guitar, Les Paul certainly had a many-sided career. His musical innovations include overlaying as many as twelve music tracks on top of each other to produce the sublime sounds featured on the hit records he made with his then-wife Mary Ford (nee Colleen Summers, 1914?–1977).

Among their eleven number one chart hits were "How High the Moon," "The World Is Waiting for the Sunrise," "I'm Sitting on Top of the World" and the 1953 mega-hit "Vaya Con Dios." Paul had had his first recordings released when he was just twenty years of age.

A professional guitarist from 1930, Paul played with Fred Waring's orchestra and on the radio as a country musician/comedian with names like Rhubarb Red and Hot Rod. During this time he steadily worked on his inventions and improvements, including the further development of the solid-body guitar. He often built his own recording equipment.

Long lionized by his fellow musicians, he was best known to the general public through his collaboration with Mary Ford. They had their own television show and were called "Mr. and Mrs. Music." Previously he played with Bing Crosby and the Andrews Sisters and had formed the Les Paul Trio in 1943.

When he was ninety years old he was still being nominated for Grammy Awards (two in 2006 alone), had been given a Lifetime Achievement Award from the Songwriter's Hall of Fame, and was an inductee of the Rock and Roll Hall of Fame. To his credit were more than 20 million recordings sold. A documentary *Chasing Sound: Les Paul at 90* was released in 2006.

Sensations of 1945 (1944)

Lew Preston and His Ranch Hands
Prairie Stranger (1941) "Ride, Cowboy, Ride" and "Scallwag"

Lewis, Gary *see* Gary Lewis and the Playboys

Lewis, Jimmie *see* Jimmie Lewis and His Texas Cowboys

Lewis, Ted *see* Ted Lewis and His Orchestra

Lewis, Texas Jim *see* Texas Jim Lewis...

Lewis and Clarke Expedition
For Singles Only (1968) "Destination Unknown"

Lewis and White [unknown]
Boarding House Blues (1948)

Lewis Lymon and the Teenchords
Lewis Lymon (lead); Ralph Vaughan (1st tenor); Rossilio Rocca (2nd tenor); Lyndon Harold (baritone); David Little (bass)

Without brother Frankie Lymon's brief fame it is a reasonable supposition that there would have been no Lewis Lymon and the Teenchords. However, they did score some small successes like "I'm So Happy" and "Honey, Honey" in the late 1950s. Their stage presence was a clean-cut one, being costumed in white shirts and black pants with black bowties.

Following two of the band members' problems with the law (a stolen car) the group disbanded in 1960. Lymon himself recorded with other groups and re-formed the Teenchords in the 1970s to cash in on rock-and-roll nostalgia. In the 21st century he performed with a revived version of the Teenagers, his late brother's group.

Jamboree (1957) "Your Last Chance" and "Gone"

Light Crust Dough Boys
Bob Wills (1905–1975) (fiddle); Herman Arnspiger (guitar); Milton Brown (vocals); Tommy Duncan

The intriguing name of the Light Crust Doughboys hardly conveyed its standing as a premier western swing band, in fact one of the progenitors of that style. They bore the name of a Fort Worth, Texas radio sponsor, a rather common occurrence for groups in the 1920s and '30s — they knew what side their bread was buttered on, so to speak.

Previously they had been known as the Aladdin Laddies. The trio was an offshoot of Bob Wills's fiddle band whose radio show was sponsored by Light Crust Flour and which became an enormous draw in the Southwest in the early

1930s. Although the original members, particularly Wills, soon went on to other opportunities, the Doughboys continued on well into the 1940s in radio and on recordings.

At one point after the original members had departed, they were called the Coffee Grinders. In latter days the Light Crust Doughboys have been resurrected and become more versatile, dabbling in gospel and other musical forms. Nominated for several Grammys, they were declared the "Official Music Ambassadors of the Lone Star State" by the Texas legislature.

The Big Show (1936) * *Oh, Susanna!* (1936)

Lilly Brothers *see* Tex Logan and the Lilly Brothers

Lionel Hampton and His Band; Lionel Hampton and Orchestra

Lionel Hampton (Louisville, Kentucky, 1908–2002)

Considered one of the true jazz greats, Lionel Hampton led his own band from 1940 and for forty years worked with a whole panoply of musicians from Benny Goodman to Quincy Jones. He was member of the Benny Goodman Quartet, which was pioneering for its racial admixture, and prior to that had played with various ensembles from 1928.

A vibraharp/vibraphone virtuoso, Hampton was credited with bringing that instrument out of obscurity, as well as playing drums and a mean two-fingered piano. Besides the many popular jazz albums he released, his 1939 recording of "Flyin' Home" (his theme song) is considered by some to have been a precursor to rock-and-roll.

Harlem Hotshots (1953) * *Harlem Jazz Festival* (1955) [documentary] * *Rhythm-and-Blues Revue* (1955) [documentary] * *Rock 'n' Roll Revue* (1955/56) [documentary] * *The Benny Goodman Story* (1956) * *Mr. Rock 'n' Roll* (1957) "Star Rocket," "Mister Rock 'n' Roll" and other songs

Little Joe's Wranglers

Fighting Mustang (1948)

Little Vagabonds [unknown]

Tuxedo Junction (1941)

Logan, Tex *see* Tex Logan and the Lilly Brothers

Lollipop Shoppe

Fred Cole (vocals); Ed Bowen (guitar); Ron Buzzell (guitar); Bob Atkins (bassist); Tom Rockson (drums)

Originally known as the Weeds, the group known as the Lollipop Shoppe supposedly changed its name to fit in with the "bubblegum" music that was in vogue in the 1960s. But the band was anything but bubblegum in its admixture of garage and psychedelic rock.

The Lollipop Shoppe backed such famous performers as Janis Joplin and the Doors and made recordings like "You Must Be a Witch" and "Someone I Knew" before breaking up in 1969. Although the band never made the charts their recordings are much sought after.

Angels from Hell (1968) "Who's It Gonna Be" and "Mr. Madison Avenue"

Lombard, Carole *see* Carole Lombard Singers

Lombardo, Guy *see* Guy Lombardo...

Lone Star Cowboys *see* Texas Jim Lewis and His Lone Star Cowboys

Long, Johnny *see* Johnny Long and His Orchestra

Lonzo and Oscar

Lonzo (aka Ken Marvin) (Lloyd George, Cordova, Tennessee, 1924–1991) (bassist); Oscar (Rollin Sullivan, Edmonton, Kentucky, 1919–) (guitar); Johnny Sullivan (Edmonton, Kentucky, 1917–1967); David Hooten

Lonzo and Oscar, comic musicians, had both been on the radio and a part of other groups before they teamed as Cicero and Oscar in the mid–1940s. Their first major gig was opening for the great country singer Eddy Arnold and His Tennessee Plowboys; it was he who re-dubbed them Lonzo and Oscar.

Their comedy, heard on the *Grand Ole Opry* from 1947 to 1967, could be fairly described as hillbilly corn. (Example: After each tells the other that there is nothing he wouldn't do for him, they conclude: "That's the way we go through life — doing nothing for each other.")

But they were exuberant musicians. The 1948 novelty song "I'm My Own Grandpa" was their big recording hit, selling more than four million copies. When Lloyd George (Lonzo) departed the act in 1950 to solo (calling himself Ken Marvin), Rollin's older brother Johnny Sullivan took over the role.

Lonzo and Oscar also had a hit with "Country Music Time" in the 1960s. Following the elder Sullivan's untimely death David Hooten assumed the mantle of Lonzo and the duo continued to perform into the 1980s.

Country Music Holiday (1958) * *Tennessee Jamboree* (1964) * *Country Music Caravan* (1964) * *Country Boy* (1966)

Lopez, Manny see Manny Lopez and His Orchestra

Lopez, Vincent see Vincent Lopez and His Orchestra

Lord Flea and His Calypsonians; Lord Flea Calypsonians; Calypsonians

Lord Flea (Norman Thomas)

Dubbed the "Calypso King of Jamaica," Lord Flea was one of the originators of "modern" calypso.

Bop Girl Goes Calypso (1957) "Calypso Jamboree" * *Calypso Joe* (1957)

Los Angeles Opera Company

Enter Madame! (1934)

Lou Bring Orchestra

Lou Bring (Robert Borsuk, New York, New York, 1907?–1961)

Pianist Lou Bring had a New York society band in the 1930s and had previously played piano with Vincent Lopez. He also was the music director for such greats as Al Jolson, Helen Morgan, Betty Hutton, Gracie Fields and Jimmy Durante.

Lady, Let's Dance! (1944)

Louis Armstrong and Band; Louis Armstrong and His Orchestra

Louis Armstrong (New Orleans, Louisiana, 1900/01–1971)

Perhaps the most famous jazz performer of his time, Louis "Satchmo" Armstrong led many bands but they were not considered to be among the great ones. It was his own trumpet playing and singing that pulled in the audiences, and some believed that his bands were a distraction from his own outstanding musicianship.

If strictly true the story of Armstrong's youth could rival a Horatio Alger novel. He learned to play the cornet at the Waifs Home after being arrested as a young teenager. Mentored by King Oliver, he became a trumpeter who in the 1920s made a series of classic recordings with groups formed just for recording sessions and given names like the Hot Five and the Hot Seven.

From 1930 he fronted his own band with its theme song of "Sleepy Time Down South." Later in the decade Satchmo (the name is perhaps a misreading of the nickname "Satchelmouth") turned more to acting in movies and on Broadway. As time went on he fine-tuned his lovable persona and became as well known for that as for his real musical accomplishments.

Armstrong continued to duet with the great singers of his time, like Bing Crosby, Ella Fitzgerald and the Mills Brothers and played solo roles in movies such as *Hello, Dolly!* Increasingly he toured Europe where American jazz was enormously popular and made films there in Germany and Denmark. In 1956 a documentary *Satchmo the Great* was released.

Ex-Flame (1930) * *Pennies from Heaven* (1936) * *Artists and Models* (1937) * *Everyday's a Holiday* (1938) * *Doctor Rhythm* (1938) * *Going Places* (1938) * *Cabin in the Sky* (1943) * *Atlantic City* (1944) * *Jam Session* (1944) * *Pillow to Post* (1945) * *New Orleans* (1947) * *The Strip* (1951) * *High Society* (1956) * *La Paloma* (Germany) * *The Night Before the Premiere* (Germany) * *A Girl, a Guitar and a Trumpet* (Denmark) * *Auf Wiedersehen* (Germany) * *When the Boys Meet the Girls* (1965)

Louis Jordan and His Orchestra; Louis Jordan and His Tympany Five; Louis Jordan and His Tympany Band

Louis Jordan (Brinkley, Arkansas, 1908–1975)

A respected master composer and performer of jazz, blues and rhythm-and-blues music from the 1930s to the '60s, alto sax player Louis Jordan had million-selling records with his various groups. He had previously played with the Chick Webb and Ella Fitzgerald bands before leading his own big band.

One of the more famous of his ensembles was the Tympany Five, which actually used up to eight players on occasion. Formed in the 1930s, it produced recordings like "Ration Blues," "What's the Use of Gettin' Sober" and "Keep A-

Knockin'." "Caldonia" was one of Jordan's biggest hits; it was covered by other bands' versions as were several of his recordings.

A World War II–era smash was "Is You Is or Is You Ain't My Baby?" Although some of his records were crossover hits, like "Choo Choo Ch'Boogie," many scored only on the so-called "race" charts that featured the music of African-American artists.

With his "jump blues" style Louis Jordan is often credited with being one of the very earliest musicians to pioneer, or at least influence, the onset of rock-and-roll. In the 1940s he had been seen in many soundies and musical shorts and was dubbed the "King of the Juke Box." He was an acknowledged mentor of such performers as Little Richard and Chuck Berry.

Follow the Boys (1944) * *Miss Bobby Socks* (1944) * *Beware* (1946) "How Long Must I Wait for You," "Long Legged Lizzie" and several other songs * *Swing Parade of 1946* (1946) * *Reet, Petite and Gone* (1947) "Caldonia," "Let the Good Times Roll," "Reet, Petite and Gone" and several other songs * *Look Out Sister* (1949) "Ten Gallon Hat," "Caldonia," "You're Much Too Fat" and numerous other songs

Louis Prima with His Band

Louis Prima (New Orleans, Louisiana, 1910–1978)

An uncharacteristically serene Louis Prima.

Certainly one of the most publicly extroverted of all bandleaders, Louis Prima was boisterous (or just plain loud, depending on one's viewpoint) with a raspy voice, and instantly identifiable by his strong Italianate features topped by a rather bad toupee. Not for him was the bland smile favored by most orchestra leaders.

Trained in the violin and later a trumpeter, he formed a Dixieland combo, Louis Prima and his New Orleans Gang, in the 1930s and had a band during the following decade. Not surprisingly his theme song was "Way Down Yonder in New Orleans."

Supposedly discovered about 1934 by suave Guy Lombardo (almost his diametric opposite in every way), Prima was initially known for his Italian-flavored novelty tunes like "Zooma Zooma," "Angelina" and "Felicia No Capecia."

He was a songwriter of some talent, having penned "A Sunday Kind of Love" and the all-time big band classic "Sing Sing Sing," popularized by Benny Goodman. But it was probably his teaming with singer, and later wife, Keely Smith (nee Dorothy Keely) that brought him to a wider audience. Together they starred in the rock and roll quickie *Hey Boy! Hey Girl!*

They also produced hit recordings like "That Old Black Magic" and were perennials on the Las Vegas showroom scene for many years. Before he was well known Louis Prima had had small roles in such '30s films as *Rhythm on the Range* and *You Can't Have Everything*. Much later he was the voice of the orangutan in Disney's animated feature *The Jungle Book*.

Manhattan Merry-Go-Round (1937) * *Start Cheering* (1938) * *Rose of Washington Square* (1939) * *Senior Prom* (1958) * *Hey Boy! Hey Girl!* (1959)

Louise Massey's Westerners

Louise Massey (aka Louise Mabie) (Midland, Texas, 1902–1983) (vocals/piano); Milt Mabie (bassist); Larry Wellington (accordion); Dott Massey (violin/trumpet); Allen Massey (guitar/banjo)

Mostly a family act, the Westerners were on radio's *National Barn Dance* in the early 1930s. They produced numerous recordings of western songs like "Round Up Time in Heaven," "Riding Down That Old Texas Trail" and "The Cowboy's Dream," and others including "Is It True

What They Say About Dixie?" and "Squeeze Box Polka."

The act's biggest hits were "When the White Azaleas Start Blooming" (a multi-million seller), "South of the Border" and "My Adobe Hacienda." The latter scored as both a western and popular tune, making it one of the early crossover hits of its day.

Louise Massey was the driving force behind the Westerners and had been dubbed the "Original Rhinestone Cowgirl." She was a professional from 1918 and thus somewhat of a pioneer as a woman in the ranks of western singers. She went to New York to appear on radio, retired in 1950, and was inducted into the National Cowgirl Hall of Fame in 1982.

Where the Buffalo Roam (1938)

Loumell Morgan Trio

Loumell Morgan (North Carolina, 1919/22–) (piano); James Jackson; Jimmy Smith (bassist)

A two-year stint with Slim Gaillard's Flat Foot Floogie Boys beginning in 1939 was one of Loumell Morgan's earlier gigs, but he had probably begun playing professionally at fifteen. He formed his own jazz trio, sometime later to be a quintet, in the early 1940s.

All By Myself (1943) * *Melody Parade* (1943)

Louvin, Charlie *see* Charlie Louvin and His Band

Lovin' Spoonful

Steve Boone (bassist); Joe Butler (drums); John Sebastian; Zal Yanovsky (Zalman Yanovsky, Toronto, Canada, 1944–2002) (guitar); Jerry Yester; Skip Boone

Nineteen sixty-five was the year that two rock musicians and two folksingers from the Mugwumps formed the Lovin' Spoonful. The teaming resulted in ten Top Twenty hits that included "Summer in the City," "Do You Believe in Magic?," "Daydream," "Did You Ever Have to Make Up Your Mind?" and "You Didn't Have to Be So Nice."

Becoming one of the most popular of the American pop groups, the Spoonfuls' smooth harmonies did not unduly suffer when their comic Zal Yanovsky was replaced by Jerry Yester. Such recordings as "Darling Be Home Soon" and "Six o'Clock" ensued. In 1969 the Lovin' Spoonful disbanded only to reunite some twenty-two years later. They were inducted into the Rock and Roll Hall of Fame in 2000.

The Big T.N.T. Show (1966) [documentary] "Do You Believe in Magic?" and "You Didn't Have to Be So Nice" * *What's Up, Tiger Lily?* (1966) "Respoken"

Lowdermilk, Romaine *see* Romaine Lowdermilk and His Ranch House Cowboys

Lowe, Bernie *see* Bernie Lowe and His Orchestra

Lucky Millinder and His Band; Lucky Millinder and His Orchestra

Lucky Millinder (Lucius Millinder, Anniston, Alabama, 1900–1966)

After working with blues orchestras as an emcee and even a dancer, Lucky Millinder formed his own big band. Despite the fact that he could not actually play an instrument, his band turned out to be an innovative one that became a link between the swing and rhythm-and-blues eras. They often played at Harlem's Apollo Theater, backing top-line acts, with their theme song "Ride, Red, Ride."

Millinder had strong views and he personally decried white bands that imitated Black-led groups, and he criticized Black arrangers for aiding them. In the 1940s, with sidemen like Dizzy Gillespie, his band had several chart hits, including "When the Lights Go on Again." What he lacked in instrumental expertise he made up for with musical taste and the personality to power the group for many successful years until 1952.

Scandal (1933) * *Paradise in Harlem* (1940) * *Harlem on Parade* (1946?) * *Boarding House Blues* (1948?)

Lucky Seven; Lucky Seven Choir

Freshman Year (1938)

Luis Arcaraz and His Orchestra

Luis Arcaraz (Mexico City, Mexico, 1905–1968)

Bandleader, pianist and songwriter Luis Arcaraz led one of the most popular Mexican orchestras of the 1940s and '50s, and was also well-known to United States fans of Mexican pop

music. He is credited with composing more than 200 songs and the scores of many Mexican movies as well as appearing in several films there.
Cha-Cha-Cha Boom (1956)

Lulu and the Luvvers

Lulu (Marie Lawrie, Glasgow, Scotland, 1948–)

In America the pop singer Lulu is undoubtedly best-known for her role as a schoolgirl in Sidney Poitier's 1967 hit movie *To Sir with Love*, and for her singing of the title song. However, in Britain her success went beyond "To Sir with Love"; the Luvvers had a big hit with "Shout!" As a solo performer she had her own television show and nine Top Ten hits, mostly in the 1960s. They included "Leave a Little Love" and "Morning Dew."

Go-Go Big Beat (1964) [documentary] "Shout" * *Gonks Go Beat* (1965)

Lulu Belle and Scotty

Scotty (aka Skyland Scotty) (Scott Wiseman, Ingalls or Spruce Pine, North Carolina, 1909–1981); Lulu Belle (Myrtle Cooper, Boone, North Carolina, 1913–1999)

A very popular duo on the radio, married singers Scott Wiseman and Myrtle Cooper called themselves Lulu Belle and Scotty. They were known as the "Sweethearts of Country Music" and the "Hayloft Sweethearts." They appeared on the National Barn Dance program for nearly twenty years from 1933 and made television appearances as well.

Scott Wiseman, a guitar and banjo player, was also a songwriter with some seventy songs to his credit, his most famous being "Have I Told You Lately That I Love You?" Myrtle had begun as a hillbilly-style comedienne in the Minnie Pearl/Judy Canova mold. Their popular recordings together included "Home Coming Time," "Mountain Dew" and "My Heart Cries for You." Lulu Belle and Scotty retired the act in 1958.

Shine on, Harvest Moon (1938) * *Village Barn Dance* (1940) * *Country Fair* (1941) * *Hi, Neighbor* (1942) * *Swing Your Partner* (1943) * *Sing, Neighbor, Sing* (1944) * *The National Barn Dance* (1944)

Luman, Bob see Bob Luman and the Shadows

Lunceford, Jimmy see Jimmy Lunceford and His Band

Luther, John J. see John J. Luther...

Luvvers see Lulu and the Luvvers

Lyman, Abe see Abe Lyman...

Lymon, Frankie see Frankie Lymon and the Teenagers

Lymon, Lewis see Lewis Lymon and the Teenchords

Lynn Proctor Trio

The Lynn Proctor trio was a vocal group.
Miracle in Harlem (1948) "Watch Out"

Lyons, Cliff see Sons of the Pioneers

Lyttle Sisters

Darlene Lyttle; Dorothy Lyttle; Elinor Lyttle; Marilyn Lyttle

The Lyttle Sisters were a vocal quartet.
(Abbott and Costello) In Hollywood (1945) "I Hope the Band Keeps Playing" and "The Cocabola Tree" * *Easy to Look at* (1945)

Mac and Ace [unknown]

Juke Joint (1947)

Mac Niles and the Calypsonians

Calypso Heat Wave (1957)

Macbeth's Calypso Band

House-Rent Party (1946?)

Macon, Uncle Dave see Uncle Dave Macon and His Son, Dorris

Madriguera, Enric see Enric Madriguera and His Orchestra

Major, Sharp and Minor

Josephine Riley; Anita Nieto; Barbara Johnstone
Major, Sharp and Minor was a vocal trio.
The Big Broadcast (1932)

Malneck, Matty see Matty Malneck and His Orchestra

Malone Sisters [unknown]
Joe Palooka in The Knockout (1947)

Mamas and the Papas
John Phillips (Parris Island, South Carolina, 1935–2001); Cass Elliott (Ellen Cohen, Baltimore, Maryland, 1941–1974); Michelle Phillips (Holly Gilliam, Los Angeles, 1944?–); Denny Doherty (Halifax, Nova Scotia, 1940–2007)

The leader of the much-lauded pop group the Mamas and the Papas was John Phillips. He had first founded the folk ensemble the Journeymen with Denny Doherty and John's wife Michelle and later helped organize the Monterey Pop Festival. Cass Elliott and Doherty had previously sung with The Mugwumps.

Pretty Michelle, who had an acting career after the group disbanded (including the biopics *Valentino* and *Dillinger*), provided the glamour. The corpulent Elliott was the earth mother figure and with her winning personality was much seen on television.

Doherty had begun his career in his native Canada with the folk group the Halifax Three. After hooking up with the other Papa and the Mamas, he wrote their hit song "I Saw Her Again." His latter-day career included a role on a public broadcasting children's show and also the authorship of the play *Dream a Little Dream: the Mamas and the Papas Musical*.

Among the other noted hits of the Mamas and the Papas (they had six Top Ten charters within two years) were "Dream a Little Dream of Me," "San Francisco (Be Sure to Wear Some Flowers in Your Hair"), which almost reached anthem status, "Kokomo," "California Dreamin'," "Words of Love" and "Monday, Monday."

The Mamas and the Papas disbanded in 1967 amid recriminations all around. It re-formed in the 1980s and was inducted into the Rock and Roll Hall of Fame in 1998 and the Vocal Hall of Fame two years later.

Monterey Pop (1969) [documentary] "California Dreamin'" and "I've Got a Feeling"

Manny Harmon and His Orchestra
Manny Harmon (Philadelphia, Pennsylvania, 1909–2003)

The musical director of Republican nominating conventions from 1956 to 1992 was Manny Harmon. (When asked what his own political affiliation was, the bandleader cracked "I belong to the cocktail party.") Beside his political stints, he was the leader of a dance orchestra and musical director at the RKO Studios for some seventeen years.

Harmon, who had played in vaudeville and as a sideman for Earl Burtnett, seemed to be the bandleader of choice for many important show biz events. He played at the Academy Awards, the Emmys, the Rose Parade, the Miss Universe contest and on many television telethons.

Walking On Air (1936) * *When's Your Birthday?* (1937) * *From This Day Forward* (1946)

Manny Lopez and His Orchestra
Cha-Cha-Cha Boom (1956)

Manone, Wingy see Wingy Manone and His Band

Maple City Four
Art Janes (LaPorte, Indiana); Fritz Meissner (Frederick Meissner, LaPorte, Indiana); Al Rice (Allan Rice, La Porte, Indiana); Pat Petterson (LeRoy Petterson, LaPorte Indiana)

Veterans of radio singing commercials, the Maple City Four (named for their home town) appeared on radio from about 1926 into the 1950s. The close harmony quartet was dubbed the "Marx Brothers of Radio" for their mix of singing, skits, barbershop harmony and eccentric instrumentals. They had also performed in vaudeville.

Git Along Little Dogies (1937) * *The Old Barn Dance* (1938) * *Under Western Stars* (1938)

Marcels
Richard Knauss (baritone); Fred Johnson (bass); Gene Bricker (2nd tenor); Ron Mundy (1st tenor); Cornelius Harp (lead singer)

Perhaps one of the few groups to be named after a hairstyle (the marcelled hair of member Fred Johnson), the Pittsburgh-based Marcels had one big hit, their 1961 doo-wop rendition of "Blue Moon." This topped both the pop and rhythm-and-blues charts and since has been heard on the sound tracks of several movies. They had a second hit with another oldie, "Heartaches."

Originally an integrated group founded in 1959, the Marcels eventually became all Black when a couple of its members departed. Despite the dearth of many big hits, they are considered to have been one of the premier vocal groups. With some new membership the group toured in nostalgia shows until the mid–1990s.

Twist Around the Clock (1961) "Blue Moon" and "Merry Twistmas"

Marie Bryant Swing Band

Marie Bryant (New Orleans, Louisiana, 1919–1978)

Marie Bryant was most famous for her sexily exotic dancing and later for her singing. It is possible she led a swing band for one film only.

The Duke Is Tops (1938)

Marimba Merry Makers

Sailor Beware (1951) * *Skirts Ahoy!* (1952)

Martha and the Vandellas

Martha Reeves (Eufaula, Alabama, 1941–) (2nd soprano); Rosalind Ashford (1943–) (soprano); Betty Kelly (1944–); Annette Beard (alto); Lois Reeves; Gloria Williamson (d. 1999)

Rock fans figuratively (and perhaps literally) did dance in the streets when Martha and the Vandellas released their smash "Dancing in the Street" in 1964. The group had been named with the odd combining of Detroit's Van Dyke Street and singer Della Reese. They were formed with members of the Del-Fi's (or Del-Phi's) and were originally used for backup with Marvin Gaye and called the Vells and then the Beljeans.

Martha Reeves had been a Motown secretary when she got her big break. She possessed a strong, almost gospel-like voice that powered other hits like "Quicksand," "Jimmy Mack," "Heat Wave" and "Nowhere to Run." In the mid–1960s, they were undeniably one of Motown's pre-eminent "girl" groups — until the Supremes came along.

"Honey Child" was the Vandellas last hit and they broke up when Reeves embarked on a solo career in the early 1970s. But they re-grouped later that decade, continue to perform sporadically, and were inducted into the Rock and Roll Hall of Fame in 1995.

The T.A.M.I. Show (1964) [documentary]

Martin, Freddy *see* Freddy Martin and Orchestra

Martinez, Tony *see* Tony Martinez and His Band

Martiniques *see* Felix and His Martiniques

Mary Kaye Trio

Mary Kaye (Mary Ka'aihue, Detroit, Michigan, 1924/28–2007) (guitar); Norman Kaye (Norman Ka'aihue) (bassist); Jules Pursley; Frank Ross (Biagio Bologna) (accordion)

The Mary Kaye Trio is credited with being the very first lounge act in Las Vegas; in fact Mary Kaye credited herself with inventing the term "lounge act." The group played mainly in Sin City venues for up to nine months a year and found time to make popular records such as "Besame Mucho," "My Funny Valentine" and "April in Paris," as well as many albums.

Mary and Norman Kaye, brother and sister, were supposedly the grandchildren of a Hawaiian prince who was the brother of Hawaii's last queen. As youngsters they had performed with their father Johnny Ka'aihue's orchestra (he was professionally known as Johnny Ukulele). The trio disbanded in 1966 at a time when they were earning a princely one million dollars a year.

Cha-Cha-Cha-Boom! (1956) * *Bop Girl Goes Calypso* (1957) "Fools Rush in" and "Calypso Rock"

Matadors

The Satin Mushroom (1969)

Mathews, Tobin *see* Tobin Mathews and the All Stars

Matty Malneck and His Orchestra

Matty Malneck (Newark, New Jersey, 1904–1981)

After playing with the Paul Whiteman orchestra for many years violinist Matty Malneck established his band in the mid–1930s. He kept it going for another thirty-five years, sometimes as an octet.

Besides being a music arranger for films and television, Malneck was the writer of songs that ran the gamut from "Stairway to the Stars" "I'm Through with Love," "Till Tomorrow" and "Shangri-La" to "Fidgety Joe" and "Goody Goody."

East Side of Heaven (1939) * *Hawaiian Nights* (1939) * *Man About Town* (1939) * *Saint Louis Blues* (1939) * *Scatterbrain* (1940) * *You're in the Army Now* (1941) * *Shantytown* (1943) * *Trocadero* (1944)

Maurel, Raymond *see* **Raymond Maurel and the Cimini Male Chorus**

Maxwell, Philip *see* **Philip Maxwell's Choristers**

May, Billy *see* **Billy May and Orchestra**

Maynard, Ken *see* **Ken Maynard's Buckaroos**

McCarthy, Dorothy *see* **Dorothy McCarthy and the Three Dots**

McIntyre, Hal *see* **Hal McIntyre...**

McKay, Scotty *see* **Scotty McKay Quintet**

McKinley, Ray *see* **Ray McKinley and His Orchestra**

McVea, Jack *see* **Jack McVea and Orchestra**

Medians [unknown]
Everybody's Dancin' (1950)

Meglin Glee Club
Ethel Meglin (1890?–1988)

The Meglin Kiddies were well-known to Hollywood producers who frequently used them in movies. Ethel Meglin, a kind of super stage mother, ran a school that trained young children for show business careers, especially one tiny discovery named Shirley Temple. Other alumni were Mickey Rooney and Judy Garland.

In the 1930s she owned the largest number of dance schools in the United States, more than 130. Mrs. Meglin (originally Moegling) was herself a former Ziegfeld Follies dancer who later had a television show called *The Meglin Review*.
Reg'lar Fellers (1941)

Mel Tormé Trio *see* **Mel-Tones**

Mellomen (aka Mello-Men)
Thurl Ravenscroft (Norfolk, Nebraska, 1914–2006); Max Smith

From a stint as a studio and radio singer in the 1930s, Thurl Ravenscroft joined the Sportsmen, a quartet, but World War II put a temporary halt to that group. The Mellomen came about in the post-war period and they did much back-up singing for big bands and artists like Elvis Presley, Frank Sinatra and Rosemary Clooney.

Ravenscroft was a talented voice artist for films, including animated movies like *The Brave Little Toaster* and *Snoopy Come Home*, but his great claim to fame was as the distinctive voice of Tony the Tiger for Frosted Flakes cereal. It is he that is heard roaring the oft-imitated "They're grrrrrreat!" Such is immortality.

The Glenn Miller Story (1954) * *It Happened at the World's Fair* (1963) * *The Sword in the Stone* (voices only) (1963)

Melodears *see* **Ina Ray Hutton and Her Melodears**

Mel-Tones (sometimes billed as the Meltones); Mel Tormé Trio
Mel Tormé (Melvin Tormé, Chicago, Illinois, 1925–1999); Les Baxter; Ginny O'Connor (later Mancini); Bernie Parke; Diz Disruhd; Betty Beveridge

Considered one of the premier singers of his generation, Mel Tormé, was dubbed the "Velvet Fog" for publicity purposes but such facile nicknames obscured his real talents. His song phrasing was legendary and his reputation as a jazz singer has endured much longer than most of the mere band singers of his day. He was also a talented pianist and drummer.

He began as a child actor on the radio and by his teen years was already singing and arranging with the Chico Marx band. The five member Mel-Tones were formed about 1943, the biggest of their hits being "What Is This Thing Called Love?" They had originally dubbed themselves the School Kids and the Skylarks.

The Mel-Tones' jazz-influenced style is considered the forerunner of such groups as Manhattan Transfer. By 1947 Tormé was off to his solo career in nightclubs, along the way amassing numerous successful albums and singles like "Careless Love," "Blue Moon" and "Mountain Greenery." He was also a composer of some 300 songs, including such standards as "The Christmas Song" with its evocative opening line "Chestnuts roasting on an open fire...."

Mel Tormé did not neglect the acting side of his career and was Emmy-nominated for his performance in the 1956 television movie *The Comedian*, starring Mickey Rooney. He appeared in several films without the Meltones, beginning with *Higher and Higher* in 1943 and ending with *The Naked Gun 2½* (1991), and numerous television shows. He was also considered a talented author, but it is for his unique singing style that he will remain memorable.

Pardon My Rhythm (1944) * *Let's Go Steady* (1945)

Men About Town Quartette
It Happened in Paris (1932)

Mendez, Sergio see Sergio Mendez and Brasil '66

Menendez, Nilo see Nilo Menendez and His Rhumba Band

Mercer Brothers
Bud Mercer (banjo); Jim Mercer (banjo)

The banjo-plunking Mercer Brothers began performing in the 1920s with their sister and became a duo when she dropped out in the late 1930s. They appeared in many tony hotels and in Las Vegas, as well as doing much television, on which they had their own show.

Casa Manana (1951)

Mercy Group (aka Mercy)
"Love Can Make You Happy" was the Mercy Group's one hit.

Fireball Jungle (1969) "Love Can Make You Happy" and "Fire Ball"

Meredith Neal and the Boot-Heel Boys
Tiger By the Tail (1970)

Meremblum, Peter see Peter Meremblum...

Merle Travis and His Bronco Busters; Merle Travis Trio
Merle Travis (Rosewood, Kentucky, 1917–1983)

As a guitarist Merle Travis was considered a nonpareil who actually had an instrumental style "Travis Picking" named for him. As a songwriter he produced the classic "Sixteen Tons" (a million seller for Tennessee Ernie Ford) and the popular novelties that must have made tobacco companies happy: "Smoke, Smoke, Smoke (That Cigarette)" and "So Round, So Firm, So Fully Packed."

About 1936 he started in radio and eventually appeared on several popular shows, including one in Cincinnati where he was teamed with the country music great Grandpa Jones as the Sheppard (or Shepherd) Brothers. He was also a member of the Brown's Ferry Four, a gospel quartet.

Travis arrived in Hollywood in 1944 and recorded hits including "Dark As a Dungeon," "Steel Guitar Rag," "Sweet Temptation" and "Merle's Boogie Woogie." Like his contemporary Les Paul, he worked on improving guitar design. He was also a member of Ray Whitley's western swing band.

Years after his solo appearances in "B" westerns like *The Old Texas Trail* and *Beyond the Pecos* and those with his own groups, Merle Travis had a role in 1953's *From Here to Eternity* in which he played "Re-Enlistment Blues." He also appeared in *Honky Tonk Man*.

The multi-talented Travis became a major influence on guitarists who succeeded him and was inducted into both the Songwriters Hall of Fame and the Country Music Hall of Fame in the 1970s.

Galloping Thunder (1946) * *Lone Star Moonlight* (1946) * *Roaring Rangers* (1946) * *Cyclone Fury* (1951)

Merry Macs
Judd McMichael (George McMichael, Minneapolis, Minnesota, 1906?–1989) (tenor); Ted

McMichael (Minneapolis, Minnesota, 1908–2001) (baritone); Joe McMichael, Minneapolis, Minnesota, 1916–1944) (tenor); Cheri McKay (melody)

As teenagers in the early 1920s the two elder McMichael brothers began singing professionally. As they gained recognition (and their much younger brother) they were known as the Mystery Trio (wearing masks, even though it was radio) and then the Personality Boys. In 1930 they added a girl singer, Cheri McKay, and thus was born the Merry Macs.

They supposedly pioneered a series of "firsts": the first four-part harmony group to include a female member; the first to appear on stage in white tie and tails, and the first to use purely rhythmic accompaniment. Although the Merry Macs appeared in relatively few films (and were top-billed in one), they had signed a ten-year contract with Universal Studio in 1938.

Among the hits of this extremely popular group, who performed extensively on the radio and with top big bands from Glenn Miller to Glen Gray, were "The Hawaiian War Chant," "Mairzy Doats," "Laughing on the Outside (Crying on the Inside)," "Spurs That Jingle, Jangle, Jingle" and "The Hut Sut Song."

During the height of World War II their "Praise the Lord and Pass the Ammunition" and "Sentimental Journey" became inspirational paeans to both the fighting and home fronts. They also introduced some jazz stylings into the act.

The Merry Macs' girl singers changed over the years (Helen Carroll, Mary Lou Cook and the longest-serving, Marjorie Garland), as did the third male member after brother Joe was killed during the war. The quartet's last chart hits came in 1946, but they remained popular through numerous personnel changes and soldiered on until the 1960s.

Love Thy Neighbor (1940) * *Melody Lane* (1941) * *Moonlight In Hawaii* (1941) * *Ride 'Em Cowboy* (1942) "Wake Up, Jacob" * *Mr. Music* (1950)

Meyer Davis and His Orchestra

Meyer Davis (Washington, D.C., 1893–1976)

Besides being a prominent society bandleader, Meyer Davis was a shrewd businessman who contracted his name out to several different bands so that many gala occasions could boast of a "Meyer Davis" orchestra. His own original band had been formed as far back as the 1910s.

With a few other such prominent orchestra leaders, like the Lanin brothers, Davis cornered the market for society bands on the East Coast in the 1950s and '60s. His brand of music could fairly be described as soothingly undistinguished but he did try to keep up with the times. He even misguidedly released an album of twist music in the early 1960s.

Advise and Consent (1962)

Meyers Sisters

The Meyers Sisters were singers.
Frozen Justice (1929)

MG's *see* Booker T and the MG's

Mickey Rooney Jr. and His Combo

Mickey Rooney, Jr. (Joseph Yule III, Birmingham, Alabama, 1945–)

The eldest son of entertainer Mickey Rooney (nee Joe Yule, Jr.), Mickey Rooney, Jr. began his show biz career as a Walt Disney Mouseketeer and also played the bass in orchestras. Unlike his diminutive five-foot dad Junior grew to be over six feet tall.

Hot Rods to Hell (1967)

Midwesterners [unknown]

The Second Greatest Sex (1955)

Mike Riley and His Musical Maniacs; Mike Riley and His Orchestra; Mike Riley's Orchestra

Originally the co-leader of a six piece band with Eddie Farley in the 1930s, Mike Riley and Farley co-wrote the enormously popular novelty tune "The Music Goes Round and Round."

Kid Dynamite (1943) * *Sleepy Lagoon* (1943) * *That's My Baby* (1944)

Miller, Dave *see* Dave Miller and His New York French Casino Band

Miller, Eddie *see* Eddie Miller and His Bobcats

Miller, Glenn *see* Glenn Miller...

Miller, Herb *see* **Herb Miller and His Orchestra**

Miller, Steve *see* **Steve Miller Band**

Millinder, Lucky *see* **Lucky Millinder...**

Mills Brothers
John Mills, Sr. (1883/89–1968); John Mills, Jr. (Piqua, Ohio, 1911–1936); Herbert Mills (Piqua, Ohio, 1912–1989); Harry Mills (Piqua, Ohio, 1913–1982); Donald Mills (Piqua, Ohio, 1915–1999)

When very young this iconic harmony group was called Four Brothers and a Kazoo and then, having gone up in the world, Four Boys and a Guitar. Originally their father stood proudly on the sidelines and only joined his sons onstage after the early death of John, Jr. (Papa had led the barbershop quartet the Four Kings of Harmony.)

The Brothers initially garnered attention through their ability to imitate musical instruments and only needed an actual guitar to accompany them (originally played by John, Jr.). They hit it big on network radio under their own name but had previously been dubbed the Steamboat Four, the Tasty Yeast Jesters, Will, Willie, Wilbur and William and other names depending on the station on which they worked.

The Mills' first recording, "Tiger Rag," was a smash and was quickly followed by standards like "Up a Lazy River," "You're Nobody's Sweetheart Now," "Ole Rockin' Chair" and numerous others. They were apparently the first Black group to appear at a command performance before British royalty and became a worldwide success.

At the end of the 1930s the Brothers' pre-eminence was challenged by the Ink Spots but they remained popular, especially after their post-war multi-million selling record of "Paper Doll." In the 1950s songs like "Glow Worm," "You're Nobody 'Til Somebody Loves You" and "Opus One" kept them in the public eye. In all they had more than seventy songs that made the charts.

The Mills Brothers remained in the spotlight through some 2,200 recordings and with new membership are probably still performing somewhere today. They became a trio with Papa Mills' retirement in 1957. The last original member, Donald, had sung in public for some seventy-five years by the time of his last performance.

The Big Broadcast (1932) * *Twenty Million Sweethearts* (1934) * *Strictly Dynamite* (1934) * *Operator 13* (1934) * *Broadway Gondolier* (1935) * *Rhythm Parade* (1942) * *Chatterbox* (1943) * *He's My Guy* (1943) * *Reveille with Beverly* (1943) * *Cowboy Canteen* (1944) * *The Fight Never Ends* (1948) * *When You're Smiling* (1950) * *The Big Beat* (1958) "You're Being Followed"

The Mills Brothers (1930s).

Milo Twins
Edward Milolen; Edwin Milolen

The identical twin Milo Brothers cashed in on the so-called "hillbilly boogie" craze of the late 1940s with their hit recording of "Truck Driver's Boogie" in 1948.

I'm From Arkansas (1944) * *Sing, Neighbor, Sing* (1944) * *Marked for Murder* (1945)

Milt Britton and His Band

Milt Britton (Winston-Salem, North Carolina, 1894–1948)

Before orchestra leader Milt Britton founded his own band, he and brother Frank had co-led a comedy band (in)famous for smashing instruments over each others' heads. The Britton band was variously called "America's Craziest Orchestra" and the "Mad Musical Maniacs."

Riding High (1943)

Milt Herth Trio

Milt Herth (Kenosha, Wisconsin, 1902–1969) (organ); Billy Kyle (piano); O'Neil Spencer (drums/vocals)

Among the recordings made by the jazz group the Milt Herth Trio were "Minuet in Jazz," "Rockin' in Rhythm," "Copenhagen" and "Looney Little Tooney."

Juke Box Jenny (1942)

Milton Delugg and His Swing Wing

Milton DeLugg (Los Angeles, California, 1918–)

A musical director for television shows in that medium's early days, Milton DeLugg and his band were regulars on one of the first late night shows, *Broadway Open House* starring Jerry Lester. There he showed a flair for comedy.

DeLugg was also an arranger and composer of film scores and such songs as "Whoop-de-Doo" and "Shanghai." His most famous composition was the novelty tune "Orange Colored Sky" with its catchy refrain of "Wham bam alakazam."

It's Great to Be Young (1946)

Milton Douglas and Orchestra

Gigolette (1935)

Minevitch, Borah *see* Borah Minevitch...

Minnie Cow and His Orchestra

With Love and Kisses (1936)

Miracles *see* Smokey Robinson and the Miracles

Miranda, Carmen *see* Carmen Miranda Band

Mr. Acker Bilk and His Paramount Jazz Band *see* Acker Bilk and His Paramount Jazz Band

Mitch Ayres and His Orchestra

Mitch Ayres (Mitchell Agress, Milwaukee, Wisconsin, 1910–1969)

Perhaps better known in latter days as a music arranger for Perry Como, the King Family and others, Mitch Ayres had been the front man for an orchestra in the 1930s and early '40s. He also toured with the Andrews Sisters, in a couple of whose films he appeared.

With its tagline of "Fashions in Music" and theme song "You Go to My Head" the Ayres orchestra proved popular in hotels and other upscale venues. It played many novelty tunes and swing versions of classical melodies; among its successful recordings was "On Treasure Island."

Moonlight and Cactus (1944) * *Swingtime Johnny* (1944) * *Lady, Let's Dance!* (1944)

Mitchell, Bob *see* Bob Mitchell...

Mitchell, George *see* George Mitchell and His Swing Orchestra

Mitchell, Robert *see* Bob Mitchell...

Modern Folk Quartet

Chip Douglas; Jerry Yester; Cyrus Faryar; Henry Diltz

Formed in the early 1960s, the Quartet specialized in four-part harmony with a bit of jazz riffing thrown in. They achieved their first measure of success as part of the hootenanny scene in Los Angeles where all of them had previously played with other groups.

After cutting a couple of albums, the Modern Folk Quartet split up and two of the members joined the soon-to-be successful groups the Turtles and the Lovin' Spoonful. "The Ox Driver Song" probably had been the Quartet's most memorable recording.

Palm Springs Weekend (1963) * *The Big T.N.T. Show* (1966) [documentary] "This Could Be the Night"

Modernaires

Hal Dickinson (lead/2nd tenor); Chuck Goldstein (1st tenor); Bill Conway (baritone); Ralph Brewster (1st tenor); Paula Kelly; June Hutton

One of the most famous of the mixed-gender vocal groups was the Modernaires. Originally a male trio at their 1935 formation, they had been dubbed with such unusual names as Don Juan-Two and Three, the Three Weary Willies and the Wizards of Ozzie (when they sang with Ozzie Nelson's orchestra).

The Modernaires also performed with Fred Waring (with whom they became a quartet) and Paul Whiteman before signing on with Glenn Miller. It was with his band that they found their greatest fame and a female member, Paula Kelly, who made them a quintet. Their first hit was "Perfidia."

A large number of their hit records were made with the Miller orchestra including the classics "Tuxedo Junction," "A String of Pearls," "Jukebox Saturday Night," "Pennsylvania 6-5000," "Song of India" and numerous others. In 1941 alone they scored ten chart hits.

In the post–World War II era the Modernaires continued their hit-making with the haunting "To Each His Own" and the lilting "Zip-A-Dee-Doo-Dah." Although their final chart single came with 1956's "April in Paris" it was far from the end.

The Modernaires performed for decades and became an extremely influential ensemble both on their own and with other great singers. Their reputation remains largely undimmed even now, and they were inducted into the Vocal Group Hall of Fame in 1999.

Sun Valley Serenade (1941) * *Orchestra Wives* (1942) * *Home in San Antone* (1949) * *When You're Smiling* (1950) * *Walking My Baby Back Home* (1953) * *The Glenn Miller Story* (1954)

Modupe, Prince *see* Prince Modupe's Congo Choir

Molina, Carlos *see* Carlos Molina...

Mongo Santamaria and His Band

Mongo Santamaria (Ramon Santamaria, Havana, Cuba, 1917/22–2003)

The Afro-Cuban percussionist Mongo Santamaria composed the jazz standard "Afro Blue" and had a hit with "Watermelon Man" in 1963, a recording later inducted into the Grammy Hall of Fame. Another success came with "Cloud Nine," and he was still recording into the 1990s. Since coming to the U.S. in 1950, he had played with the bands of Perez Prado, Cal Tjader and Tito Puente.

Made In Paris (1966)

Monkees

Michael Nesmith (Robert Nesmith, Houston, Texas, 1942/43–) (guitar/lead singer); Micky Dolenz (Los Angeles, California, 1945–); David Jones (Manchester, England); Peter Tork (Peter Thorkelson, Washington, D.C., 1942–) (guitar, ukulele, banjo, piano, etc.)

The four Monkees came together as the result of a casting call for a 1966 television show that was supposed to emulate the style of The Beatles' wildly successful film *A Hard Day's Night*. Producers had advertised for "four insane boys, age 17–21."

Most of the quartet had had some show business background. Micky Dolenz was the son of character actor George Dolenz and already had done much television work, including his starring series *Circus Boy*. He had also sung with a group known as the Missing Links.

Nesmith, who sported a green knit cap throughout their television series and was dubbed "Wool Hat," was a songwriter and folk singer. Diminutive Davy Jones, who had been a jockey, was also a veteran of British theater and BBC radio. Peter Tork was a folk singer. They all used their own names as those of their goofy characters.

Initially the group was scorned as a bunch of non-musicians whose songs were written by others and whose instrumentation was largely played by professional musicians. Eventually they did coalesce as a fairly talented band among whose hits were "The Last Train to Clarksville," a million seller in 1966. The film *Head*, designed to capture their anarchic antics, was just a mishmash and failed.

Other recording successes were "Pleasant Valley Sunday," "Daydream Believer" and "I'm a Believer." Indeed there was a time that they outsold both the Beatles and Elvis Presley *combined*, but by 1969 the novelty had dissipated and they disbanded. During the 1980s and '90s there were several reunion concerts that drew large crowds.

Monroe

The Monkees at the height of their fame.

Head (1968) "Circle Sky," "As We Go Along," "Daddy's Song," "Do I Have to Do This All Over Again," "Porpoise Song" and "Can You Dig It?"

Monroe, Vaughn *see* **Vaughn Monroe and His Orchestra**

Monroe Singers
Big Boy (1930)

Montclairs
Phil Perry (Springfield, Missouri, 1952–); David Frye; George McLellan; Kevin Sanlin (1953–); Clifford Williams

Among the better-known recordings of the Montclairs, who came together about the mid–1960s, were "Dreaming Out of Season" and "Make Up for Lost Time." Their casting in a film followed their win in a Massachusetts Battle of the Bands contest. They split up in 1975.

Feelin' Good (1966) "Feelin' Good" and "Summertime"

Moonglows
Prentiss Barnes (Magnolia, Mississippi, 1925–2006) (bass); Harvey Fuqua (1929–) (baritone/piano); Bobby Lester (Bobby Dallas, 1930–1980) (lead); Billy Johnson (guitar); Alexander Graves (1930–) (tenor); Marvin Gaye (Washington, D.C., 1939–1984)

Among the Moonglows' hit recordings (after uber–DJ Alan Freed changed their name from the Crazy Sounds) were "Sincerely," "Most of All," "We Go Together" and their biggest, "See Saw" and "The Ten Commandments of Love." The rhythm-and-blues septet cut their first record in 1952 and are considered to be a seminal doo-wop group.

They actually recorded for two record companies. For one they used their own name, and for the other were called Bobby Lester and the Moonlighters. Their sound was rather unique for its time: the lead tenor would musically cry and plead, and they sometimes blew into the microphone.

Before disbanding about eight years later, the Moonglows (by now known as Harvey and the Moonglows) added young Marvin Gaye to their roster. He went on to a very distinguished if troubled fame as a solo. New versions of the group sprang up led by one or another of the original members. The first — and best — were inducted into the Rock and Roll Hall of Fame in 2000.

Rock, Rock, Rock (1956) "Over and Over Again" and "I Knew from the Start" * *Go Johnny Go* (1957) * *Mr. Rock 'n' Roll* (1957) "Barcelona Rock" and "Confess It to Your Heart"

Moore, Phil *see* **Phil Moore...**

Morales, Esy *see* **Esy Morales and His Rhumba Band**

Moran, Jackie *see* **Jackie Moran's Band**

Moreau Choir of Notre Dame
Knute Rockne—All American (1940)

Morella Brothers [unknown]
It Can't Last Forever (1937)

Morgan, Loumell *see* Loumell Morgan Trio

Morgan, Russ *see* Russ Morgan and His Orchestra

Morton Gould and His Orchestra
Morton Gould (Queens, New York, 1913–1996)

Pianist Morton Gould was a child music prodigy who supposedly published his first composition at the age of six and had a full scholarship to the predecessor of the Julliard School at age eight. He undertook his first professional concert tour at seventeen. During his illustrious career he composed numerous ballets, film scores and Broadway musicals.

Gould was particularly known for his ballet *Fall River Legend.* Among his other works were the "Latin American Symphonette" and "Boogie Woogie Etude." He was awarded a Grammy in 1966 and in his final decade his career was topped off by the Kennedy Center Honors in 1994 and a Pulitzer Prize for his piece "Stringmusic" the following year.
Delightfully Dangerous (1945)

Mosby, Curtis *see* Curtis Mosby and His Orchestra

Moscow Conservatory Orchestra
Song of Russia (1944)

Mother Maybelle and the Carter Family
Maybelle Addington Carter (Nickelsville, Virginia, 1909–1978) (guitar); Sara Dougherty Carter (Virginia, 1898/99–1979) (autoharp); Alvin "Doc" Carter (Maces Springs, Virginia, 1891–1960) (fiddle); June Carter (Maces Spring, Virginia, 1929–) (guitar/autoharp); Anita Carter; Helen Carter

All the original Carters performed double duty on instruments and vocals during their personal appearances, on recordings and on the radio. They were Maybelle, her brother-in-law Alvin and his wife Sara. The trio's maiden records were made in 1927 and they performed together until 1942 or '43. During that time it is estimated they released some 250 to 300 songs.

At that juncture the matriarch replenished the act with her three daughters Anita, Helen and June as Mother Maybelle and the Carter Sisters. Daughter June later married Johnny Cash for whom she wrote "Ring of Fire."

Dubbed the "Queen of Country Music," Mother Carter took her family to the pinnacle of country and gospel music fame upon which they still remain. This fame is at least partly based on Maybelle's virtuoso and much-imitated guitar style.

In subsequent years, many other singers covered or rewrote songs that the Carters had either composed or made famous, like "Foggy Mountain Top," "Can the Circle Be Unbroken," "Wayworn Traveller," "Gospel Ship" and "When This World's on Fire." They have been inducted into the Country Music Hall of Fame, the Grammy Hall of Fame and the International Bluegrass Hall of Honor.

The original Carter trio of Maybelle, Alvin and Sara received the signal honor of being portrayed on a U. S. postage stamp and generations of the family have now performed. Justifiably,

A very suave Morton Gould.

they are called the "First Family of Country Music."

The Road to Nashville (1966) * *Johnny Cash! The Man, His World, His Music* (1969) [documentary]

Moving Star Hall Singers

The Moving Star Hall Singers were a gospel group.

Festival (1967) [documentary]

Mulcays

Jim Mulcay (d. 1969); Mildred Mulcay

The Mulcays were dual harmonicists who had two successful records in the mid–1950s, "My Happiness" and "Alabamy Bound."

Night Club Girl (1945) * *Variety Girl* (1947)

Murad, Jerry *see* Jerry Murad and His Harmonicats

Murtah Sisters

The three Murtah Sisters were singers.

Freshman Year (1938)

Muse, Clarence *see* Clarence Muse Singers

Music City All Stars

Music City U.S.A. (1966)

Music Maids

Bobbie Canvin; Jeanne Darrell; Virginia Erwin; Patt Hyatt; Alice Ludes; Bonnie McRaven; Dottie Messmer; Alice Sizer; Denny Wilson

East Side of Heaven (1939) * *Broadway Melody of 1940* (1940) * *Ziegfeld Girl* (1941) * *Babes on Broadway* (1942) * *Panama Hattie* (1942) * *DuBarry Was a Lady* (1943) * *The Hit Parade of 1943* (1943) * *Hoosier Holiday* (1943) * *Broadway Rhythm* (1944) * *Jamboree* (1944) * *Meet Me in St. Louis* (1944) * *A WAVE, a WAC and a Marine* (1944)

Music Masters

Animal Crackers (1930)

Musical Cowhands *see* Nick Cochran's Musical Cowhands

Musical Tornados

Sundown on the Prairie (1939)

Mustard and Gravy

Mustard (Frank Rice, Wilson, North Carolina); Gravy (Ernest Stokes, Wilson, North Carolina)

The tastily-named duo of Mustard and Gravy joined up in 1933 and were a popular team for twenty years thereafter. Radio was their primary medium, and they also recorded such songs as "Be Bop Boogie," a departure from their usual country/hillbilly style of music. Western movie sidekick Smiley Burnette was primarily responsible for getting them into films.

West of Dodge City (1947) * *The Lone Hand Texan* (1947) * *Bandits of El Dorado* (1949) * *Feudin' Rhythm* (1949)

Nadon Singers

Sweet Surrender (1935)

Nappy La Mare and His Dixieland Band

Nappy La Mare (Hilton La Mare, New Orleans, Louisiana, 1907/10–1988)

Starting out as a teenager playing guitar and banjo, Nappy La Mare appeared with the bands of Ben Pollack and Bob Crosby from the mid–1930s to the early '40s. Among his own Dixieland ensembles were the Straw Hat Strutters and the Riverboat Dandies.

Holiday Rhythm (1950)

Nash, Len *see* Len Nash and His Country Boys

Nashville Teens

Arthur Sharpe (vocals); John Hawken (keyboard); Barry Jenkins (drums); Ray Phillips (bassist); John Allen (guitar); Pete Shannon (guitar)

The Nashville Teens were a British rock group, founded in 1962, who obviously wanted to pay homage to American music. Indeed they did play many American songs and backed up such artists as Jerry Lee Lewis and Bo Diddley on their European tours.

Like many another British rock group, the Teens spent some time in their early years in

Hamburg, Germany clubs. Their biggest hit proved to be "Tobacco Road" which was later covered by many other bands. Less successful recordings included "Google Eye" and "This Little Bird" prior to their split in 1973. They reformed seven years later.

Beach Ball (1965) * *Be My Guest* (1965) "My Baby Loves Nobody But Me" and "Whatcha Gonna Do" * *Gonks Go Beat* (1965) * *Pop Gear* (1965) [documentary] "Tobacco Road" and "Google Eye" * *Run with the Wind* (1966)

Nathaniel Shilkret Orchestra

Nathaniel Shilkret (New York, 1895/1899–1982)

As a young man Nathaniel Shilkret (known as Nat) was a clarinetist with several orchestras, including those of John Philip Sousa and Victor Herbert. Then as a popular bandleader himself in the late 1920s and early '30s, he was a presence on radio and in Hollywood. He had also been the director of so-called "light music" for the RCA Talking Machine Company (later RCA Victor).

In the film capital, Shilkret became a composer for Laurel and Hardy movies, adapting classic pieces for some of their film operettas like *The Bohemian Girl* and penning original music for one of their best, *Way Out West*. He also scored other films, including Fred Astaire–Ginger Rogers vehicles, and received an Academy award nomination for *Winterset* (1936).

Ultimately Nathaniel Shilkret went to the CBS network in the mid-'40s to become its music director. His most famous song was "The Lonesome Road" (recorded at least 100 times) and he also composed some classical pieces.

It Happened in Paris (1932)

Navy Blues Sextet(te)

Georgia Carroll (Blooming Grove, Texas, 1919–); Peggy Diggins (Margaret Diggins, New York, New York, 1921–1957); Marguerite Chapman (Chatham, New York, 1918–1999); Leslie Brooks (Lorraine Gettman, Lincoln, Nebraska, 1922–); Claire James (Minneapolis, Minnesota, 1920–1986); Kay Aldridge (Tallahassee, Florida, 1917–1995)

Warner Brothers studio formed the Navy Blues Sextet(te) as publicity for the 1941 movie *Navy Blues*. They did sing, but they mostly looked pretty as set dressing. Almost all the ladies, particularly Marguerite Chapman, went on to screen careers of various worthiness. Singer Georgia Carroll, was soon to be the vocalist, then wife, of bandleader Kay Kyser.

Navy Blues (1941) * *You're in the Army Now* (1941)

Neal, Meredith *see* Meredith Neal and the Boot Heel Boys

Nelson, Ozzie *see* Ozzie Nelson and His Orchestra

Nestor Amaral and Orchestra; Nestor Amaral and His Samba Band

Nestor Amaral (1913–1962)

The Brazilian composer-singer Nestor Amaral was the musical director for fellow country(wo)man Carmen Miranda, with whom he came from Sao Paulo to Hollywood about 1939. He also played several instruments.

Pan-Americana (1945) * *The Three Caballeros* (1945) * *Holiday for Lovers* (1959)

New Age

The Love-Ins (1967)

New Society Band

Joe Siracusa

After bandleader Spike Jones's death some remnants of his band formed the New Society Band in the 1960s. That it was very much in the style of Jones's City Slickers was apparent in its later name change to the Phunharmonic Orchestra.

Musical Mutiny (1970) "Up in the Air"

New Vaudeville Band

Geoff Stephens; Robert Kerr; Pete Cooper; Mike Wilsher; Stan Haywood; Neil Korner; Hugh Watts; Henry Harrison; Alan Klein

An artificially-created British band that existed solely to record a novelty tune, the New Vaudeville Band was composed of a random bunch of recording studio musicians. The song turned out to be the bouncy "Winchester Cathedral" which went on to become a major hit in 1966.

This unexpected success made touring a profitable venture for the hastily thrown-together ensemble that now became an actual group. For publicity the newest member Alan Klein was dubbed Tristan, the Seventh Earl of Cricklewood, presumably to impress American audiences.

Interestingly, Klein had not even sung on the hit recording that turned out to be their only major success. After a few more indifferently-received records the group that had been so hastily assembled now as quickly disbanded.

The Bliss of Mrs. Blossom (1968)

New York French Casino Band *see* **Dave Miller and His New York French Casino Band**

New York Philharmonic
Carnegie Hall (1947) * *Of Mice and Music* (1951)

New York Philharmonic Quintette *see also* **New York Philharmonic**
John Corigliano; Leonard Rose; Michael Rosenker; William Lincer; Nadia Reisenberg

Quintette member John Corigliano was the father of the current-day composer of the same name.

Carnegie Hall (1947)

New York Square Library
Robert Lewis

New York Square Library was a 1960s garage band. The fact that member Robert Lewis (who was also in the band Fly-By-Nytes) was the son of the director undoubtedly helped them get into the film.

Just for the Hell of It (1968)

New Yorkers *see* **Paul Vincent and His New Yorkers**

Newman, Frank *see* **Frank Newman and His Orchestra**

Nichols, Red *see* **Red Nichols and His Five Pennies**

Nick Cochran's Musical Cowhands
Crazy House (1943)

Night Jumpers *see* **Jimmy Bryant and the Night Jumpers**

Niles, Mac *see* **Mac Niles and the Calypsonians**

Nilo Menendez and His Rhumba Band
Nilo Menendez (Matanzas, Cuba, 1903?–1987)

In the U.S. from 1924, Menendez was the composer of the big band standard "Green Eyes" made famous by singer Helen O'Connell. He composed much music for Hollywood films and had his own band during the 1940s.

Music in Manhattan (1944)

Nilsson Sisters
Eileen Nilsson (1925–); Elsa Nilsson (1925–)

Prior to their entrée into films, the singing Nilsson twins did U.S.O. tours with Bob Hope and Spike Jones.

Hi Ya, Sailor (1943) * *Meet the People* (1944)[†]
* *Double Rhythm* (1946) * *Ladies Man* (1947)

[†]Their appearance in the film is not confirmed.

Nitty Gritty Dirt Band
Jeff Hanna (multi-instruments); Chris Darrow (fiddle); John McEuen (banjo); Ralph Burr (guitar/clarinet); Les Thomson (guitar/mandolin); Jackson Browne; Jimmie Fadden (multi-instruments); Bruce Kunkel (guitar/kazoo)

The Nitty Gritty Dirt Band began life in 1966 as a so-called country/folk jug band and had a hit with "Mr. Bojangles" and the album "Will the Circle Be Unbroken," recorded with several country artists. Their first recording to have made a splash was "Buy for Me the Rain."

As a Long Beach, California, high school band they had called themselves the Illegitimate Jug Band. Ultimately they retreated from the jug band image and were known just as the Dirt Band in the 1980s, their greatest period of popularity. In 1992 at an awards ceremony ex–President George H.W. Bush, in a howler of a malapropism, referred to them as the Nitty Ditty Nitty Gritty Great Bird.

For Singles Only (1968) * *Paint Your Wagon* (1969) "Hand Me Down That Can of Beans"

Nitwits [unknown]
Juke Box Rhythm (1959)

Noble, Leighton *see* **Leighton Noble and His Orchestra**

Noble, Ray *see* **Ray Noble and His Band**

Noble Sissle and His Orchestra

Noble Sissle (Indianapolis, Indiana, 1889–1975)

Known primarily for his long collaboration with pianist Eubie Blake, Noble Sissle had a worthy career on his own as well. As a teenager he toured with a gospel quartet and during World War I was a drum major in the famous overseas band of James Reese Europe.

Sissle's teaming with Blake came in 1915. Together they wrote songs and were pioneers in bringing African-American showmanship to mainstream Broadway. This they did with the musical *Shuffle Along*, a sensation in 1921 with its serious romance between an African-American man and woman. The songs included "I'm Just Wild About Harry."

"Harry" became the theme song of Sissle's orchestra, along with "Hello, Sweetheart, Hello." Before the team of Blake and Sissle broke up they had appeared in an early experimental Lee de Forest sound short in 1923, so were truly pioneers in musical talking pictures as well.

During his career Noble Sissle fronted many bands in the 1920s and '30s, Lena Horne being one of his vocalists. He performed in previously white-only clubs and hotels, owned his own nightclub, was a disc jockey, and ran a publishing company. A man of many parts indeed, he had dubbed himself the "colored Rudy Vallee."

Mistaken Identity (1941); re-released as *Murder with Music* (1948)

Nomads

The Nomads performed French-Canadian songs.

Nikki, Wild Dog of the North (1961)

Noone, Jimmie *see* Jimmie Noone and His Band

Nooney Rickett Four

Nooney Rickett (Everett Rickett); Kent Dunbar; Tommy Funk; Tommy Poole

The Nooney Rickett Four was a Los Angeles–based band, active in the mid–1960s, which made appearances on the television show *Shindig*.

Pajama Party (1964) "Beach Ball" * *Winter-a-Go-Go* (1965) "Ski City" and "Do the Ski (with Me)"

Nora Lou Martin and the Pals of the Golden West *see* Pals of the Golden West

Norman, Lee *see* Lee Norman...

Northwesterners

J. Brier; Buck Rasch; Merle Scobee; Ray Scobee; Charles Davis

Starlight Over Texas (1938) * *Down the Wyoming Trail* (1939)

Norvo, Red *see* Red Norvo Trio

Notables; Notables Quartet; Four Singing Notables

Law and Order (1940) * *West of Carson City* (1940) * *Arizona Cyclone* (1941) * *Babes on Broadway* (1942) * *Down Missouri Way* (1946)

Novelites [unknown]

Art Terry; Frankie Carr (1925–1986); Joe Mayer

I Surrender Dear (1948) * *The Bellboy* (1960)

Novelle Brothers [unknown]

You're a Sweetheart (1937)

Oak Ridge Boys

Wally Fowler; Lon Freeman; Curly Kinsey; Johnny New

The Oak Ridge Boys, originally known as the Country Cut-Ups and the Oak Ridge Quartet, have ten gold records to their credit, including "Elvira," "Bobbie Sue," "Fancy Free" and "Gonna Take a Lot of River." They also have added a Grammy Award to their accomplishments.

Formed in 1945, the Boys were originally a gospel group that gradually evolved into country/western music in the 1970s and performed with the likes of Paul Simon and Johnny Cash. With numerous personnel changes over the years the Boys have continued to perform well into the 21st Century.

Sing a Song, for Heaven's Sake (1966) [documentary]

O'Conner Family [unknown]

It Can't Last Forever (1937)

O'Dell, Doye *see* Doye O'Dell and the Radio Rangers

O'Donnell and Blair [unknown]
Charles O'Donnell; Jack Blair
   The team of O'Donnell and Blair appeared on the Broadway stage and in musical shorts.
   Always Leave Them Laughing (1949)

Offbeets
David Duff (bassist/guitar); Tommy Wynn (drums); Dennis Messimer (guitar); Tommy Talton (guitar)
   Originally named the Nonchalants, the Offbeets was an Orlando, Florida garage band. In 1966 they merged with the Trademarks to become We the People.
   Daytona Beach Weekend (1965) "Double Trouble" "She Lied" and "Hey Little Girl"

Ohman, Phil *see* Phil Ohman and His Orchestra

Oklahoma Outlaws *see* Al Clauser and His Oklahoma Outlaws

Oklahoma Rangers
The Oklahoma Rangers were a group of western musicians.
   Ambush Valley (1936)

Oklahoma Wranglers *see* Willis Brothers

Olenn, Johnny *see* Johnny Olenn and His Group

Olsen, George *see* George Olsen and His Orchestra

Original California Collegians *see* California Collegians

Original New Orleans Ragtime Band
New Orleans (1947)

Orphan Egg
There was only one album released by the California Bay Area band Orphan Egg. Formed in San Jose in 1967, the psychedelic rock group did not long exist but had a very listenable sound produced by, among other instruments, the harpsichord and recorder.
   Born Wild (1968) "In Big Letters" * *The Angry Breed* (1969)

Orrin Tucker's Orchestra
Orrin Tucker (St. Louis, Missouri, 1911–)
   Handsome Orrin Tucker, with his trademark pompadour, played the saxophone. His first band was formed in college and mainly appeared on the Midwest and Southern theater circuits. He sometimes sang with the band as well.
   Tucker differentiated his group from countless others by gimmicks such as flashing music notes to designate different sections of the orchestra. But it was no gimmickry that finally brought the band success, it was his then-vocalist the winsome Wee Bonnie Baker (nee Evelyn Nelson).
   Her piping-voiced version of "Oh, Johnny" in 1939 was a smash hit and the band rode along on that fame, however temporarily. With its popular theme song "Drifting and Dreaming," Orrin Tucker's Orchestra went on for a few more years. The leader himself remained active in one musical endeavor or another until the 1990s.
   You're the One (1941) * *Tender Is the Night* (1962)

Osborne, Will *see* Will Osborne and His Orchestra

Osborne Brothers
Bobby Osborne (Robert Osborne, Hyden, Kentucky, 1931–) (tenor/ mandolin); Sonny Osborne (Roland Osborne, Hyden, Kentucky, 1937–) (banjo); Benny Birchfield (guitar)
   Considered one of the best progressive bluegrass groups to arise in the 1950s, the Osborne Brothers distinguished themselves from other such bands by their innovative use of instrumentation and amplification (i.e., electrifying their instruments). Younger brother Sonny started his professional life at the age of thirteen, playing with bluegrass pioneer Bill Monroe before joining his older brother on radio programs like the *Grand Ole Opry*.
   The Osbornes formed a band and scored their first hit recording with 1956's "Once More."

That brought them to a wider audience and they began touring college campuses, further exposing bluegrass to a new demographic. They have been honored by the adoption of two of their songs as official state songs: "Rocky Top" for Tennessee and "Kentucky" for that state.

Other Osborne hits, many featuring their high tenor voices, over the years have included "Midnight Flyer," "Take Me Home, Country Roads," "Muddy Bottom" and "Tennessee Hounddog." In the 1990s they were inducted into the International Bluegrass Music Hall of Fame and continued to tour until Sonny retired in 2005.

Music City U.S.A. (1966) [documentary] * *The Road to Nashville* (1966) * *Festival* (1967) [documentary]

Our Lady of the Angels Choir
The Firefly (1937)

Outcasts [unknown]
The Shocking Miss Pilgrim (1947)

Owens, Harry *see* Harry Owens...

Ox Road Co-eds [unknown]
College Humor (1933)

Oxford Boys
When they were not singing the forte of the Oxford Boys was imitating musical instruments.

DuBarry Was a Lady (1943)

Ozie Waters and His Colorado Rangers
Ozie Waters (Vernon Waters, Missouri, 1903–1978)

From the mid–1940s Ozie Waters and the Colorado Rangers lent their talents to "B" westerns with such stars as William (Hopalong Cassidy) Boyd and Charles Starrett, two non-singing cowboy actors. Waters had begun his career with a Hawaii radio show.

Landrush (1946) * *Terror Trail* (1946) * *Prairie Riders* (1947) * *Phantom Valley* (1948) * *Outcast of Black Mesa* (1950) * *Streets of Ghost Town* (1950)

Ozzie Nelson and His Orchestra
Ozzie Nelson (Oswald Nelson, Jersey City, New Jersey, 1906–1975)

However popular Ozzie Nelson had been as a fresh-faced bandleader in the 1930s, it was eclipsed several years later by his overwhelming success as the idealized dad in *The Adventures of Ozzie and Harriet*. The show began on radio and later settled in for a long run on television.

The "Harriet" was Harriet Hilliard (nee Peggy Lou Snyder) whom he hired as a vocalist and married in 1935. Their two sons David and Eric (better known as Ricky or Rick) were also a part of their hit television show and starred with them in the 1951 film *Here Come the Nelsons*. Rick Nelson was to become a talented pop icon in his own right.

Before such undreamt of fame Ozzie Nelson had played the banjo and ukulele, and vocalized through his nose a la Rudy Vallee, in small groups like the Syncopation Four. His theme song "Loyal Sons of Rutgers" paid homage to his palmy college days.

Nelson had his own radio show from 1930 and the band enjoyed bookings in some of the top venues in the country. A gig at the Glen Island Casino especially brought him a measure of prominence. He gave up the band in 1944, the year his to-be famous show began on radio.

Always a shrewd businessman, Nelson had conceived the idea of portraying a family roughly based on his own (albeit without the single-minded ambition of the real-life family). It is perhaps well he did so because the conventional music his band produced would probably not have enabled it to survive much longer.

Sweetheart of the Campus (1941) * *Strictly in the Groove* (1942) * *The Big Street* (1942) * *Honeymoon Lodge* (1943) * *Hi, Good Lookin'!* (1944) * *Take It Big* (1944)

Pacemakers *see also* Gerry and the Pacemakers
The Pacemakers were western musicians and singers.

Ride, Tenderfoot, Ride (1940)

Pacheco, Jose *see* Jose Pacheco and His Continental Orchestra

Pacific Palisades High School Madrigals
Pacific Palisades High School is in an upscale part of Los Angeles adjacent to the Pacific Ocean.

The Trouble with Girls (1969)

Padilla Sisters [unknown]
Pan-Americana (1945)

Page Cavanaugh Trio
Page Cavanaugh (Walter Cavanaugh, Cherokee, Kansas, 1922–); Al Viola (guitar); Lloyd Pratt; Robert Morgan (guitar); Charles Parnell (bassist); Alvin Stoller (drums)

Before they became the Page Cavanaugh Trio the three singers were known as the Three Sergeants, courtesy of the U.S. Army during World War II. They modeled their easy-listening vocal style on the (Nat) King Cole Trio and began making records of what they dubbed "cocktail-type jazz" in the late 1940s.

Besides their own recordings, which included "The Three Bears" and "All of Me," the Trio backed many a famous singer the likes of Frank Sinatra and Mel Tormé. They appeared much on radio and by the early '50s were a big draw in nightclubs as well.

Page Cavanaugh gradually expanded the size of his ensemble throughout the 1960s, at times leading a septet, and they released many albums that experimented with several musical forms. Although never having a breakout hit they remained a top favorite with fans.

The Big City (1948) * *A Song Is Born* (1948) * *Romance on the High Seas* (1948) * *Lullaby of Broadway* (1951) * *Frankenstein's Daughter* (1958)

Paige, Raymond *see* Raymond Paige and His Orchestra

Pair Extraordinaire
Carl Craig (vocals); Marcus Hemphill (bassist)

The singing Pair Extraordinaire was active for only two or three years during the mid–1960s and made four albums during that time. They generally performed as a duo, while occasionally adding a drummer.

C'mon, Let's Live a Little (1966)

Palan Brothers Cuban Orchestra *see* Ernesto Lecuona and the Palan Brothers Cuban Orchestra

Palmer, Fred *see* Fred Palmer's Orchestra

Pals of the Golden West
The Pals of the Golden West were singers.

Rovin' Tumbleweeds (1939) * *Stage to Chino* (1940) * *Rancho Grande* (1940) * *The Silver Bullet* (1942) * *The Boss of Hangtown Mesa* (1942) * *Laugh Your Blues Away* (1942)

Pancho and Dolores
Pancho (Kenny Hagood, Strait, Michigan, 1926–1989); Dolores (Dolores Brown)

A ballad singer in the Billy Eckstine mode and also a virtuoso of "scat" singing, Kenny Hagood was the "Pancho" of Pancho and Dolores. He sang with the orchestras of Benny Carter and Dizzy Gillespie starting in the 1940s; among his recordings was "All the Things You Are."

Jivin' in Be-Bop (1947)

Paramount Jazz Band *see* Acker Bilk and His Paramount Jazz Band

Paris Sisters
Albeth Paris (San Francisco, California); Priscilla Paris (San Francisco, California, 1945–2005) (lead vocals); Sherell Paris (San Francisco, California)

Although it sounds like part of a movie plot, the Paris Sisters were supposedly discovered in the audience of an Andrews Sisters performance. They were called up on stage, sang the Andrews' own hit "Rum and Coca Cola," and were signed by a record executive who happened to be in attendance!

The Sisters began recording in the mid–1950s and worked in Las Vegas lounges with the likes of Frank Sinatra and Elvis Presley, even though they were all under age and had to be disguised. In 1961 they scored their first minor hit with "Be My Boy" but it was their follow-up "I Love How You Love Me" that was the break-out success.

Part of the Phil Spector "stable," and one of the first of his successful girl groups, the Parises never again matched the heights reached by that tune. But they continued to record singles and albums, and toured with rock groups until disbanding in the early 1970s. Following this Priscilla Paris launched a solo career.

It's Trad, Dad! (1962)

Parris, Fred *see* Fred Parris and His Satins

Pastor, Tony see Tony Pastor and His Orchestra

Pat and Lolly Vegas

Pat Vegas (Pat Vasquez, Fresno, California); Lolly Vegas (Lolly Vasquez, Fresno, California)

The Vegas brothers, supposedly of Yaqui Indian heritage, founded the band Redbone in the late 1960s, one of the first Native American groups to find commercial success. At one time they also had a group called the Crazy Cajun Cakewalk Band. Among their hits was "Come and Get Your Love." They also wrote songs for many other performers.

The Nasty Rabbit (1964) "The Robot Walk" * *It's a Bikini World* (1967) "Walk on (Right Out of My Life") and "Long Gone"

Paul, Les see Les Paul Trio

Paul Butterfield Blues Band

Paul Butterfield (Chicago, Illinois, 1942–1987) (flute/harmonica); Elvin Bishop (guitar); Jerome Arnold (bassist); Sam Lay (drums); Michael Bloomfield (guitar); Mark Naftalin (keyboard)

A leading exponent of the so-called electric blues style, harmonica virtuoso Paul Butterfield formed a biracial ensemble in the mid–1960s. Their first and subsequent albums were critically praised and proved influential at music festivals, such as Newport, and with icons like Bob Dylan. Butterfield appeared solo in *You Are What You Eat* prior to the group's disbanding in 1970.

Festival (1967) [documentary] "Maggie's Farm" and "I Was Born in Chicago"

Paul Hargett and the Bikini Sweethearts

Bad Girls for the Boys (1966)

Paul Lavert and His Swinging Cavemen

50,000 B.C. (Before Clothing) (1963)

Paul Specht and His Orchestra

Paul Specht (Sinking Springs, Pennsylvania, 1895–1954)

One of the pioneering bandleaders, Paul Specht had his own six-piece ensemble as early as 1916 in the Midwest. He enlarged it a few years later and it became one of the most popular bands in the Chicago of the early 1920s. It was supposedly the first band to be heard on the radio and played mostly in hotels and ballrooms.

The orchestra's theme songs were "Evening Star" and "Sweetheart Time." Specht, who led his band until the early 1930s, was a songwriter too, his most famous being "Moonlight on the Ganges." Among the sidemen who went on to found their own orchestras were Artie Shaw, Russ Morgan and Charlie Spivak.

Love at First Sight (1930)

Paul Vincent and His New Yorkers

Enlighten Thy Daughter (1934)

Paul Whiteman and His Band with Ramona; Paul Whiteman and His Orchestra

Paul Whiteman (Denver, Colorado, 1890–1967)

Portly Paul Whiteman was the (self?)-crowned "King of Jazz" in the 1920s; it was, after all, the Jazz Age. But in actuality his had not been primarily a jazz orchestra and there were certainly far greater jazz musicians than he. Nevertheless his band did have some sidemen who were very distinguished in that musical style.

Fully deserving or not, Whiteman was considered one of the top bandleaders of his day and occupies an honored place even today. He had been trained as a classical violinist and played with the San Francisco Symphony, but after he conducted a Navy band during World War I he found his true vocation.

After his 1918 discharge he formed a dance band and soon had million-seller hits with "Japanese Sandman" and "Whispering." Throughout his tenure he was supported by sidemen including Bix Beiderbecke, the Dorsey brothers, Henry Busse, Jack Teagarden and Matty Malneck.

The landmark achievement for which Paul Whiteman is known today is his famous 1924 Aeolian Hall concert (dubbed "An Experiment in Modern Music") in which he debuted George Gershwin's "Rhapsody in Blue," later adopted as his theme song. He was also responsible for introducing Bing Crosby to a wider public as a member of his trio the Rhythm Boys.

Ultimately his group did become a more distinguished jazz ensemble. Whiteman's sobriquet was recognized in his 1930 starring movie *King of Jazz* but his appeal was already beginning to wane and by the middle of that decade he had been overshadowed by the giants of the swing era. In later years he was musical director for the American Broadcasting Company and he did occasionally revive his orchestra. He also appeared as "himself" in biographical films like *Rhapsody in Blue* and *The Fabulous Dorseys*.

King of Jazz (1930) * *Thanks a Million* (1935) * *Strike Up the Band* (1940) * *Atlantic City* (1944)

Pebbles
Hell's Playground (1967)

Pee Wee King and His Golden West Cowboys

Pee Wee King (Julius Kuczynski, Milwaukee or Abrams, Wisconsin, 1914–2000)

Best-known as the composer of the multi-million selling evergreen "Tennessee Waltz" (later the state song of Tennessee), accordionist Pee Wee King also penned "You Belong to Me," "Slow Poke," "The Arkansas Traveler" and "Bonaparte's Retreat." His band the Golden West Cowboys, formed in the mid–1930s, played an amalgam of country/western music, polkas and even waltzes.

Many of the Cowboys had been members of Gene Autry's band before the oater star went to Hollywood. They were a staple on the *Grand Ole Opry* program, and unusually for a country band incorporated drums, electric guitars and trumpets.

They also backed up such country artists as Minnie Pearl, Ernest Tubb and Cowboy Copas, who at one time had been Pee Wee King's vocalist. For many years beginning in the late 1940s the ensemble had its own television show before disbanding in 1959. King was elected to the Country Music Hall Of Fame in 1974.

Flame of the West (1945) * *Riding the Outlaw Trail* (1951) * *The Rough, Tough West* (1952)

Pennsylvanians *see* Fred Waring and His Pennsylvanians

Penny, Hank *see* Hank Penny and His Plantation Boys

Pepe Guizar and the Flores Brothers *see* Flores Brothers

Peppermint Loungers [unknown]
Hey, Let's Twist! (1961)

Perez Prado and His Orchestra

Perez Prado (Damaso Perez Prado, Mantanzas, Cuba, 1916–1989)

The popularizer of a major dance craze of the 1950s, diminutive Perez Prado was ultimately dubbed the "Mambo King." A pianist and organist, he became a master of the Afro-Cuban rhythm which is the basis of the mambo. He had found his first successes in Mexico where he formed a band and became a music arranger and an actor in Mexican cinema. Such was his popularity there that he actually became known as the "Glenn Miller of Mexico." A well-known trademark of his was a loud grunt or "ugh" sound that was heard during pauses in the music.

Prado's first tour of the United States came in 1951. Four years later he scored a sensational success with the lively cha cha recording "Cherry Pink and Apple Blossom White" that reached the top of the pop charts and remained there for half a year. A second chart topper "Patricia" came in 1958. He was top-billed in his one American film but by the middle of the following decade

Pee Wee King.

his popularity began to decline along with much of the mania for Latin-themed music.

Cha-Cha-Cha-Boom (1956)

Pete Daily and His Chicagoans

Pete Daily (Portland, Indiana, 1911–1986)

Before establishing the Chicagoans in the post–World War II era jazz cornetist Pete Daily played with several bands in the Chicago area and with Ozzie Nelson in California. He also tootled on the tuba. Thereafter he concentrated on Dixieland music with the Chicagoans, and from 1952 with smaller-size groups, remaining active until the 1970s.

Daily, who helped to revive the popularity of jazz in the late 1940s with his big selling record of "South," supposedly was the model for Jack Webb's character in *Pete Kelly's Blues*. He was ultimately dubbed the "Emperor of Jazz." Ironically, his theme song was "I Want to Linger"— ironic because he spent the last seven years of his life paralyzed and speechless from a stroke.

Yes Sir, Mr. Bones (1951)

Peter and Gordon

Peter Asher (London, England, 1944–); Gordon Waller (Braemar, Scotland, 1945–)

In 1964 the British pop duo of Peter and Gordon had a big record hit in both the U.K. and the U.S. with the poignant "A World Without Love." They recorded several songs written by Beatle Paul McCartney (some co-composed with John Lennon) and had further success with "True Love Waits" and "I Go to Pieces."

They actually had more hits in the American market than they did at home. Their last recording success came in 1967 and they disbanded about a year later. In 2005 they reunited on stage for the first time in thirty years.

Pop Gear (1965) [documentary] "A World Without Love" * *Disk-O-Tek Holiday* (1966) "Leave Me Alone" and "Soft As the Dawn"

Peter Meremblum California Junior Symphony Orchestra; Peter Meremblum Junior Orchestra

Peter Meremblum (Batum, Georgia (later U.S.S.R.), 1890–1966)

In 1936 immigrant music teacher Peter Meremblum gathered some young student musicians together to form a string ensemble that a short time later metamorphosed into a full symphony orchestra. It was founded as a venue to train young people for musical careers and is still going strong into the 21st Century.

They Shall Have Music (1939) * *Song of Russia* (1944) * *Mexicana* (1945)

Peter, Paul and Mary

Peter Yarrow (New York, New York, 1937–); Noel Paul Stookey (Baltimore, Maryland, 1937–); Mary Travers (Louisville, Kentucky, 1936/37–)

Their teaming in 1961 was surely one of the most fortuitous in folk music history. Although they were formed by a manager who wanted to create a successful (read: profitable) folk music group, Peter, Paul and Mary became the musical social conscience of the anti–Vietnam War protest movement in America.

None of them were tyros in music; Mary Travers, for instance, had been a member of the Song Swappers folk ensemble. The trio's recordings and live appearances in places like Carnegie Hall, the Hollywood Bowl and, memorably, in front of the Lincoln Memorial during Martin Luther King's March on Washington, stirred the nation.

They had started performing in small clubs and their fame grew rapidly, helped along by their first Top Ten hit the anthem-like "If I Had a Hammer." This was followed by "Lemon Tree," "Blowin' in the Wind," "Don't Think Twice (It's All Right)," the much-beloved "Puff the Magic Dragon," and one of their last hits "Leaving on a Jet Plane." Many of their albums turned platinum and gold; at one time three occupied Billboard's top six slots at the same time.

Peter, Paul and Mary disbanded in 1970 but each stayed active in music; Mary Travers alone released five albums in the 1970s. However, they were too iconic and beloved for the public to allow them to stay separated forever. Since their 1960s heyday they have reunited several times for concerts and for multitudes remain *the* voice of social justice. They were inducted into the Vocal Hall of Fame in 1999.

Festival (1967) [documentary] "If I Had a Hammer," Blowin' in the Wind" and several other songs

Peters Brothers

Peter Peters (Peter Piotrowski, Jr., Milwaukee, Wisconsin); Ronald Peters (Ronald Piotrowski, Milwaukee, Wisconsin)

Peter Peters honed his vocal and dancing talent in amateur shows, winning first prize in a Major Bowes competition. In 1939 he worked at the New York World's Fair. Joining forces with his brother Ronnie they headed off to Hollywood and fairly quickly got singing gigs at theaters and top nightspots like the Cocoanut Grove.

Sing Another Chorus (1941) * *Babes on Broadway* (1942)†

†Their appearance in this film has not been confirmed.

Peters Sisters

The Peters Sisters were vocalists.

With Love and Kisses (1936) * *Ali Baba Goes to Town* (1937) * *Love and Hisses* (1937) * *Happy Landings* (1938)† * *Hi De Ho* (1947)

†Their appearance in this film has not been confirmed.

Pharaohs *see* Sam the Sham and the Pharaohs

Phelps Brothers

Norman Phelps (Virginia, d. 1981) (bass) (bassist/guitar); Willie Phelps (Virginia, 1914–2004) (baritone) (guitar/drums/washboard); Earl Phelps (Virginia, d. 1971) (tenor) (fiddle/mandolin)

The Phelps boys performed in clubs and on the radio before heading to New York in 1936 where they won a contest on a Fred Allen radio program. This garnered them a recording deal as well as more radio and rodeo appearances.

Upon joining Ray Whitley as part of his outfit the Bar-Six Cowboys it was off to Hollywood to make musical shorts and "B" westerns. They were "the boys" for oater stars like Tex Ritter and George O'Brien before striking off on their own again in 1940 and returning to their home state to record western and gospel music.

Many years of club dates and radio again ensued as well as television, on which they were known as Norman Phelps and the Virginia Rounders. They were also songwriters; Norman is believed to have co-written "Back in the Saddle Again" for which Ray Whitley is usually given solo credit.

Hittin' the Trail (1937) * *Border G-Man* (1938) * *The Painted Desert* (1938) * *The Renegade Ranger* (1938) * *Where the West Begins* (1938) * *Trouble in Sundown* (1939)

Phil Harris and His Orchestra

Phil Harris (Wonga Harris, Linton, Indiana, 1904–1995)

Multi-talented Phil Harris was a bandleader, songwriter, singer and actor/comedian whose distinctive extroverted personality set him apart from most of his bland orchestra leader contemporaries. He was an integral part of Jack Benny's troupe and their banter (usually beginning with his tagline "Hiya, Jackson!") was a highlight of that comedian's hugely successful radio and television shows.

Adopting a Southern-style hip persona, one of Harris's theme songs "That's What I Like About the South" perfectly encapsulated his style. (The other theme song was "Rose Room.") His marriage to movie singer Alice Faye, and their subsequent 1940s radio show purporting to show their "real life" domestic situation, added to his popularity.

Phil Harris had begun his career as a drummer, in the 1920s led a band jointly with one Carol Lofner (aka Laughner), and for many years in the 1930s his was the house band at the Cocoanut Grove nightclub. He began appearing in acting roles without his band, generally in Jack Benny movies like *Man About Town* and *Buck Benny Rides Again*.

In the latter years of his career Phil Harris's

Phil Harris flashes his million dollar smile (1940s).

distinctive voice was much heard in animated features like *The Jungle Book* and *Robin Hood* well into his late eighties. Among his hit records was the novelty tune "The Thing."
Turn Off the Moon (1937)

Phil Moore and His Orchestra; Phil Moore Four

Phil Moore (Portland, Oregon, 1918–1987)

Pianist Phil Moore played with dance bands and then became a music arranger for MGM before founding his own short-lived ensembles. Among his albums were "Fantasy for Girls and Orchestra" and "Moon Mist Blues." He perhaps had more success backing up singers like Frank Sinatra and Lena Horne.

Gang Smashers (1939) * *Stars on Parade* (1946) * *The Joint Is Jumpin'* (1949?)

Phil Ohman and His Orchestra

Phil Ohman (Philmore Ohman, New Britain, Connecticut, 1896–1969)

Better known as half of the piano duo of Ohman and Arden, Phil Ohman was a popular entertainer in the 1920s and '30s. Before teaming with Victor Arden (whom he fittingly met when they worked for a piano roll manufacturer), he was an arranger and composer for classical singers and a pianist with Paul Whiteman's orchestra.

Ohman and Arden (nee John Fulks) were vaudeville headliners as well as pit conductors for several George Gershwin shows on Broadway. They also were heard on the radio and formed their own jointly-led big band until going their separate ways in 1934.

As a busy solo artist Phil Ohman went on to found his own big band, playing at Hollywood's famous Trocadero nightclub, and worked at the movie studios scoring and composing music for films. His best-known song was "Lost" with Johnny Mercer.

Sweethearts of the U.S.A. (1944)

Phil Spitalny and His Hour of Charm All Girl Orchestra, Featuring Evelyn and Her Magic Violin

Phil Spitalny (Odessa, Russia, 1890–1970)

Many orchestras had a gimmick, Phil Spitalny's had two: Evelyn's "magic" violin (she was also his wife) and the fact that he was a man leading an all-girl orchestra. For the most part the gimmick caught the public's attention, but the orchestra, with its theme song of "My Isle of Golden Dreams," was not considered to be particularly distinguished. He had previously led a conventional male radio and dance band orchestra.

When Johnny Comes Marching Home (1943) * *Here Come the Coeds* (1945)

Philadelphia Orchestra

In their single on-camera appearance, the Philadelphia Orchestra was conducted by Leopold Stokowski.

Fantasia (1940)

Philharmonic Orchestra of Los Angeles

The Star Maker (1939)

Philharmonic Symphony Orchestra [of New York] *see* New York Philharmonic

Philharmonic Trio

Hollywood Barn Dance (1947) * *Rose of Santa Rosa* (1947) * *Two Guys from Texas* (1948)

Philip Maxwell's Choristers

The Choristers was a boy's choir.

Kind Lady (1935) "Silent Night"

Pickard Family

Obed Pickard (1874–1954) (banjo/guitar)

The patriarch of the Pickard Family of musicians, Obed Pickard was one of the first performers on the *Grand Ole Opry* program in 1926. A while later some family members joined him on various radio shows around the country, thence to Hollywood and later to television. Obed, familiarly known as "Dad" Pickard, appeared on his own in a few character roles in films including *Sea Of Grass*, *Riders of the Dawn* and *Frontier Vengeance*.

Rawhide Rangers (1941)

Pickens Sisters

Helen Pickens (Macon, Georgia, 1910–), Jane (aka Georgia) Pickens, Macon, Georgia, 1909?–

1992); Patti Pickens (Macon, Georgia, 1914–1995)

The melodious Pickens Sisters followed the three Brox Sisters as one of the premier singing sister acts and were contemporaries of the close-harmony Boswell Sisters. They first performed professionally in 1932 and initially were billed as the "Three Little Maids from Dixie."

They conquered nightclubs, radio and theater before the marriages of Patti and Helen ended the act after a few years and Jane soldiered on as a solo act. She found success on Broadway in the *Ziegfeld Follies*, and especially in the musical version of *The Little Foxes*, called *Regina*, in which she played the title character to considerable acclaim. She also had her own radio and television shows.

Sitting Pretty (1933)

Pickett Sisters

One of the Pickett Sisters' popular records was the title song from their one film *Take Me to Town*.

Take Me to Town (1953)

Pied Pipers

Jo Stafford; John Huddleston; Billy Wilson; Chuck Lowry; Clark Yocum; June Hutton (Chicago, Illinois, 1920–1973); Hal Hopper (Oklahoma, 1912–1970); Bud Hervey; George Tait; Woody Newbury; Dick Whittinghill (Montana, 1913–2001); Sue Allen; Virginia Marcy

The acclaimed quartet the Pied Pipers was once an octet, seven men and one lone lady, the result of the merger in 1938 between the Four Rhythm Kings, the Three Esquires and the soon-to-be-famous Jo Stafford. The octet was a hit on Los Angeles radio with its unusual vocal arrangements during which members could sing in harmony with one another or "against" each other. However, when they got to New York they were unceremoniously fired after one show.

They attracted Tommy Dorsey's attention but he would only employ them as a quartet. It was thus that the foursome consisting of Jo Stafford, John Huddleston, Chuck Lowry and Billy Wilson was hired for his orchestra in 1939. One of the young singers they backed (on "I'll Never Smile Again") was band vocalist Frank Sinatra, a former member of the Hoboken Four.

After a run-in with the notably volatile Dorsey, the group decamped in 1942 to make recordings with songwriter/singer Johnny Mercer. Further hits included "The One I Love Belongs to Somebody Else," "Stardust," "There Are Such Things" and "Let's Get Away from It All."

Jo Stafford began her stellar solo career in 1944 and the Pipers soldiered on with replacement June Hutton and scored several hit records, the first being "Dream," a million seller. Among the others were "Dolores," "My Happiness," "Candy" and "Blues in the Night."

Down Beat Magazine's annual poll selected the Pipers as the top vocal group for the years 1944 to '49. Although the 1950s saw the group's popularity in a decline, the name has been carried on by new members to the present day.

Honolulu (1939) * *Las Vegas Nights* (1941) * *Ship Ahoy* (1942) * *DuBarry Was a Lady* (1943) * *Gals, Incorporated* (1943) * *I'm from Arkansas* (1944) * *Sweet and Low-Down* (1944) * *Jam Session* (1944) * *Rhythm Round-Up* (1945) * *Make Mine Music* (voices only) (1946) * *Luxury Liner* (1948) * *Hoedown* (1950)

Pinafores

The Pinafores was a vocal trio that accompanied Gene Autry on some of his recordings and appeared in one of his films.

Riders of the Whistling Pines (1949)

Pink Floyd

Syd Barrett (Roger Barrett, Cambridge, England, 1946–2006) (lead guitar); Roger Waters (1944–) (bass guitar); Nick Mason (1945–) (drums); Richard Wright (1943–2008) (keyboard); David Gilmour (1944–) (lead guitar); Bob Klose (lead guitar)

The intriguing name of Pink Floyd is actually a combination of the first names of two Southern blues guitarists of the early twentieth century, Pink Anderson and Floyd Council. The band (originally called Tea Set) proved to be one of the most influential psychedelic groups; at least one of their albums, "The Dark Side of the Moon," remained on the pop charts for an astounding eight years running. To date, total album sales are said to exceed some 200 million copies.

Pink Floyd, said to personify the "drug, sex and rock and roll" era, toured extensively and produced hit albums one after the other. Their reclusive but innovative guitarist Syd Barrett would produce music by means such as sliding a cigarette lighter down his strings, an echo chamber and other electronic gizmos. He had founded the group in 1965 with former members of a band variously called the Megga Deaths and the Screaming Adabs.

The band eventually eased out of its psychedelic period and in the 1970s assumed a more mellow sound. At the end of the decade — like their confreres the Who — they essayed a rock opera called *The Wall*. The 1982 film *Pink Floyd: the Wall* is considered a classic of its kind about a rock band. A previous self-titled documentary appeared in 1971. The group was inducted into the Rock and Roll Hall of Fame in 1996.

Tonite Let's All Make Love in London (1968) [documentary] "Interstellar Overdrive" * *European Music Revolution* (1970) [documentary] * *Stamping Ground* (1971) [documentary] "Saucerful of Secrets"

Plainsmen *see* Andy Parker and the Plainsmen

Plantation Boys *see* Hank Penny and His Plantation Boys

Plantation Club Chorus
Policy Man (1938) * *The Spirit of Youth* (1938) * *Gone Harlem* (1939)

Plantation Singers
In their single film, a part-talkie, the singing was done by the Plantation Singers in a prologue which contained all the music but did not show the performers.

Show Boat (1929) (voices only)

Platters
David Lynch (St. Louis, Missouri, 1929–1981); Paul Robi (1932?–1989); Herbert Reed (bass); Tony Williams (1928?–1992) (lead tenor); Alex Hodge; Zola Taylor (1938?–2007); Cornel Gunter

Formed in 1953, the Platters were one of the great harmony groups of the 1950s, well on a par with predecessors like the Inkspots and the Mills Brothers. They had innumerable gold records for enduring romantic hits like "Only You," "Smoke Gets in Your Eyes," "The Great Pre-

The Platters at the beginning of a glorious career.

tender," "Twilight Time," "The Magic Touch" and "My Prayer."

The Platters' final Top Ten record proved to be "Harbor Lights," although into the 1960s they still produced records that charted. All told they scored sixteen gold records and three albums that sold over a million copies.

Internal dissension caused the group to splinter and led to competing groups bearing the Platters name. Ultimately original member Herb Reed legally won the right to the Platters name. They were inducted into the Rock and Roll Hall of Fame in 1990 and the Vocal Hall of Fame in 1998.

Rock Around the Clock (1956) "Only You" and "The Great Pretender" * *The Girl Can't Help It* (1956) "You'll Never Never Know" * *Rock All Night* (1957) * *Carnival Rock* (1957) "Remember When" * *Girls Town* (1959) "Wish It Were Me"

Playboys *see* J. B. and the Playboys; Gary Lewis and the Playboys

Pleasant Valley Boys
Two Thousand Maniacs! (1964) †

†The well-known western ensemble the Pleasant Valley Boys was presumably formed by country music star Alvin Crow in 1969, so apparently is not be the same group that appeared in this film.

Plowboys see Polly Jenkins and Her Plowboys

Poison Gardner Trio
Among the recordings of the Poison Gardner Trio were "Poison's Boogie," "Second Piece of Pie" and "Noisin' (or Noisen) With Poison"
My Buddy (1944)

Polly Jenkins and Her Plowboys
Polly Jenkins (Mary Zoller, Mohawk, New York, 1903–1983); Walter Lewis; Jimmy Ames; Cliff Japhet; Erlau Wilcox

A veteran of vaudeville, Polly Jenkins was said to be the first woman to headline a country music act in that medium. To create their raucous music, the Plowboys utilized such exotica as rakes, hat racks, funnels and cowbells, as well as discs that hit different notes as they were spun. The band remained popular from the 1930s through World War II, during which time they toured with the U.S.O.
The Man from Music Mountain (1938)

Poole, Brian see Brian Poole and the Tremeloes

Pope Sisters
Una Pope; Odele Pope; Inez Pope

In the 1930s the glamorous Pope Sisters trio performed in fashionable nightspots around the country. They were one of the first African-American sister acts comparable to the then-popular Boswell Sisters. Their two features were directed by Black pioneer Oscar Micheaux, and they also sang in a musical short.
Temptation (1936) * *Underworld* (1937)

Powell, Teddy see Teddy Powell and His Orchestra

Prado, Perez see Perez Prado and His Orchestra

Preacher Smith and the Deacons; Preacher Smith's Deacons
Rock Baby, Rock It! (1957) "Roogie Doogie" and "Eat Your Heart Out"

Preservation Hall Jazz Band of New Orleans
A group that is almost the very symbol of New Orleans jazz is the Preservation Hall Jazz Band. They have performed in the most prestigious venues around the world since their founding in the early 1960s, as well as having a home base in the theater after which the band is named.

Some of the original members have performed well into their eighties and the ensemble is a multi-ethnic, multi-generational mirror of the populace of New Orleans itself. Trumpets, trombones, clarinets, a piano, banjos, drums and bass fiddle all meld into an irresistible sound that has been heard on the soundtrack of many a film, including those of aficionado Woody Allen.
WUSA (1970)

Preston, Lew see Lew Preston and His Ranch Hands

Pretty Things
Dick Taylor (Richard Taylor, Dartford, England, 1943–); Phil May (Phillip Kattner, Dartford, England, 1944–); Brian Pendleton (Wolverhampton, England, 1944–2001) (rhythm guitar); John Stax (John Fullegar, Crayford, England, 1944–) (bassist); Viv Prince (Vivian Prince), Loughborough, England, 1944–) (drums)

Dick Taylor was a member of the fledging Rolling Stones but left before worldwide fame came to that iconic rock and roll band. Instead he formed the Pretty Things which did respectably enough. It was a popular group in Europe and an influence on the so-called garage bands in the U.S. Indeed their name was a homage to rocker Bo Diddley's song "Pretty Thing."

Although the long-haired band began as a standard rock group it soon found psychedelic music more to its liking, as well as the raucous behavior that went with it. They were infamous for setting fires backstage, breaking up furniture and impinging rudely on other acts on the same bill.

The Pretty Things reached their acme in the mid-to-late 1960s, after which their new heavy metal/hard rock style faced increasing competition from many other bands. They continued to perform into the 21st century and were the subjects of a book wittily titled *Growing Old Dis-*

gracefully. In 1966 a self-titled short film containing much of their music was released.

What's Good for the Goose (1969) * *The Monster Club* (1981)

Prima, Louis *see* Louis Prima with His Band

Prince Modupe's Congo Choir

Prince Modupe (French Guinea?)

The true life history of the man who called himself Prince Modupe is hard to uncover, but what is certain is that he worked at MGM as an actor and "consultant." He advised that studio about the authenticity of films it set in exotic Africa.

Drums of the Congo (1942) †

†Their appearance in this film has not been confirmed.

Proctor, Lynn *see* Lynn Proctor Trio

Pyramids

Steve Leonard (bassist)

A rather late arrival on the surf band scene, the Long Beach, California–based Pyramids had one Top Twenty hit with "Penetration." They were publicized as "America's Answer to the Beatles" and, as such, they shaved their heads rather than grow their hair long. During concerts, however, they wore Beatles "mop top" wigs which they then removed and flung into the audience. Further publicity involved their arrival at concerts in such conveyances as helicopters, or even atop elephants.

Bikini Beach (1964) "Record Run" and "Bikini Drag"

Quartet [unknown]

Follies Girl (1943)

Quatros Latinos

Los Quatros Latinos was a gospel group.

Sing a Song, for Heaven's Sake (1966) [documentary]

Quicksilver Messenger Service

Dino Valenti (Chester Powers, 1937?–1994) (lead singer); John Cipollina (Berkeley, California, 1943–1989); Gary Duncan (guitar); David Freiberg (Boston, Massachusetts, 1938–) (bassist); Greg Elmore (Coronado, California, 1946–) (drums); Nicky Hopkins (London, England, 1944–1994) (piano)

Quicksilver vocalist Dino Valenti had played with iconic '60s groups such as Jefferson Airplane, Big Brother and the Holding Company and the Grateful Dead. He is known today for his song "Get Together" which contains the line that seems to perfectly summarize the 1960s: "C'mon people now, smile on your brother, everybody get together to love one another right now."

The band he helped co-found, the Quicksilver Messenger Service, was a San Francisco Bay–area psychedelic group that recorded five albums in their heyday, which was from 1965 to about 1971. Their one chart hit "Fresh Air" came in 1970. There were occasional reunions of some members as recently as 1987 but they never recaptured their early success.

Revolution (1968) [documentary] "Babe I'm Gonna Leave You" and "Codine" * *Captain Milkshake* (1970) * *Fillmore* (1972) [documentary]

Radio Pictures Beauty Chorus *see* Doris Eaton and the Radio Pictures Beauty Chorus

Radio Rangers *see* Doye O'Dell and the Radio Rangers

Radio Rogues; Three Radio Rogues

Eddie Bartell (Brooklyn, New York, 1907–1991); Syd Chalton; Jimmy Hollywood; R. D. Bartell; Henry Taylor

In its time the Radio Rogues was an enormously popular act that was heard on the radio and was seen on Broadway and in live theater appearances. Their particular shtick was imitating radio performers — and sometimes singing — at a time when that medium was becoming a major entertainment force in homes across the country: the 1920s. They continued on until radio itself was overtaken by newer technology.

Going Hollywood (1933) * *Every Night at Eight* (1935) * *Hats Off* (1936) * *Blossoms on Broadway* (1937) * *Reveille with Beverly* (1943) * *Harvest Melody* (1943) * *O, My Darling Clementine* (1943) * *She Has What It Takes* (1943) * *Spotlight Scandals* (1943) * *Trocadero* (1944)

Raiders *see* Paul Revere and the Raiders

Rainbow Four
Jack Barbee; Jack Frost; Chick Madden; Art Smith
Bowery to Broadway (1944) * *The Naughty Nineties* (1945)

Rainbow Ramblers *see* Jimmie Davis and His Rainbow Ramblers

Rainwater Wranglers
The Wranglers were western swing musicians.
Song of the Trail (1936)

Ramos, Bobby *see* Bobby Ramos Band

Ramsay Ames and Her Tropicanans
Ramsay Ames (Rita Phillips, New York, New York, 1924–1998)

Auburn-haired Ramsay Ames was primarily known as a "B" actress in serials and such films as *The Mummy's Ghost* and *Calling Doctor Death*. However, the former model and dancer had worked with Xavier Cugat and had led her own rumba band. It supposedly disbanded because so many of its members were off fighting in World War II.
Crazy House (1943)

Ranch Boys
Joe "Curly" Bradley (Raymond Courtney, Oklahoma, 1914–1985) (guitar); Ken Carson (Hubert Flatt, Oklahoma, 1914–1994); Jack Ross (Mexico, ca. 1904–)

At their prime in the 1930s the Ranch Boys even rivaled the Sons of the Pioneers in popularity. Former members of the Beverly Hillbillies, they struck out on their own about 1934 and made records, performed on the radio and toured until about 1940.

That was about a year before they disbanded. Ken Carson later joined the Sons of the Pioneers and then went into television, most notably as a permanent cast member of Garry Moore's show. Curly Bradley portrayed Tom Mix on a long-running radio show.
In Old Monterey (1939)

Ranch Hands *see* Lew Preston and His Ranch Hands

Ranch House Cowboys *see* Romaine Lowdermilk and His Ranch House Cowboys

Randall Sisters
The Randalls were a singing trio.
Stand Up and Cheer! (1934)

Randi, Don *see* Don Randi Trio Plus One

Range Ramblers *see* Ray Whitley and His Range Ramblers

Range Ranglers Band *see* Arizona Wranglers

Ranger Chorus; Ranger Chorus of Forty
Ride 'Em Cowboy (1942)

Rangers (1930s)
The Rangers, active in the 1930s, were an octet.
Going Hollywood (1933)

Rangers (1960s)
The Rangers, active in the 1960s, were a gospel group.
Sing a Song, for Heaven's Sake (1966) [documentary]

Ray Anthony and Band; Ray Anthony and Orchestra
Ray Anthony (Raymond Antonini, Bentleyville, Pennsylvania, 1922–)

One of the few successful bandleaders to become prominent after the Big Band era had already declined, Ray Anthony formed his band about 1946. Its theme song, appropriate to the fact that he was trumpeter, was "The Man with the Horn." His style was an homage to — or imitation of— Glenn Miller, for whom he had been a sideman, and/or Harry James.

He also had played trumpet with Jimmy Dorsey. His own brand of music was more pop than jazz, with "The Bunny Hop" being a million seller. With his dark good looks Anthony was somewhat of a sex symbol as well, his mar-

Ray Anthony (at right) and band in *This Could Be the Night*.

riage to Hollywood "B" actress Mamie Van Doren garnering much publicity.

Without his band he appeared in such films as *High School Confidential* and *Sun Valley Serenade*. As apt a businessman as he was a musician, in the 1980s Ray Anthony formed franchised swing bands to play Big Band–era music in schools and on the radio.

Daddy Long Legs (1955) * *The Girl Can't Help It* (1956) * *This Could Be the Night* (1957)

Ray Charles Orchestra

Ray Charles (Ray Robinson, Albany, Georgia, 1930–2004)

Considered one of the very great pop singers, Ray Charles survived a hard childhood during which he lost his eyesight to glaucoma at the age of seven, and not too long thereafter was orphaned. He performed in Midwest clubs and had a trio in the late '40s that he modeled after that of Nat "King" Cole, about the time Charles first started making records.

He had a band from about 1954 that played everything from gospel music to rhythm-and-blues, rock-and-roll and jazz. His first hit record was 1955's "I Got a Woman" and it was ultimately followed by such successful recordings as "I Can't Stop Loving You," "Born to Lose," "Unchain My Heart" and the iconic "Georgia." By the end of his life it was estimated that he had sung on some 250 albums.

He was even bruited to be the first entertainer to have done a musical show in the Roman Coliseum — or at least the first one in 2,000 years! In a career that spanned some fifty-five years Ray Charles was showered with numerous honors, including a Grammy Lifetime Achievement Award, dozens of Grammys, induction into the Rock and Roll Hall of Fame in its first year (1986), the Rhythm and Blues Foundation in 1991, and the Jazz Hall of Fame in 2004.

The capstone to a distinguished career was perhaps the biographical film *Ray*, starring Jamie Foxx, who was awarded a Best Actor Oscar in 2005 for his portrayal. Charles also had the singular honor of having a Los Angeles post office named for him. In 2007 the controversial musical *Ray Charles Live!* debuted in California; it emphasized (some said *over*-emphasized) his somewhat colorful private life.

The Big T.N.T. Show (1966) [documentary] "One Two Three" * *Blues for Lovers* (1966)

Ray Charles.

Ray Eberle and His Orchestra

Ray Eberle (Hoosick Falls, New York, 1919–1979)

The younger brother of band singer Bob Eberly (who had changed the spelling of the family name for ease of pronunciation), Ray Eberle joined Glenn Miller's famed ensemble as a vocalist in 1938. Among his big selling records were "At Last," "Serenade in Blue" and "Moonlight Cocktails."

After being summarily fired by the stern taskmaster in 1942, Ray Eberle joined the Gene Krupa band and then formed his own orchestra. Even though Glenn Miller had dismissed him Eberle modeled his group's arrangements after those of Miller and played many of his big hits. His theme song was even "Serenade in Blue." He continued with the band into the 1950s.

In 1970 Eberle joined the Tex Beneke–led Glenn Miller band, which toured many prestigious venues, and so came full circle. In the 1940s he had been seen in a few movie musicals like *Sun Valley Serenade*, *Honeymoon Lodge* and *Orchestra Wives* before forming his band, and later he made many television appearances.

Hi'Ya, Sailor (1943) * *This Is the Life* (1944)

Ray McKinley and His Orchestra

Ray McKinley (Fort Worth, Texas, 1910–1995)

A sideman in the bands of Red Nichols and the Dorsey brothers, drummer Ray McKinley co-led a boogie-woogie orchestra from 1939 with Will Bradley. Among their recordings was the famous "Beat Me Daddy, Eight to the Bar"; others included "Bounce Me Brother with a Solid Four" and "Scrub Me Mama with a Boogie Beat."

With such songs the band acquired quite a following, but Bradley left in 1942 to form his own group and McKinley rebuilt what remained. His own successes included "Hard Hearted Hannah" and "You've Come a Long Way from St. Louis."

At some point his theme song was "Howdy, Friends." When he went into the military he joined Glenn Miller's Army Air Force band as a drummer and kept it going as leader after the latter's disappearance in 1944.

"The Most Versatile Band in the Land" was the name given to Ray McKinley's post-war orchestra and it performed until disbanding in 1952. He again took over the Glenn Miller orchestra about 1956, led it for some ten years, and was still going into the 1970s.

Hit Parade of 1943 (1943)

Ray Noble and His Band

Ray Noble (Brighton, England, 1903/07–1978)

The leader of the "sweet" New Mayfair Dance Orchestra and music director/arranger at the BBC in his native England, Ray Noble launched his American, primarily jazz, band in 1935. They played the prestigious Rainbow Room in Manhattan before disbanding in 1937; among its renowned sidemen were Glenn Miller, Claude Thornhill and Charlie Spivak.

That same year he regrouped and became the bandleader for top radio shows with Edgar Bergen, Jack Benny, and George Burns and Gracie Allen. Noble segued to television where he continued playing off of his stiff upper-lip English image as both bandleader and actor.

Mustachioed Ray Noble was also the composer of classic songs like "Love Is the Sweetest Thing," "The Very Thought of You" and "Goodnight Sweetheart," the latter two of which were his theme songs.

The Big Broadcast of 1936 (1935) * *A Damsel in Distress* (1937) * *Here We Go Again* (1942) * *The Pride of the Yankees* (1942) * *Lake Placid Serenade* (1944)

Ray Whitley and His Bar-Six Cowboys; Ray Whitley and His Orchestra; Ray Whitley and His Range Ramblers

Ray Whitley (Atlanta, Georgia, 1901–1979); Earl Phelps; Willie Phelps; Norman Phelps; Ken Card; Ken Carson; Spade Cooley; Merle Travis

Ray Whitley was a man of many parts, being a singer, yodeler, songwriter and actor. He arrived in New York and found his niche there singing on radio's *National Barn Dance* with the Range Ramblers about 1930. They later became the Bar-Six Cowboys.

By about 1936 Whitley was in Hollywood where he would appear in more than fifty movies both solo and with his bands, the first being *Hopalong Cassidy Returns*. He also found time to record and work on improved guitar design.

Although a good singer, he never had his own oater series like several of his contemporaries but did appear in some eighteen western musical shorts for RKO. His proficiency with a bullwhip, honed on the rodeo circuit, could well have made him a rival of the oater hero Whip Wilson.

Ray Whitley appeared frequently on Roy Rogers' television show and his film career ended on a high note when he was cast in *Giant* (1956). As a songwriter he is famed for composing the Gene Autry perennial "Back in the Saddle Again" and "I Hang My Head and Cry." He was posthumously inducted into both the Nashville Songwriters Hall of Fame and the Western Music Association Hall of Fame.

Hittin' the Trail (1937) * *Mystery of the Hooded Horseman* (1937) * *Where the West Begins* (1938) † * *Boss of Boomtown* (1944) * *The Old Texas Trail* (1944) * *Riders of the Santa Fe* (1944) * *Trail to Gunsight* (1944) * *Trigger Trail* (1944) * *Beyond the Pecos* (1945) * *Renegades of the Rio Grande* (1945)

†Their appearance in this film is not confirmed.

Raymond Maurel and the Cimini Male Chorus

Raymond Maurel (Mario Cozzi, Florence, Italy)

A well-known opera singer, Raymond Maurel had small acting roles in several early talkies.

Street Girl (1929)

Raymond Paige and His Orchestra

Raymond Paige (Wausau, Wisconsin, 1900?–1965)

Paige was somewhat of a master at conducting large-scale orchestras, sometimes up to 100 members strong. During the 1930s he had been a conductor on the radio and at movie studios, and for the fifteen years after 1950 he was the music director at New York's Radio City Music Hall. He also conducted the Hollywood Bowl Orchestra.

Hollywood Hotel (1938)

Raymond Scott and His Quintet; Raymond Scott Quintet

Raymond Scott (Harry Warnow, Brooklyn, New York, 1908/10–1994); John Williams (drums); Fred Whiting (bassist); Eric Hoex (saxophone); Pat Pimiglio (clarinet); Dave Wade (trumpet)

Pianist Raymond Scott played in the CBS radio orchestra and in the mid–1930s formed his swing "quintet," which was actually a *sextet*. For it he composed pieces with names like "New Year's Eve in a Haunted House," "War Dance for Wooden Indians," "Confusion Among a Fleet of Taxicabs Upon Meeting with a Fare" and "Dinner Music For a Pack of Hungry Cannibals." He was obviously a man of some humor.

The quintet (sextet) lasted only a couple of years but had some record hits, even though the critics disdained it as not being serious music. In the early 1940s Scott sold his music rights to Warner Brothers which then proceeded to use it widely in their cartoons. To this day his music is still being heard in animated features, especially his composition "Powerhouse."

Other Raymond Scott compositions included "In an Eighteenth Century Drawing Room," "Mountain High, Valley Low" and "The Toy Trumpet." He had formed a big band in the 1940s but ultimately settled into composing for Broadway shows and leading the orchestra on television's *Your Hit Parade*.

Scott was also a noted inventor of electronic gadgetry, his major one being the Electronium, one of the first synthesizers. Other gizmos included the so-called Karloff, which produced a range of sounds, and the Clavinox, a type of electronic keyboard. Although eccentric, Raymond Scott had proved himself to be a real Renaissance man.

Ali Baba Goes to Town (1937) * *Sally, Irene and Mary* (1938) * *Happy Landings* (1938) * *Rebecca of Sunnybrook Farm* (1939)

Rebel Rousers *see* Duane Eddy and the Rebel Rousers

Red Arnall and His Western Aces

Red Arnall (T. J. Arnall)

Blazing Across the Pecos (1948)

Red Caps *see* Steve Gibson's Redcaps

Red Foley and His Saddle Pals

Red Foley (Clyde Foley, Blue Lick or Berea, Kentucky, 1910–1968)

From about 1930 Red Foley sang and played the guitar on radio, including the *National Barn Dance* program with the group the Cumberland Ridge Runners, and on recordings. One of his early efforts "Old Shep" became somewhat of a classic and it was far from the only one; he was to become one of the most famous country/western singers of all time.

In 1938 he became one of the first country performers to have a network radio program. Foley first made the charts during World War II with the patriotic "Smoke on the Water" and it was all upwards from there. He became a regular on *Grand Ole Opry* and later had a television show.

His string of hits included over forty country and gospel chart records, many in the top ten, among them "Peace in the Valley," "Steal Away," "One By One" and "Just a Closer Walk with Thee." Red Foley's 1950s renditions of "Chattanoogie Shoeshine Boy," "Candy Kisses" and "Don't Let the Stars Get in Your Eyes" were pop favorites as well.

He often teamed with both country and popular music singers like the Andrews Sisters and Ernest Tubb. He also essayed a few rock-and-roll tunes. On television Red Foley co-starred in the television series *Mr. Smith goes to Washington* and on *Ozark Jubilee*. He was elected to the Country Music Hall of Fame and had been designated the top U.S. folk artist in 1950.

The Pioneers (1941)

Red Mountain Jug Band

Pat May; Bill Boelk; Randy Thornally; Pat Rooney

The Strawberry Statement (1970)

Red Nichols and His Five Pennies

Red Nichols (Ernest Nichols, Ogden, Utah, 1905–1965)

Cornetist Red Nichols' first recordings came in 1922 with many of the same jazz musicians playing under different names, including the Syncopatin' Five, the Redheads, the Varsity Eight, the Six Hottentots, the Alabama Red Peppers and even Miff Mole and his Little Molers.

Nichols also worked under bandleaders like Paul Whiteman and was supposedly heard on more than 4,000 recordings in the 1920s alone. His first Five Pennies group was launched in the mid–'20s and their recording of "Ida" in 1927 sold more than one million copies. He also led the pit band for a George Gershwin musical and was on radio with chanteuse Ruth Etting.

Later on Nichols led an unsuccessful swing band before returning to his more tried-and-true jazz ensemble with its theme song "Wail of the Winds." Danny Kaye portrayed him in the highly fictionalized 1959 biopic *The Five Pennies*, in which Nichols dubbed the trumpet playing, and he continued to lead small groups into the 1950s.

Quicksand (1950) * *Wabash Avenue* (1950) * *Disc Jockey* (1951) * *The Gene Krupa Story* (1959)

Red Norvo Trio

Red Norvo (Kenneth Norville, Beardstown, Illinois, 1908–1999) (vibes); Mundell Lowe (guitar); Red Kelly (bassist); Tal Farlow (guitar); Charles Mingus (bassist); Jimmy Raney; Red Mitchell

Norvo (his stage name was supposedly an announcer's mispronunciation of Norville) is credited with introducing the xylophone and vibraphone to jazz music. He also was a master of the marimba. With his then-wife, the great blues singer Mildred Bailey, he founded an orchestra in 1941 and they were thereafter known as "Mr. and Mrs. Swing," also the title of their theme song.

Red Norvo had appeared in vaudeville and first recorded in 1933. He had previously established an all-marimba band, performed with a group called the Collegians and was a sideman in Paul Whiteman's orchestra. He formed his Trio in 1949 after leading a quintet and sextet. Following its break-up he played with Benny Goodman, Dizzy Gillespie, Charlie (Bird) Parker and Teddy Wilson.

Texas Carnival (1951) * *Screaming Mimi* (1958)

Red River Valley Boys *see* Johnny Bond and His Red River Valley Boys

Red Tops *see* Rosco Gordon and His Red Tops

Redcaps *see* Steve Gibson's Redcaps

Reflections; Joni Lyman and the Reflections

Joni Lyman; Ray Steinberg

Somewhat of a one-hit wonder, that one being the smash ("Just Like) Romeo and Juliet," the Reflections were a Detroit-based quintet. They also recorded "Poor Man's Son" and "Like Columbus Did." In the 1970s they merged with the Larados.

Winter-a-Go-Go (1965) ("I'm) Sweet on You"

Regency Three

The Regency Three was a singing group.
I Walk Alone (1948)

Reichman, Joe *see* Joe Reichman and His Orchestra

Reisman, Leo *see* Leo Reisman and His Band

Remo Four *see* Tommy Quickly and the Remo Four

Renegades

Bruce Johnston; Sandy Nelson; Richard Podolor; Nik Venet
Ghost of Dragstrip Hollow (1959) "Geronimo," "He's My Guy" and several other songs

Republic Rhythm Riders

George Bamby (accordion); Darol Rice (clarinet); Buddy Dooley (guitar); Michael Behan, Jr. (bassist); Slim Duncan (fiddle)

Working primarily with oater star Rex Allen at the very end of the movies' "B" western era, the Republic Rhythm Riders were a group of musicians cobbled together by the Republic Studio to appear in films. (This would have been less expensive for the studio than hiring a pre-existing group.) Some members had previously appeared with another three-R group, the Roy Rogers Riders.

Border Saddlemates (1952) * *Colorado Sundown* (1952) * *The Last Musketeer* (1952) * *Old Oklahoma Plains* (1952) * *South Pacific Trail* (1952) * *The WAC from Walla Walla* (1952) * *Old Overland Trail* (1953)

Revuers

Betty Comden (Elizabeth Cohen, Brooklyn, New York, 1917?–2006); Judy Holliday (Judith Tuvim, 1921?–1965); Adolph Green (1915?–2002); John Frank; Alvin Hammer

In the late 1930s Judy Tuvim (later Holliday) brought in a group of her friends, including Betty Comden and Adolph Green, to perform with her in a satirical musical act at the New York nightclub the Village Vanguard. They called themselves The Revuers and went on to have a weekly radio show, as well as being seen in other top nightspots.

The Revuers broke up in the mid–1940s after their single film in which most of their material was left in the cutting room. Holliday then began a successful Broadway and Hollywood career. She was lauded for her "dumb blonde" roles in *Born Yesterday* (winning an Oscar for Best Actress), *Adam's Rib*, *Bells Are Ringing* and others.

Comden and Green also conquered Broadway and then the movies. Together they wrote numerous screenplays (*Singin' in the Rain*, *Auntie Mame* and *The Band Wagon* among them) and stage musicals. During their sixty-plus years of collaboration they garnered seven Tonys and wrote enduring hit songs like "Make Someone Happy," "Just in Time" and "The Party's Over."

Greenwich Village (1944)

Rey, Alvino *see* Alvino Rey and His Orchestra

Reyes, Chuy *see* Chuy Reyes...

Rhythm Boys *see* Bing Crosby and His Rhythm Boys

Rhythm Cowgirls *see* Judy Clark and Her Rhythm Cowgirls

Rhythm Masters

Get Yourself a College Girl (1964)

Rhythm Rangers *see* Cal Shrum's Rhythm Rangers

Rhythm Rascals

Will Jones; James Turner; Lloyd George; [first name unknown] Howell

Rhythm Rascals founder Lloyd George went on to become the first Lonzo in the hillbilly act Lonzo and Oscar.

The Girl from Chicago (1932) * *Nobody's Baby* (1937) * *Hollywood Bound* (1946) †

†This film was compilation of three film shorts that featured Betty Grable early in her career. The Rhythm Rascals appeared in the 1935 two-reeler *A Night at the Biltmore Bowl*.

Rhythm Riders *see* **Art Davis and His Rhythm Riders**

Rhythm Wranglers *see* **Cal Shrum's Rhythm Wranglers**

Rhythmaires

The Rhythmaires were a female singing group that appeared in Walt Disney films.

The Reluctant Dragon (1941) (voices only?) * *The Adventures of Ichabod and Mr. Toad* (1949) (voices only) * *So Dear to My Heart* (1949)

Rich, Buddy *see* **Buddy Rich and His Orchestra**

Rich, Freddie *see* **Freddie Rich and His Orchestra**

Rickett, Nooney *see* **Nooney Rickett Four**

Riders of the Purple Sage *see* **Foy Willing and the Riders of the Purple Sage**

Righteous Brothers

Bill Medley (Santa Ana, California, 1940–) (baritone); Bobby Hatfield (Beaver Dam, Wisconsin, 1940–2003) (tenor); Jimmy Walker

Among the premier exponents of so-called "blue-eyed soul" were the Righteous Brothers, who of course were not really brothers. Their recording of "You've Lost That Loving Feeling" is a classic that will probably never fade from the ranks of all-time greatest hits. It is said to be the most performed song on radio even today.

Formed in 1962 as the Paramours, Medley and Hatfield adopted their new name about a year later for such recordings as "Little Latin Lupe Lu" and other minor rhythm-and-blues numbers. They had supposedly adopted the name after a fan yelled "That was righteous, brothers!" during one of their performances.

After establishing themselves with "Loving Feeling" their clean-cut image and singing style more befit such powerfully dramatic songs as "Unchained Melody," "Just Once in My Life" and "Ebb Tide." The Brothers' last big success came with ("You're My) Soul and Inspiration."

There was one last minor hit, "He," before Medley embarked on a solo career in 1967 or '68. Hatfield and Jimmy Walker carried on as the Righteous Brothers for a few years before the originals re-teamed for "Rock and Roll Heaven" in the 1970s. They continued performing together off and on until Hatfield's death.

Apart, Medley and Hatfield never reclaimed the chemistry that they had together. Their voices had a special blending that was all too rare in rock-and-roll. The Righteous Brothers were inducted into the Rock and Roll Hall of Fame in 2003.

A Swingin' Summer (1965) "Justine" * *Beach Ball* (1965) "Baby, What You Want Me to Do"

Riley, Mike *see* **Mike Riley...**

Rio Brothers; Three Rio Brothers; Eddie Rio and Brothers

Frank Rio (1925?–2005); Eddie Rio; Larry Rio

The Rio "Brothers" were actually a father (Eddie), his brother (Larry) and Eddie's son Frank. They were a triple-threat act of comedy, singing and dancing.

New Faces of 1937 (1937) * *Hollywood Varieties* (1950) * *Casa Manana* (1951)

Rip Chords

Phil Stewart; Rich Rotkin; Arnie Marcus

Bobby Hatfield (left) and Bill Medley, the Righteous Brothers.

The rock group that most memorialized the Southern California car culture was the Rip Chords trio. With their smash hit "Hey Little Cobra" and others like "409," "Three Window Coupe" and "Red Hot Roadster" they enjoyed a short period of popularity following their 1962 formation. They also charted with "Here I Stand" and "Gone."

Although the Chords made personal appearances as a threesome, their records often had additional singers (including Terry Melcher and Bruce Johnston) and credit for who sang on what singles and albums is somewhat murky. The original group split up in 1965 but various members still tour today.

A Swingin' Summer (1965) "Red Hot Roadster"

Rippling Rhythm Orchestra *see* **Shep Fields and His Orchestra**

Riptides
Mondo Hollywood (1967)

Ritter, Tex *see* **Tex Ritter's Tornadoes**

Robert B. Mitchell and His St. Brendan's Boys Choir *see* **Bob Mitchell's Boys Choir**

Robertos [unknown]
A Song for Miss Julie (1945)

Roberts Brothers [unknown]
Tin Pan Alley (1940)

Robinson, Smokey *see* **Smokey Robinson and the Miracles**

Rocco and Saulter
Maurice Rocco; Dorothy Saulter
   Maurice Rocco was a pianist and Dorothy Saulter a soprano.
   52nd Street (1937); *Walter Wanger's Vogues of 1938* (1937)

Rocco and the Saints; Rocco and His Saints
Bobby Rydell (Robert Ridarelli, Philadelphia, Pennsylvania, 1942–) (drums); Frankie Avalon (Francis Avallone, Philadelphia, Pennsylvania, 1940–) (trumpet)

In the 1950s Rocco and the Saints, a Philadelphia and summer resort dance band, boasted two teenaged future bubblegum rock stars. Francis Avallone (later Frankie Avalon) became known on local television and went on to become a staple in the beach movies of the 1960s and a credible actor in more serious fare until the 1980s.

Robert Ridarelli (later Bobby Rydell) also appeared on television as a teen and was later an occasional actor (*Bye Bye Birdie*). He produced solo hits like "Wild One," "Swingin' School" and "Sway" and had the signal honor of having the fictional high school in the popular musical *Grease* named after him.

Jamboree (1957) "Twenty Four Hours a Day"

Rocket Trio [unknown]
The Music Goes 'Round (1936)

Rocking R's
The Hot Bed (1965)

Rocky Twins
The Rocky Twins were drag entertainers.
   Blondie of the Follies (1932)

Rodeo Rangers *see* **Curly Clements and His Rodeo Rangers**

Rodeo Revelers
Sunset Carson Rides Again (1947)

Rodeoliers
The Rodeoliers were radio singers.
   Home on the Prairie (1939) "I'm Gonna Round Up My Blues" and "She'll Be Comin' Round the Mountain"

Rodik Twins
Verna Rodik; Verda Rodik
   The Rodik Twins were singers.
   The Return of Daniel Boone (1941)

Rogers, Roy *see* **Roy Rogers Riders**

Rogers, Shorty *see* **Shorty Rogers and Band**

Romaine Lowdermilk and His Ranch House Cowboys

Romaine Lowdermilk (Kansas, 1890–1970)

Most active in the 1920s and '30s as a radio singer (*The National Barn Dance*) and songwriter, Romaine Lowdermilk wrote such tunes as "Mr. Cowboy Goes to Town" and "The Rodeo Parade."

Arizona Frontier (1940) * *Rainbow Over the Range* (1940)

Ronettes

Veronica Bennett (aka Ronnie Spector) (New York, New York, 1943–); Estelle Bennett (New York, New York, 1944–); Nedra Talley (New York, New York, 1946–)

Described as "urban hot and urban cool," and one of the most influential of the rock-and-roll "girl groups," was the Ronettes, the Bennett sisters and cousin Nedra. Their hits were to include "Be My Baby," "Baby, I Love You" and "Walking in the Rain." Calling themselves the Darling Sisters as young teenagers, the trio piled their long black hair up as high as it could go, donned tight skirts and plentiful makeup and set out to conquer show business.

They supposedly got their professional start when a club manager mistook them for another act. One of their first gigs was as dancers at the famous Peppermint Lounge, home of the Twist. Renamed Ronnie (for Veronica) and the Relatives, they played local theaters, began recording with little initial success, and backed other singers, including Bobby Rydell and Del Shannon.

This all changed when record producer Phil Spector, famous for his "wall of sound" music, discovered the Ronettes and personally fell for Veronica, whom he later married. The trio became world-famous after touring with the Beatles and Rolling Stones, but Spector eventually turned to shepherding other talents and their popularity slowly declined,

The Ronettes disbanded in 1966. Veronica Bennett launched a solo career that lasted into the 1980s and she is still considered one of the great ladies of rock-and-roll. She also had a few solo acting roles in films. The Ronettes were inducted into the Rock and Roll Hall of Fame in 2007.

The T.A.M.I. Show (1964) [documentary] * *The Big T.N.T. Show* (1966) [documentary] "Be My Baby" and "Shout"

Rooney, Mickey Jr. *see* Mickey Rooney Jr. and his Combo

Rosco Gordon and His Red Tops

Rosco Gordon (Memphis, Tennessee, 1928/34–2002)

Pianist and singer Rosco Gordon was on local radio by 1950 and began recording about a year later. One of his songs "Booted" became a top rhythm-and-blues hit; another was "No More Doggin'." Yet another, "The Chicken," begat a dance fad of that name.

Throughout the 1950s and '60s Gordon toured and recorded, both with the Red Tops and as a solo performer. After a lengthy retirement he re-emerged in the 1980s to appear at many music festivals and was still recording as late as 2000.

Rock Baby, Rock It (1957) "Bop It" and "Chicken in the Rough"

Rough Riders *see* Jimmy Wakely and His Rough Riders; Roy Knapp Rough Riders

Rounders [unknown]

The Rounders may have been dancer-singers. They provided background for the Brox Sisters and Cliff Edwards when they performed the classic song "Singin' in the Rain" in its first film appearance in MGM's *Hollywood Revue of 1929*.

Hollywood Revue of 1929 (1929) * *Blaze o' Glory* (1929)

Roundup Boys *see* Eddie Cletro and His Roundup Boys

Routers

The Routers may not have been an actual band but a group of studio musicians brought together for one film.

Surf Party (1964) "Great White Water" and "Crack Up"

Roy Acuff and His Smoky Mountain Boys; Roy Acuff and His Smoky Mountain Boys and Girls; Roy Acuff and His Smoky Mountain Boys, with Rachel

Roy Acuff (Maynardsville, Tennessee, 1903–1992) (fiddle); Rachel Veach (banjo); Oswald

Veach (guitar); Jess Easterday (guitar); Lonnie Wilson; Velma Williams

Beginning his career in touring medicine shows and on local Tennessee radio, fiddler Roy Acuff eventually had one of the most popular of the western swing bands and was considered the first country superstar. His group became regulars on radio's *Grand Ole Opry* in 1938.

His original band, formed in 1933, had been called the Tennessee Crackerjacks and the Crazy Tennesseans. (The "Crazy" possibly came from Acuff antics like yo-yo tricks and balancing a fiddle on his nose.) During World War II Acuff actually eclipsed Frank Sinatra in some popularity polls.

Roy Acuff was involved with music, either performing or running his own music publishing company, until the 1970s. He received the prestigious Kennedy Center Honors in 1991 and was supposedly the first living person to be inducted into the Country Music Hall of Fame.

Known as the "King of Country," and trading on that popularity, in 1948 he ran unsuccessfully for governor of Tennessee. Among the Acuff groups' recordings were "Wabash Cannonball," "Great Speckled Bird," "Night Train to Memphis," "Wreck on the Highway" and "Beneath That Lonely Mound of Clay."

Grand Ole Opry (1940) * *Hi Neighbor* (1942) * *O, My Darling Clementine* (1943) * *Sing Neighbor Sing* (1944) * *Cowboy Canteen* (1944) * *Night Train to Memphis* (1946) * *Smoky Mountain Melody* (1948) * *Home in San Antone* (1949)

Roy Rogers Riders

Pat Brady (Robert O'Brady, Toledo, Ohio, 1914–1972); Jimmy Bryant (guitar); George Bamby (accordion); Buddy Dooley (guitar); Michael Burton (bassist); Darol Rice (clarinet)

Roy Rogers (1911–1998) was Republic's "King of the Cowboys" and one of the most popular of the singing cowboys. Although possessed of a fine voice (and yodeling ability) of his own he usually was backed by a western swing group, the most famous being the Sons of the Pioneers which he co-founded.

The Sons were replaced in his pictures in 1948 by Foy Willing and the Riders of the Purple Sage for financial reasons (i.e., they cost the Republic Studio less). For the same reason the Roy Rogers Riders then replaced the Riders of the Purple Sage in 1951 as the singing "boys" in Rogers' few remaining films.

It is most probable that there were a group of disparate musicians specifically hired for the Roy Rogers Riders, rather than being a previously established group of their own. Several later appeared with the Republic Rhythm Riders and with other groups.

In Old Amarillo (1951) * *Pals of the Golden West* (1951) * *South of Caliente* (1951)

Royal Canadians see Guy Lombardo and His Royal Canadians

Royal Hawaiian Orchestra see Harry Owens and His Royal Hawaiians

Royal Hawaiian Serenaders

Barney Isaacs (Alvin Isaacs, Jr., 1924–1996) (steel guitar); Alvin Isaacs, Sr. (1904–1984) (multiple instruments); Benny Kalama; George Kainapau

Alvin Isaacs, Sr., the sire of a large (ten children) musical family, was the leader of the Royal Hawaiian Serenaders, a quartet that performed at Honolulu's Royal Hawaiian Hotel and on radio. He was also credited with being the composer of more than 300 songs and had been part of music ensembles from the age of thirteen.

His son Alvin was considered a master of the steel guitar and had been a part of the radio show *Hawaii Calls* for many years before joining his father's Serenaders in 1948. His guitar was heard on hundreds of recordings and he toured widely, as well as serving as music director for a Hawaiian record company.

Million Dollar Weekend (1948)

Royal Hawaiians see Harry Owens and His Royal Hawaiians

Royal Rogues see Cecil Stewart and His Royal Rogues

Royal Teens

Bob Gaudio (Bronx, New York, 1942–); Billy Dalton (bassist); Bill Crandall (saxophone); Tom Austin (drums); Larry Quagliano; Al Kooper; Joe Villa; Ray Mariani

The one-shot wonders who were the Royal Teens captured the public's fancy with the catchy song "Short Shorts" (it sounded more like "Shawt Shawts" as they sang it). The New Jersey–based quartet was formed in 1956 or '57, and was originally dubbed the Royal *Tones.*

The group had backed-up various rhythm-and-blues groups before making the record that went to number three on the charts. They became a quintet prior to producing the minor "Harvey's Got a Girlfriend" and "Believe Me." The latter song marked a departure in the band's style in an unsuccessful effort to repeat their initial success.

Let's Rock! (1958) "Short Shorts"

Rubini, Jan *see* **Jan Rubini Orchestra**

Rudy Sooter and His Californians
Riders of Pasco Basin (1940)

Ruloff, Follette and Lunard [unknown]
Melody Parade (1943)

Runaway Pancake
Wanderlove (1970)

Russ Morgan and His Orchestra
Russ Morgan (Scranton, Pennsylvania, 1904–1969)

Trombonist Russ Morgan was the co-writer of the standard "You're Nobody Till Somebody Loves You." A former coal miner, he had begun his music career as an arranger for luminaries like John Philip Sousa and Victor Herbert, and played in various bands including those of Freddie Martin, Ted Fio Rito and Phil Spitalny.

During Morgan's career as a sideman he developed his signature "wah wah" sound on the trombone. He was encouraged to form his own band by crooner Rudy Vallee and thus launched the much-publicized "Music in the Morgan Manner" in 1936. The orchestra's theme song was "Does Your Heart Beat for Me?" and their record hits included "Cruising Down the River" and "Sunflower."

The Russ Morgan ensemble played in the top hotels and theaters well into the 1950s, although the band size was reduced, and then in Las Vegas for a dozen years in the '60s and '70s. He was a multi-talented man who played several instruments, arranged music and sang. Among his other compositions was "Somebody Else Is Taking My Place."

Cigarette Girl (1947) * *Sarge Goes to College* (1947)

Russian Cossack Choir
Balalaika (1939)

Russo and the Samba Kings
Russo Do Pandeiro (Antonio Cardoso Martins, Rio de Janeiro, Brazil, 1913–1985)

Russo Do Pandeiro was a stage name that was taken from the pandeiro, the tambourine-like percussion instrument of which Antonio Cardoso Martins was master. Before coming to the U.S. from his native Brazil he had accompanied such star personalities as Carmen Miranda and Josephine Baker. He was active in music from the late 1920s and had appeared in a few Brazilian movies.

Romance on the High Seas (1948) * *A Song Is Born* (1948)

Sacred Harp Singers
Festival (1967) [documentary]

Saddle Kings *see* **Hank Caldwell and His Saddle Kings**

Saddle Pals *see* **Red Foley and His Saddle Pals; Jimmy Le Fevre and His Saddle Pals; Jimmy Wakely...**

Saddle Tramps *see* **Buster Fite and the Saddle Tramps**

Sagebrush Serenaders
Enright Busse; John Scott; John Wilder
Man from Rainbow Valley (1946)

St. Brendan's Boys Choir *see* **Bob Mitchell Boys Choir**

St. Joseph's Choir
The Wizard of Oz (voices only?) * *Forty Little Mothers* (1940)

St. Luke's Choristers *see* **Dorr's St. Luke's Choristers**

Saints *see* **Rocco and His Saints**

Sal Hoopii and His Hawaiian Band

Sal Hoopii (Solomon Ho'opi'i Ka'ai'ai (Honolulu, Hawaii, 1902?–1953)

The youngest of twenty-one children, Sal Hoopii still managed to make himself heard over the crowd by his musical ability on the ukulele and Hawaiian guitar. He parlayed this talent into a trio that began recording blues-influenced and Hawaiian music in 1927; "Hula Girl" was one of their most popular tunes.

He was also a respected music arranger, but in the latter 1930s Hoopii effectively gave up music to join with evangelist Aimee Semple McPherson. He did issue a few more recordings and resumed a music career again after her death. His reputation as one of the foremost Hawaiian steel guitarists remained strong even after his own death.

Flirtation Walk (1934) * *Hawaiian Nights* (1939)

Sam and the Ape Men

Dr. Goldfoot and the Bikini Machine (1965)

Sam Butera and the Witnesses

Sam Butera (New Orleans, Louisiana, 1926/27–)

Saxophone player Sam Butera gained a reputation as an arranger, conductor and comic foil for Louis Prima. His band the Witnesses made recordings and was also Prima's sometime backup group.

Senior Prom (1958) * *Hey Boy! Hey Girl!* (1959) * *Twist All Night* (1962)

Sam the Sham and the Pharaohs

Domingo Samudio (Dallas, Texas, 1937–) (organ/guitar); Jerry Patterson; Ray Stinnett; Butch Gibson; Frank Carabetta (multi-instruments); Tony Gerace (bassist); Billy Bennett (d. 2000) (drums); Andrew Kuha (guitar); Louis Vilardo (drums)

Domingo Samudio (aka Sam the Sham) took over the leadership of Andy and the Night Riders, the band in which he was playing. He renamed it after himself and in tribute to the then-popular movie *The Ten Commandments*. The "Sham" may come from the slang word "shamming" that apparently meant cutting up while performing.

Whatever the derivation of their name, the Pharaohs recorded the novelty tune "Woolly Bully" in 1965 and had a three million seller. The sly "Li'l Red Riding Hood" was another big hit in 1966. A while later the band added a female vocal trio called the Shamettes.

A bunch of not-too memorable novelty songs followed, e.g., "Ring Dang Doo" and "The Hair on My Chinny Chin Chin." Samudio ultimately went on to a solo career as a gospel singer and was still active into the 21st century. He also appeared solo in the film *The Border* (1982).

When the Boys Meet the Girls (1965) "Monkey See Monkey Do"

Sam the Soul and the Inspirations

Mondo Mod (1967) [documentary] "Mary Lou"

Samba Kings *see* Russo and the Samba Kings

Sammy Kaye and His Orchestra

Sammy Kaye (Samuel Zarnocay, Lakewood, Ohio, 1910–1987)

"Swing and sway with Sammy Kaye" was that orchestra leader's famous tagline. During some of his performances he employed a well-known gimmick whereby an audience member would be called up to conduct his band. It was effective enough to earn him an early television program called "So You Want to Lead a Band?"

Kaye's sweet music sound earned him much popularity in the 1930s and '40s in elegant New York hotels and on the radio. The orchestra, whose theme song was "Sammy's Melody," was never considered top-drawer by other musicians, but under his strict discipline it maintained a strong niche with fans. He himself played the clarinet and saxophone.

Although he exhibited a smiling, easygoing persona, at one point Sammy Kaye's dictatorial ways almost had the entire band quitting en masse. However its easily danceable music kept it going into the 1960s and after the leader himself retired the group has continued to perform to this day.

Iceland (1943) * *Song of the Open Road* (1945)

San Cristobal Marimba Band

Dominguez Brothers
Tropic Holiday (1938)

San Francisco Opera Company
The Lost Weekend (1945)

Sandpipers
Richard Shoff; Michael Piano; Jim Brady; Pamela Ramcier

The male members of the Sandpipers quartet were graduates of the Robert (Bob) Mitchell Boys Choir. First calling themselves the Four Seasons, they learned about the other group of that name and so changed theirs to the Grads before assuming their final name.

The folk singers had one hit with the enduring standard "Guantanamera" and lesser successes with "Kumbaya" and others of that ilk. The Sandpipers memorably sang the poignant "Come Saturday Morning" on the soundtrack of the film *The Sterile Cuckoo*, but that was somewhat of a last hurrah. They struggled into the mid–1970s before disbanding.

Beyond the Valley of the Dolls (1970)

Santamaria, Mongo *see* Mongo Santamaria and His Band

Santana
Carlos Santana (Autlan de Navarro, Mexico, 1947–) (guitar); Tom Frazier (guitar); Mike Carabello (1947–) (congas/percussion); Rod Harper (drums); Gus Rodriguez (bass guitar); Greg Rolie (1947–) (organ); Jose Areas (1946–) (timbales); Michael Shrieve (1949–) (drums); David Brown (1947–) (bassist)

World-famous Latin-rock guitarist Carlos Santana and the group that began as the Santana Blues Band reputedly had sold some 80 million albums by the end of the 20th Century. Although formed in 1966 under Santana's name he was not necessarily the leader of the group. The band was more of a collective effort even after it was simply dubbed Santana.

At the Woodstock Festival Santana was one of the standouts. Their success helped propel their first album into the stratosphere, as did many of the ones that followed. In 1973, after internal dissension, Carlos Santana formed a new group and ultimately settled on a Latin funk sound that came to memorialize the band.

The Grammy Award–winning ensemble has gone through its ups and downs over the years but persevered to retain its place among the great bands of its type. Santana's hit singles over the years included "Evil Ways," "Maria, Maria," "Smooth," "Soul Sacrifice" and "Black Magic Woman." In 1998 the group was inducted into the Rock and Roll Hall of Fame

Woodstock (1970) [documentary] "Soul Sacrifice" * *Soul to Soul* (1971) [documentary] "Jingo," "Black Magic Woman" * *Stamping Ground* (1971) [documentary] "Gumbo" * *Fillmore* (1972) [documentary]

Satch Gould and His Boys
The Lusting Hours (1967)

Satins *see* Five Satins

Saturday Revue
Wild Wheels (1969) "Holiday Right Here"

Savannah Club Chorus *see* "Shootsie" Keith and the Savannah Club Chorus

Savitt, Jan *see* Jan Savitt...

Sawyer, Terri *see* Terri Sawyer Quartet

Schnicklefritz Band *see* Corn Colonel and His Band

Scobey, Bob *see* Bob Scobey and His Band

Scott, Raymond *see* Raymond Scott and His Quintet

Scotty McKay Quintet
The Scotty McKay Quintet was a Texas garage band that recorded from about 1959 into the '70s.

The Black Cat (1966) "Bo Diddley," "Brown Eyed Handsome Man" and "Sinner Man" * *Creature of Destruction* (1967) "All Around the World" and "Watch Out for the Batman"

Seckler Group
Marvin Bailey; Justin Conlon; Mack McLean; Bill Seckler

The Seckler Group was a vocal ensemble.
Lost in a Harem (1944) * *Meet Me in St. Louis* (1944)

Seeds

Sky Saxon (vocals/bass guitar); Jan Savage (guitar); Daryl Hooper (keyboard); Rick Andridge (drums)

"You're Pushin' Too Hard" was one of the Seeds' first singles, coming about a year after their formation in 1965. It was a notable debut but was also the high point of their record careers. Much later it was designated as one of the Rock and Roll Hall of Fame's 500 Songs That Shaped Rock and Roll.

Further singles and albums did not match that auspicious beginning, with releases like "Mr. Farmer" and "A Thousand Shadows" only scoring modestly. The band, which had gone heavily toward a raw psychedelic sound, broke up in 1970.

Leader Sky Saxon (who later called himself Sky Sunlight) re-formed the Seeds in the late 1980s and they have continued to pop up every now and then into the current century.

Psych-Out (1968) "Two Fingers Pointing on You."

Sentimentalists

Ann Clark; Jean Clark; Peggy Clark; Judy Clark

Before the Clark Sisters decided to perform under their own names they were the Sentimentalists who sang with Tommy Dorsey's band. Their specialty was imitating musical instruments, a talent used on several recordings including "Sugar Blues." They had several chart songs, most of them covers of others groups' hits.

Broadway Rhythm (1944)

Sergio Mendes and Brasil '66

Sergio Mendes (Niteroi, Brazil, 1941–) (piano); Jose Soares (percussion); Joao Palma (percussion); Bob Matthews (bassist); Lani Hall (vocals)

Originally trained as a classical pianist, Sergio Mendes founded his so-called "Latin-Rock" group Brasil '66 in — not surprisingly — 1966. It initially consisted of four men and two women and was U.S. based, Mendes having emigrated from Brazil earlier in the decade. In his native land he had led the Bossa Nova Trio.

Brasil '66's first two albums shot up on the pop charts but their ascendance was short-lived, although cover singles like "The Look of Love," "Fool on the Hill" and "Look Around" did well. Their last hit was 1968's "Scarborough Fair" though the group continued to remain very popular in South America.

Mendes staged a comeback in the 1980s with "Never Gonna Let You Go" and had several successful albums thereafter. By that time Brasil '66 had been replaced by Brasil '77. In the early 1990s he was several years too early for his newest incarnation: Brasil '99.

Sullivan's Empire (1967)

Seven Singing Buckaroos

The Singing Buckaroo (1937)

Sextetto Habanero *see* Habanera Sextette

Seymour and Corncob

Seymour and Corncob were "hayseed" musicians.

Here Comes Cookie (1935) * *Way Down East* (1935)

Shadows *see* Bob Luman and the Shadows

Shamrock Cowboys

The Shamrock Cowboys were members of the Spade Cooley band but he did not perform with this group.

Singin' Spurs (1949)

Sha-Na-Na

Donny York; Jocko Marcellino (drums); Scott Simon (piano); Henry Gross (guitar); David Ryan; Mal Gray; Jon Bauman; Scott Powell; Lennie Baker; Denny Green; Johnny Contardo; Richie Jaffe; Bruce Clark; Elliot Cahn; Henry Gross; Chris Donald

Yet another group that started out calling itself the Kingsmen, Sha-Na-Na took its new moniker from the refrain of the rock-and-roll standard "Get a Job." Kind of a faux 1950s doowop parody group, they started performing at Columbia University about 1968 or '69 and appeared at the now-legendary Woodstock Festival.

For about five years from the late 1970s Sha-

Na-Na had a popular television show. Although they made recordings they were most successful in live concerts in which their comedy, choreography and costuming could be seen to great advantage. They continue to benefit from the nostalgia for early rock songs, mixing music and comedy in pleasing proportions in their touring shows.

Woodstock (1970) [documentary] "At the Hop" * *Grease* (1978)

Shane Fenton and the Fentones

Shane Fenton (Bernard Jewry, London, England, 1942–); Mick Eyre (guitar); Jerry Wilcock (guitar); Bill Bonney (Walter Bonney) (bassist); Tony Hinchcliffe (drums)

The Fentones were a British pop band called the Tremelos when Shane Fenton joined them and eventually they became his renamed back-up group. Their onstage presence was enlivened by their costuming: Fenton wore a silver lame suit and the rest were "pretty in pink."

The Fentones had four British chart songs: "I'm a Moody Guy," "Walk Away," "It's All Over Now" and "Cindy's Birthday," their biggest success. The group disbanded in 1965.

Play It Cool "It's Gonna Take Magic" (1962) * *It's All Happening* (1963)

Shaw, Artie *see* Artie Shaw and His Band

Shaw, Freita *see* Freita Shaw...

Shearing, George *see* George Shearing Quintet

Shep Fields and His Orchestra

Shep Fields (Brooklyn, New York, 1910–1981)

With his memorably-named Rippling Rhythm Orchestra, Shep Fields literally opened his radio show the *Rippling Rhythm Revue* with the sound of bubbles being blown through a straw in a pot of water. Naturally enough one of their theme songs was "Rippling Rhythm"; the other was "Ritual Fire Dance."

The "sweet" dance band was formed in the early 1930s and had record hits like "Jersey Bounce," "Cathedral in the Pines" and "Thanks for the Memory." (The latter, from Fields' film, became Bob Hope's theme song.) The band was credited with producing some 300 recordings, fifty of which were hits.

In 1936 and '37 the Fields band placed number one in the Paramount Theatre Big Band poll. In the 1940s Fields formed an all-reed orchestra that featured future comedy great Sid Caesar. Fields himself was a saxophone and clarinet player. Eventually he returned to the musical sound that had made him famous and the band continued on into the 1950s. In latter years he became a disc jockey.

The Big Broadcast of 1938 (1937)

Shepp, Hobie *see* Hobie Shepp and the Cowtown Wranglers

Sheriff's Boys Band

The "Sheriff" of the Sheriff Boys Band was longtime Los Angeles County lawman Eugene Bizcailuz. He encouraged the formation of a band with young musicians who were then trained by a veteran conductor.

Good Luck, Mr. Yates (1943) * *Magic Town* (1947) †

†Their appearance in this film is not confirmed.

Sherrell Sisters (aka Sherrill Sisters)

Doris Sherrell; Grace Sherrell

The Sherrell Sisters were singers.

Follow the Leader (1944) "Now and Then" * *Moon Over Las Vegas* (1944)

Sherrill Sisters *see* Sherrell Sisters

Sherven Brothers Rodeoliers *see* Rodeliers

Sherwood, Bobby *see* Bobby Sherwood and His Orchestra

Sherwood Singers

The Young Swingers (1963)

Shilkret, Nathaniel *see* Nathaniel Shilkret Orchestra

Shirelles

Shirley Owens (1941–) (lead vocals); Adeline "Micki" Harris (1940–1982); Beverly Lee (1941/42–); Doris Coley (1941–2000)

Originally dubbed the Poquellos, the trailblazing New Jersey quartet the Shirelles began harmonizing in 1958. Their first hit "I Met Him on a Sunday" was actually written by them for a high school talent show but became a big national smash after they got a recording contract.

The Shirelles' name was a combination of Shirley Owens's first name and part of the last syllable of the then-popular group the Chantels. In contrast to girl groups like the Ronettes who opted for a sexy, almost tough, look, they were outfitted demurely.

On the strength of that first record the Shirelles toured in theaters and then had other successes with "Tonight's the Night" and especially "Will You Still Love Me Tomorrow?" This was the first-ever number one chart hit by a black female group.

Other songs like "Dedicated to the One I Love" "Baby It's You," "Soldier Boy" "Foolish Little Girl" and "Mama Said" cemented their place as a leading girls group. However by 1964 the English Invasion had breached American shores and the Shirelles' popularity began to wane.

Somewhat ironically Beatle John Lennon named them as his favorite group and the Beatles featured two of their songs on their first album. In the late 1960s the Shirelles became a trio (billed as Shirley and the Shirelles) and toured with other fading rock groups, already kind of a nostalgia item.

But the Shirelles still carried a cachet and in the 1990s there were three separate ensembles calling themselves by that name, with each having one original member. They were inducted into the Rhythm-and-Blues Hall of Fame in 1994 and the Rock-and-Roll Hall of Fame three years later.

It's a Mad, Mad, Mad, Mad World (1963) * *Let the Good Times Roll* [documentary] (1973)

"Shootsie" Keith and the Savannah Club Chorus

Harlem Follies (1949?)

Shorty Rogers and Band

Shorty Rogers (Milton Rajonsky, Laurel or Great Barrington, Massachusetts, 1922/24–1994)

Jazz musician Shorty Rogers played trumpet with, and did musical arrangements for, such big bands as those of Woody Herman and Stan Kenton in the 1940s. He had his own big band for a while and then formed a smaller combo, releasing several jazz albums with a "bop" flavor. He is considered a pioneer of the West Coast jazz scene.

Somewhat of an innovator, Rogers experimented with bi-tonality and twelve tone composition. By the 1960s he had disbanded his ensemble in order to write music for television and films, as well as doing music scoring for those media. He did occasionally return to performing in the 1980s and into the '90s, even taking up the flugelhorn.

The Glass Wall (1953) * *The Man with the Golden Arm* (1955)

Shorty Thompson and His Saddle Rockin' Rhythm

Shorty Thompson; Chet Atkins; Zed Tennis
El Dorado Pass (1948)

Shrum, Cal *see* Cal Shrum...

Shrum, Walt *see* Walt Shrum...

Sid Catlett's Band

Sid Catlett (Evansville, Indiana, 1910–1951)

Jazz drummer "Big" Sid Catlett played in bands both large and small prior to joining Benny Goodman in 1941. But he never stayed with anyone for very long and a few years later he formed his own band. In 1947 he joined Louis Armstrong's All Stars. He was known for his showy drum work during which he frequently tossed his sticks into the air.

Boy! What a Girl! (1947) * *Harlem Follies* (1950)

Silly Symphonists *see* Al Trace and His Silly Symphonists

Simon and Garfunkel

Paul Simon (Queens, New York, 1941–); Art Garfunkel (Queens, New York, 1941–)

Although the duo of Paul Simon and Art Garfunkel have long since gone their separate ways some of their songs endure as virtual anthems to the period in which they were written. Their phenomenal career began in an unprepossessing way with the 1950s twosome they called Tom and Jerry that produced the bubblegum hit "Hey, Schoolgirl."

Lasting fame as folk singers came under their own names with "The Sound of Silence" in 1965. Their soundtrack music for the 1968 mega-hit film *The Graduate* further cemented it. Among the hits that flowed from them were "Scarborough Fair," "Parsley, Sage, Rosemary and Thyme," "Bridge Over Troubled Waters," "I Am a Rock" and "Homeward Bound."

Simon and Garfunkel's emergence at a time of national upheaval over the Vietnam War made their music a symbol for antiwar forces, along with that of Peter, Paul and Mary and other folk groups. Their song "Mrs. Robinson," from *The Graduate*, earned a Grammy for record of the year and Simon won one for best original score for the movie.

Their album "Bridge Over Troubled Water" proved a major hit, winning additional Grammy Awards. However, Simon and Garfunkel's increasingly rocky personal relationship caused them to split in 1970. In subsequent years both continued to be very active musically.

Paul Simon garnered a reputation as an innovator working in various musical forms. Many of his songs have been recorded by other performers and he has essayed Broadway musicals. He also has made an occasional movie appearance, notably in *One-Trick Pony* and *Annie Hall*.

Art Garfunkel also dabbled with acting in *Catch-22* and *Carnal Desire*. From time to time the duo reunited for concerts but each has continued to thrive as individual performers. Although perhaps better known as folk singers, they were inducted into the Rock-and-Roll Hall of Fame.

Monterey Pop (1969) [documentary] "Fifty-Ninth Street Bridge Song"

Simp-Phonies
Country Fair (1941) * *The Medico of Painted Springs* (1941)

Sims, Artie *see* Artie Sims and His Band

Singing Buckaroos *see* Jimmie Davis and His Singing Buckaroos

Singing Constables *see* Arizona Wranglers

Singing Cowboys
Lloyd Perryman; Rudy Sooter; Curley Hogg

It is likely that the Singing Cowboys was a group put together for this one film only from members of existing western swing groups.
Santa Fe Rides (1937)

Singing Guardsmen
Wagon Wheels (1934)

Singing Indian Braves
Singin' in the Corn (1946)

Singing Riders
The Singing Riders all dressed alike and rode white horses.
Westward Ho (1935)

Singing Strings
The Singing Strings was a six member female vocal ensemble.
Pot O' Gold (1941)

Sissle, Noble *see* Noble Sissle and His Orchestra

Sistine Chapel Choir
Holy Year 1950 (1950) [documentary]

Six Bar-B Cowboys
Gun Law (1938) * *Where the West Begins* (1938)

Six Candreva Brothers [unknown]
William Candreva
Here Comes Cookie (1935)

6-Harlem Beauties-6 [unknown]
Dirty Gertie from Harlem, U.S.A. (1946)

Six Hits; Six Hits and a Miss
Marvin Bailey; Pauline Byrne; Vincent Degen; Lee Gotch; Phil Hanna; Frank Howard; Howard Hudson; Betty McCabe; Mack McLean; Tony Paris; Jerry Preshaw; Charles Schrouder; Bill Seckler; Conrad Taylor

Broadway Serenade (1939) * *Down Argentine Way* (1940) * *If I Had My Way* (1940) * *Hit Parade of 1941* (1940) * *Hellzapoppin'* (1941) * *Keep 'Em Flying* (1941) * *The Big Store* (1941) * *Lady Be Good* (1941) * *Time Out for Rhythm* (1941) * *Ziegfeld Girl* (1941) * *Babes on Broadway* (1942) * *Butch Minds the Baby* (1942) * *Call Out the Marines* (1942) * *For Me and My Gal* (1942) * *Panama Hattie* (1942) * *Springtime in the Rockies* (1942) * *DuBarry Was a Lady* (1943) * *Presenting Lily Mars* (1943)

Six Saddle Tramps *see* Buster Fite and His Six Saddle Tramps

Six Sizzlers Orchestra
Underworld (1937)

Six Solid Senders *see* Judy Clark and the Six Solid Senders

Six Spirits of Rhythm [unknown]
Gambling (1934)

Six Sweethearts [unknown]
Swing It Soldier (1941)

Skinnay Ennis and His Band; Skinnay Ennis and the Groove Boys

Skinnay Ennis (Robert Ennis, Salisbury, North Carolina, 1907–1963)

Orchestra leader Skinnay Ennis was really very thin, hence his accurate nickname. (The unorthodox spelling apparently was the result of a misspelling on a record label.) As a member of Bob Hope's radio family he developed the knack of exchanging barbs with the comic and thus was allowed to exhibit more of his personality than many bandleaders.

Ennis had also appeared with Bob Crosby and was later to work with Abbott and Costello on their late '40s radio show. He had been a drummer and vocalist with the Hal Kemp band before forming his own orchestra in 1938. His vocals had a distinctive "out-of-breath" quality about them and when he recorded the hit "Got a Date with an Angel" it became Kemp's theme song.

Because of his comedy skills Skinnay Ennis was a better film actor than most of his confreres so he occasionally played a character other than "himself." He and his band also appeared in some musical shorts and produced hit recordings like "Deep in a Dream" and "Garden of the Moon." He also played solo roles in films such as 1937's *College Swing*.

After leading a service band during World War II, Ennis managed to find work throughout the 1950s, including a lucrative several years conducting the house band at the Los Angeles Statler-Hilton. Unfortunately, he died in a Beverly Hills restaurant after choking on some food.

College Swing (1938) * *Blondie Meets the Boss* (1939) * *Swing It Soldier* (1941) * *Sleepytime Gal* (1942) * *Follow the Band* (1943) * *Radio Stars on Parade* (1945) * *Let's Go Steady* (1945)

Slack, Freddie *see* Freddie Slack and His Orchestra

Slam Stewart Trio *see* Slim and Slam

Slate Brothers

Syd Slate (Russia, 1907–1976); Henry Slate (New York, New York, 1910–1996); Jack Slate (1909–1989)

The multi-talented Slate Brothers were singers and dancers.

Happy Days (1930) * *College Swing* (1938) * *Harlem Follies* (1950) * *Meet Me in Las Vegas* (1955)

"Sleepy" Williams and His Three Shades of Rhythm [unknown]
"Sleepy" Williams; Lucius Smith; Alice Haynes Marcus; Louise Harris

Hoosier Holiday (1943)

Slick and Slack [unknown]
The Joint Is Jumpin' (1949?)

Slim and Slam; Slim Gaillard Trio; Slam Stewart Trio

Slim Gaillard (Bulee Gaillard, Santa Clara, Cuba or Detroit, Michigan, 1916?–1991); Slam Stewart (Leroy Stewart, Englewood, New Jersey, 1914–1987); Bam Brown; Beryl Booker; Johnny Collins; Billy Taylor

His entrée into show business was somewhat

inauspicious (tap dancing while playing the guitar in vaudeville) but Slim Gaillard rose above those modest beginnings. He formed a duo with Slam Stewart as Slim and Slam in 1937 or '38 and they had some hit recordings, including "Flat Foot Floogie (with a Floy, Floy"). They also essayed "Tutti Frutti" and other novelties.

Gaillard, who also played piano and vibes, invented a kind of jive language that he dubbed "vout" or "vout oreenie," and even composed a lengthy work called *Opera in Vout*. As a songwriter he produced the classic "Down By the Station" and the less-than-classic but catchy "Cement Mixer, Put-ti, Put-ti."

He and Stewart had a radio show where he played the guitar and Stewart the bass. When they split in 1942 Bam Brown became the bassist and they teamed for several years thereafter. Gaillard was an extremely colorful performer, doing things like playing the piano with his hands turned upside down.

Conservatory-trained Slam Stewart got his nickname from the sound his bass fiddle made while he was plucking the strings. He was one of the premier and most recorded jazz musicians of his day. Before and after teaming with Gaillard he played in several small ensembles.

One of them was his own Trio (piano, bass, guitar) which at times included Billy Taylor, Beryl Booker and Johnny Collins. Stewart also played with such giants as Benny Goodman, Art Tatum and Charlie Parker and sometimes essayed classical pieces. One of his specialties was humming while plucking the bass.

When his brand of music became somewhat passé Slim Gaillard left the music industry but took some television acting jobs, including *Roots: the Next Generation*. He had appeared in several movies in the 1940s and also had later roles in films like *Planet of the Apes*. Acting was a natural for the 6'4" man who in his youth had been known as the "Dark Gable."

Returning in the 1980s to the music scene, Gaillard made some new recordings and was a familiar figure at festivals around the world. In 1989 the BBC aired a documentary called *The World of Slim Gaillard*. He had lived in England since 1983.

Hellzapoppin' (1941) * *Almost Married* (1942) * *Stormy Weather* (1943) * *Star Spangled Rhythm* (1943) * *Stairway for a Star* (1946?) * *Sweetheart of Sigma Chi* (1946) * *Boy! What a Girl!* (1947)

Slim Gaillard Trio *see* Slim and Slam

Sly and the Family Stone

Sly Stone (Sylvester Stewart, Dallas or Denton, Texas, 1944–) (organ); Freddie Stone (guitar); Larry Graham (bassist); Vaetta Stewart (tambourine/piano); Mary McCreary (vocals); Elva Mouton (vocals); Rose Stone (vocals/keyboard); Greg Errico (drums); Jerry Martini (saxophone)

As youngsters Sylvester Stewart and three siblings formed the Stewart Four and made a recording of gospel songs. Later he and his brother belonged to the San Francisco Bay–area group The Viscaynes. Subsequently, for a gig as a San Francisco radio disc jockey Sylvester changed his name to Sly Stone.

Both Sly and his brother formed their own bands — the former's was called Sly and the Stoners. After they merged their groups in 1967 Sly and the Family Stone was launched as a racially integrated band. Their first major record success was the rocking "Dance to the Music." Others included "Everyday People," "Hot Fun in the Summertime" and "Sing a Simple Song"; several albums also scored in the millions of copies.

The band had a mélange of styles that ranged from funk to show tunes to psychedelic music (their onstage costuming also tended to be psychedelic.) They were a most colorful ensemble during their major period of activity from 1967 to 1975, and were considered groundbreakers in both their music and their racial and gender mix. Woodstock was one of the venues at which they appeared.

In the 1970s Sly and the Family Stone's music became darker as drug abuse crept into the fabric of the band. After the initial group's dissolution, the reclusive Stone formed another with which he toured until the late 1980s. They were inducted into the Rock-and-Roll Hall of Fame in 1993.

Woodstock (1970) [documentary] "I Want to Take You Higher" and "Hey Music Lover"

Smart Set [unknown]
Lone Star Moonlight (1946)

Smiley and Kitty
Smiley Wilson; Kitty Carson Wilson

Smiley and Kitty Wilson sang on radio in Texas and Nashville. In latter days Smiley became a top talent agent for country singers like Loretta Lynn.

Square Dance Jubilee (1949) "Mocking Bird" and "It's a Boy"

Smith, Hubert *see* **Hubert Smith and His Coral Islanders**

Smith, Jimmy *see* **Jimmy Smith...**

Smith, Preacher *see* **Preacher Smith's Deacons**

Smith Ballew and the Sons of the Sage

Smith Ballew (Palestine, Texas, 1902–1984)

It definitely was not John Wayne singing in his early 1930s "B" westerns as the character "Singing Sandy," but it may well have been Smith Ballew. He later also had his own brief oater series in the latter 1930s that included *Hawaiian Buckaroo* and *Panamint's Bad Man*.

Starting out in college bands, Ballew sang and played the banjo in several big orchestras including those of Ted Fio Rito, Ben Pollack and Freddie Rich. He also had his own radio show, *Shell Chateau*. Familiarly known as "Sykes," he also led his own band in which Glenn Miller played trombone.

Tall (at least 6'5") and matinee-idol handsome, Ballew was perhaps an unconvincing oater lead but an able enough second lead and supporting player in films like *I Killed Geronimo* and *The Red Badge of Courage*. He appeared in movies up to the early 1950s; his first had been 1937's *Palm Springs*.

In one of his starring western films, *Rawhide*, Ballew had a most unusual co-star: baseball legend Lou Gehrig. Supposedly the vocalist on more than 5,000 recordings using different names, Smith Ballew also appeared on Broadway and in nightclubs.

Under Arizona Skies (1946)

Smokestack Lightnin'

Kelly Green; Ric Eiserling; Art Guy (drummer); Ron Darling

A rock band of the mid–1960s, Smokestack Lightnin' frequently played at the famed Sunset Strip club Whiskey-A-Go-Go, the "in" place in Los Angeles for several years. Their album "Off the Wall" has gained respect over the years since the group disbanded in 1970.

Dreams of Glass (1968) "Well Tuesday"

Smokey Robinson and the Miracles

Smokey Robinson (William Robinson, Jr., Detroit, Michigan, 1940–); Clarence Dawson; Warren "Pete" Moore (bass); Ronnie White (1938?–1995) (baritone); James Grice; Claudette (Rogers) Robinson; Bobby Rogers (tenor); Emerson Rogers (tenor); Marv Tarplin (guitar)

In the mid–1950s some of the men who were to become the Miracles began in a high school group called the Chimes (later the Matadors). Berry Gordy, the young Motown entrepreneur-to-be, liked their sound and indeed they became a symbol of the so-called "Motown sound." He renamed them the Miracles, with the addition of a female member.

The group's success was

Smith Ballew (tall man at center) in one of his starring westerns (late 1930s).

not the proverbial overnight one; their first hit "Shop Around" did not come for a few years but once going the Miracles never looked back. A string of hits followed, including "The Track of My Tears," "You Really Got a Hold on Me," "Going to a Go-Go," "What's So Good About Goodbye" and "I'm the One You Need."

In the mid–1960s they became Smokey Robinson and the Miracles and had one of their biggest successes with "I Second That Emotion." "Tears of a Clown" was the Miracles' final hit. Robinson, a songwriter for many other rock groups as well as a talented singer, embarked on a solo career in 1972. Among his own compositions were "My Guy" and "The Way You Do the Things You Do."

In 1996 he received a Lifetime Achievement Award from the National Academy of Songwriters. Smokey Robinson was inducted into the Rock-and-Roll Hall of Fame in 1987 and received Kennedy Center honors in 2006. The Miracles remained together for a few more years with "Love Machine" being their best seller during that time. They were inducted into the Vocal Group Hall of Fame in 2001.

The T.A.M.I. Show (1964) [documentary] "That's What Love Is Made of," "You Really Got a Hold on Me" and "Mickey's Monkey"

Smoky Mountain Boys *see* **Roy Acuff...**

Smoky Mountain Boys and Girls *see* **Roy Acuff...**

Smoky Mountain Boys, with Rachel *see* **Roy Acuff...**

SMU 50 *see* **Southern Methodist University 50**

Solidaires *see* **Leo Diamond and His Solidaires**

Song Spinners

The Song Spinners' biggest moment in the limelight came during a musicians' strike in 1943. The popular song "You'll Never Know" was recorded by crooner Dick Haymes without instrumentation and the Spinners provided a cappella background accompaniment. Unusually for that era they received credit on the recording for their contribution.

Follies Girl (1943)

Sonny and Cher

Sonny Bono (Salvatore Bono, 1935–1998); Cher (Cherilyn LaPiere, El Centro, California, 1946–)

One of the most popular (some might say bizarre) boy-girl teamings in music history were Sonny and Cher, who were originally dubbed Caesar and Cleo. After an uncertain start — and a well-advised name change — they hit the jackpot with "I Got You Babe." Sonny, thirty years old, was a fairly successful songwriter. Cher, who was nineteen, had previously made records under the name of Bonnie Jo Mason.

Of course it was not only their music-making but their contrasting personalities, often cornball humor, and evolving relationship that made the duo famous. Their celebrity was cemented by a long-running Emmy-nominated variety show in the early 1970s. They had previously headlined a poorly-received movie called *Good Times*; Cher alone starred in *Chastity*.

Other Sonny and Cher hits were "The Beat Goes on," "Little Man" and "Baby, Don't Go." By 1974 their always-in-the-limelight marriage was ending and so their variety show fell by the wayside. They each got their own television shows and thereafter rarely reunited professionally.

Diminutive Sonny Bono went on to a semi-successful career as a singer and film actor (*Hairspray*), became the mayor of Palm Springs and then a U.S. congressman. Cher continued her successful career as a solo performer, and with an unerring flair for publicity managed to stay in the public eye for many years longer while proclaiming many "final" tours.

She made such well-received movies as *Come Back to the Five and Dime, Jimmy Dean, Jimmy Dean, Silkwood, The Witches of Eastwick* and *Mask* and had an acclaimed Oscar-winning role in *Moonstruck*. She also continued to issue well-received albums.

Wild on the Beach (1965) "It's Gonna Rain" * *Good Times* (1967) "It's the Little Things," "Trust Me" and several other songs

Sonny Dunham and His Orchestra

Sonny Dunham (Elmer Dunham, Brockton, Massachusetts, 1911/14–1990)

The New York Yankees are not only a baseball team but also the name of Sonny Dunham's first, short-lived orchestra in the early 1930s. He was originally a trombonist but made his reputation playing the trumpet as a sideman in various bands, particularly Glen Gray's Casa Loma orchestra.

His fellow musicians called him the "Man from Mars" because he blew such high notes. In 1940 Dunham established the band that would be his most successful, with its theme song "Memories of You." The group recorded and toured until being disbanded in the early 1950s. He thereafter led various bands but his time in the limelight had passed.

Behind the Eight Ball (1942)

Sons of Adam

Michael Stuart-Ware (drums); Mike Port; Randy Holden; Jack Tanna

The Sons of Adam were a garage band active in the mid–1960s.

The Slender Thread (1965)

Sons of the Pioneers; Cliff Lyons and the Sons of the Pioneers

Roy Rogers (Leonard Sly [later Slye], (Cincinnati, Ohio, 1911–1998); Bob Nolan (Clarence Nobles, Point Hatfield or Winnipeg, Canada, 1908–1980); Tim Spencer (Vernon Spencer, Webb City, Missouri, 1908–1974); Hugh Farr (Thomas Farr, Plano, Texas, 1903–1980); Karl Farr (Rochelle, Texas, 1909–1961) (lead guitar); Lloyd Perryman (Ruth, Arkansas, 1917–1977); Ken Curtis (Curtis Gates, Colorado, 1916–1991); Pat Brady; Ken Carson; Tommy Doss; George Fisher; Cliff Lyons

Without doubt the most famous (if not necessarily the greatest) western swing ensemble, the Sons of the Pioneers were founded during the heart of the Great Depression. One of them was Leonard Sly(e), later to become famous after his first starring vehicle, 1938's *Under Western Stars.*

As Roy Rogers he became Republic Studio's "King of the Cowboys." Previously he had played small parts in other stars' westerns under the name of Dick Weston. He and Bob Nolan had been members of the Rocky Mountaineers and several other groups before they and Tim Spencer got together to form the International Cowboys, then the O-Bar-O Cowboys, and finally the Pioneer Trio in Los Angeles in 1933.

It was not long before their singing and yodeling attracted radio listeners far and wide. The Pioneer Trio became the Sons of the Pioneers through a radio announcer's error and as such they went to recording and movie fame, first providing support in many Charles Starrett oaters. The talented Farr brothers, who played what they termed "cowboy jazz," became important additions to the group. "Tumbling Tumbleweeds," written by Bob Nolan, was the Pioneers' theme song.

They began appearing in Roy Rogers films in 1941 (with *Red River Valley*) and continued with him until 1948's *Night Time in Nevada.* Foy Willing and the Riders of the Purple Sage then replaced them. Unlike many other western swing groups who were strictly anonymous background in films the Pioneers often had speaking parts. Bob Nolan sometimes played the second male lead.

Roy Rogers went on to make some ninety films and had a popular television show in the early 1950s with his wife, and frequent leading lady, Dale Evans. As late as the mid-'70s Rogers had a hit record with "Hoppy, Gene and Me" and was inducted into the Country Music Hall of Fame in 1988.

In 1979 the Sons of the Pioneers were designated a "National Treasure" by the Smithsonian Institution and their recordings of "Cool Water" and "Tumbling Tumbleweeds" were placed in the National Archives. They were also inducted into the Country Music Hall Of Fame. With new members they have continued performing into the 21st century.

The Gallant Defender (1935) * *The Old Homestead* (1935) * *Tumbling Tumbleweeds* (1935) * *The Big Show* (1936) * *The Old Corral* (1936) * *California Mail* (1936) * *Rhythm on the Range* (1936) * *Ride, Ranger, Ride* (1936) * *Song of the Saddle* (1936) * *The Mysterious Avenger* (1936) * *The Old Barn Dance* (1936) * *The Old Wyoming Trail* (1937) * *Outlaws Of the Prairie* (1937) * *Springtime in the Rockies* (1937) * *Call of the Rockies* (1938) * *Law of the Plains* (1938) * *The Cattle Raiders* (1938) * *The Colorado Trail* (1938) * *West of Cheyenne* (1938) * *West of the Santa Fe* (1938) * *Rio Grande* (1938) * *South of Arizona* (1938) * *Riders of the Black River* (1939) * *Western Caravans* (1939) * *The Stranger from Texas* (1939) * *Texas Stampede* (1939) * *Spoilers of the Range* (1939) * *North of the Yukon* (1939) * *The

170 Sons

Thundering West (1939) * *Outpost of the Mounties* (1939) * *The Man from Sundown* (1939) * *Blazing Six Shooters* (1940) * *Two-Fisted Rangers* (1940) * *The Thundering Frontier* (1940) * *Bullets for Rustlers* (1940) * *West of Abilene* (1940) * *The Durango Kid* (1940) * *Texas Stagecoach* (1940) * *The Pinto Kid* (1941) * *Outlaws of the Panhandle* (1941) * *Red River Valley* (1941) * *Romance on the Range* (1942) * *Ridin' Down the Canyon* (1942) * *The Man from Cheyenne* (1942) * *Heart of the Golden West* (1942) * *Call of the Canyon* (1942) * *South of Santa Fe* (1942) * *Sons of the Pioneers* (1942) * *Sunset on the Desert* (1942) * *Sunset Serenade* (1942) * *Silver Spurs* (1943) * *The Man from Music Mountain* (1943) * *Idaho* (1943) * *Song of Texas* (1943) * *King of the Cowboys* (1943) * *San Fernando Valley* (1944) * *Yellow Rose of Texas* (1944) * *Hands Across the Border* (1944) * *The Cowboy and the Senorita* (1944) * *Lights of Old Santa Fe* (1944) * *Song of Nevada* (1944) * *Hollywood Canteen* (1944) * *Sunset in El Dorado* (1945) * *The Man from Oklahoma* (1945) * *Don't Fence Me In* (1945) * *Along the Navajo Trail* (1945) * *Utah* (1945) * *Bells of Rosarita* (1945) * *Song of Arizona* (1946) * *Under Nevada Skies* (1946) * *Rainbow Over Texas* (1946) * *Roll on, Texas Moon* (1946) * *My Pal Trigger* (1946) * *Heldorado* (1946) * *Ding Dong Williams* (1946) * *Home In Oklahoma* (1946) * *Home on the Range* (1946) * *On the Old Spanish Trail* (1947) * *Bells of San Angelo* (1947) * *Springtime in the Sierras* (1947) * *Apache Rose* (1947) * *The Hit Parade of 1947* (1947) * *The Gay Ranchero* (1948) * *Melody Time* (1948) (voices only) * *Under California Stars* (1948) * *Night Time in Nevada* (1948) * *Eyes of Texas* (1948) * *Rio Grande* (1950) * *Wagonmaster* (1950) * *Everybody's Dancin'* (1950) * *The Fighting Coast Guard* (1951)

Sons of the Sage *see* Smith Ballew and the Sons of the Sage

Sooter, Rudy *see* Rudy Sooter and His Californians

Southern Methodist University 50

The "50" was a college choir.
The Big Show (1936)

Spade Cooley and His Orchestra

Spade Cooley (Donnell Cooley, Pack Saddle or Grand, Oklahoma, 1910–1969)

Originally trained as a classical cellist and violinist, Spade Cooley played fiddle in western bands from 1934 and formed his own western swing ensemble in 1941. He was eventually dubbed (perhaps by himself) the "King of Western Swing." His nickname of "Spade" supposedly came about because of an extended run of spades he once held in a poker game.

Cooley appeared in films both with and without his band, including three minor starring westerns in 1950 (*Border Outlaws*, *The Silver Bandit*, *The Kid from Gower Gulch*). At the time of his death he was on leave from prison where he had been incarcerated for murdering his wife in 1961. In fact he is the only known convicted killer who has a star on Hollywood's Walk of Fame.

The Sons of the Pioneers.

In 1946 Spade Cooley starred on what was supposedly the first television show to feature ballroom dancing. He also had a television western variety show from 1948 to '56. At one time he had been Roy Rogers' stand-in.

Chatterbox (1943) * *The Singing Sheriff* (1944) * *Senorita from the West* (1945) * *Rockin' in the Rockies* (1945) * *Vacation Days* (1947) * *Square Dance Jubilee* (1949)

Specht, Paul *see* Paul Specht and His Orchestra

Spencer Davis Group

Spencer Davis (Swansea, Wales, 1939–) (guitar); Muff Winwood (bassist); Steve Winwood (vocals); Pete York (drums)

Founded in the heady days just before the British Invasion, the Spencer Davis Group had U. S. hits in the mid–'60s like "Gimme Some Lovin'" and "I'm a Man." They also did recordings in German.

The popularity of the Group diminished after the Winwood brothers left to play with the band Traffic, but Spencer Davis soldiered on. He continued to release albums periodically and found renewed success in the 1980s and beyond with new ensembles.

Pop Gear (1965) [documentary] "My Babe" * *Go Go Mania* (1965) * *The Ghost Goes Gear* (1966) * *Here We Go 'Round the Mulberry Bush* (1968)

Spike Jones and the City Slickers; Spike Jones and His Orchestra

Spike Jones (Lindley Jones, Long Beach, California, 1911–1965)

Supposedly earning his nickname because he was as thin as a railroad spike, the bandleader Spike Jones carved a unique place for himself as a master of cacophony. He played in several orchestras, and was a studio drummer, before establishing the City Slickers which gained a reputation for "murdering" classic melodies.

It was no classic that first brought Jones to prominence but a ditty entitled "Der Fuhrer's Face," originally from a Disney cartoon, which accomplished the feat. A follow-up, "Cocktails for Two," became his signature song. The Slickers' recordings, including "Chloe," contained many of their trademark "instruments": a washboard, cowbells, foghorns, pistol shots, bird calls, belches, barking dogs and even a toilet seat (dubbed the "latrinophone").

The public responded enthusiastically to Jones' eccentric music-making and earned him several number one records in the 1940s, including "All I Want for Christmas Is My Two Front Teeth." Among other popular songs were "The Sheik of Araby" and "Dance of the Hours." He always prefaced his (mis)playing of such classics as "The William Tell Overture" and "Liebestraum" by gravely intoning, "Thank you, music lovers."

Besides his extreme gauntness, Spike Jones was possessed of an angular face, red hair and a wardrobe usually consisting of garish, tight-fitting checked suits. This made him a natural for character roles in films besides those in which the City Slickers appeared. The orchestra also had long-running radio and television shows.

Thank Your Lucky Stars (1943) * *Meet the People* (1944) * *Bring on the Girls* (1945) * *Breakfast in Hollywood* (1946) * *Ladies Man* (1947) * *Variety Girl* (1947) * *Fireman, Save My Child* (1954)

Spirit

The Model Shop (1969) "Nothing to Do and Little to Say"

Spitalny, Phil *see* Phil Spitalny and His Hour of Charm All Girl Orchestra, Featuring Evelyn and Her Magic Violin

Spivak, Charlie *see* Charlie Spivak and His Orchestra

Spooky Tooth

Mike Harrison (Carlisle, England, 1942–) (keyboard); Greg Ridley (Alfred Ridley, England, 1942–2003) (bassist); Luther Grosvenor (Eversham, England, 1946–) (guitar); Mike Kellie (Birmingham, England, 1945–) (drums); Gary Wright (Creskill, New Jersey, 1943–) (organ)

The British rock band Spooky Tooth flourished from 1967 to the mid–1970s. Among their more successful recordings were "Society's Child" and "Here I Lived So Well," but "You Broke My Heart So I Busted Your Jaw" has to be the most memorable. They reunited in the late 1990s.

Groupies (1970) [documentary]

Sportsmen; Sportsmen Quartet

John Rarig (baritone); Thurl Ravenscroft; Gurney Bell (Los Angeles, California, 1912–1976)

The singing group the Sportsmen, formed in the late 1930s, were regulars on Jack Benny's radio and television shows.

Puddin' Head (1941) * *Lost Canyon* (1942) * *Here Comes Elmer* (1943) * *O, My Darling Clementine* (1943) * *Moon Over Las Vegas* (1944) * *Weekend Pass* (1944) * *Feudin', Fussin' and a-Fightin'* (1948) * *Make Believe Ballroom* (1949) * *Footlight Varieties* (1950) * *Walking My Baby Back Home* (1952) * *Paris Follies of 1956* (1955)

Spriggins, Deuce *see* Deuce Spriggins and His Band

Stabile, Dick *see* Dick Stabile and His Band

Stafford, Jesse *see* Jesse Stafford and His Orchestra

Stafford Quartet; Stafford Sisters; Stafford Trio

Jo Stafford (Coalinga, California, 1917–2008); Christine Stafford (Gainesboro, Tennessee, 1903?–1990); Pauline Stafford (d. 1988); Vivian Edwards; Mary Mahoney; Judy Matson; Dorothy Wilkerson

The Stafford Sisters made their debut on radio in 1935 but as an ensemble they were not destined to endure for very long. Pauline and Christine left the group for marriage and the one who was to be the most famous, Jo, joined the Pied Pipers in the mid–1940s. While the sisters were in films they performed some comedy singing, in one picture playing the sour-voiced "Levinsky Trio."

Jo Stafford went on to a distinguished solo career and a reputation as one of the 20th century's greatest chanteuses with such smash records as "My Happiness," "Shrimp Boats," "Jambalaya," "Temptation" and especially "You Belong To Me." She was supposedly the first female singer to sell 25 million records.

Stafford also had another string to her bow and was a successful comedienne under the unlikely rubric of Cornelia C. Stump. With husband Paul Weston she established a fictional comic duo called Darlene and Jonathan Edwards, one of their albums winning an Emmy.

Avenging Waters (1936) * *The Old Barn Dance* (1938) * *Gold Mine in the Sky* (1938) * *Babes on Broadway* (1942) * *Girl Crazy* (1943)

Stamps

V. O. Stamps; Ed Enoch

Among Elvis Presley's most favored gospel groups was the Stamps quartet. Having been professionally active since 1924 they are one of the longest-surviving white gospel ensembles. "Give the World a Smile" was one of their first major record successes.

They began appearing with Presley in 1971 and often backed him at his live performances and on records. They have also sung with luminaries like Tammy Wynette, Willie Nelson and Ricky Skaggs.

The Stamps continue to make music to this day, touring throughout the world in major venues and garnering Grammy nominations and numerous awards. They were inducted into the Gospel Music Hall of Fame in 1997.

Sing a Song, for Heaven's Sake (1966) [documentary] * *Elvis on Tour* (1972) [documentary]

Stan Kenton and His Orchestra

Stan Kenton (Wichita, Kansas, 1911/12–1979)

Pianist Stan Kenton formed his own ensemble about 1941 after playing in other orchestras (e.g., Gus Arnheim, Johnny "Scat" Davis) for many years. Almost from the first he distinguished himself with his super-sized groups and their somewhat unconventional music. (At 6'6" in height he was also super-sized!) "Artistry in Rhythm" was his evocative and prescient theme song and the band's descriptive name.

In the era of the sweet big bands his groups sometimes played Afro-Cuban rhythms with a variety of percussive instruments. Later, often composing his own music, Kenton experimented with different sounds and sometimes pure dissonance. For two years running in the late '40s his was declared Band of the Year.

As the 1940s drew to a close Kenton had formed his Innovations in Modern Music orchestra that contained more than forty players (later drastically reduced in size). His choice of music continued to be eclectic and unconventional for its time, but he eventually came to be best known for his progressive jazz stylings.

Following his New Concepts in Rhythm and New Era in Modern Music Orchestras, Stan Kenton's last great ensemble was his Mellophonium band of the 1960s. Increasingly, he turned to music education in high school and colleges and thereby influenced a new generation of musicians with his own passion for innovation. His will specified that no band use his name after his death.

Talk About a Lady (1946)

Standells

Larry Tamblyn (vocals); Tony Valentino; Gary Lane (bassist); Gary Leeds (drums); Dick Dodd (vocals)

Believe it or not, the Standells who came together in 1962 were named thusly for all the times they were *standing* around waiting for work! Eventually they stopped standing and started working in local Los Angeles clubs, occasionally on television, and making recordings.

They finally hit the big time with the song "Dirty Water" and the more modest successes "Sometimes Good Guys Don't Wear White" and "Why Pick on Me?" They disbanded in the early 1970s, except for a couple of reunion gigs, but today are credited with having been one of the first garage (punk) bands. Their songs were sometimes banned on radio for being obscene.

Get Yourself a College Girl (1964) "The Swim" and "Bony Maronie" * *Riot on Sunset Strip* (1967) "Riot on Sunset Strip" and "Get Away from Here"

Staple Singers

Roebuck "Pop" Staples (Winona, Missouri, 1915–2000); Mavis Staples (contralto); Cleotha Staples; Pervis Staples; Yvonne Staples

A gospel, rhythm-and-blues and soul group, the Staple Singers were composed of a father and eventually four of his children. They were active from 1951 but did not achieve much renown until the latter '60s. Among their hits from that era were "I'll Take You There," "Respect Yourself," "Uncloudy Day," and "Let's Do It Again."

The Staples also released several albums and in the 1960s expanded into rhythm-and-blues. They toured abroad extensively with the Bee Gees and others. Their last charted song came in 1985.

Festival (1967) [documentary] "Up Above My Head," "I Ain't Gonna Let No One Turn Me Around" and "Go Tell It on the Mountain" * *Soul To Soul* (1971) [documentary] "When Will We Be Paid?" and "Are You Sure?" * *Wattstax* (1973) [documentary]

Stardusters

June Hutton (Chicago, Illinois, 1920–1973); Glenn Calyon; Curt Purnell; Dick Wylder

The most famous member of the Stardusters vocal group was undoubtedly its only female member, chanteuse June Hutton. She was related to the showy bandleader Ina Ray Hutton (her half-sister).

The Stardusters were the quartet attached to Charlie Spivak's orchestra and had a couple of record hits with "This Is No Laughing Matter" and "Brother Bill." When Jo Stafford departed from the Pied Pipers in 1944, Hutton replaced her and eventually went on to a solo career until the mid–1950s.

Slightly Terrific (1944) * *Trocadero* (1944)

Starlighters

The Starlighters was a vocal group.

Fun and Fancy Free (voices only?) (1947) * *It Happened in Brooklyn* * (1947) * *Song of Idaho* (1948)

Starliters *see* Joey Dee and the Starliters

Statesmen; Statesmen Quartet; Hovie Lister and the Statesmen Quartet

Mosie Lister (lead vocals); Hovie Lister (d. 2001) (piano); Gordon Hill (bass); Jake Hess; A.D. Soward; Jim Wetherington (d. 1973) (bass); Denver Crumpler (d. 1957) (tenor); Doy Ott (baritone)

A Southern gospel group, the Statesmen was formed by Hovie Lister in 1948. Although he was a Baptist minister his frantic piano-playing style was a precursor of such showmen as Jerry Lee Lewis.

The Statesmen influenced many who followed them, including Elvis Presley. They are still active in the new century and are considered to have been one the premier gospel groups. Among their more than 100 recordings are "Get Away Jordan" and "Happy Rhythm."

Sing a Song, for Heaven's Sake (1966) [documentary]

Statler Brothers

Don Reid (Staunton, Virginia, 1945–) (lead vocals); Harold Reid (Staunton, Virginia, 1939–) (bass); Phil Balsley (Staunton, Virginia, 1939–) (baritone); Lew DeWitt (1938–1990) (tenor); Jimmy Fortune (tenor)

The Statler Brothers are neither named Statler nor are all of them brothers; in fact they claimed to be named after a brand of facial tissues! (They were initially called the Kingsmen at their formation in 1955, a name later made famous by a folk music group.) Whatever the true origin of their name, they were a highly-regarded country music (tinged with gospel) ensemble who won several Grammys and numerous other honors and awards.

The Statlers had more than forty albums to their credit, some having gone double and triple platinum, including a couple of comedy albums. Their hit singles are less numerous, being composed of "Flowers on the Wall," "Class of '57," "Don't Wait on Me" and "Bed of Roses." They presumably have sold more than 15 million records.

With their admixture of songs and comedy the Brothers also had a popular variety show on television prior to announcing their retirement in 2002. In their early days, they toured extensively with Johnny Cash.

That Tennessee Beat (1966)

Steve Gibson's Red Caps

Jimmy Springs (lead tenor/drums); David Patillo (2nd tenor/bassist); Richard Davis (baritone/piano); Steve Gibson (bass/guitar); Beryl Booker (piano); Doles Dickens; Romaine Brown; Damita Jo; Emmett Mathews (tenor/saxophone)

Steve Gibson's Red Caps featured instrumentals and comedy as well as vocals. About 1940 they came together from several other groups that had been active in the Los Angeles area in the 1930s. Originally called the Four Toppers (although there were sometimes more than four members) they renamed themselves the Red Caps (traditionally, railway porters) about 1943.

This name was apparently assumed so it would be understood they were a Black group and perhaps be compared to the popular Ink Spots. They turned out numerous recordings and soon came up with the hit "I Learned a Lesson I'll Never Forget."

Later successes in the 1940s were "Blueberry Hill," "Boogie Ball" and "Wedding Bells Are Breaking Up That Old Gang of Mine." They were also the first to record "I Went to Your Wedding," later covered and popularized by Patti Page.

The Red Caps continued to tour and record pop and rhythm-and-blues tunes into the 1950s, and were by then known as Steve Gibson and the Original Red Caps. They added girl singer Damita Jo to their lineup and played clubs throughout the country before their long run finally came to an end in 1961.

Son of Inagi (1940) * *Mystery in Swing* (1940) * *Murder with Music* (1941) * *Mantan Messes Up* (1946) * *Excess Baggage* (1949) * *Destination Murder* (1950)

Steve Miller Band

Steve Miller (Milwaukee, Wisconsin, 1943–), James Cook (guitar); Tim Davis (drums); Lonnie Turner (bassist); Jim Peterman (keyboard); Boz Scaggs

The Marksmen was the name of Steve Miller's first band, formed in 1955 when he was twelve. That was followed by the Ardells, the World War Three Band and the Miller-Goldberg Blues Band. He was nothing if not persistent and it paid off with an appearance on the television show *Hullabaloo*.

With that exposure Miller migrated to San Francisco during the height of the hippie era and the "Summer of Love" days. It was there he assembled his Steve Miller Blues Band, later shortened to the Steve Miller Band. By 1967 they were headliners at local clubs; eventually they were to tour the world with sellout performances everywhere.

The Miller Band also had a lucrative record contract that led to several multimillion-selling gold and platinum albums, one of which went an amazing thirteen-times platinum. Their landmark single was "The Joker." The band was still going strong and remains a highly-influential music group well into the 21st Century.

Revolution (1968) [documentary] "Your Old Lady"

Stevens Sisters

Cecile Stevens; Leonetti Stevens; Charmaine Stevens

The Steven Sisters were young singers and dancers.

Broken Strings (1940) "Kentucky Babe"

Stewart, Cecil *see* **Cecil Stewart and His Royal Rogues**

Stewart, Slam *see* **Slim and Slam**

Stokowski, Leopold *see* **Leopold Stokowski and His Symphony Orchestra**

Stone Country
Steve Young (guitar); Don Beck; Denny Conway

A short-lived band, Stone Country was formed in 1967 and by 1969 was already kaput. In that time the group released but a single, self-titled, album.

Skidoo! (1968)

Stonemans
Ernest Stoneman (Monarat, Virginia, 1893–1968); Roni Stoneman; Van Stoneman; Jimmy Stoneman; Donna Stoneman

There could potentially have been a whole lot of Stonemans because father Ernest and his wife Hattie had fourteen children. (In practice they broke up into separate groups.) A master of the autoharp, harmonica and Jew's harp, the patriarch had a very successful recording of "The Sinking of the Titanic" in 1924. During the remainder of that decade he recorded some 200 songs, but not always under his own name.

By 1930 Stoneman had begun to include other members of his family in the act, thus making them one of the longest continuously-performing country-western acts ever (along with the Carter Family). They have appeared much on radio and television, on which they had their own show, and have won awards as the best vocal group.

The Road to Nashville (1966) * *Hell on Wheels* (1967)

Stop, Look and Listen Trio [unknown]
Swing It Soldier (1941) * *Babes on Broadway* (1942)

Strangers
From Nashville with Music (1969) * *Killers Three* (1969)

Strawberry Alarm Clock
Ed King (lead guitar); Lee Freeman (rhythm guitar); Gary Lovetro (bassist); Mark Weitz (organ); Randy Seol (drums); George Bunnell (bassist)

"Incense and Peppermints" was the title of Strawberry Alarm Clock's biggest hit, a song redolent of the psychedelic music era. Interestingly, it was vocalized by a sixteen year old, Greg Munford, who was not even a member of the band. It was sung in both their films, one of which is now the uber-cult movie *Beyond the Valley of the Dolls*.

The Alarm Clock released a couple of albums in the late 1960s and had one or two minor hits but never again had a success like their million seller. They toured and were briefly considered one of the top rock bands before disbanding in 1971. Several members regrouped in the '80s for what were already considered "oldies" tours.

Psych-Out (1967) "Incense and Peppermints," "Rainy Day Mushroom Pillow" and "The Pretty Song from Psych-Out" * *Beyond the Valley of the Dolls* (1970) "A Girl from the City," "I'm Coming Home" and "Incense and Peppermints"

Stream of Consciousness
Hells Angels '69 (1969)

Sunkissed Brown Skin Chorus [unknown]
Sunday Sinners (1941)

Sunset Riders *see* **Art West and His Sunset Riders**

Sunshine Band *see* **Jimmie Davis and His Sunshine Band**

Sunshine Boys; Sunshine Boys and Girls
Andy Parker (1913–1977); George Bamby (accordion); Paul Smith; Earl Murphey; Charlie Morgan; Ed Wallace (accordion/piano); Fred Daniel; Ace Richman (bassist); J. D. Sumner; A. L. Smith (guitar); J. O. Smith (fiddle)

One of the western swing bands that appeared in films with oater stars Eddie Dean and Charles Starrett in the 1940s and early '50s were the Sunshine Boys. They later played with a minor singer by the name of Elvis Presley. The group had begun its life in 1938 as the Red River Rangers.

As the Rangers they sang on the radio as a western group, and were known as the Sunshine Boys when they sang gospel tunes. Simultaneously they became yet another incarnation of the western band the Light Crust Doughboys, so performed under *three* different names at the same time. They combined with the Sunshine Girls for one film, *Song of Idaho*.

Driftin' River (1946) * *Stars Over Texas* (1946) * *Tumbleweed Trail* (1946) * *Range Beyond the Blue* (1947) * *West to Glory* (1947) * *Wild Country* (1947) * *West of Sonora* (1948) * *Song of Idaho* (1948) * *Challenge of the Range* (1949) * *Quick on the Trigger* (1949) * *Prairie Roundup* (1951) * *Junction City* (1952)

Sunshine Company
Maury Manseau (keyboard); Larry Sims (guitar); Mary Nance (vocals); Merle Brigante (drums)

Starting out as a folk singing group in the mid–1960s, the Sunshine Company ventured into pop-rock, something that may have blurred their identity in the long run. Their recordings included many covers of previously-released material rather than original songs.

Among their best-remembered recordings are "Look, Here Comes the Sun" and "Back on the Street Again." Whatever the reasons for their failure to find breakout success, they were considered a very talented ensemble and were the opening act for Jefferson Airplane on one tour. The Sunshine Company disbanded in 1970.

For Singles Only (1968)

Sunshine Girls
June Wiedner; Colleen Summers (later Mary Ford) (Pasadena, California, 1921–1977); Vivian Earls; Marilyn Myers

The Sunshine Girls appeared in Jimmy Wakely westerns and were known for their strong harmony. The guitar playing was furnished by Colleen Summers, who later went on to become the Mary Ford of Les Paul and Mary Ford fame. In the latter 1940s they apparently combined with the Sunshine Boys to appear in *Song of Idaho* billed as the Sunshine Boys and Girls.

I'm from Arkansas (1944) * *Song of the Range* (1944) * *The Lonesome Trail* (1945)

Sunshine Serenaders
Louisiana (1947) "All Aboard for Louisiana"

Supremes
Diana Ross (Diane Ross, Detroit, Michigan, 1944–); Florence Ballard (1943–1976); Mary Wilson (1944–); Cindy Birdsong; Jean Terrell

If the hit 1981 Broadway show and subsequent 2006 film *Dreamgirls* is to be believed, the lives of girl singers are replete with triumph and tragedy. In the case of the real-life Supremes, on whom the show is based, there probably is more than a dollop of truth in that belief.

In 1959 the Primettes was formed by Florence Ballard and Mary Wilson, both fifteen at the time. Three other girls were soon added, including Diane (later Diana) Ross. Two dropped out, relegating them to obscurity and the rest of the group to rock history. But that was in the future; at first they had to be content to sing at local clubs and talent shows.

Nineteen sixty-one was the year of their signing by Motown boss Berry Gordy and the change of name to the Supremes. Their breakthrough came with "Where Did Our Love Go?" in 1964. From then on it was one hit after another — twelve number one records in all — that included "Baby Love," "Come See About Me," "Back in My Arms Again," "Stop! In the Name of Love," "The Happening," "You Can't Hurry Love," "I Hear a Symphony," "My World Is Empty Without You" and "Love Is Here and Now You're Gone."

Florence Ballard was considered by many to have the best voice but Diana Ross was given the lead vocals and by 1967 the group had been renamed Diana Ross and the Supremes. Ballard, volubly discontent, was fired and replaced by Cindy Birdsong. It is this upheaval that the famous *Dreamgirls* anthem "And I Tell You I'm Not Going" memorializes.

The reconstituted Supremes gave their final concert in 1970 and Diana Ross embarked on a very successful solo career that included such movies as *Lady Sings the Blues*, *The Wiz* and *Mahogany*. These were expensive "A" pictures that were far different from the rock-and-roll quickies in which the young Supremes had appeared. Among her singles were "Do You Know Where You're Going to" and "Ain't No Mountain High Enough."

The T.A.M.I. Show (1964) [documentary] "Run Run Run," "Baby Love" and other songs * *Beach Ball* (1965) "Come on to the Beach Ball with Me" and "Surfer Boy" * *American Music— from Folk to Jazz to Pop* (1967) [documentary]

Surfaris

Ron Wilson (1944–1989) (drums); Jim Fuller (guitar); Bob Berryhill (guitar); Pat Connolly (bass); Jim Pash (1949?–2005) (saxophone)

There are perhaps a few iconic recordings of surfing music, but surely the Surfaris' instrumental "Wipe Out" is very high, if not first, on the list. The Southern California band was formed in 1962 and had a moderate success with "Surfer Joe."

On the "B" side was "Wipe Out" with its rollicking guitar sound and only two spoken words — the title — preceded by a raucous laugh. It is often heard as background on commercials and movie sound tracks. The Surfaris had disbanded by 1966 but reunited from time to time and were still performing into the 21st century.

One Man's Challenge (1962) "Surf Bash"

Surftones

The Surftones were a Florida-based band.

Hell's Playground (1967?)

Swan Silvertones

Claude Jeter (lead tenor/falsetto); Eddie Boroughas; John Myles (baritone); Paul Owens (tenor); Leroy Watkins; Solomon Womack; John Manson; Robert Crutcher; William Connor (bass); Robert Crenshaw

Formed in the coal country of West Virginia in the late 1930s, the a cappella ensemble the Swan Silvertones were popular gospel singers in the 1940s and '50s. Originally dubbed the Four Harmony Kings, the group changed its name to the very apt Silvertone Singers and later added the "Swan" for the name of their radio program sponsor the Swan Bakeries.

National popularity first came in the late 1940s when the Silvertones released several gospel recordings that included "I Cried Holy" and "Go Ahead." During the following decade they added instrumentation to the ensemble and added more hits as well, the most memorable being "Oh Mary Don't You Weep."

It was the latter song's lyric "I'll be a bridge over deep water" that supposedly inspired Paul Simon's "Bridge Over Troubled Water." Indeed, the Swan Silvertones were an inspiration to many artists both before and after initially disbanding in the mid–1960s. They ultimately continued on in one form or another into the 1980s and were inducted into the Vocal Group Hall of Fame in 2002.

Festival (1967) [documentary]

Swanee River Boys

Buford Abner (Alabama, 1917–) (lead singer); Merle Abner (Alabama, 1913–) (bass); George Hughes (Texarkana, Arkansas, 1911–) (tenor); Billy Carrier (Arthur, Kentucky, 1913–) (baritone/guitar)

A white harmony group that sang in the style of such Black groups as the Mills Brothers, the Swanee River Boys were originally known as the Vaughn Four. They performed on the radio from about 1938 until the onset of World War II caused them to disband.

The Boys reunited in the postwar period to sing again on radio and recordings. Among their gospel-tinged songs were "He Lifted Me from Sin," "I Have Desire" and "Was He Quiet or Did He Cry?"

Sing a Song, for Heaven's Sake (1966) [documentary]

Swanee Swingsters

Active from the 1930s, the Swanee Swingsters recorded such tunes as "Slappin' the Bass" and "Take It Easy."

Swanee Showboat (1947)

Sweet Gum Sisters and Brothers [unknown]

Moonshine Mountain (1964)

Sweet Inspirations

Dionne Warwick (Marie Warrick, East Orange, New Jersey, 1940–); Dee Dee Warwick (Delia Warrick, Newark, New Jersey, 1945–2008); Emily Houston; Lee Warwick; Doris Troy; Sylvia Shemwell; Myrna Smith; Estelle Brown

As their name might imply the Sweet Inspirations specialized in soul music. The original members of the ensemble had come from two other soul groups in the 1960s, the Drinkard Singers and the Gospelaires. Two of them were the mothers of the future singing stars Dionne Warwick and Whitney Houston.

They gained considerable cachet as back-up singers to such artists as the Drifters, Wilson Pickett, Elvis Presley and Aretha Franklin, but the Inspirations were anxious to record on their own. They first did so in 1967 after some of their number had departed, most notably Dionne Warwick who had gone on to a notable solo career.

Among the Sweet Inspirations' singles were "Why Am I Treated So Bad," "To Love Somebody," one of their biggest hits "Sweet Inspiration" and "Gotta Find Me a Brand New Lover." By the mid–1970s the group had begun to break up but periodically reunited into the 1990s. Emily Houston, who recorded into the 1990s, was awarded a special Grammy.

This Is Elvis — the Concert (1970) [documentary] * *Elvis — That's the Way It Is* (1970) [documentary] * *Elvis on Tour* (1972) [documentary]

Swingin' Medallions

Charlie Webber (trumpet); Steve Caldwell (saxophone); Jimmy Perkins (saxophone/bass guitar); John McElrath (keyboard); Carroll Bledsoe (trumpet); Jim Doares (guitar); Brent Fortson (saxophone/flute); Joe Morris (drums)

A South Carolina–based band, the Swingin' Medallions had the record hit "Double Shot (of My Baby's Love") but little else that excited the pop charts. Formed in the early 1960s, they toured college campuses before their million-seller in 1966. Other records included "She Drives Me Out of My Mind" and "Hey, Hey, Baby." With numerous personnel changes, they are still touring to the present time.

Weekend Rebellion (1970) [documentary]

Swing Wing *see* Milton Delugg and His Swing Wing

Swinging Cavemen *see* Paul Lavert and His Swinging Cavemen

Sylte Sisters

The Sylte Sisters were singers.
Madison Avenue (1962)

Tailor-Maids

Joline Westbrook; Marilyn Myers; Marian Bartel

The Tailor-Maids were a vocal group.
So's Your Uncle (1943) * *Down Missouri Way* (1944) * *Cowboy Canteen* (1944)

Tams

Joseph Pope (Atlanta, Georgia, 1933–1996) (lead vocals); Charles Pope (Atlanta, Georgia, 1936–); Robert Lee Smith (1936–); Horace Key (Atlanta, Georgia, 1936–); Floyd Ashton

Named for the colorful tam o'shanters they wore while performing, the Tams were formed in the late '40s or early 1950s. It was quite a while, eight years or so, until they had their first record hit "Untie Me" but it was "What Kind of Fool (Do You Think I Am?") that put them high on the charts.

Although a Southern-based group they seemed to have had their greatest success in England where some of their recordings reached high on British pop charts. Among them were "Hey Girl, Don't Bother Me," "Be Young, Be Foolish, Be Happy" and "There Ain't Nothing Like Shaggin'," referring to the Shag a popular dance craze in the U.K. in the late 1980s.

Weekend Rebellion (1970)

Tarriers

Alan Arkin (New York, New York, 1934–); Bob Carey; Erik Darling; Carl Carlton

Supposedly the first folk group to have a hit record on the Billboard pop chart with 1956's "The Banana Boat Song," the Tarriers were briefly in the midst of the folk music revival that the Weavers began. Bob Carey and Erik Darling, members of the defunct Tunetellers, formed the Tarriers as a quartet. The name was derived from the (presumably) Irish folksong "Drill, Ye Tarriers, Drill."

The group had become a trio when Carl Carlton left and they made their first impression as back-up singers on the hit record "Cindy, Oh Cindy." Their own hit song soon followed. However, Alan Arkin decided to pursue an acting career and did become a much-lauded, Oscar-winning film (Best Supporting Actor in *Little Miss Sunshine* in 2007) and Broadway actor.

Erik Darling replaced Pete Seeger with the Weavers and then founded the Rooftop Singers who scored the number one hit "Walk Right in." With all new members, the Tarriers soldiered on

into the 1960s but could be said to finally have been a casualty of the British Invasion.
Calypso Heat Wave (1957)

Taylor and Sinclair

Taylor and Sinclair were xylophonists.
The Picture of Dorian Gray (1945)

Taylor Twins [unknown]

Hollywood Bound (1946) †

†This film is a compilation of three Betty Grable musical shorts made in the 1930s. The Twins appeared in 1934's *Ferry-Go-Round*.

T-Bones

Dan Hamilton (1946?–1994) (vocals/guitar); Joe Carollo (bassist); Tommy Reynolds (multi-instruments); George Dee (Arnold Rosenthal) (bassist); Richard Torres (keyboard/saxophone); Gene Pello (drums)

The rollicking instrumental "No Matter What Shape (Your Stomach's in)" was originally the theme of an Alka-Seltzer commercial and was also a big hit for the T-Bones. It was a short-lived group, forming in 1965 and disbanding about two years later when its latest album failed to impress.

The group was revived a couple of years later when a record producer heard an old demo they had made and recalled them to life. The song "Don't Pull Your Love" became another hit for them as was "Fallin' in Love." By the 1970s success was once again eluding them and they disbanded about 1980, this time apparently for keeps.

Nightmare in Wax (1969) "Look for the Rainbow"

Teagarden, Jack *see* Jack Teagarden and His Orchestra

Ted Dahl and His Orchestra

Girl o' My Dreams (1934)

Ted Dawson and Orchestra

High Hat (1937)

Ted Fio Rito and His Band

Ted Fio Rito (originally Fiorito), Newark, New Jersey, 1900–1971)

A pianist and organist, bandleader Ted Fio Rito was also a prolific songwriter who collaborated on "Toot, Toot, Tootsie, Goodbye," one of Al Jolson's standards, as well as over 100 others. Among them were "Now That You're Gone" and "Laugh Clown Laugh." He also had many recording hits with such ditties as "My Little Grass Shack" and "I'll String Along with You."

Fio Rito's sweet band, which was based at the Cocoanut Grove nightclub, had its peak popularity in the 1930s when he had such future movie stars as Betty Grable and June Haver as his vocalists. The group was also a regular on the *Hollywood Hotel* radio show.

Their theme song, no doubt meant to be in harmony with "Fio Rito," was "Rio Rita." In the early days the band was known for its showy arrangements, including whistling and tricky rhythms. In later years Ted Fio Rito led smaller combos that performed in places like Las Vegas.

The Sweetheart of Sigma Chi (1933) * *Twenty Million Sweethearts* (1934) * *Young and Beautiful* (1934) * *Broadway Gondolier* (1935) * *Rhythm Parade* (1942) * *King of the Cowboys* (1943) * *Silver Skates* (1943) * *Melody Parade* (1943) * *Reveille with Beverly* (1943) * *Out of This World* (1945)

Ted Fio Rito.

Ted Lewis and His Orchestra

Ted Lewis (Theodore Friedman, Circleville, Ohio, 1890/92–1971)

A veteran of vaudeville and a bandleader from about 1910, Ted Lewis was famous for his tagline "Is e-e-everybody happy?" and the battered top hat that he wore (and rolled down his arm) for decades. He was dubbed the "High-Hatted Tragedian of Jazz."

A clarinet player but not a great musician, Lewis led what was probably one of the most popular bands of the 1920s and into the '30s. It was jazz-oriented and featured such up-and-comers as Jimmy Dorsey, Fats Waller, Jack Teagarden and Benny Goodman. The orchestra's recording of "Tiger Rag" sold in the millions and they performed in clubs and Broadway shows.

The band was winding down by the 1950s but even after that was seen on television and in Las Vegas for another decade or so. Ted Lewis himself was primarily a showman who talk-sang songs like "Me and My Shadow" (a Black youngster generally "played" the shadow), "On the Sunny Side of the Street" and "When My Baby Smiles at Me," his theme song.

As part of his act Lewis often waxed sentimental about his life. It was strictly cornball, but apparently what audiences supported in those days. His tagline was used as the title for no less than three films, including a musical short.

Is Everybody Happy? (1929) * *The Show of Shows* (1929) * *Here Comes the Band* (1935) * *Manhattan Merry-Go-Round* (1937) * *Hold That Ghost* (1941) * *Is Everybody Happy?* (1943) * *Follow the Boys* (1944)

Ted Weems and His Orchestra

Ted Weems (Pitcairn, Pennsylvania, 1901–1963)

Violinist/trombonist Ted Weems founded his band in 1923 while still a college student. From the mid–1920s to the early '30s they were primarily a Chicago-based organization appearing in ballrooms and hotels. The ensemble's theme song was "Out Of the Night," but they found greater success with "Piccolo Pete" and especially the standard "Heartaches" which featured a considerable amount of whistling.

Beginning on big-time radio with Jack Benny, Weems continued to establish his reputation while working with other luminaries such as the popular radio duo of Fibber McGee and Molly and opera singer James Melton. Although he was not a bad instrumentalist he did not play with his orchestra.

Ted Weems' most famous vocalist was undoubtedly silky-voiced Perry Como who joined him in 1936. Another was actress-to-be Marvell (later Marilyn) Maxwell. When Weems joined the service during World War II the orchestra disbanded, but it was eventually re-established and continued playing into the 1950s.

Swing Sister Swing (1938) * *Hat Check Honey* (1943)

Teddy Buckner and His All-Stars; Buckner All-Stars

Teddy Buckner (John Edward Buckner, Sherman, Texas, 1909–1994)

Resembling and emulating Louis Armstrong, and even once his movie stand-in, trumpeter Teddy Buckner and his Dixieland band were active during World War II. Some forty years later they were still playing — at Disneyland.

Buckner had begun his professional life in the '30s with Kid Ory, Benny Carter and Lionel Hampton. He also played with bands in Mexico and China. Considered an excellent, and possibly even a great musician, he was also one who rarely strayed from tried-and-true musical stylings.

Pete Kelly's Blues (1955) * *Hush, Hush Sweet Charlotte* (1964)

Teddy Powell and His Orchestra

Teddy Powell (Teodoro Paolella, Oakland, California, 1905/06–1993)

Supposedly forming his first band at the age of fifteen, for a short time in the late 1930s Teddy Powell led one of the top jazz bands. A violinist, banjo and guitar player, he had previously been with Abe Lyman's orchestra among others. Although it made no recordings after 1942 the band managed to keep going for a couple of years more before disbanding. Its theme song had been "Sans Culottes."

Teddy Powell wrote songs including "Bewildered" and "If My Heart Could Only Talk" and had his own music publishing business. He continued to lead regional bands into the 1950s but never regained the brief hour of fame during which his had been considered one of the finest ensembles.

Jam Session (1944)

Teddy Wilson and His Band

Teddy Wilson (Theodore Wilson, San Francisco, California or Austin, Texas, 1912–1986)

An important milestone was set by jazz pianist Teddy Wilson when he became the first African-American musician to perform publicly with a racially-mixed jazz ensemble. It was initially composed of Benny Goodman (who called Wilson "the greatest musician in dance music today"), Gene Krupa and Wilson, and then expanded to include another Black musician, Lionel Hampton.

From about 1929 Wilson had played with the Benny Carter, Chick Webb and "Satchmo" Armstrong orchestras. He was also a much sought-after accompanist to such African-American chanteuses as Ella Fitzgerald, Lena Horne and Billie Holiday, as well as numerous white musicians.

Teddy Wilson had formed his own big swing band in 1939 but aficionados termed it "too white" and it only lasted a year. (In view of that, his theme song "Jumpin' on the Blacks and Whites" could be interestingly interpreted.)

Wilson then led a sextet that lasted through the war years. Considered one of the greatest swing pianists of his time, Teddy Wilson remained active in music to near the time of his death. Besides the movies in which he appeared with his orchestra, Wilson had a role in *The Benny Goodman Story*, and had also been in at least one Broadway show.

Something to Shout About (1943) * *Harlem on Parade* (1946?)

Teenagers *see also* Frankie Lymon and the Teenagers

The credits of the Teenagers' one film read: "Radio's newest and youngest band."

One Exciting Week (1946)

Teenchords *see* Lewis Lymon and the Teenchords

Ten Years After

Alvin Lee (Graham Barnes, Nottingham, England, 1944–) (vocals/harp); Leo Lyons (David Lyons, Mansfield, England, 1943–) (bassist); Chuck Churchill (Michael Churchill, Mold, Wales, 1946–) (keyboard); Ric Lee (Richard Lee, Cannock, England, 1945–) (drums)

The core of the British rock group Ten Years After was formed about 1960 and underwent some name changes that included Ivan Jay and the Jaymen, Blues Trip and Blues Yard. In 1966 they assumed their final one.

One story about the origin of the name is that the band wanted to commemorate the ten years since Elvis Presley had catapulted to fame in 1956. Their initial album was released in 1967, the first of many until 1974.

They continued to be issued sporadically into the 21st century when the group presumably reunited for concerts. Among their better-known singles were "I'm Going Home," "Love Like a Man" and "Hear Me Calling." They appeared at the Newport Jazz Festival and the legendary Woodstock.

Woodstock (1970) [documentary] "I'm Going Home" * *Groupies* (1970) [documentary] "Good Morning Little Schoolgirl" and "Help Me Baby"

Tennessee Ramblers

Harry Blair (New Martinsville, West Virginia, 1913?–); "Montana Jack" Gillette (Providence, Rhode Island, 1908?–) (violin and a variety of instruments including musical saw, bicycle pump and balloon); Cecil "Curly" Campbell (Belew's Creek, North Carolina, 1912?–) (guitar/banjo/mandolin); "Happy Tex" Martin (Martin Schopp, Chenoa, Illinois, 1915?–) (guitar/bassist); "Kid" Clark (Leland Clark); Claude Casey; Don White

First heard on the radio about 1928, the Tennessee Ramblers made numerous recordings, among them "Grab Your Saddle Horn and Blow," "Sweet Mama Treetop Tall," "The Preacher Got Drunk and Laid His Bible Down" and "Midnight Boogie," as well as more traditional western songs. "Montana Jack" Gillette had previously been with a vaudeville act called the Rodeo Boys, while "Happy Tex" Martin had played with several groups including a Spanish orchestra.

Ride, Ranger, Ride (1936) * *Yodelin' Kid from Pine Ridge* (1937) * *Ridin' the Cherokee Trail* (1941) * *O, My Darling Clementine* (1943) * *Swing Your Partner* (1943) * *Sundown Valley* (1944)

Tennessee Three

W. S. Holland (drums); Luther Perkins (d. 1968) (electric guitar); Bob Wootton (bass guitar); Marshall Grant (bass guitar)

Frequently the backup band for Johnny Cash, the Tennessee Three developed the so-called "boom chicka boom" or "freight train" musical effect that characterized that singer's unique sound. They remained with him some forty years until his retirement in 1996.

The Three had begun as the Tennessee Two with Luther Perkins and Marshall Grant in the mid–1950s and have continued to perform into the 21st century. They were portrayed by actors in the 2005 film bio of Johnny Cash called *Walk the Line*.

Johnny Cash! The Man, His World, His Music (1969) [documentary]

Terri Sawyer Quartet
The Block (1964)

Terry Twins
Perhaps the Terry Twins greatest claim to fame is their 1946 soundie called *Chiquita Banana* in which they warbled a song of the same name. With different words it later became a famous commercial for the banana company which urged you to "never put bananas in the refrigerator."

Stairway for a Star (1946?)

Tex Logan and the Lilly Brothers
Tex Logan (Benjamin Logan, Coahoma, Texas) (fiddle); Everett Lilly (Clear Creek, Washington) (mandolin/banjo/fiddle); Bea Lilly (Clear Creek, Washington) (guitar)

Tex Logan was a noted bluegrass fiddler and a major presence at folk festivals. The Lilly Brothers began playing and singing on radio as the Lonesome Holler Boys in 1938 and continued to about 1970. They made their first recording in the latter '40s.

Everett Lilly had also been a member of the Foggy Mountain Boys. He, brother Bea, and Tex Logan teamed up about 1952. The Lillys' career was highlighted in the 1979 documentary *True Facts in a Country Song*.

Festival (1967) [documentary]

Tex Ritter's Tornadoes
Cowboy star and western singer ("High Noon") Tex Ritter (1905–1974) made a long series of "B" oaters from 1936 to 1945. His singing group the Tornadoes appeared on the radio as well as in his films.

Sing, Cowboy, Sing (1937) * *Hittin' the Trail* (1937) * *Riders of the Rockies* (1937) * *Trouble in Texas* (1937) * *The Utah Trail* (1938) * *Rollin' Westward* (1939)

Texas Cowboys see Texas Jim Lewis...

Texas Jim Lewis and His Lone Star Cowboys; Texas Jim Lewis and His Band; Jimmie Lewis and His Texas Cowboys
Jim Lewis (Meigs, Georgia, 1909–1990); Smoky Rogers; Cactus Soldi

Texas Jim Lewis formed the Lone Star Cowboys in the mid–1930s and they played mostly in the New York area, popularizing western swing on the East Coast. The 1944 release "Too Late to Worry, Too Blue to Cry" was one of their bigger hits.

In later years Lewis recorded country and novelty tunes and was a Seattle children's show host on television, as well as working in nightclubs. He re-formed a western band in the 1960s that thrived for another decade.

Bad Man from Red Butte (1940) * *Carolina Moon* (1940) * *Down Mexico Way* (1941) * *Pardon My Gun* (1942) * *The Old Homestead* (1942) * *Law of the Canyon* (1947) * *The Stranger from Ponca City* (1947)

Texas Playboys see Bob Wills and His Texas Playboys

Texas Rangers
Tex Owens (guitar); Herb Kratuska (banjo/guitar); Paul Sells (accordion); Francis Mahaney (or Mahoney); Roderick May; Robert Crawford; Edward Cronenbold; Gomer Cool

On the radio the Texas Rangers were known as the CBS-KMBC Texas Rangers. They were basically a quartet but sometimes expanded to as many as eight for various picture appearances, the great majority of which were with western star Johnny Mack Brown.

Ghost Town Riders (1938) * *Colorado Sunset* (1939) * *Oklahoma Frontier* (1939) * *Chip of the Flying U* (1939) * *Scatterbrain* (1940) * *Ragtime Cowboy Joe* (1940) * *Son of Roaring Dan* (1940) *

Rawhide Rangers (1941) * *Law of the Range* (1941) * *The Last Round-Up* (1947) * *The Arkansas Swing* (1948)

Texas Stars *see* Wesley Tuttle and His Texas Stars

Texas Troubadors *see* Ernest Tubb and His Texas Troubadors

Texas Wanderers

Cliff Bruner (Texas City, Texas, 1915–2000) (fiddle); Bob Dunn (steel guitar); Leo Raley (mandolin); Dick McBride (vocals/guitar); Moon Mullican (vocals/piano); Hezzy Bryant (bassist); J. R. Chatwell (fiddle)

Considered one of the pioneers of western swing, Cliff Bruner had been a fiddler with Milton Brown's Musical Brownies, a group considered to be the first true western swing band. He formed the Texas Wanderers in 1937 and they appeared in local clubs and on radio.

Before disbanding in the mid–1940s their hit recordings included "It Makes No Difference Now" and "Truck Driver's Blues." Rather than playing traditional western songs, the Texas Wanderers' music focused on the hardscrabble lives of working class people. Bruner himself remained active in music into the early 1990s.

Village Barn Dance (1940)

Thirteenth Committee
Wild Wheels (1969) "I Hear Music"

Thomas Sisters [unknown]
Sugar Daddy (1968)

Thompson, Bill *see* Bill Thompson Singers

Thompson, Kay *see* Kay Thompson and Her Radio Choir

Thompson, Shorty *see* Shorty Thompson and His Saddle Rockin' Rhythm

Three Ambassadors

Jack Smith (Seattle, Washington, 1913?–2006); Marty Sperzel; Al Teeter; Art Wilson

Jack Smith (called the "Man with a Smile in His Voice") had his own radio show for eight years as well as hosting the popular television show "You Asked for It." His debut in show business had come much earlier, in 1931, when he and two friends (all still in high school) replaced Bing Crosby's Rhythm Boys at the legendary Cocoanut Grove nightclub. They dubbed themselves the Three Ambassadors, named for the hotel which housed the club.

The erstwhile students found themselves in heady company indeed as they performed at venues like San Francisco's Mark Hopkins Hotel. They also appeared frequently on the radio with stars like Kate Smith before disbanding in 1939. Jack Smith later had roles in *Make Believe Ballroom* and *On Moonlight Bay*. He also sang on several successful recordings.

Strange Justice (1932) [†] * *The Constant Woman* (1932) * *Walking on Air* (1936)

[†]Their appearance in this film is not confirmed.

Three Blue Keys [unknown]
The Sweetheart of Sigma Chi (1933)

Three Brian Sisters *see* Brian Sisters

Three Brown Girls [unknown]
Fools for Scandal (1938)

Three Cheers [unknown]
Okay America (1932) * *Swing It Soldier* (1941) * *The Hit Parade of 1943* (1943)

Three Diamond Brothers *see* Leo Diamond...

Three Dots *see* Dorothy McCarthy and the Three Dots

Three Harmonettes *see* Harmonettes

Three Heat Waves
The Three Heat Waves were singer/dancers.
Follies Girl (1943)

Three Hits and a Miss
Martha Tilton (Corpus Christi, Texas, 1915–2006)

The most prominent member of the singing group Three Hits and a Miss was the "Miss," i.e., Martha Tilton, who joined it in the early 1930s. Later known for her recordings of "And the Angels Sing," "I Should Care" and "That's My Desire," she was dubbed "Liltin'" Martha Tilton.

After she departed Three Hits and a Miss Tilton vocalized with major bands such as those of Benny Goodman and Jimmy Dorsey and was supposedly the first non-classical female singer to appear in Carnegie Hall. She had radio and television shows and on her own appeared in such movies as *Swing Hostess*, *Crime, Inc.* and *The Benny Goodman Story*.

Topper (1937)

Three Jays

The Three Jays were a vocal ensemble.
Call Out the Marines (1942)

Three Lieutenants [unknown]

Frank McKee; Herbert Hall; Jack Frost
Girl O'My Dreams (1934)

Three Midshipmen [unknown]

Billy McDonald; Bob Farrell; Max Terrill
The Sweetheart of Sigma Chi (1933)

Three Mountain Boys [unknown]

Sing While You're Able (1937)

Three Nelsons [unknown]

Henry Johnson; Roy Dove; Harry Johnson
Keep Smiling (1938)

Three of August

Wild Wheels (1969)

Three Oxford Boys *see* Oxford Boys

Three Peppers

Walter Williams (bassist); Bob Bell (guitar); Roy Branker (piano)

Formed in St. Louis in the mid–1930s, the Three Peppers were a swing instrumental and vocal group. They tended to do tried-and-true tunes like "The Sheik of Araby" and "Down By the Old Mill Stream," but there were also novelty numbers such as "Swing Out Uncle Wilson" and "It's a Puzzle to Me (So What)." They disbanded about 1950.

Straight To Heaven (1939) * *A Lady Takes a Chance* (1943)

Three Radio Rogues *see* Radio Rogues

Three Rio Brothers *see* Rio Brothers

Three Shades of Rhythm *see* "Sleepy" Williams and His Three Shades of Rhythm

Three Sisters *see* Fontane Sisters

Three Suns

Al Nevins (Albert Tepper, Washington, D.C., 1915–1965) (guitar); Morty Nevins (Morton Tepper, Washington, D.C., 1919–1990) (accordion); Artie Dunn (Dorchester, Massachusetts, 1922–1996) (organ)

There were few instrumental groups of their time as famous as the melodious Three Suns. Composed of two brothers and their cousin, the trio began their professional lives in 1939 and by the next year had established themselves at a New York hotel for a seven-year engagement.

In the mid-'40s the Suns and their soaring organ sound scored two recording hits with the million-selling "Twilight Time" and "Peg o' My Heart." Although continuing to call themselves the *Three* Suns, the group was sometimes a quintet with a rhythm guitar and bass added for recording sessions. Becoming less traditional, they later added such instruments as a Celestine, castanets, pipe organ and vibes.

The Suns broke up and re-formed at least once before disbanding in the 1980s. However the mini-revival of lounge music in the 1990s brought their name to the fore once again, helped by the fact they had made a great number of albums. They had also done several 1940s soundies, along with their one feature film appearance.

Two Gals and a Guy (1951)

Three Thorntons [unknown]

Youth Aflame (1945)

Three Tones *see* **Herb Jeffries and the Four Tones**

Thunderbirds *see* **Gay Land and the Thunderbirds**

Tic Toc Girls
Yvonne Manoff; Mildred Winston; Barbara Johnston
The Hit Parade (1937) "Love Is Good for Anything That Ails You"

Tico Tico Guitars
The Gay Senorita (1945)

Tipica Orchestra *see* **Jose Arias and His Mexican Tipica Orchestra**

Titans
Larry Green (bass); Charles Wright (1st tenor); Sam Barnett (2nd tenor); Alvin Branom (tenor/baritone); Curtis McNair (baritone)
Originally called the Egyptians, the Titans was founded in 1956 by Larry Green, its name supposedly coming from the then-new Titan missile. They remained Los Angeles–area performers throughout their brief tenure as a rock group.
The Titans' first recording to make even a mild impression was "G'wan Home Calypso." Like their follow-up records this really did not put them on the map but may have given them the chance to appear in their one film together. They continued on as a quartet starting in 1958 and then as a trio before disbanding about 1960.
Bop Girl Goes Calypso (1957) "Rhythm in Blues" and "So Hard to Laugh, So Easy to Cry"

T.J. and the Fourmations
The Cool Ones (1967) "Hey Hey Ronnie"

Tjader, Cal *see* **Cal Tjader...**

Tobin Mathews and the All Stars
Twist All Night (1961)

Tommy Atkins Sextet [unknown]
Hollywood Revue of 1929 (1929)

Tommy Christian and His Band
From 1925 to 1930 New York–based orchestra leader Tommy Christian and his band recorded such novelty tunes as "Bolshevik," "Elsie Shultzen-heim" and "How I Love Bulgarians." They also did more traditional ditties like "In a Little Spanish Town" and "Show Me the Way to Go Home."
Howdy Broadway (1929)

Tommy Dorsey and His Orchestra
Tommy Dorsey (Thomas Dorsey, Jr., Shenandoah or Mahanoy Plane, Pennsylvania, 1905–1956)
If his publicity tagline "The Sentimental Gentleman of Swing," his theme song "I'm Getting Sentimental Over You," and his owlish appearance made bandleader Tommy Dorsey sound like an easygoing man it was most misleading. He was temperamental to the point of being volcanic, was not above getting into fistfights, and was known for firing people with very little provocation.
However, he was undeniably one of the most popular orchestra leaders of the Big Band days and supposedly sold about 110 million records, among them "Marie," "Opus No.1," "Song of India," "I'll Never Smile Again" and "Boogie Woogie." His vocalists included Frank Sinatra and Jo Stafford.
Before Tommy went out on his own he had co-led a band with older brother Jimmy after they had been sidemen for Paul Whiteman, Vincent Lopez and others. After numerous physical scraps they broke up their band to go solo in 1935 but reunited in 1953. He had disbanded his original band in 1946, then re-formed it two years later.
As a film performer Tommy Dorsey was somewhat more animated than many of his confreres. Among his roles he played "himself" in the biopic *The Fabulous Dorseys*, but it was always his fantastic trombone playing that distinguished him. After his sudden death a band under his name continued touring.
Las Vegas Nights (1941) * *Ship Ahoy* (1942) * *Presenting Lily Mars* (1943) * *DuBarry Was a Lady*

186 Tommy

Tommy Dorsey.

(1943) * *Girl Crazy* (1943) * *Broadway Rhythm* (1944) * *Thrill of a Romance* (1945) * *The Fabulous Dorseys* (1947) * *Disc Jockey* (1951)

Tommy Duncan and His Western All-Stars

Tommy Duncan (Hillsboro, Texas, 1911–1967)

A longtime vocalist with Bob Wills' Texas Playboys, Tommy Duncan had been a member of the Light Crust Dough Boys starting about 1933. He went out on his own in 1948 and his All-Stars had an almost immediate hit with "Gamblin' Polka Dot Blues." He also was the composer of such songs as "Bubbles in My Beer," "Time Changes Everything" and "Stay a Little Longer."

Duncan's time with the Western All-Stars was a relatively brief one and he joined the Miller Brothers band in the early '50s before embarking on a solo career. This time success eluded him but he continued to tour and record to the time of his death.

South of Death Valley (1949)

Tomorrow

Steve Howe (electric/acoustic guitar); Keith West (vocals); John Wood (bass guitar); John Alder (drums)

A British psychedelic rock band, the Tomorrow had been previously called the In Crowd and the Four Plus One. They did a few singles, among them "My White Bicycle" and "Revolution," as well as a couple of albums. In their one film they appeared as a fictitious band called the Snarks.

Smashing Time (1967)

Tony Martinez and His Band

Tony Martinez (San Juan, Puerto Rico, 1920–2002)

Better known in later years as a character actor on the television show *The Real McCoys*, Tony Martinez was one of the few Latinos then appearing on any series. He also played on Broadway as Sancho Panza in the long-running *Man of La Mancha*.

He turned to acting after giving up his band Tony Martinez and His Mambo–USA, which he had formed in the 1940s. A performer on five instruments, he was actually "discovered" as an actor while he and his band were performing in a Hollywood club. Thereafter he scored several minor roles in movies besides the one he made with the band.

Rock Around the Clock (1956) "Cubros," "Mambo Capri" and other songs

Tony Pastor and His Orchestra

Tony Pastor (Antonio Pestritto, Middletown, Connecticut, 1907–1969)

A tenor saxophonist with Artie Shaw's band in the mid-'30s, Tony Pastor started his own ensemble about 1940 and led it well into the 1950s. Its theme song was "Blossoms." Aided by his rather impish personality and good singing voice, the band was especially popular on radio.

Among Pastor's vocalists were the Clooney sisters, Betty and Rosemary. As the years passed Pastor turned more and more to singing and eventually formed a vocal group with his sons, ending his music career playing Las Vegas lounges in the 1960s.

Two Blondes and a Redhead (1947)

Top Hatters *see* Jan Savitt and His Top Hatters

Tormé, Mel *see* Mel-Tones

Tornadoes *see* Johnny and the Tornadoes; Tex Ritter's Tornadoes

Town Criers

The Town Criers was a vocal quartet.

Radio Stars on Parade (1945) * *Song of the Prairie* (1945) * *Cowboy Blues* (1946)

Toys

June Montiero (Queens, New York, 1946–) (2nd soprano); Barbara Harris (lead singer); Barbara Parritt (Wilmington, North Carolina, 1944–) (alto); Dottie Berry

The three-girl singing group the Toys (a name they incidentally disliked) was a product of Queens, New York. They had come together in the early 1960s as the back-up quartet called the Charlettes but became a trio when Dottie Berry dropped out. Their catchy recording of "A Lover's Concerto," which was "borrowed" from a melody by Johann Sebastian Bach, sold more than a million copies in 1965.

By the time they disbanded in 1968 they had not duplicated that success, but other songs like "Attack" (that also utilized classical themes), and especially "Sealed with a Kiss," did respectably well. They also appeared on television shows like *Shindig, American Bandstand* and *Hullaballoo!* and briefly reunited in the 1980s.

It's a Bikini World (1967) "Attack"

Trace, Al see Al Trace...

Tracy and Elwood [unknown]

Love at First Sight (1930)

Traffic

Steve Winwood (vocals/keyboard); Jim Capaldi (Nicola Capaldi, Evesham, England, 1945?–2005); Chris Wood (d. 1983) (saxophone/flute); Dave Mason (guitar)

Formed by some ex-members of the Spencer Davis Group in 1966, Traffic was a Birmingham, England–based band whose first recordings "Paper Sun" and "Hole in My Shoe" were hits in Britain. The group also toured the United States.

Racked by internal dissension, the band disbanded and re-grouped several times, released eleven albums, and were still recording into the 1990s. Traffic was inducted into the Rock and Roll Hall of Fame in 2004.

Popcorn: an Audio/Visual Rock Thing (1969) [documentary]

Trail Riders see Jimmy Dean and His Trail Riders

Trailsmen see Curt Barrett and the Trailsmen

Tramp Band; Cotton Club Tramp Band

The Tramp Band was kind of a Spike Jones–ish group, playing on exotic "instruments" like washboards and kazoos.

Stormy Weather (1943)

Trans Love Airways

Captain Milkshake (1970)

Travis, Merle see Merle Travis and His Bronco Busters

Tremeloes see Brian Poole and the Tremeloes

Treniers

Claude Trenier (Mobile, Alabama, 1919–2003); Cliff Trenier (Mobile, Alabama, 1919–1983), Milt Trenier, Buddy Trenier

Identical twins Claude and Cliff Trenier, together with their older and younger brothers, turned out several rock-and-roll records in the 1950s as The Treniers. In the 1940s the twins had done an act as the Trenier Twins and then were part of the Gene Gilbeaux Orchestra. Apart, they each had also performed with orchestras and in nightclubs.

The Treniers were known for their extremely hyperactive antics onstage, complete with acrobatic dancing, as they delivered songs the ilk of "Rockin' Is Our Business," "Rockin' on Saturday Night" and "It Rocks, It Rolls, It Swings." They were also specialists in risqué fare like "Poon-Tang" and "Uh Oh, Get Out of the Car."

When the rock-and-roll craze began slowing, the Treniers found new life as early pioneers on the casino circuit in Las Vegas (where they were one of the first African-American groups to perform) and Atlantic City. There they could cut loose as they had not necessarily been able to do in their television appearances. They remained active into the 1990s with others of the Trenier clan joining them from time to time.

Don't Knock the Rock (1956) "One of These Days" and "The House Will Rock" * *The Girl Can't Help It* (1956) "Rockin' Is Our Business" * *Calypso Heat Wave* (1957) "Rock Joe" and "Day Old Bread and Canned Beans" * *Juke Box Rhythm* (1959) "Uh Oh, Get Out of the Car"

Trio Calaveras

The Trio were singers.
The Three Caballeros (voices only?) (1945) * *The Torch* (1950)

Tropicanans *see* Ramsay Ames and Her Topicanans

Trotter, John Scott *see* John Scott Trotter [and His Orchestra?]

Trovadores Chinacos

Nicandro Castillo Gomez (Xochiatipan, Mexico, 1914–1990); Roque Castillo Gomez

The Trovadores Chinacos were guitarists and a successful singing group from at least the early 1930s, ultimately appearing in both the Mexican and American cinema and touring widely in both countries.
The Gay Desperado (1936)

True, Bobby *see* Bobby True Trio

Tubb, Ernest *see* Ernest Tubb and His Texas Troubadors

Tubby Hayes Quintet

Tubby Hayes (Edward Hayes, London, England, 1935–)

Tubby Hayes, master of the tenor saxophone, vibes and flute, has led ensembles of varying sizes from an octet in the 1950s to a quartet.
All Night Long (1961)

Tucker, Orrin *see* Orrin Tucker's Orchestra

Tudor Williams Male Chorus
Winter Carnival (1939)

Tumbleweed Tumblers [unknown]
Square Dance Jubilee (1949)

Tune Twisters

The Tune Twisters were singers.
Sweet Surrender (1935)

Turner, Ike and Tina *see* Ike and Tina Turner

Turtles

Howard Kaylan (1947–) (vocals); Mark Volman (1947–) (vocals); Al Nichol (lead guitar); Don Murray (drums); Chuck Portz (bassist); Jim Tucker (rhythm guitar)

Some members of the band that was to become the famous Turtles started out as the Nightriders in high school, and then dubbed themselves the Crossfires. By 1965 they were known as the Tyrtles (a sly homage to the Byrds), but soon assumed the name by which they were best-known.

After some moderate cover hits like "It Ain't Me Babe" and "Let Me Be" the Turtles hit the big time with "Happy Together," a number one charter in 1967. Other Top Twenty recordings including "She's My Girl" and "You Know What I Mean" followed.

The Turtles metamorphosed from a straight pop sound, becoming a proponent of psychedelic music, before disbanding in 1970. Many of its members continued their music careers, Howard Kaylan and Mark Volman, for instance, formed the interestingly-named ensemble Phlorescent Leech and Eddie.
Out of Sight (1966) "She'll Come Back"

Tuskegee Choir

The tradition of choral singing at the historically Black Tuskegee Institute in Alabama goes back to 1884 when the first group was founded by Booker T. Washington himself. Originally a quartet, the group mainly varied from four to eight over the years as they toured the country into the 1940s. At times, however, they expanded into a 100-strong ensemble.

The Choir also performed for many Presidents from Herbert Hoover to Bill Clinton, and in 1946 were the first African-American group to be allowed to perform at Washington's Constitution Hall (from which contralto Marion Anderson had been barred years before). They also were much heard on radio and television.
George Washington Carver (1940)

Tuttle, Wesley *see* **Wesley Tuttle and His Texas Stars**

Two Fat Men [unknown]
Tall, Tan and Terrific (1946)

Tyrones
Tyrone DeNittis; George Lesser
A Philadelphia rock-and-roll group, the Tyrones (named after their lead singer Tyrone DeNittis) were helped along by Bill Haley of the Comets fame and recorded some of his songs. Two of their hits were "Blast Off" and "I'm Shook"; other recordings included "Pink Champagne" and "My Rock 'n' Roll Baby."
Let's Rock! (1958) "Blast Off"

U.F.O.'s
The Love-Ins (1967)

Ukonu and His Afro-Calypsonians
Ukonu (A. E. Ukonu)
Panama Sal (1957)

Uncle Dave Macon and His Son, Dorris
Dave Macon (Smart Station, Tennessee, 1870–1952)
Considered a *Grand Ole Opry* pioneer, "Uncle" Dave Macon was a renowned banjo player who influenced many who followed. He was almost fifty years old when he turned professional with a vaudeville act, and a few years later he joined the *Opry*'s radio family.
Macon's recordings were legendary and he was inducted into the Country Music Hall of Fame in 1966. The annual "Dave Macon Days" music and dance festival is staged in Murfreesboro, Tennessee to honor his memory and invariably attracts at least 40,000 people.
Grand Ole Opry (1940)

University of Arizona Glee Club
Tumbledown Ranch in Arizona (1941)

Vagabonds
Attilio Risso; Dom Germano; Peter Peterson; Till Riaso; Al Torrieri
A comic musical group, the four Vagabonds played and clowned their way through several movies of the 1930s and '40s, with 1943 being a banner year before the cameras. Following their screen career they opened a Miami nightspot.
Something to Sing About (1937) * *The Spirit of Stanford* (1942) * *She Has What It Takes* (1943) * *Swing Out the Blues* (1943) * *It Ain't Hay* (1943) * *Hey, Rookie!* (1943) * *Tahiti Nights* (1944) * *People Are Funny* (1946)

Vagrants
Disk-O-Tek Holiday (1966) * *Blonde on a Bum Trip* (1968) "I Love You, Yes I Do"

Vandellas *see* **Martha and the Vandellas**

Vanilla Fudge
Carmine Appice (drums); Tim Bogert (bassist); Mark Stein (organ); Vince Martell (guitar)
A psychedelic rock band originally called the Electric Pigeons (later abbreviated to the Pigeons), the Vanilla Fudge was formed about 1967. They recorded for several years, many of their songs being "cover" records of other groups' hits. These included the Beatles' "Ticket to Ride" and "Eleanor Rigby." "You Keep Me Hangin' on," formerly a Supremes' success, garnered a gold record for the Fudge.
The group played many of the important club venues across the country and released other albums and singles, but with somewhat less than their initial success. Vanilla Fudge split up in 1970 but reunited for albums and tours a few times, one as late as 2005.
Popcorn: an Audio/Visual Rock Thing (1969) [documentary]

Vass Family [unknown]
Country Fair (1941)

Vaughn Monroe and His Orchestra
Vaughn Monroe (Akron, Ohio, 1911–1973)
At the height of its success the Vaughn Monroe band was on the road more than 200 days a year, and was the highest-earning orchestra of its kind. Monroe won a Wisconsin trumpet competition at the age of fifteen and had begun playing trumpet and singing in big bands about 1937. The radio show *Camel Caravan* featured the band which had been formed in 1940.

Its leader was a tall and handsome baritone whose hits included "There, I've Said It Again," "Ghost Riders in the Sky," "Ballerina" "Let It Snow" and his signature theme song "Racing with the Moon." They were all sung through the nose in his inimitable semi-operatic style.

Monroe was known as "Old Mellow Bellow" and "Old Leather Tonsils" in tribute to his extremely deep voice. In the early 1950s, perhaps because of his western-themed "Ghost Riders" hit, someone got the bright idea of starring him in movie westerns. He proved himself an adequate actor in *Singing Guns* and *The Toughest Man in Arizona*.

Meet the People (1944) * *Carnegie Hall* (1947)

Vegas, Pat and Lolly *see* Pat and Lolly Vegas

Velvet Underground

Lou Reed (Freeport, New York, 1942–) (vocals/songwriter); Sterling Morrison (Holmes Morrison, Jr., East Meadow, New York, 1942?–1995) (guitar); John Cale (viola); Maureen Tucker (drums); Nico (Christa Paffgen, Cologne, Germany, 1938–1988) (vocals)

The best-known Velvet Underground alumnus today is probably the often controversial Lou Reed. In its heyday from 1965 to 1973 the band was a considerable influence on other groups, and is considered the progenitor of punk rock. Starting out as the Warlocks and the Falling Spikes, the group finally named itself after a book about sadomasochism.

For a while the Underground was managed by artist/tastemaker Andy Warhol, which certainly gave it added visibility. They became a part of his traveling multimedia show (some would say circus) called *Exploding. Plastic. Inevitable.* and appeared in his movies. Warhol's protégée, the German singer Nico, was their vocalist for this period.

It is easy to imagine the Velvet Underground's leanings from such memorable songs as "Venus in Furs" (a further exploration of the S&M theme), "The Black Angel's Death Song," "Femme Fatale" and "Heroin." They continued to further experiment with their music and gradually their sound became even rawer, more intense, and even wildly improvised on occasion. After Reed and then John Cale left the group in 1970 it slowly began to lose steam, basically disbanding in 1973. Various members have continued to re-team for concerts, however, and their best albums of the 1960s (e.g., "White Light/White Heat") are still considered classics of their kind. A documentary about one of their reunions, *Velvet Redux*, was released in 1993.

The Velvet Underground and Nico (1966) [documentary] * *Diaries, Notes and Sketches* (1969)

Vendells

The Vendells were a Los Angeles garage band.

Psycho-A-Go-Go (1965)

Ventures

Bob Bogle (Robert Bogle, Wagoner, Oklahoma, 1934–) (lead vocalist/bass guitar); Don Wilson (Tacoma, Washington, 1933–); Gerry McGee (Gerald McGee, Eunice, Louisiana, 1937–) (lead guitar); Melvin Taylor (Brooklyn, New York, 1933–1996) (drums); Nokie Edwards (Nole Edwards, Lahoma, Oklahoma, 1935–) (bass)

Founded in the 1950s by Bob Bogle and Don Wilson as the Versatones, the Ventures are still going strong today, although they probably found their greatest success in the 1960s. Their new version of "Walk Don't Run" became an international smash hit, with some two million records sold. Another version called "Walk Don't Run '64" was also a big seller.

They were particularly popular in Japan, way outselling the Beatles there, and with about 150 albums and 110 million copies sold are considered the best selling instrumental rock group ever. Other hits included "Lullaby of the Leaves" and "Telstar."

Beloved Invaders (1965) [documentary] "Apache," "Wipe Out," "Pipeline" and numerous other songs

Victor Young and His Orchestra

Victor Young (Chicago, Illinois, 1899–1956)

Multi-talented violinist Victor Young was a noted arranger and composer whose numerous song standards included "When I Fall in Love," "Sweet Sue," "My Foolish Heart," "Stella By Starlight" and "Love Letters." He had begun his distinguished career as a concert violinist in Poland where he moved as a child.

Returning to the States, Young joined the orchestra of Ted Fio Rito after touring as a classical violinist. Later, with his own orchestra that he had established in 1935 he performed on radio. Having migrated to Hollywood in the mid–1930s, he worked on numerous film scores (e.g., *Samson and Delilah, Shane, For Whom the Bell Tolls, The Quiet Man*).

Victor Young was ultimately nominated for twenty-two Academy Awards but won the coveted Oscar just once — and that posthumously — for the score to *Around the World in 80 Days*. He had also composed for, and occasionally performed in, many Broadway shows from the 1930s until shortly before his death.

Walter Wanger's Vogues of 1938 (1937)

Vienna Boys Choir

The origins of the Vienna Boys Choir probably date back to the 15th century but the modern version was established in 1924. The Choir consists of boys between ten and fourteen who, divided into four touring choirs, give some 300 concerts a year.

The Big Broadcast of 1936 (1935)

Vigilantes [unknown]

Harvest Melody (1943)

Vincent, Gene *see* Gene Vincent...

Vincent, Paul *see* Paul Vincent and His New Yorkers

Vincent Lopez and His Orchestra

Vincent Lopez (Brooklyn, New York, 1895–1975)

Although the big bands all had theme songs few are so associated with an orchestra as was the catchy "Nola" with suave Vincent Lopez. For many years his was the house band of New York's Hotel Taft and he himself played a smooth piano. (It was said he perfected his playing at the monastery in which he was studying for the priesthood.)

He formed his band in 1917 and in the early '20s was one of the pioneers of the burgeoning medium of radio on which he grandly announced himself by intoning "Lopez speaking!" The Vincent Lopez band remained very popular into the 1940s, when he had an early television show.

Lopez was said to have influenced Liberace and Eddie Duchin with his piano stylistics. Among his vocalists were the Thornburg sisters — Elizabeth and Marion — whom he renamed Betty and Marion Hutton. Sidemen included the Dorsey brothers, Xavier Cugat, Artie Shaw and Glenn Miller.

The Big Broadcast (1932)

Vito's Group

You Are What You Eat (1968) [documentary]

Vronsky and Babin

Vitya Vronsky (Kiev, Ukraine, 1909–1992); Victor Babin (Moscow, Russia, 1908–1972)

Vronsky and Babin, dual pianists, concertized all over the world and were considered among the foremost piano teams of their era. It was the music of their mentor, the renowned composer Sergei Rachmaninoff, which they frequently recorded and from which they became famous. It is estimated that they gave more than 1,200 concerts in North America alone before becoming affiliated with the Cleveland Institute of Music.

Adventures in Music (1944) [documentary]

Vulcanes

Don Roberts (Los Angeles, California) (saxophone)

The Vulcanes were a California-based surf/instrumental band that became briefly popular following an appearance on local television in the early 1960s.

I'll Take Sweden (1965)

Wakely, Jimmy *see* Jimmy Wakely...

Wald, Jerry *see* Jerry Wald and His Orchestra

Walker Brothers

Scott Engel (Noel Engel, Hamilton, Ohio, 1943–) (vocals/bass guitar); John Maus (New York, New York, 1943–) (vocals/guitar); Gary Leeds (Glendale, California, 1942–) (drums)

The Walker Brothers was formed in Southern California in 1964 by Scott Engels, John Maus and Gary Leeds who all professionally assumed the surname of Walker. Ultimately they found greater success in Great Britain than they did in their home country and even borrowed the "mop-top" hairstyles of the Beatles. For a brief time the Brothers were almost as popular as the Fab Four in England.

Their two big hits in the U.S. were "Make It Easy on Yourself" and "The Sun Ain't Gonna Shine Anymore," but they had nine chart hits abroad before disbanding in 1967. Each went on to solo but only Engel, who was still known as Scott Walker, met with some success with a new group called the Rain. The original trio later reunited briefly in the 1970s.

Beach Ball (1965) "Doin' the Jerk"

Walt Shrum and His Colorado Cowboys; Walt Shrum and His Colorado Hillbillies

Walt Shrum (Oklahoma or Missouri, 1912–1991); Rusty Cline; Chuck Peters; Jeannie Akers; Robert Hoag

Walt Shrum was professionally linked with his brother Cal playing western swing and appearing in movies for many years. His Hillbillies had a number three record in 1945 with "Triflin' Gal" and among his well-known sidemen was Spade Cooley.

The Old Barn Dance (1937) * *Blue Montana Skies* (1939) * *The Lost Trail* (1945) * *The Desert Horseman* (1946) * *Swing, Cowboy, Swing* (1946)

Walter Fuller and Orchestra; Walter Fuller's Orchestra

Walter Fuller (Los Angeles, California or Dyersburg, Tennessee, 1920–2003)

One of the first band arrangers to work in the "bop" idiom, Walter Fuller worked with such greats as Billy Eckstine and Dizzy Gillespie. He also had a big band until the early 1950s.

Sepia Cinderella (1947)

Walter Wanderley Trio

Walter Wanderley (Recife, Brazil, 1932–1986)

An organist, pianist and composer, Walter Wanderley cashed in on the bossa nova craze in the United States after moving from Brazil in 1966. In his native country, he had made a career juxtaposing modern American music with Afro-Cuban rhythms.

Wanderley's one U.S. hit record, a single from one of his albums, was "Summer Samba," but all his albums sold well. One was certified platinum for at least one million sales.

For Singles Only (1968)

Wanderers

Bob Yarborough (tenor); Alfonso Brown (tenor); Frank Joyner (baritone); Sheppard Grant (bass); Ray Pollard (1931?–2005) (tenor)

Before settling on the name of the Wanderers, the pop/jazz quartet was known as the Barons, the Barons and Betty (their then-singer), the Larks, and finally the Singing Wanderers. They had formed about 1950 and were singing in small Harlem nightspots in the style of the Mills Brothers.

They began recording in 1953 and continued performing in nightclubs all over the Eastern seaboard and Midwest. In the meantime, they found success with records such as "A Teenage Quarrel," "Shadrach, Meshach and Abednego" and their biggest charter "For Your Love" in 1961. They also did a well-received version of "I'll Never Smile Again."

The Wanderers also made several television appearances with Ed Sullivan, on whose show they were allegedly the first Black group to dance as well as sing. After they disbanded Ray Pollard went on to have a minor solo career, appearing in the Broadway musical *Purlie* and ultimately heading an Ink Spots spin-off group in the 1980s.

Rockin' the Blues (1956) "My Sweetie Pie"

Wanderley, Walter *see* Walter Wanderley Trio

Ward, Clara *see* Clara Ward Singers

Ward and Van [unknown]

Crazy House (1943)

Waring, Fred *see* Fred Waring and His Pennsylvanians

Waters, Ozie *see* Ozie Waters and His Colorado Rangers

Watson, Deek *see* Deek Watson and the Brown Dots

Watts, Cotton and Chick *see* **Cotton and Chick Watts**

Wayne Cochran and the C.C. Riders

Wayne Cochran (Thompson or Macon, Georgia, 1939–)

Having led bands since 1955, Wayne Cochran formed the C. C. Riders (i.e., Cochran's Circuit Riders) in 1963. Playing a combination of soul and rhythm-and-blues music, the band toured in the South and Midwest and released recordings like "Harlem Shuffle" and "Get Down with It." They were among the first white groups to play Harlem's Apollo Theater and other traditionally Black venues, and he himself was called the "White Otis Redding."

The Riders began appearing in venues like Las Vegas and on major television programs where Cochran paraded his bizarre outfits and white pompadour. (Publicity claimed that he spent $50,000 a year styling it.) Eventually there was a film, starring ex-footballer Joe Namath, which bore the group's name as a motorcycle gang.

C. C. and Company (1970) "I Can't Turn You Loose"

Weaver Brothers and Elviry

Abner Weaver (Leon Weaver, Ozark, Missouri, 1882–1950); Cicero Weaver (Frank Weaver, Ozark, Missouri, 1891–1967); Elviry Weaver (June Weaver, Chicago, Illinois, 1891–1977)

In the late 1930s and early '40s hillbilly-themed movies enjoyed a brief popularity. One of the main beneficiaries (or perhaps the progenitors) of this short-lived phenomenon was the country act the Weaver Brothers and Elviry. They were veterans of the radio show *Grand Ole Opry*, on which Leon was a virtuoso of the musical saw.

The Weavers were known in their vaudeville and *Opry* days as the "Arkansas Travelers." June had been married to Leon and then became Frank's wife. June and Leon's daughter Loretta accompanied them to Hollywood in 1938 to play their daughter "Violey" in some of their films.

Before they left the screen some five years later, the Weaver Brothers and Elviry had sung — or rather, *twanged* — and clowned their way through numerous films at Republic Pictures. As bottom-of-the-bill, "B" picture attractions they were at the same studio as Judy Canova, their slightly more "A" picture "rival" in this subgenre. In the late 1940s Leon appeared in films on his own.

Down in "Arkansaw" (1938) * *Swing Your Lady* (1938) * *Jeepers Creepers* (1939) * *Friendly Neighbors* (1940) * *Grand Ole Opry* (1940) * *In Old Missouri* (1940) * *Arkansas Judge* (1941) * *Mountain Moonlight* (1941) * *Tuxedo Junction* (1941) * *The Old Homestead* (1942) * *Shepherd of the Ozarks* (1942) * *Mountain Rhythm* (1943)

The Weaver Brothers and Elviry in their first film *Down in "Arkansaw."*

Weavers

Ronnie Gilbert (New York, New York, 1926–); Lee Hays (1914–1981), Fred Hellerman (Brooklyn, New York, 1927–), Pete Seeger (1919–); Erik Darling (1933–2008), Bernie Krause; Frank Hamilton (1934–)

It is very probable that the Weavers will always be considered one of the most iconic folk-singing groups of all time. No less a personage than poet Carl Sandburg said "When I hear America singing, the Weavers are there." The group was founded by Pete Seeger and Lee Hays who had been members of a similar group, the Almanac Singers.

The Weavers performed a wide variety of music, were politically active, and inspired many folksingers who followed. Among them were certainly Peter, Paul and Mary and the Kingston Trio. Their first major appearance came at the Village Vanguard in New York's Greenwich Village in 1948, and the 1949 recordings of "Tzena, Tzena, Tzena" and "Goodnight, Irene" were huge sellers.

They also hit it big with, among others, "On Top of Old Smoky," "Kisses Sweeter Than Wine" and "So Long (It's Been Good to Know Ya"). Placed under government surveillance during the height of the Cold War and brought before the House Committee on Un-American Activities because of their undoubted leftist beliefs, the Weavers eventually lost access to a large part of their audience and disbanded in 1952.

There were a few reunions of the original members thereafter but Seeger, who became the best known member, largely pursued a solo career. The documentary *The Weavers: Wasn't that a Time!* came out in 1982 to general acclaim. They were inducted into the Vocal Group Hall of Fame, and in 2006 were awarded the Grammy's Lifetime Achievement Award.

Disc Jockey (1951)

Weeks, Anson *see* Anson Weeks and His Orchestra

Weems, Ted *see* Ted Weems and His Orchestra

Welsh Singers

The Oscar-winning 1941 John Ford film *How Green Was My Valley* is a classic for many reasons, not the least of which are the magnificent voices of the Welsh Singers. Although the film itself was not actually shot in the coal-rich but poverty-stricken vales of Wales, the ambiance of that region was convincingly portrayed.

The Welsh Singers establish the authentic tone of the film over the opening credits and are seen off and on throughout harmonizing their movingly beautiful melodies. It is abundantly clear they are not just a random selection of Hollywood singers, but the genuine article.

How Green Was My Valley (1941)

Weno A-Go-Go
Music City U.S.A. (1966)

Wesley Tuttle and His Texas Stars
Wesley Tuttle (Lamar, Colorado, 1917–2003)

A professional gig on Los Angeles radio was guitarist/singer/yodeler Wesley Tuttle's entrée into show business at the age of fifteen. His burgeoning career was extraordinary in that he had lost three fingers of one hand at the age of six.

Tuttle soon was appearing with western bands like the Beverly Hill Billies, the Saddle Pals and, briefly, the Sons of the Pioneers that featured his yodeling skill. He even dubbed the yodeling of Dopey in Walt Disney's *Snow White and the Seven Dwarfs* in 1937.

By the mid–1940s Wesley Tuttle had appeared in films with such oater stars as Tex Ritter, Johnny Mack Brown and Jimmy Wakely. He recorded the hits "With Tears in My Eyes," "Never" and "Detour" and had been recording western songs like "Strawberry Roan" since the 1930s.

Tuttle also continued doing his radio shows and subsequently went into television as well. In the 1950s he became a minister and issued several gospel albums. Considered a major influence on many prominent western singers who followed him he was inducted into the Western Music Association Hall of Fame in 1997.

Riders of the Dawn (1945) * *Song of the Sierras* (1946) * *Rainbow Over the Rockies* (1947)

West, Art *see* Art West and His Sunset Riders

West Virginia Ramblers
The West Virginia Ramblers were a hillbilly act.
Bad Boy (1935)

Western Aces *see* Red Arnall and the Western Aces

Western All Stars *see* Tommy Duncan and His Western All Stars

Western Caravan Band *see* Tex Williams and His Western Caravan Band

Westerners *see* Louise Massey's Westerners

White and Stanley [unknown]
It All Came True (1940)

Whiteman, Paul *see* Paul Whiteman...

Whitley, Ray *see* Ray Whitley...

Who
Pete Townshend (London, England, 1945–) (guitar); Roger Daltrey (London, England, 1944–) (lead vocals); John Entwhistle (1945?–2002) (bass guitar); Keith Moon (Wembley, England, 1946–1978) (drums)

To this day, more than forty years after its founding, the British rock band Who is still considered one of the greatest of its kind. Originally called the Detours (and briefly the High Numbers), they adopted their current name in 1964. They were both dynamic performers and musical innovators, notably with their rock opera *Tommy*. Pete Townshend especially tried to push the envelope musically.

With Townshend as the primary writer of their music, the Who had hit after hit: "My Generation," "I Can't Explain," "I Can See for Miles," "The Kids Are Alright" and very successful albums. Their vociferous onstage antics also created a stir, the group's destruction of their instruments and sound equipment being a common occurrence. They had the dubious honor of being named the loudest rock band in the world by the *Guinness Book of Records*.

It was with 1969's *Tommy*, and the subsequent 1975 film version with Roger Daltrey (who later appeared in many other films) that the Who's major fame became cemented. The film received an Oscar nomination for best original score. The films *The Kids are Alright* and *Quadrophenia* were also based on their compositions.

There was a downside to their fame as well, particularly their 1979 concert in Cincinnati that resulted in eleven fan trampling deaths before the performance began. The Who was inducted into the Rock and Roll Hall of Fame in 1990 and has continued to be an influential presence on the music scene and the inspiration for many another rock band.

Monterey Pop (1969) [documentary] "My Generation" * *Woodstock* (1970) [documentary] "See Me, Feel Me" and "Summertime Blues"

Wiere Brothers
Herbert Wiere (Vienna, Austria, 1908–1999); Sylvester Wiere (Prague [later Czechoslovakia], 1909–1970); Harry Wiere (Berlin, Germany, 1906–1992)

The zany Wiere Brothers were a multi-talented group, singing and dancing and performing acrobatics. Their main shtick was eccentric physical comedy which their odd foreign accents further emphasized. They had a television sitcom called *Oh Those Bells* in the early 1960s.

The Great American Broadcast (1941) * *Take It or Leave It* (1944) * *Hands Across the Border* (1944) * *Road to Rio* (1947) * *Double Trouble* (1967)

Wilburn Brothers
Doyle Wilburn (Virgil Wilburn, Thayer, Missouri or Hardy, Arkansas, 1930–1982); Teddy Wilburn (Thurman Wilburn, Thayer, Missouri or Hardy, Arkansas, 1931–2003)

Beginning as child performers with the Wilburn Family act that included their older brothers and sister, Doyle and Teddy appeared on such major radio shows as *Grand Ole Opry* and *Louisiana Hayride*. They continued on as a duo when the rest of the family left show business in the 1950s. Among their recording hits were "Sparkling Brown Eyes," "Roll Muddy River," "Go Away with Me" and "Hurt Her Once for Me."

In all they had some thirty records on the country music charts and were the back-up group for many another country/western star. From 1964 to '74 the Wilburns had a television show that produced more than 350 episodes and also had a series in Australia. They also established a well-known music publishing house and talent agency; it was through these that country music queen Loretta Lynn got a major push toward stardom.

Country Music on Broadway (1964) [documentary] * *Music City U.S.A.* (1966) [documentary] * *Nashville Rebel* (1966)

Wild Affair Trio
Doctor, You've Got To Be Kidding (1967) "Little Girl"

Wild Ones
The Wild Ones were a pop vocal group.

The Fat Spy (1965) "People Sure Act Funny,"

"Do the Turtle," "Wild Way of Living," "Come on Down" and "Let's Dance, Let's Dance" * *Lord Love a Duck* (1966)

Will Osborne and His Orchestra
Will Osborne (Canada, 1905–1981)

At one time a singer who was considered a rival to crooner Rudy Vallee in the 1930s, drummer Will Osborne also was a bandleader and well-regarded composer. (He was purported to be a member of the nobility, supposedly the son of a lord and heir to a Scottish barony.)

He led several groups in his thirty-year career, beginning in 1924, which ranged from dance to swing orchestras. For a while his was the house band on the Abbott and Costello radio show in the 1940s. His ensemble featured the so-called "Will Osborne sound," produced by the playing of trombones into cardboard megaphones.

"Dry Bones," "On a Blue and Moonless Night" and "Pompton Turnpike" were among Osborne's well-regarded compositions. His orchestra's theme songs were the lesser-known "The Gentleman Awaits" and "Beside an Open Fireplace." In the 1950s he turned his talents to being the musical director at clubs in Las Vegas and Lake Tahoe.

Blues in the Night (1941) * (*Abbott and Costello*) *In Society* (1944) * *Swing Parade of 1946* (1946)

Williams, Curly *see* Curly Williams and His Georgia Peach Pickers

Williams, "Sleepy" *see* "Sleepy" Williams and His Three Shades of Rhythm

Williams, Tex *see* Tex Williams and His Western Caravan Band

Williams, Tudor *see* Tudor Williams Male Chorus

Williams Brothers; Four Williams Brothers
Bob Williams; Don Williams; Dick Williams; Andy Williams (Wall Lake, Iowa, 1927–)

The Williams Brothers quartet was formed in the late 1930s and was much heard on Midwestern radio stations. The boys became well-known enough to back Bing Crosby on his recording of "Swinging on a Star" and then went on to a nightclub act with comedienne/chanteuse Kay Thompson. In the meantime they made a couple of films.

The elder Williams brothers faded into domesticity in the early '50s, while youngest brother Andy started his solo career in 1952. Television appearances were his road to greater recognition and his success was sealed with the ballad "Canadian Sunset." This was followed up with "Butterfly," "Are You Sincere?" and "Lonely Street" among others.

Andy Williams hit his stride in the 1960s with several major albums and continued to produce such chart singles as "Can't Get Used to Losing You" and "Days of Wine and Roses," as well as starring on his own Emmy-winning variety show from 1962 to 1971.

An attempt was made to make Williams into a movie leading man with 1964's *I'd Rather Be Rich* but it was unsuccessful. His mellow public persona was much more suited to the intimacy of the television screen and the recording medium.

Kansas City Kitty (1944) * *Something in the Wind* (1947)

Willing, Foy *see* Foy Willing and Riders of the Purple Sage

Willis Brothers
Guy Willis (James Willis, Alex, Arkansas, 1915–1981) (vocals/guitar); Skeeter Willis (Charles Willis, Coalton, Oklahoma, 1917–1976) (vocals/fiddle); Vic Willis (John Willis, Schulter, Oklahoma, 1922–1995) (accordion/piano/vocals); Joe Willis

The Oklahoma Wranglers was the name that the Willis Brothers chose on their entrée into western swing about 1932. At that time it was oldest brother Joe who was a member, Vic joined in 1939. They performed on local Oklahoma radio until World War II intervened, then reunited in 1946 to join *Grand Ole Opry* on which the group was heard, off and on, until the 1990s.

Eventually the Willises decided to expand beyond their western music base and dropped the Oklahoma Wranglers name in favor of their own. As such they toured and appeared in movies with western star Eddy Arnold. They had also backed country legend Hank Williams in his first recordings.

The Brothers finally achieved a country music hit of their own with "Give Me 40 Acres (to

Turn This Rig Around") in 1964. When one Willis died and the other retired, youngest brother Vic formed the Vic Willis Trio.

Hoedown (1950) * *Forty Acre Feud* (1965)

Wills, Bob *see* **Bob Wills and His Texas Playboys**

Wilson, Teddy *see* **Teddy Wilson and His Band**

Wingy Manone and His Band

Wingy Manone (Joseph Manone, New Orleans, Louisiana, 1900/04–1982)

Despite losing an arm at the age of ten (hence the unsubtle nickname of "Wingy"), Joseph Manone played trumpet on riverboats and with the Crescent City Jazzers, later known as the Arcadian Serenaders. His own first band, formed in the mid–1930s, was called Joe Manone's Harmony Kings that had a hit with "The Isle of Capri," later to be his theme song. He also composed several tunes.

One of his early recordings was "Tar Paper Stomp" that was to become a massive hit under its new name: "In the Mood." As Manone became better known he was dubbed "The Juke Box King of Jive" and evolved into a comedic performer and sidekick to Bing Crosby on the singer's *Kraft Music Hall* radio show. He later became a staple on the Las Vegas music scene.

In the early 1950s Manone became somewhat of an unusual household name because of comic Jackie Gleason, one of whose recurring television characters was an obnoxious late-night movie pitchman. He kept offering, as a bonus, a recording of Wingy Manone's "There Are Fairies at the Bottom of My Garden"—along with the unforgettable three-pound wedge of (the fictional) Facciamara's mozzeroni cheese.

Rhythm on the River (1940) * *Juke Box Jenny* (1942) * *Hi'Ya Sailor* (1943) * *Trocadero* (1944) * *Sarge Goes to College* (1947)

Winslow, Dick *see* **Dick Winslow and His Orchestra**

Winstons

Richard Spencer (lead vocalist); Ray Maritano; Quincy Mattison; Phil Tolotta; Sonny Peckrol; G. C. Coleman

A 1960s "soul" ensemble, the Winstons came and went rather quickly but did have a hit with "Color Him Father" in 1969. It made the Top Ten in the pop and rhythm-and-blues charts, and won a Grammy for best R-and-B song. This was ample proof that their previous well-regarded efforts "Amen Brother" and "Need a Replacement" were not just flashes-in-the-pan.

It's Your Thing (1970) [documentary]

Witnesses *see* **Sam Butera and the Witnesses**

Woode, Henri *see* **Henri Woode and His Sextet**

Woody Herman and His Orchestra

Woody Herman (Woodrow Herman, Milwaukee, Wisconsin, 1913–1987)

Clarinetist Woody Herman was one of the most respected bandleaders of his time with his so-called Herd, billed as the "Band That Plays the Blues." He had played clarinet and alto sax professionally from the age of nine, first in vaudeville and then as a sideman for Gus Arnheim and Isham Jones.

In 1939 his group's big hit "The Woodchoppers' Ball" appeared to great acclaim; other early hits included "Blues in the Night" and "Blue Flame," his theme song. Later successful recordings were "Caldonia" and "Four Brothers."

The Woody Herman band was a cooperative effort in which all received an equal share of profits and Herman was elected by them as their front man. Until the mid–1940s the Herman Herd remained near the top of popularity polls with its combination of Dixieland, blues and swing. Even Russian composer Igor Stravinsky wrote a piece for it.

The first Herd was disbanded in 1946 after a Carnegie Hall concert but in time the Second, Third and Thundering Herds succeeded it. Although they flirted with different musical genres, jazz was always the mainstay and Woody Herman remained active well into the 1970s, having led bands for almost fifty years.

What's Cookin'? (1942) * *Wintertime* (1943) * *Sensations of 1945* (1944) * *Earl Carroll's Vanities* (1945) * *The Hit Parade of 1947* (1947) * *New Orleans* (1947)

Wranglers see Arizona Wranglers

Xavier Cugat and His Orchestra

Xavier Cugat (Francisco de Asis Javier Cugat Minall de Brue y Deulofeo, Girona, Spain, 1900–1990)

Latin American bandleader Xavier Cugat was certainly one of the most colorful of his kind, both onstage and in the movies. His personality translated well to the screen and he was often rewarded with lengthy speaking parts which he delivered in his theatrically garbled English. He offered moviegoers a distinctive avuncular persona; as a result he had one of the most successful film careers of any orchestra leader.

Known for cradling a diminutive Chihuahua as he conducted, Cugat was dubbed the "Rhumba King," though he had been trained as a classical violinist. The orchestra, which was originally a four piece combo called the Gigolos, was dressed in showy pseudo–Latin style. A pretty girl, often Lina Romay, sang and gyrated around the stage fetchingly.

Xavier Cugat succeeded in establishing himself as the face of Latin American music but others, like Tito Puente, were considered more authentic. He was also a talented cartoonist and had worked as one before becoming a sideman with the Phil Harris and Vincent Lopez orchestras. "Cugie," as he was called, formed a tango band in the mid–1920s and found success playing at the Cocoanut Grove in Hollywood.

Relocating to New York, Cugat's group became the house band at the posh Waldorf-Astoria hotel for many years, with its theme song "My Shawl." He embellished his credentials with hits like "Perfidia," but found greatest fame with Latin-flavored tunes like "El Manicero" and generally followed (or led) the crazes for dances like the cha cha, conga and mambo.

Xavier Cugat had more than one string to his bow: his own line of candy dubbed "Cugat's Nougats." He was active well into his eighties, forming an orchestra to tour through Spain in 1986, and he made solo film appearances in 1960s American films as well as Spanish films some two decades later.

Go West, Young Man (1936) * *You Were Never Lovelier* (1942) * *The Heat's on* (1943) * *Bathing Beauty* (1944) * *Two Girls and a Sailor* (1944) * *Week-End at the Waldorf* (1945) * *No Leave, No*

Xavier Cugat.

Love (1946) * *Holiday in Mexico* (1946) * *This Time for Keeps* (1947) * *On an Island with You* (1948) * *Luxury Liner* (1948) * *A Date with Judy* (1948) * *Neptune's Daughter* (1949)

X-L's

A Time to Sing (1968)

Yacht Club Boys

Charles Sadler (New York, New York); George Kelly; James V. Kern (1909–1966); Billy Mann (New York, New York, 1901–1974)

The Yacht Club Boys sang comedy songs and indulged in comic patter in vaudeville and nightclubs. In addition to their feature films, they appeared in many musical short subjects dating back to the late 1920s. One member, James Kern, latterly established a successful career as a director of early-day television shows, notably *I Love Lucy*.

Thanks a Million (1935) * *The Singing Kid* (1936) * *Pigskin Parade* (1936) * *Stage Struck* (1936) * *Artists and Models* (1937) * *Artists and Models Abroad* (1938) * *Cocoanut Grove* (1938) * *Thrill of a Lifetime* (1938)

Yardbirds

Keith Relf (d. 1976) (vocals/harmonica); Eric Clapton (lead guitar); Jimmy Page (lead guitar);

Jeff Beck (lead guitar); Chris Dreja (rhythm guitar); Paul Samwell-Smith (bassist); Jim McCarty (drums)

A British Invasion band, the Yardbirds are perhaps more famous for some of the individual members than they are as an ensemble. Certainly Eric Clapton is considered one of the greats on guitar, as are Jimmy Page and Jeff Beck. Formed about 1963 as the Metropolitan Blues Quartet, the band evolved from the rhythm-and-blues music popular in the early 1960s to the psychedelic phenomenon later in that decade.

The Yardbirds' hits included "For Your Love," "Over, Under, Sideways, Down" and "Heart Full of Soul." They disbanded in 1968, some of its members going on to form the Led Zeppelin, but the Yardbirds name was reconstituted in 1992 with a couple of the original musicians. They were inducted into the Rock and Roll Hall of Fame the same year.

Blow-Up (1966) "Stroll on"

Young, Ed *see* Ed Young Fife and Drum Corps

Young, Victor *see* Victor Young and His Orchestra

Young Americans

As its name implies, the Young Americans were a clean-cut ensemble that had its first nationwide exposure on a Bing Crosby television special in 1962. Many more appearances on variety shows would ensue. They were supposedly the first group to popularize a combination of choral singing and dancing.

The Americans' apparel invariably consisted of sweaters and ties for the male members and skirts for the girls, outfits to make any parent proud in the tie-dyed '60s. To date, there are some 3,000 alumni who were Young Americans when they were between the ages of fifteen and twenty-four. A film about them, not surprisingly called *The Young Americans*, won the Academy Award for Best Documentary in 1968.

The Young Americans (1967) [documentary]

Young Gents

It's Your Thing (1970) [documentary]

Young Giants

The Young Giants were a garage band.

The Wild World of Batwoman (1966)

Yukon Belles [unknown]

Belle of the Yukon (1944)

Zombies

Rod Argent (St. Albans, England, 1945–) (keyboard); Paul Atkinson (Cuffley, England, 1946–2004) (guitar); Colin Blunstone (Hatfield, England, 1945–) (lead vocalist); Chris White (Barnet, England, 1943–) (bassist); Hugh Grundy (Winchester, England, 1945–) (drums)

Considered one of the more musically sophisticated of British Invasion bands, the Zombies had hits with "She's Not There" and "Tell Her No." Their period of activity spanned 1961 to 1968, the year they released their much-lauded album "Odyssey and Oracle." They always seemed to have been more popular in the States than in their own land.

"Time of the Season," a single from that album, became a very big hit at a time when the group had already broken up. In order to capitalize on this unexpected turn of fortune, other musicians toured under the Zombies' name. Rod Argent went on to establish the band Argent, but the original Zombies were not forgotten. The use of one of their album tracks in the 2004 film *The Life Aquatic with Steve Zissou* led to renewed interest in the band and some of the members reunited in 2006.

Bunny Lake Is Missing (1965)

Appendix One: Other United Kingdom Bands

Many bands originating in the United Kingdom made at least one film, mostly in the 1960s. This is a representative sample of those not included in the main part of the book.

Andy Cavell and the Saints
Band of Angels
Bead Game
Billy Fury and the Satellites
Blackwells
Blue Mountain Boys
Bob Wallace and His Storyville Jazzmen
Chantelles
Charles McDevitt and His Skiffle Group
Chris O'Brien and His Caribbeans
Cliff Richard and the Shadows
Don Sollash and His Rocking Horses
Dudley Moore Trio
Earl Royce and the Olympics
Elaine and Derek
Embers
Four Pennies
Gamblers
Gojos
Graham Bond Organisation
Hedgehoppers Anonymous
Humphrey Lyttleton and His Band
Incredible String Band
Jackie and the Raindrops
John Barry Seven
John Lennon and the Plastic Ono Band
Kenny and the Wranglers
King Brothers
Leroys
Les Allen and His Band
Les Flambeaux Steel Band
Long and the Short
Longhairs
M6
Mellowkings (aka Mello-Kings)
Merseybeat
Migil Five
Mindbenders
Mojos
Niteshades
Orchids
Outlaws
Plebs
Rapiers
Rey Anton and the Pro Form
Rockin' Berries
Rockin' Ramrods
Rolling Stones
Rory Blackwell and the Blackjacks
Searchers
Small Faces
Sounds Incorporated
Spotniks
Springfields
Steelemen
Swinging Blue Jeans
Television Toppers
Temperance Seven
Three Bells
Tommy Eytle and His Calypso Band
Tommy Quickly and the Remo Four
Tony Crombie and His Rockets
Tony Lightfoot and His New Orleans Jazz Band
Tornadoes (aka Heinz Burt and the Tornados)
Trekkers
Trolls
Twice As Much
Vagrants
Vaqueros
Vernon Girls
Wackers
Warriors
Zephyrs

Appendix Two: Dance Teams, Skaters and Other Specialty Acts

In the "golden era" from the dawn of sound to the 1950s, Hollywood seemed always to be searching for musical novelties. Most of the non-instrumental/non-singing groups that appeared in movies were dance teams, but there were also skaters, acrobats and other "specialty" acts. Although they did not directly create music it certainly emanated from the screen during their performances, and thus contributed to filmgoers' enjoyment during their (usually) brief appearances in the limelight.

This is a representative listing of such groups into the 1960s, with the decades in which they appeared in films.

DANCE TEAMS

Aida Broadbent Girls (1940s)
Alan K. Foster Girls (1920s)
Albertina Rasch Ballet (1920s–1930s)
Alex Nahera Dancers (1940s)
Alfredo Alaria's Ballet (1960s)
Alston and Young (1940s)
American Ballet of the Metropolitan Opera (1930s)
Archie Savage Trio [aka Archie Savage Dancers] (1950s–1960s)
Armand and Diana (1930s)
Armando and Lita (1930s–1950s)
Ashburns (1940s)
Ashton and Co'ena (1930s)
Barnett and Clark (1920s)
Belcher Child Dancers (1920s)
Ben Tyber Ballet Troupe (1960s)
Berry Brothers (1940s)
Betty Jane Cooper and the Lathrop Brothers (1930s)
Big Apple Dancers (1930s)
Blackburn Twins (1940s–1950s)
Blue Ridge Mountain Dancers (1960s)
Boscoe Holder Dancers (1960s)
Brown and Brown (1930s)
Buck and Bubbles (1930s–1940s)
Burton and Kay (1940s)
Cappella and Patricia (1940s)
Car-Bert Dancers (1940s)
Carlyle Dancers (1940s–1950s)
Carmen Amaya and Her Dance Company (1940s)
Carolina Cloggers (1960s)
Catron and Popp (1940s)
Chamberlin and Hines (1930s)
Chandra Kaly and His Dancers (1940s)
Charles Teske Dancers (1930s)
Charles Weidman Dance Group (1940s)
Chester Hale Girls (1920s–1930s)
Chez Paree Adorables (1950s)
Chilton and Thomas (1930s)
Christianis (1940s)
Clark and Dexter (1930s)
Collenette Ballet (1930s)
Collier Sisters (1920s)
Condos Brothers (1930s–1940s)
Cortez and Galante (1930s)
Cosmic Daddy Dancers (1960s)
Costello Twins (1940s)
Cotten Sisters (1940s)
Countess Sonia and Company (1930s)
Covan Studio Dancers (1930s)
Crane Sisters (1930s)
Cuban Dancers (1950s)
Dancing Debonairs (1940s)
DeMarcos (1930s)
Devi Dja and Her Balinese Dancers (1940s)
Diana Nellis Dancers (1950s)
Don and Ernie (1930s)
Dunhills (1950s)

Appendix Two: Dance Teams, Skaters, Others

Earl and Francis (1930s)
Estil McNew and His Kentucky Briar Hoppers (1960s)
Fanchon and Marco (1920s–1930s)
Fanchonettes (1930s)
Florence and Alvarez (1930s)
Four Blackbirds [aka Jeni LeGon with the Four Blackbirds] (1930s)
Four Congaroos (1940s)
Four Covans (1920s)
Four Dandies (1940s–1950s)
Four Hot Shots (1930s)
Four Step Brothers [aka Step Brothers; Loren B. Brown and the Four Step Brothers] (1940s–1960s)
Four Sweethearts (1940s)
Fox Movietone Studio Dancers (1930s)
G Sisters (1920s–1930s)
Galante and Leonarda (1930s)
Gamby-Hall Dancers (1920s)
Garcias (1940s)
Gazzari Dancers (1960s)
Georges and Jalna (1930s)
Gillian Lynn Dancers (1960s)
Harlem Congeroo Dancers (1940s)
Hi-Hatters [aka High Hatters?] (1940s)
Hollywood Exhibition Square Dancers (1940s)
Igor and Yvette (1940s)
International Jitterbugs (1940s)
Jack Cole and Company (1940s)
Jester and Mole (1930s)
Jitterbug Johnnies (1940s)
Jivin' Jacks and Jills (1940s)
Johnny and Henny (1940s)
Johnny Conrad and Dancers (1950s)
Johnny Coy and his Lassies and Pipers (1940s)
Johnson Brothers [aka Johnson and Johnson?] (1940s)
Jose Cansino Dancers (1940s)
Jovada and Jimmy Ballard (1950s)
Katherine Dunham and Her Troupe (1940s)
Kay, Kay and Katya (1940s)
Kit and Kit (1940s)
Lathrops (1930s)
Lazara and Castillano (1940s)
Lee Scott Dancers (1950s?)
Leonard Harper and His Chorines (1930s)
Leonidoff Ballet (1920s)
Lester Horton Dancers [aka Lester Horton Dance Group] (1940s–1950s)
Liliane and Marlo (1940s)
Lindy Hoppers (1940s)
Lionel Blair and His Dancers (1960s) [UK]
Lola and Fernando (1940s)
Loria Brothers (1930s)
Lorraine and Rognan (1940s)
Lowe, Hite and Stanley (1930s)
Lucienne and Ashour (1940s)
Manhattan Twisters (1960s)
Marge and Gower Champion (1950s)
Marion Morgan Dancers (1920s)
Maritza Dancers (1940s)
Mata and Hari (1940s)
Mayris Chaney and Her Dance Trio
Mazzone Abbott Dancers (1940s)
Meglin Kiddies (1930s)
Meriel Abbott Dancers (1930s–1940s)
Mescalero Apache Horn Dancers (1960s)
Miller Brothers and Lois (1940s)
Millie and Bubbles (1930s)
Moore and Allen (1930s)
Music Hall Rockettes (1930s)
Natacha Natova and Company (1920s)
Ned Wayburn Dancing Girls (1930s)
New York City Ballet Company (1960s)
Nicco and Tanya (1940s)
Nicholas Brothers (1930s–1940s, 1960s)
Norman Davis Dancers (1960s)
Ozzy Mallon's Jitterbugs (1940s)
Paramount Gypsy Dancers (1930s)
Parisian Twisters (1960s)
Patterson and Jackson (1940s)
Paul and Paulina (1930s)
Paxton Sisters (1930s)
Pearl Twins (1930s)
Peppy and Peanuts (1940s)
Peter and Pan (1930)
Phil and Audrey (1940s)
Pops and Louis (1940s)
Pork Chops and Kidney Stew (1950s)
Ramon and Dolores (1930s)
Ramon and Rosita (1930s)
Ramsdell Dancers (1930s)
Reed-Schapar Dancers (1960s)
Rene and Estelle (1930s)
Rhoda and Peppino (1930s)
Rita and Rubin (1930s–1940s)
Rochelle and Beebe (1940s)
Rogers Trio [aka Rogers Adagio Trio; Rogers Dancers]
Rosalean and Seville (1930s)
Rosario and Antonio (1940s)
Roxyettes (1920s)
Rubenettes (1940s)
Russell Markert Girls (1920s)
Ruth and Lester (1930s)
St. Clair and Day (1940s)
St. Clair and Vilova (1940s)
Sara Mildred Strauss Dancers (1930s)
Searles and Galian (1940s)
Sterner Sisters (1930s)
Stoney Mountain Cloggers (1960s)
Stump and Stumpy (1940s)

Sujata and Asoka (1950s–1960s)
Sultana Dancers (1960s)
Ted French and His Hollywood Dancers (1940s)
Ted Williams Adagio Dancers (1920s)
Theodores (1930s–1940s)
Thomas and Catherine Dowling (1940s)
Thomas and Chilton (1930s)
Three Chocolateers (1930s–1940s)
Three Dunhills (1940s)
Three Martels and Mignon (1930s)
Tip, Tap and Toe (1930s–1940s)
Tommy and Betty Wonder (1930s)
Tyler Twins (1930s)
Velasco and Lenee (1940s)
Velascos (1930s)
Veloz and Yolanda (1930s–1940s)
Vernon and Draper (1940s)
Wayne and Teska (1930s)
Western Theatre Ballet Company (1960s)
Whitey's Savoy Lindy Hoppers (1930s)
Will and Gladys Ahern (1930s)
Windy City Twisters (1960s)
World Champion Boogie Woogie Dancers (1940s)
Ygor and Tanya (1930s)
Zarco and D'lores (1950s)

Skaters (Ice and Roller Skaters)

Condon and Bohland (1940s)
Dench and Stewart (1940s)
Frick and Frack (1940s)
Jackson and Lyman (1940s)
Merry Meisters (1940s)
Olympic Trio (1930s)
Rolling Robinsons (1950s)
Skating Vanities (1940s)
Three Hollywood Blondes (1940s)
Twirl, Whirl and a Girl (1940s–1950s)

Other Specialties Acts

George Ryan Winslow High-Steppers (1960s) (drill team)
Maidie and Roy (1930s) (rope act)
Maxellos (1930s–1940s) (acrobats)
Olive Hatch Water Ballet (1940s) (synchronized swimming)
Pina Troupe (1930s) (acrobats)
Six De Waynes (1940s) (acrobats)
Six Willys (1940s) (jugglers)
Three Swifts (1940s) (jugglers)
Tongas (1960s) (acrobats)
Water Waltzers (1930s) (synchronized swimming?)
Y-Knot Twirlers (1950s) (rope act?)

Bibliography

Betrock, Alan. *Girl Groups: The Story of a Sound.* New York: Delilah Books, 1982.

The Billboard Illustrated Encyclopedia of Music. New York: Billboard, 2003.

Brown, Len, and Friedrich, Gary. *The Encyclopedia of Country and Western Music.* New York: Tower, 1971.

Clemente, John. *Girl Groups.* Iola, WI: Krause, 2000.

Crenshaw, Marshall. *Hollywood Rock: A Guide to Rock and Roll in the Movies.* New York: HarperPerennial, 1994.

Crowther, Bruce, and Pinfold, Mike. *The Big Band Years.* New York: Facts on File, 1988.

Feather, Leonard. *The Encyclopedia of Jazz.* New York: Horizon, 1960.

Fetrow, Alan. *Feature Films, 1950–1959.* Jefferson, NC: McFarland, 1999.

Garfield, Brian. *Western Films: A Complete Guide.* New York: Rawson Associates, 1982.

Green, Douglas B. *Singing in the Saddle: The History of the Singing Cowboy.* Nashville: Country Music Foundation Press/Vanderbilt University Press, 2002.

Groia, Philip. *They All Sang on the Corner: A Second Look at New York City's Rhythm and Blues Vocal Groups.* West Hempstead, NY: Phillie Dee Enterprises, 1983.

The Harmony Illustrated Encyclopedia of Country Music. New York: Crown, 1994.

Hirschhorn, Clive. *The Hollywood Musical.* New York: Crown, 1981.

Holland, Ted B. *B Western Actors Encyclopedia: Facts, Photos and Filmographies for More Than 250 Familiar Faces.* Jefferson, NC: McFarland, 1989.

Lisanti, Thomas. *Hollywood Surf and Beach Movies: The First Wave, 1959–1969.* Jefferson, NC: McFarland, 2005.

Logsdon, Guy, Mary Rogers, and William Jacobson. *Saddle Serenaders.* Layton, UT: Gibbs-Smith, 1995.

Miller, Lee O. *The Great Cowboy Stars of Movies and Television.* New Rochelle, NY: Arlington House, 1979.

Oermann, Robert. *The Listener's Guide to Country Music.* New York: Facts on File, 1983.

Pitts, Michael. *Western Movies: A TV and Video Guide to 4200 Genre Films.* Jefferson, NC: McFarland, 1986.

Rothel, David. *The Singing Cowboys.* South Brunswick, NJ: Barnes, 1978.

Simon, George T. *The Big Bands.* 4th edition. New York: Schirmer, 1981.

Stanfield, Peter. *Horse Opera: The Strange History of the 1930s Singing Cowboy.* Urbana: University of Illinois Press, 2002.

Warner, Jay. *The Billboard Book of American Singing Groups.* New York: Billboard Books, 1992.

Index

Abbott and Costello in Hollywood 121
The Adventures of Ichabod and Mr. Toad 154
Advise and Consent 126
Aguilar, Dave 40
Albers, Ken 69
Albert, Don 55
Alberts, Al 68
Albin, Peter 20
Alexander's Ragtime Band 111
Alguire, Danny 65
Ali Baba Goes to Town 142, 151
All-American Sweetheart 69
All By Myself 120
All Night Long 188
Allergic to Love 82
Allison, Jerry 45
Almost Married 166
Along the Navajo Trail 170
Along the Oregon Trail 71
Always a Bridesmaid 11
Always in My Heart 27
Always Leave Them Laughing 38, 136
Ambush Valley 136
American Music — From Folk to Jazz to Pop 49, 177
The Amorous Sex 66
Anderson, Ivie 45
Anderson, Perry 15
Andrew, Sam 20
Andrews, Laverne 10
Andrews, Maxene 10
Andrews, Patty 10
Andrijasevich, Gary 40
Angels from Hell 117
The Angry Breed 136
Animal Crackers 132
Anthony, Dan 68
Anything Goes 14
Apache Country 37
Apache Rose 170
Apollon, Dave 48
Appell, Dave 48
Argentine Nights 10
Arizona Cyclone 135
Arizona Frontier 156
Arizona Trail 105
Arkansas Judge 193
The Arkansas Swing 91, 183
Armstead, Josephine 93
Arnaz, Desi 52

Arnheim, Gus 82
Arnold, James 69
Around the World 95, 108
Artists and Models 10, 35, 118, 198
Artists and Models Abroad 198
Ascencio, Ofelia 14
Ascencio, Sara 14
Ashlock, Jesse 25
Assunto, Frank 58
Assunto, Fred 58
Assunto, Jac 58
Atkins, Essie 51
Atlantic City 112, 118, 140
Atwater, Clem 69
Auf Wiedersehen 118
Avenging Waters 172
Azpiazu, Don 86

The Babe Ruth Story 25, 112
Babes on Broadway 49, 56, 135, 142, 165, 172, 175
Babes on Swing Street 74
Backus, Donald 51
Baczek, Ted 43
Bad Boy 194
Bad Girls for the Boys 139
Bad Man from Red Butte 182
Bad Men of Thunder Gap 33
Badlands of Dakota 99
Bailey, Donald 102
Bailey, John 42
Baker, Bill 66
Baker, Ginger 45
Balalaika 158
Baldra, Chuck 13
Balin, Marty 98
Ball, Ernie 59
Ball of Fire 76
Bamby, George 11
Bandits of El Dorado 132
Banjo on My Knee 83
Bar 20 Rides Again 14
Barber, Chris 40
Barbour, Don 69
Barbour, Ross 69
Bardelli, Joe 59
Barefield, Eddie 59
Bargain with Bullets 44, 59, 115
Barksdale, Chuck 37
Barnet, Charlie 9, 38
Barrett, Curt 46

Barris, Harry 22
Barry, Len 56
Barry, Ray 38
Bartley, William 66
Basie, Count 43
Bathing Beauty 82, 86
Beach Ball 70, 90, 133, 154, 177, 192
Beach Blanket Bingo 90
Beach Party 53
Beale Street Mama 9, 55
Beat the Band 76
The Beautiful Blonde from Bashful Bend 11
Beaver, Paul 62
Because They're Young 57
Becker, John 50
Beecher, Frank 21
Been Down So Long It Looks Like Up to Me 66
Behind the Eight Ball 169
Behind the Mike 113
Belew, Benny 18
Belew, Bobby 18
Bell, Freddie 73
Belland, Bruce 69
The Bellboy 135
Belle of Old New Mexico 36
Belle of the Nineties 58
Belle of the Yukon 199
Bells of Coronado 71
Bells of Rosarita 25, 170
Bells of San Angelo 170
Beloved Invaders 190
Bennett, Patricia 40
Bennett, R. 64
The Benny Goodman Story 86, 117
Benti, Phil 40
Bergman, Nat 35
Bernie, Ben 18
Berry, Jan 97
Besito a Papa 21
Best, Denzil 77
Best, William 50
Best Foot Forward 86
Betty Co-Ed 98
Beware 119
Beyond the Pecos 151
Beyond the Valley of the Dolls 160, 175
The Big Beat 21, 34, 51, 53, 68, 74, 77, 86, 112, 127
Big Boy 130

208   Index

The Big Broadcast 28, 33, 122, 127
The Big Broadcast of 1936 47, 71, 94, 150, 191
The Big Broadcast of 1937 20, 115
The Big Broadcast of 1938 162
The Big City 138
The Big Cube 65
The Big Hangover 44
The Big Show 20, 66, 117, 169, 170
The Big Show-Off 13
The Big Store 56, 165
The Big Street 137
The Big T.N.T. Show 32, 92, 93, 120, 128, 149, 156
The Biggest Bundle of Them All 45
Bikini Beach 64, 147
Bilk, Acker 7
Billy (William Hinsche) 54
The Bishop's Wife 25
Bitter Sweet 44
Black, Bill 21
Black, David 98
Black, Johnny 105
The Black Cat 160
The Black Hills 11
Blackwood, Cecil 23
Blackwood, Doyle 23
Blackwood, James 23
Blackwood, R.W. 23
Blackwood, Roy 23
Blake, Eubie 63
Blakely, Alan 29
Blast-Off Girls 38, 64
Blaze o' Glory 156
Blazing Across the Pecos 151
Blazing Six Shooters 170
Blazing the Western Trail 26
The Blazing Trail 84
The Bliss of Mrs. Blossom 134
The Block 182
Block Busters 101
Blonde on a Bum Trip 23, 63, 189
Blondie Goes Latin 112
Blondie in Society 25
Blondie Meets the Boss 165
Blondie of the Follies 155
Bloomfield, Mike 62
Blossoms on Broadway 147
Blow-Up 199
Blue Canadian Rockies 37
Blue Hawaii 107
Blue Montana Skies 192
Blue Suede Shoes 21
Blues for Lovers 149
Blues in the Night 102, 196
Boarding House Blues 113, 116, 120
Bob Hope Vietnam Christmas Show 115
Boettcher, Carl 79
Boettcher, Curt 90
Boggs, Noel 11
Bond, Johnny 102, 105
Bone, Ralph 31
Bonham, Guy 99
Bookbinder, Tony 22
Bop Girl Goes Calypso 46, 80, 118, 123, 185
Border G-Man 142
Border Saddlemates 153
Born Reckless 106

Born Wild 9, 136
Boss of Boomtown 151
Boss of Bullion City 82
The Boss of Hangtown Mesa 138
Boswell, Connee (Connie) 27
Boswell, Martha 27
Boswell, Vet 27
Both Barrels Blazing 99
Bower, Joey 71
Bowery to Broadway 148
Boy! What a Girl! 50, 163, 166
Boys Town 28, 56
Brandt, William 82
Branford, Mifflin 37
Brann (Braun), Erik 95
Bratton, Creed 80
Bray, Curly 8
Breakfast in Hollywood 110, 171
Bregman, Buddy 31
Brewster, Barbara 28
Brewster, Gloria 28
Brian, Betty 29
Brian, Doris 29
Brian, Gwen 29
Bring on the Girls 171
Britt, Elton 20
Broadway 82
Broadway Gondolier 35, 127, 179
Broadway Melody of 1936 101
Broadway Melody of 1938 45
Broadway Melody of 1940 132
Broadway Rhythm 82, 132, 161, 186
Broadway Serenade 108, 165
Broadway Thru a Keyhole 7
Broken Strings 46, 174
Bronson, Johnny 85
The Bronze Buckaroo 87
Brook, Geoffrey 29
Brook, Ricky 29
Brookins, Don 14
Brooks, Charles 33
Brooks, Danny 56
Brooks, Harvey 62
Broome, Lee 29
Broome, Ray 29
Brown, Bill 85
Brown, Eddie 103
Brown, James 96
Brox, Bobbe 30
Brox, Lorayne 30
Brox, Patricia 30
Bruce, Jack 45
Bryant, Jack 64
Bryant, Jimmy 101
Buck Privates 10
Buckaroo from Powder River 37
Buckley, Frank 84
Buckner, Teddy 31
Buffalo Gun 107
Bullets for Rustlers 170
Bundesen, Jayne 54
Bunny Lake Is Missing 199
Burdon, Eric 12
Burke, Alohe 66
Burke, Clarence, Jr. 66
Burke, Cubie 66
Burke, Dennis 66
Burke, James 66
Burke, Kenneth 66
Burlison, Paul 105

Burnette, Dorsey 105
Burnette, Johnny 105
Burns, Ritchie 90
Burroughs, Clark 89
Burtnett, Earl 58
Burton, Gary 77
Bury Me Not on the Lone Prairie 103
Bush, Eddie 22
Bushy, Ron 95
Busse, Henry 87
Busse, Hi 32
Busseri, Frank 69
Butch Minds the Baby 165
Butler, Rhett 50
Butterworth, Mabel 61
Byers, Billy 89
Byrd, Billy 62

Cabin in the Sky 58, 83, 118
The Caddy 54
Café Metropole 97
Cairo 82, 112
Caldwell, Hank 11, 52, 84
California Firebrand 71
California Mail 169
Call of the Canyon 170
Call of the Prairie 14
Call of the Rockies 69, 169
Call Out the Marines 112, 165, 184
Callahan, Bill 34
Callahan, Joe 34
Calloway, Ann 34
Calloway, Cab 32
Calloway, Liz 34
Calypso Heat Wave 89, 121, 188
Calypso Joe 59, 87, 118
Campbell, Glen 90
Campus Sleuth 25
Can This Be Dixie? 66, 69
Cannon, Gus 16
Canova, Anne 35
Canova, Judy 35
Canova, Pete 35
Canova, Zeke 35
Cantanzarita, Artie 29
Captain Milkshake 108, 147, 187
Carefree 25
Carey, Ezikial 66
Carey, Jacob 66
Carle, Frankie 72
Carlson, Wamp 99
Carlucci, Billy 47
Carnegie Hall 134, 190
Carnival 145
Carnival in Costa Rica 63
Carnival Rock 23, 25
Carolina Blues 85, 108, 113
Carolina Moon 182
Carpenter, Ike 92
Carroll, Earl 33
Carroll, Fran 88
Carroll, Jimmy 32
Carroll, Johnny 105
Carroll, Pete 36
Carter, Ben 18
Carter, Benny 18
Carter, Johnny 66
Carver, Bob 49
Carver, Eddie 59
Casa Manana 20, 49, 61, 125, 154

Castillon, Jesus 81
Catalina Caper 36
Catskill Honeymoon 65
The Cattle Raiders 169
Cauchi, Les 29
Cavaliere, Jack 65
Cavallaro, Carmen 36
Cavallo, Jimmy 101
C.C. and Company 193
Celebration at Big Sur 46, 61, 67
Cha-Cha-Cha Boom 20, 107, 121, 122, 123, 141
Chadwick, Les 77
Challenge of the Range 176
Champagne Waltz 34
Chandler, Charles 12
Chaplin, Blondie 16
Chapman, Milt 75
Chappaqua 75
Chatterbox 127, 171
The Cheaters 56
Check and Double Check 44, 58
Check Your Guns 11
Chellette, Carolyn 39
Chellette, Judy 39
Chellette, Mary Jo 39
Cherebin, Curtis 85
Cheyenne Roundup 103
Chip of the Flying U 182
A Christmas Carol 56
Christmas Holiday 25
Cigarette Girl 158
The Cisco Kid in Old New Mexico 99
Cita, Raoul 85
Clapton, Eric 45
Clark, Dave 48
Clark, Gene 32
Clark, James 33
Clark, Nicky 85
Clarke, Alan 89
Clarke, Michael 32
Clauser, Al 8
Cletro, Eddie 59
Cline, Rusty 13
Close Harmony 99
Club Havana 36, 95
Cluskey, Conleth 14
Cluskey, Declan 14
C'mon, Let's Live a Little 138
Cobb, Ed 69
Cocker, Joe 104
Cocoanut Grove 198
Codarini, Corrado 69
The Cohens and the Kellys in Hollywood 101
Colacrai, Cirino 41
Coleman, Eddie 49
College Holiday 34
College Humor 137
College Swing 25, 69, 165
Collette, Buddy 39, 51
Colorado Sundown 153
Colorado Sunset 182
The Colorado Trail 169
Columbus, Christopher 40
Colvert, Bernie 89
Compton, Bob 38
Concert Magic 90
Coney Island 114

Confessions of a Co-Ed 23
A Connecticut Yankee 25
Connecting Rooms 64
Connell, Jim 100
The Constant Woman 183
Convention Girl 95
Cook, Frank 34
Cook, Wally 64
The Cool Ones 15, 113, 185
Coonce, Rick 80
Cooper, Alice 8
Copacabana 50
The Corn Is Green 56
Corneal, John 67
Corn's-a-Poppin' 89
Coronado 60
Correo, Vinnie 104
Costell, David 75
Costello, Laverne 13
Cotton, Carolina 52
Country Boy 78, 118
Country Fair 121, 164, 189
Country Music Caravan 107, 118
Country Music Holiday 107, 112, 118
Country Music Jamboree 45
Country Music on Broadway 11, 195
Country Western Hoedown 39, 42
The Courtship of Eddie's Father 104
The Cowboy and the Senorita 170
Cowboy Blues 11, 52, 91, 187
Cowboy Canteen 30, 127, 157, 178
Cowboy from Lonesome River 103
Cowboy in the Clouds 99
Craddock, Zeke 20
Craig, Judy 40
Crash Donovan 111
Craswell, Dennis 37
Crawford, Marjorie 36
Crawford, Traverse 51
Crazy House 44, 51, 65, 79, 113, 114, 134, 148, 192
Creach, John 98
Cream's Farewell Concert 45
Creature of Destruction 160
Crime Without Passion 26
Criss Cross 63
Cropper, Steve 27
Crosby, Bing 22
Crosby, Bob 24
Crosby, David 32, 45
Crosby, Israel 77
Crowe, Bill 23
Cruisin' Down the River 18
Cuban Love Song 63
Cuban Pete 52, 111
Cuckoo Patrol 73
Curse of the Voodoo 26
Curtis, Sonny 45
Cyclone Fury 125
Cyclone of the Saddle 13
Cyclone Prairie Rangers 100

Daddy Long Legs 149
Dale, Dick 53
D'Amato, Maria 100
D'Ambrosia, Joey 21
A Damsel in Distress 150
Danchik, Howard 64
The Dancing Co-Ed 14
Dancing Feet 98

Dancing in Manhattan 49
Dancing Lady 92
Dandridge, Dorothy 47
Dandridge, Louis 15
Dandridge, Vivian 47
Daniel, Howard 38
Daniels, Freddie 23
Daniels, Jerry 94
Dannermann, Don 46
The Dark Corner 60
Darling, Maryellen 47
Darling, Polly 47
D'Artega, Alfonso 48
Davidson, Lenny 48
Davis, Art 13
Davis, Billy, Jr. 65
Davis, Gary 43
Davis, Jimmie 100
Davis, Ross 31
Davis, Shelly 29
Davis, Willie 104
Dawes, Tom 46
Day, Charles 63
Day, Jack 63
A Day at the Races 45, 46
The Day the Music Died 17, 56
Daytona Beach Weekend 92, 136
Dean, Eddie 59
Dean, Jimmy 71, 101, 105
Deane, Sandy 98
DeCastro, Babette 49
DeCastro, Cherie 49
DeCastro, Peggy 49
Dee, Joey 104
Dee Dee 53
Deep in the Heart of Texas 103
Deere, Carol 77
DeFranco, Buddy 31
Dehne, Ace 13
Dehr, Rich 59
De la Parra, Adolfo 34
D'Ell, Dennis 90
Delfield, Bill 31
Delightfully Dangerous 131
DeLoach, Darryl 95
Del Rio, Emmy 14
DeMarco, Ann 51
DeMarco, Arlene 51
DeMarco, Gloria 51
DeMarco, Joan 51
DeMarco, Terry 51
Demmon, Bob 14
Dempsey, William 85
Denby, Al 66
Dennis, Mike 56
Denny, Jack 95
Densmore, John 55
DeRose, Joe 59
The Desert Horseman 192
Desert Vigilante 84
Desi (Desi Arnaz IV) 54
Destination Murder 174
Devil Rider! 88
The Devil's Playground 102
De Vito, Nick 70
De Vito, Tommy 70
Diamond, Leo 27
Diaries, Notes and Sketches 75, 190
Diary of a Mad Housewife 9
Dillard, Dottie 12

Dimples 83
Ding Dong Williams 170
Dinning, Ginger 54
Dinning, Jean 54
Dinning, Lou 54
Dinning, Tootsie 54
Dino (Dean Paul Martin) 54
Diodati, Fred 68
Dirty Gertie from Harlem, U.S.A. 164
Disc Jockey 71, 77, 152, 186, 194
Disk-O-Tek Holiday 15, 40, 48, 73, 141, 189
Dixie Jamboree 18
Do You Love Me? 86
Dr. Goldfoot and the Bikini Machine 159
Doctor Rhythm 118
Doctor, You've Got to Be Kidding 195
Dodson, Bert 36
Donahue, Al 8
Donna, James 37
Donner, Dave 20
Don't Fence Me In 170
Don't Knock the Rock 21, 48, 72, 188
Don't Knock the Twist 36, 57
Dooley, Clarence 46
The Doors Are Open 56
Dorman, Lee 95
Dorr, Ripley 56
Dorsey, Jimmy 101
Dortch, Stanley 66
Dossey, Len 13
Double Rhythm 134
Double Trouble 75, 195
Doubleday, Marcus 62
Douglas, Harry 50
Douglas, Steve 14, 57
Down Argentine Way 15, 67, 165
Down Dakota Way 71
Down in "Arkansaw" 75, 193
Down Mexico Way 88, 182
Down Missouri Way 135, 178
Down the Wyoming Trail 135
Drake, Dona 55
Drake, Jack 62
Drake, Lavern 33
Dreams of Glass 167
Driftin' River 176
Drifting Along 46
Driscoll, Greg 21
Drums of the Congo 147
Dryden, Spencer 98
DuBarry Was a Lady 132, 137, 144, 165, 185
Duchess of Idaho 107
Duchin, Eddie 60
Duke, Maurice 35
The Duke Is Tops 16, 37, 84, 123
Duncan, Harry 46
Duncan, Slim 84
Duncan, Tommy 25
Dunn, Donald 27
Duran, Carlos 33
Duran, Manuel 33
The Durango Kid 170

Eadie Was a Lady 83
Earfin, Gene 43
Earl Carroll's Vanities 197
Earnshaw, Ernie 68

The East Side of Heaven 124, 132
Easy to Look at 51, 121
Easy to Take 47
Eaton, Doris 56
Eboli, Osvaldo Moraes 15
Eddy, Buck 30
Eddy, Chickie 30
Eddy, Duane 57
Edgar, Ron 79
Eidson, Ken 90
El Dorado Pass 163
Ellington, Duke 57
Elliott, Don 88
Elliott, Ron 17
Ellison, Stanley 46
Elsa Maxwell's Hotel for Women 28
Elvis on Tour 172, 178
Elvis—That's the Way It Is 93, 94, 178
Enchanted Island 69
Enlighten Thy Daughter 139
Entner, Warren 80
Eppolito, Tom 38
Errair, Ken 69
Ethridge, Chris 67
European Music Revolution 145
Ever Since Venus 94
Every Night at Eight 147
Everybody Sing 25
Everybody's Dancin' 41, 124, 170
Everyday's a Holiday 118
Everything's Ducky 89
Excess Baggage 174
Ex-Flame 118
The Exile 55
Eyes of Texas 170

The Fabulous Dorseys 87, 102, 186
Fagg, Elmo 23
Family Jewels 75
Fantasia 115, 143
The Far Frontier 71
Farmer, Jimmy 88
The Farmer's Other Daughter 110
The Fat Spy 195
Fataar, Rick 16
Fazio, Ralph 104
Feast of Friends 56
Feder, Miriam 65
Feder, Sylvia 65
Feelin' Good 28, 130
Felton, John 53
Ferrara, Fred 29
Ferry Cross the Mersey 23, 71, 77
Festival 59, 74, 77, 100, 132, 137, 139, 141, 158, 173, 177, 182
Feudin', Fussin' and a-Fightin' 172
Feudin' Rhythm 132
Fields, George 35
Fields, Vanetta 93
Fiesta 27, 82, 107
Fifield, Rich 14
52nd Street 43, 155
50,000 B.C. (Before Clothing) 139
The Fight Never Ends 14, 127
Fighting Bill Fargo 60
Fighting Buckaroo 62, 104
The Fighting Coast Guard 170
The Fighting Frontiersman 84
Fighting Mustang 117

Fillmore 81, 99, 147, 160
Fiore, Al 27, 99
Fiore, Tony 13
Fireball 500 36, 55
Fireball Jungle 125
The Firefly 56, 137
Fireman, Save My Child 171
Fisher, Freddie 43
Fisher, Stan 53
Fisherman's Wharf 56
Fite, Buster 32
Five Bad Men 66
Flame of the West 140
Flanigan, Bob 69
The Fleet's In 102
Flennoy, Lorenzo 67
Flick, Bob 30
Flirtation Walk 159
Flores, Bill 40
Flying Down to Rio 28
The Flying Fool 58
Flying High 82
Flying with Music 60
Flynn, Bill 59
Foley, Dick 30
Follies Girl 106, 147, 168, 183
Follow Me 55
Follow the Band 27, 111, 165
Follow the Boys 11, 51, 74, 112, 119, 180
Follow the Leader 162
Follow Your Heart 83
Folschow, Robert 37
Fools for Scandal 115, 183
Footlight Varieties 72, 99, 172
For Me and My Gal 112, 165
For Singles Only 34, 116, 134, 176, 192
Forbes, Wes 66
Ford, Robert 79
Foreman, Speed 8
Forever Yours 114
Forty Acre Feud 197
Forty Little Mothers 158
Fountain, Pete 58
Four Jills in a Jeep 102
Francis, Ritchie 64
Frankenstein's Daughter 138
Frauenfelder, Betty 72
Frauenfelder, Reinhardt, Jr. 72
Frauenfelder, Reinhardt, Sr. 72
Frauenfelder, Ruth 72
Frauenfelder, William 72
Freddie Steps Out 38
Free, White and 21 104
Freeman, Ernie 63
Freeman, Jim 66
Freeman, Rich 66
Freshman Year 114, 120, 132
Fried, Marty 46
Friendly Neighbors 193
From Nashville with Music 30, 107, 175
From This Day Forward 122
Frontier Fury 100
Frontier Gun Law 8
Frontier Justice 20
Frontier Law 105
Frontier Outpost 84
Frontier Town 102
The Frontiersman 25
Frozen Justice 126

Fry, Bobby 64
Fugitive Valley 57
Fuller, Bobby 26
Fuller, Randy 26
Fun and Fancy Free 54, 112, 173
Fun in Acapulco 68
Fuqua, Charles 94
Furlong, Terry 80

Gaines, Lee 51
Gaining, Cub 33
Gallagher, Jim 14
The Gallant Defender 169
Galli, Norma 75
Galloping Thunder 125
Galloway, Bill 85
Gallup, Cliff 76
Gals, Incorporated 78, 144
Gambling 165
Gang Smashers 143
The Gang's All Here 15, 20
Gannon, Mary 7
Garber, Jan 97
Garcia, Jerry 81
Gardner, Ivanetta 61
Gardner, Vernon 50
Garnes, Sherman 72
Garrity, Freddie 73
Gas-s-s-s 45, 80, 105
Gates, Kenny 23
Gaucho Serenade 107
Gauchos of El Dorado 80
Gaudio, Bob 70
The Gay Desperado 188
The Gay Ranchero 170
The Gay Senorita 185
Gayle (Gayle Caldwell) 96
The Gene Krupa Story 152
General Spanky 62, 74
Gentleman from Arizona 80
Gentleman from Dixie 41
The Gentleman from Texas 46
Gentry, Art 63
George Washington Carver 188
George White's Scandals 76
Get Yourself a College Girl 12, 49, 73, 102, 153, 173
Ghost Catchers 112
The Ghost Goes Gear 171
The Ghost in the Invisible Bikini 26
Ghost of Dragstrip Hollow 153
Ghost Town Riders 182
G.I. Blues 107
Gibb, Barry 17
Gibb, Maurice 17
Gibb, Robin 17
Gibbons, Paul 22
Gibson, Steve 15
Gidget 70
Gift of Gab 16, 57, 82
Gigolette 128
Gilbert, Joe 103
Gilberto, Tommy 40
Giles, Lem 20
Gilkyson, Terry 59
Gimme Shelter 67, 92, 99
Girard, Chuck 90
A Girl, a Guitar and a Trumpet 118
The Girl Can't Help It 41, 76, 106, 145, 149, 188

Girl Crazy 112, 172, 186
The Girl from Chicago 153
Girl Happy 107
Girl o' My Dreams 179, 184
The Girl of the Golden West 56, 65
The Girl, the Body and the Pill 67
Girls on the Beach 16, 45
Girls Town 145
Git Along Little Dogies 33, 122
Give Out, Sisters 11
Glamour Girl 76
Glaser, Chuck 78
Glaser, Jim 78
Glaser, Tompall 78
The Glass Wall 163
The Glenn Miller Story 124, 129
Go Down, Death! 86, 100
Go-Go Beat Beat! 12, 29, 42, 48, 89, 121
Go, Johnny, Go! 33, 67, 101, 130
Go West, Young Lady 25, 71
Go West, Young Man 198
Godchaux, Keith 81
God's Step Children 114
Goff, Harper 65
Goin' Places 37
Going Hollywood 111, 147, 148
Going My Way 25
Going Places 118
Gold Diggers in Paris 44
Gold Mine in the Sky 172
Goldberg, Barry 62
The Golden Stallion 71
Goldmine in the Sky 103
Goldstein, Chuck 68
Gone Harlem 145
Gonks Go Beat 121, 133
Good Luck, Mr. Yates 25, 162
Good Neighbor Sam 89
Good Times 168
Goodman, Al 8
Goodman, Benny 9, 19
Gordon, Jimmy 50
Grand Canyon Trail 71
Grand Ole Opry 157, 189, 193
Grande, John 21
Grant, A. 51
Grant, Earl 59
Gravenites, Nick 62
Graves, Fred 67
Gray, Glen 78
Grayson, Hal 83
Grease 162
The Great American Broadcast 94, 195
The Great Caruso 56
The Great Morgan 111
The Great Waltz 25, 72
Green, Art 14
Green, Johnnie 105
Green, Karl 88
Green, Lennie 36
The Green Light 56
The Green Pastures 83
Greene, Alan 35
Greenwich Village 15, 153
Gregorakis, James 68
Gregorio, Mike 29
Grier, Jimmie (Jimmy) 100
Griffin, A.C. 79

Griffiths, Ken 23
Grill, Rob 80
Grimes, Lloyd 37
Grounds for Marriage 65
Groupies 57, 104, 171, 181
Gruesome Twosome 67
Guercio, Joe 94
Guizar, Pepe 67
Gummoe, John 36
Gun Law 164
Gunning for Vengeance 46

Haas, Gene 13
Hail the Conquering Hero 82
Hairston, Jester 99
Haley, Bill 21
Half Marriage 82
Hall, Harry 67
Hall, Jim 39
Hall, Sammy 23
Hall, Willie 27
Hallelujah! 46, 55
Hamilton, Chico 39, 51
Hands Across the Border 28, 82, 170, 195
Hanson, Maria 7
Happy Days 77, 165
Happy Landings 142, 151
A Hard Day's Night 17
Hargrave, Don 64
Harlem Follies 50, 89, 104, 163, 165
Harlem Hotshots 117
Harlem Is Heaven 64
Harlem Jazz Festival 42, 44, 113, 117
Harlem on Parade 59, 114, 120, 181
Harlem on the Prairie 87
Harlem Rides the Range 87
Harmony Lane 74
Harper 62
Harrell, Dickie 76
Harrell, Scotty 71, 102
Harris, Bill 42
Harris, Clyde 46
Harris, Jet 100
Harris, Rutha 74
Harrison, George 16
Hart, Jimmy 76
Hart, Mabel 61
Hart, Mickey 81
Harvest Melody 61, 147, 191
Harvey, Bob 98
Haslett, Hank 37
Hat Check Honey 74, 86, 180
Hats Off 147
Hatton, Billy 70
Havana Rose 65
Having a Wild Weekend 49
Hawaiian Nights 124, 159
The Hawk of Powder River 11
Hawkins, Edwin 61
Hawkins, Gabrielle 90
Haydock, Eric 89
Hayes, Isaac 27
Hayman, Richard 27
Head 130
Heading West 84
Heart of the Golden West 83, 170
Heart of the Rio Grande 103
Heart of the Rockies 71, 88
Hearts Divided 83

Index

The Heat's On 198
Heavenly Days 112
Heidt, Horace 91
Heldorado 57, 170
Hell Harbor 82
Hell on Wheels 175
Hell's Angels '69 175
Hell's Highway 63
Hell's Playground 140, 177
Hellzapoppin' 165, 166
Help! 17
Hemmingway, Gabe 20
Henderson, Jimmie 37
Hensley, Roy 37
Her Lucky Night 11
Here Come the Coeds 143
Here Comes Cookie 30, 161, 164
Here Comes Elmer 97, 110, 172
Here Comes the Band 180
Here We Go Again 150
Here We Go Round the Mulberry Bush 171
Herron, Red 62
He's My Guy 56, 114
Hess, Jake 93
Hester, Eloise 93
Hey Boy! Hey Girl! 119, 159
Hey, Let's Twist! 104, 140
Hey, Rookie! 83, 89, 108, 189
Heywood, Eddie 60
Hi, Buddy 112
Hi, Good Lookin' 51, 96, 137
Hi, Neighbor 121, 157
Hicks, Tony 89
Hideaway Girl 14
Hi-De-Ho 33, 142
Hier Bin Ich — Hier Bleib'ich 21
High Hat 57, 74, 179
High School 29
High School Hero 74, 98
High Society 118
Hill, Bill 98
Hillman, Chris 32, 67
Hilly, Joe 25
Hirsch, Chicken 45
His Fighting Blood 13
The Hit Parade 35, 58, 60, 185
Hit Parade of 1941 27, 165
Hit Parade of 1943 74, 80, 132, 150, 183
Hit Parade of 1947 170, 197
Hit Parade of 1951 26, 65
Hit the Deck 107
Hit the Ice 70, 106
Hite, Bob 34
Hits and Bits of 1938 84
Hittin' the Trail 142, 151, 182
Hi'Ya, Sailor 35, 51, 83, 114, 134, 150, 197
Hoedown 144, 197
Hoeptner, Tex 8
Hoff, Carl 35
Hold Everything 7
Hold On! 88
Hold That Co-Ed 28
Hold That Ghost 10, 180
Holiday for Lovers 133
Holiday in Mexico 198
Holiday Rhythm 37, 41, 93, 132
Holland, Clinton 51

Hollinsworth, Pods 15
Holly, Buddy 45
Holly, Dave 21
Hollywood Barn Dance 62, 143
Hollywood Bound 101, 153, 179
Hollywood Canteen 36, 80, 102, 170
Hollywood Hotel 20, 151
Hollywood Revue of 1929 22, 30, 156, 185
Hollywood Varieties 91, 154
Holmberg, Dottie 79
Holmberg, Sheri 79
Holmes, Jake 100
Holy Year 1950 164
Home in Oklahoma 68, 170
Home in San Antone 57, 129, 157
Home on the Prairie 155
Home on the Range 170
Homer (Henry Haynes) 90
Honeymoon Lodge 137
Honolulu 11, 111, 144
The Hooked Generation 15
Hooray for Love 33
Hoosier Holiday 91, 132, 165
Hootenanny Hoot 30, 76, 103
Hopkins, Charles 66
Hopkins, Gary 64
Hopkins, Sy 66
Hopwood, Keith 88
Horror of Party Beach 51
The Hot Bed 155
Hot Rod Gang 76
Hot Rods to Hell 126
Hot Thrills and Warm Chills 79
Hotel Imperial 55
House-Rent Party 121
How Green Was My Valley 194
How to Commit Marriage 43
How to Stuff a Wild Bikini 111
Howard, Alan 29
Howdy Broadway 185
How's About It? 11, 31
Huggins, Harley 25
Hunsaker, Earl 82
Hunt, Gregg 65
Hunt, Tommy 67
Hunter, Charles 13
Hush, Hush Sweet Charlotte 180
Hutcherson, Sam 15
Hutton, Ina Ray 93
Huxley, Rick 48
Hyams, Margie 77

I Cover Chinatown 11
I Dood It 102
I Love a Bandleader 70
I Surrender Dear 135
I Walk Alone 153
Iblings, Henry 82
Iceland 159
Idaho 25, 170
Idea Girl 38
If I Had My Way 165
If I'm Lucky 86
I'll Get By 86
I'll Sell My Life 60
I'll Take Sweden 191
I'll Tell the World 101
I'm from Arkansas 128, 144, 176
In Caliente 35

In Old Amarillo 157
In Old Missouri 83, 193
In Old Monterey 91, 148
In Society (aka Abbott and Costello in Society) 68, 196
In the Navy 10
Ingle, Doug 95
Ingram, Marv 69
Innes, Louis 84
International House 33, 78
Intorella, Oreste 104
Iona, Andy 11
Is Everybody Happy? 180
Isley, Ernie 95
Isley, Marvin 95
Isley, O'Kelly 95
Isley, Ronald 95
Isley, Rudolph 95
Isley, Vernon 95
Isn't It romantic? 61
It Ain't Hay 189
It All Came True 18, 61, 112, 195
It Can't Last Forever 23, 47, 96, 131, 135
It Happened at the World's Fair 107, 124
It Happened in Brooklyn 173
It Happened in Paris 125, 133
It Happened on Fifth Avenue 112
It's a Bikini World 12, 37, 76, 139, 187
It's a Date 86
It's a Gift 14
It's a Great Life 69
It's a Mad, Mad, Mad, Mad World 163
It's a Wonderful Day 77
It's All Happening 42
It's All Over Town 7, 15, 89
It's Great to Be Young 128
It's Trad, Dad! 7, 29, 40, 58, 108, 138
It's Your Thing 29, 41, 61, 66, 92, 95, 197, 199
I've Gotta Horse 15
Ivins [Ivans], Joe 13

Jackie (Jackie Miller) 96
Jackson, Al 27
Jackson, Don 51
Jackson, Eddie 38
Jailhouse Rock 107
Jam Session 9, 38, 78, 97, 118, 144, 180
Jamboree 38, 44, 62, 68, 116, 132, 155
James, Eddie 85
James, Harry 9, 85
Jardine, Al 16
Jaroff, Serge 55
Jazz Festival 58
Jazz on a Summer's Day 39
Jeepers Creepers 193
Jeffries (Jeffreys), Herb 87
Jethro (Kenneth Burns) 90
Jivin' in Be-Bop 92, 138
Joan of Paris 25
Joe Palooka in The Knockout 122
John Lair's Renfro Valley Barn Dance 65
Johnny Cash! The Man, His World, His Music 132, 182

Johnny Doughboy 63
Johnny Rocco 25
Johnson, Bernice 74
Johnson, Candy 64
Johnson, Delores 93
Johnson, Gwen 36
Johnson, Hall 83
Johnson, Kripp 51
Johnson, Ray 71
Johnson, Wayne 25
Johnson, Willie 79
Johnston, Bruce 16
The Joint Is Jumpin' 9, 76, 107, 143, 165
Jolly, Pete 31
The Jolson Story 25
Jones, Booker T. 27
Jones, Carl 51
Jones, Etta 47
Jones, Gary 50
Jones, Isham 95
Jones, Jack 13
Jones, Matt 74
Jones, Orville 94
Jones, Ralph 21
Jones, Ray 22
Joplin, Janice 20
Jordao, Itelio 15
Juke Box Jenny 38, 111, 128, 197
Juke Box Rhythm 59, 134, 188
Juke Joint 58, 121
Junction City 176
Junior Prom 7, 60
Just for Fun 29, 45, 100, 103
Just for the Hell of It 134
Juventud Rebelde 21

Kane, Howard 98
The Kansan 112
Kansas City Kitty 196
Kantner, Paul 98
Karstein, Jimmy 75
Katz, Fred 39
Kaufman, Denise 7
Kaukonen, Jorma 98
Kay, John 21
Kaye, Andy 98
Keep 'Em Flying 165
Keep Punching 113
Keep Smiling 184
Keith, Bill 100
Kelley, Kevin 32
Kelly, Joe 90
Kemp, Hal 83
Kenny, Bill 23, 94
Kentucky Blue Streak 18
Kentucky Jubilee 30
Kentucky Moonshine 29
Kerr, Anita 12
Kettering, Frank 90
Kid Dynamite 126
The Kid from Amarillo 37
Kiffle, Karl 89
Killer Diller 11, 42, 110
Killers Three 175
Kimball, Ward 65
Kind Lady 143
King, Henry 87
King, Joe 50
King, Phil 35

King Creole 107
King of Jazz 23, 30, 140
King of the Cowboys 170, 179
Kirby, John 104
Kirchner, Fritz 15
Kirchner, Jeff 15
Kirchner, Mike 15
Kirk, Andy 11
Kirk, Jack 13
Kirkland, Mike 30
Kirkpatrick, Ches 22
Kiss the Boys Goodbye 105
Kissin' Cousins 107
Klein, Dave 65
Kleinow, Pete 67
Knights of the Range 111
Knute Rockne—All American 131
Kostelanetz, Andre 10
Kowalski, Ted 53
Kramer, Billy J. 22
Kratzsch, Hal 69
Kreutzmann, Bill 81
Krieger, Robby 55
Kruble, Leroy 11
Krupa, Gene 9, 76
Kupferberg, Tuli 75
Kuzzell, Dudley 82
Kweskin, Jim 100

Ladies Man 134, 171
The Ladies Man 86
Ladies of the Chorus 26
Lady Be Good 165
Lady for a Night 83
Lady, Let's Dance! 61, 87, 118, 128
A Lady Takes a Chance 184
Lafell, Leon 35
Lake Placid Serenade 86, 150
Landrush 137
Langford, William 79
Langham, Roy 84
Lantree, Honey 90
Lantree, John 90
Larceny with Music 9, 111
Larson, Glen 69
LaRue, Florence 65
Las Vegas Nights 144, 185
The Last Days of Boot Hill 37
The Last Frontier Uprising 57, 71
The Last Horseman 26
The Last Musketeer 153
The Last Round-Up 183
Latham, Red 99
Lattimore, Carlton 104
Laugh Your Blues Away 140
Lauritsen, Jack 64
Law and Lawless 80
Law and Order 135
The Law of 45's 13
Law of the Canyon 182
Law of the Pampas 111
Law of the Plains 169
Law of the Range 183
Lawless Empire 26
Lawless Land 40
Lawless Range 13
The Lawless Rider 84
Lawless Valley 70
Laws, Maury 88
Lawson, George 50

Lebak, Jim 21
LeBaron, Eddie 60
Leckenby, Derek 88
Lecuona, Ernesto 63
Lee, Barbara 40
Lee, Billy 22
Leighton, Charles 35
Lennon, John 16
Lerchey, David 51
Leroy, Greg 43
Les, Don 99
Lesh, Phil 81
Let It Be 17
Let the Good Times Roll 21, 47, 66, 163
Let's Go Collegiate 96
Let's Go Steady 125, 165
Let's Make Music 24
Let's Rock! 47, 158, 189
Levitt, Phil 53
Levy, John 77
Lewis, Earl 67
Lewis, Gary 75
Lewis, Noah 16
Lewis, Robert 67
Leyva, Lamberto 81
Liebert, Billy 71
Life Begins in College 28
Lights of Old Santa Fe 170
Linares, Ronnie 50
Linda, Be Good 34
Lindsey, Dennis 14
The Little Joe Wrangler 103
Little Miss Broadway 28, 29, 99
Live It Up! 108
Living Venus 25
Loaded Pistols 37
Lombardo, Carole 36
Lombardo, Carmen 82
Lombardo, Guy 82
Lombardo, Lebert 82
Lombardo, Victor 82
The London Rock and Roll Show 21
Lone Hand Texan 132
The Lone Prairie 25
Lone Star Moonlight 91, 108, 125, 166
The Lone Star Trail 103
The Lonesome Trail 176
Longnecker, Ezra 20
Look Back in Anger 40
Look Out Sister 119
Loomis, Mark 40
Lord Love a Duck 196
Lost Canyon 172
Lost in a Harem 102, 161
Lost Lagoon 92
The Lost Trail 192
The Lost Weekend 160
The Loud Speaker (aka *The Loudspeaker*) 30
Louisiana 176
Louvin, Charlie 39
Love, Mike 16
Love Affair 25, 29
Love and Hisses 18, 28, 142
Love at First Sight 139, 187
The Love-Ins 40, 133, 189
Love That Brute 112
Love Thy Neighbor 126
Love Under Fire 27

Lovelady, Dave 71
Loving You 86, 107
Lowe, Bernie 20
Lubahn, Doug 42
Lucas, Harold 42
Lucy Gallant 69
Lullaby of Broadway 138
Luman, Bob 24
Lunceford, Jimmy (Jimmie) 102
Lundy, Jimmy 50
The Lusting Hours 160
Luxury Liner 144, 198
Lyles, Bill 23
Lyman, Abe 7
Lyman, Mel 100
Lymon, Frankie 72
Lytle, Marshall 21

MacDonald, Robin 22
Macioci, Jim 29
Mack, Red 51
Maclaine, Pete 22
MacMurray, Fred 34
Mad About Music 35
Mad Dogs and Englishmen 104
Madam Satan 7
Made in Paris 44, 129
Madison Avenue 178
Madriguera, Enric 62
Maestro, Johnny 29
Maffei, Frank 47
Magic Town 162
Maguire, Les 77
Mahoney, Dave 68
Mahramas, George 68
Mahramas, Michael 68
Majewski, Hank 70
Make a Wish 56
Make Believe Ballroom 172
Make Mine Laughs 44, 72
Make Mine Music 11, 108, 112, 144
Mallery, Clark 65
Malneck, Matty 123
Mama Steps Out 56
Man, Betty 75
Man About Town 124
The Man from Montana 111
Man from Music Mountain 146, 170
The Man from Oklahoma 170
Man from Rainbow Valley 57, 158
The Man from Sundown 170
Manhattan Merry-Go-Round 33, 108, 119, 180
Mantalis, George 68
Mantan Messes Up 174
Many Happy Returns 82
Manzarek, Ray 55
Marie Antoinette 56, 65
Marked for Murder 128
Marks, David 16
Marriage Is a Private Affair 56
Marsden, Freddy 77
Marsden, Gerry 77
Marsh, Warne 89
Marshal of Gunsmoke 105
Marshall, Jackie 23
Martin, Don 104
Martin, Eddie 66
Martin, Fred 36
Martin, Freddie (Freddy) 73

Mask of the Dragon 46
The Masked Rider 82
Masquerade in Mexico 82
Massi, Nick 70
Mauldin, Joe 45
Maxfield, Mike 22
May, Billy 22
Mayo, O.W. 25
Maytime 55
McAuliffe, William 25
McCartney, Paul 16
McCaslin, George 67
McCoo, Marilyn 65
McDonald, Joe 45
McElroy, Sollie 67
McGuinn, Roger 32
McIntyre, Hal 83
McKernan, Ron 81
McLean, Dave 104
McLemore, Lamonte 65
McPeters, Curtis 13
McQuarter, Matthew 42
McSpadden, Gary 93
McVea, Jack 96
Meagher, Ron 17
The Medico of Painted Springs 164
Meeks, Johnny 76
Meet Danny Wilson 36
Meet John Doe 9, 25, 49, 83
Meet Me in Las Vegas 165
Meet Me in St. Louis 132, 161
Meet Miss Bobby Sox 110
Meet the Baron 28
Meet the Boyfriend 20
Meet the People 111, 134, 171, 190
Melody Lane 126
Melody Parade 13, 120, 158, 179
Melody Time 11, 54, 73, 170
Melton, Barry 45
Men of Boys Town 56
Merchant, Jimmy 72
Merrill, Jack 64
Merry-Go-Round of 1938 48
Mershon, Gil 71
Metzger, Hal 84
Mexican Hayride 67
Mexicana 56, 141
Midnight Frolics 28, 38
Miles, Buddy 62
Miles, Herbie 37
Miller, Eddie 61
Miller, Elmaurice 51
Miller, Frank 59
Miller, Glenn 78
Miller, Herb 87
Million Dollar Weekend 157
Millward, Mike 70
Minevitch, Borah 27
Minstrel Man 11
The Minx 47
Miracle in Harlem 107, 121
Mirandy 20
Miss Bobby Socks 119
Mississippi 33
Mississippi Rhythm 100
Mistaken Identity (aka *Murder with Music*) 135
Mr. Ace 67
Mr. Big 18, 61
Mr. Broadway 60, 95

Mr. Music 126
Mr. Rock and Roll 72, 117, 130
Mitchell, Lloyd 15
Mitchell, Robert 25
The Model Shop 171
Molloy, John 64
Mondo Hollywood 155
Mondo Mod 81, 159
The Monkey's Uncle 16
The Monster Club 147
Monterey Pop 12, 21, 27, 35, 45, 99, 122, 164, 195
Montgomery, Robbie 93
Monticello, Here We Come 31
Moon Over Harlem 40
Moon Over Las Vegas 162, 172
Moonlight and Cactus 11, 128
Moonlight and Pretzels 63, 71, 78, 95
Moonlight in Hawaii 126
Moonshine Mountain 37, 76, 177
Moore, Shirley 37
Morales, Armond 93
Morales, Esy 63
Moran, Jackie 96
More American Graffiti 45
Morgan, Bob 84
Morgan, Charlie 11, 71
Morrison, Jim 55
Morse, Bob 89
Mosby, Curtis 46
Moulin Rouge 28
Moulton, Victor 15
Mountain Justice 114
Mountain Moonlight 193
Mountain Rhythm 193
Mountjoy, Monte 65
Mrs. Brown, You've Got a Lovely Daughter 88
Mrs. Miniver 56
Mrs. Parkington 56
Muldaur, Geoff 100
Mullendore, Joe 35
Mulligan, Declan 17
Munden, Dave 29
Murad, Jerry 27, 99
Murder at the Vanities 58
Murder with Music 174
Murderers Row 55
Murphey, Earl 11
Murphy, Jesse 66
Murray, Martin 90
Murray, Steve 21
Murray, Tom 20
Muscle Beach Party 53
Muse, Clarence 41
Music City, U.S.A. 34, 39, 132, 137, 194, 195
The Music Goes 'Round 155
Music in Manhattan 38, 134
Music in My Heart 10, 29
Music Man 102
The Music Man 31
Musical Mutiny 65, 81, 95, 133
My Buddy 146
My Favorite Spy 108
My Friend Irma Goes West 54
My Lucky Star 28
My Old Kentucky Home 83
My Pal Trigger 170
My Tale Is Hot 86

Mydland, Brent 81
The Mysterious Avenger 169
Mystery in Swing 38, 174
The Mystery of the Hooded Horseman 151

Nabbie, Jimmy 50
The Naked Zoo 35
Nancy Goes to Rio 15
Nash, Graham 45, 89
Nashville Rebel 195
The Nasty Rabbit 139
The National Barn Dance 54, 91, 121
The Naughty Nineties 148
The Navy Way 81
Naylor, Jerry 45
Neal, Jack 76
Neblett, Charles 74
Negroni, Joe 72
Neilsen, Sherrill 93
Neilson, Ron 79
Nelson, Nate 67
Neptune's Daughter 198
New Faces of 1937 29, 69, 154
New Orleans 118, 136, 197
New Wine 56
Newman, Bob 84
Newman, Hank 84
Newman, Slim 84
Ney, Michael 42
Nicholls, Alan 98
The Night Before the Premiere 118
Night Club Girl 51, 132
Night Time in Nevada 170
Night Train to Memphis 157
Night World 83
Nightmare 22
Nightmare in Wax 179
Nikki, Wild Dog of the North 135
No Leave, No Love 82, 198
No Nukes 46
Nobody's Baby 14, 101, 153
Noone, Jimmie (Jimmy) 101
Noone, Peter 88
North of the Great Divide 71
North of the Yukon 169
Northwest Outpost 9
Notkoff, Bobby 62
The Notorious Elinor Lee 72
Nunley, Louis 12
The Nutty Professor 75, 115

O, My Darling Clementine 147, 157, 172
O'Dell, Doye 57
Of Men and Music 143
Ogden, Larry 64
Oh, Susanna! 117
O'Hara, Brian 70
Okay, America! 24, 64, 183
Oklahoma Frontier 182
Oklahoma Raiders 105
The Old Barn Dance 33, 122, 169, 172, 192
The Old Chisholm Trail 103
The Old Corral 169
The Old Homestead 169, 182, 193
Old Oklahoma Plains 153
Old Overland Trail 153
The Old Texas Trail 151

The Old Wyoming Trail 169
Oliveira, Aloysio 15
Olsen, George 77
On an Island with You 198
On Stage Everybody 111
On the Old Spanish Trail 170
On Top of Old Smoky 37
On with the Show 84
Once Upon a Coffeehouse 74, 79, 100
One Dark Night 87
One Exciting Week 181
One Foot in Heaven 25
One Hundred Men and a Girl 115
One in a Million 27
One Man's Challenge 16, 76, 177
One Too Many 114
Operator 13 127
The Opposite Sex 86
Orchestra Wives 79, 129
Osborne, Bobby 50
Osorio, Afonso 15
Osorio, Stenio 15
Out California Way 56, 71
Out of Sight 14, 73, 75, 112, 188
Out of This World 78, 87, 104, 179
Outcast of Black Mesa 137
Outlaws of the Panhandle 170
Outlaws of the Prairie 169
Outpost of the Mounties 170
Over the Santa Fe Trail 13, 50, 91
Owens, Harry 86
Owens, Henry 79

Paige, Tommy 62
Paine, John 30
Paint Your Wagon 134
The Painted Desert 142
Pajama Party 135
Palm Springs Weekend 128
Palmer, Bill 67
La Paloma 118
Palooka 82
Pals of the Golden West 157
Pals of the Range 104
Panama Hattie 20, 132, 165
Panama Sal 189
Pan-Americana 84, 133, 138
Paradise for Three 72
Paradise in Harlem 107, 120
Paradise Valley 20
Pardon My Gun 7, 182
Pardon My Rhythm 24, 125
Pardon My Sarong 94
Pardon Us 63
Parham, Kitty 41
Parker, Andy 11
Parris, Fred 66
The Parson of Panamint 82
Parsons, Gram 32, 67
Parsons, Ray 21
Party Girl 58
Pass, Joe 77
Patterson, J.E. 13
Patterson, John 14
Patterson, Samuel 51
Paul, Johnny 71
Payton, Denis 48
The Peanut Man 83
Peeples, Lewis 66
Penner, Ed 65

Pennies from Heaven 118
Penny, Hank 84
Penrod, Jerry 95
People Are Funny 189
The People Next Door 16, 78
Perilous Holiday 61
Pete Kelly's Blues 95, 180
Petersen, John 17, 85
Peterson, Sylvia 40
Petulia 21, 43, 81
Phantom Valley 137
Pharr, Kelsey 51
Phillips, Bobby 33
Phillips, Gene 67
Pickens, Earl 46
The Picture of Dorian Gray 179
Pigskin Parade 198
Pillow to Post 118
Pin Up Girl 39
The Pinto Kid 170
The Pioneers 57, 152
The Playgirl Killer 98
Playmates 82, 108
Plumb, Neely 71
Policy Man 44, 145
Pompilli, Rudy 21
Poole, Brian 29
Pop Gear 12, 17, 22, 71, 88, 90, 133, 141, 171
Popcorn: An Audio/Visual Rock Thing 16, 18, 65, 81, 187, 189
Pope, Joe 46
Porter, Del 71
Porter, Nancy 78
Pot o' Gold 91, 164
Powell, Austin 37
The Powers Girl 20
Prairie Riders 137
Prairie Roundup 176
Prairie Stranger 116
Presenting Lily Mars 24, 165, 185
The President's Analyst 42
Price, Alan 12
Price, Ernie 37
The Pride of the Yankees 150
Primitive London 22
The Prince and the Pauper 56
Priorities on Parade 49
Private Buckaroo 11, 86
Provisor, Dennis 80
Pruitt, Marvin 69
Psych-Out 161, 175
Psycho-a-Go-Go 190
Puddin' Head 111, 172
Puerling, Gene 89
Puleo, Johnny 27

Quick, Clarence 51
Quick on the Trigger 176
Quicksand 152
Quirico, DeWayne 26
Quirk, Charlie 20

Racing Blood 66
Radio City Revels 83
Radio Stars on Parade 35, 165, 187
Radle, Carl 75
Ragtime Cowboy Joe 182
Rainbow on the River 56, 83
Rainbow Over Texas 170

216 Index

Rainbow Over the Range 156
Ramos, Bobby 26
Ramsay, Al 75
Rancho Grande 28, 138
Randazzo, Teddy 40
Randi, Don 55
Random Harvest 56
Range Beyond the Blue 176
The Rangers Take Over 33
Rapp, Danny 47
Rascals 27
Raspberry, Larry 76
Rat Fink 75
Rathbone, Donald 89
Rawhide Rangers 143, 183
Reagon, Cordell 74
Rebecca of Sunnybrook Farm 151
Rebel in the Ring 53
The Reckless Age 51
Rector, Jim 64
Red River Valley 170
Reed, Bill 53
Reed, Vern 31
Rees, Wyndam 64
Reese, Jim 26
Reet, Petite and Gone 119
Reg'lar Fellers 22, 124
Reichman, Joe 104
Reinhart, Dick 71, 102
The Reluctant Dragon 154
The Renegade Ranger 142
The Renegade Trail 111
Renegades of the Rio Grande 151
The Return of Daniel Boone 155
The Return of the Durango Kid 99
Reveille with Beverly 24, 44, 74, 127, 147, 179
Revolution 7, 45, 108, 174
Revolution Is in Your Head 65, 75
Rex, Al 21
Rey, Alvino 9
Rhapsody in Blue 87, 147
Rhythm-and-Blues Revue 42, 51, 58, 110, 117
Rhythm Inn 13
Rhythm on the Range 169
Rhythm on the River 105, 197
Rhythm Parade 127, 179
Rhythm Round-Up 26, 50, 91, 144
Rice, Darol 71
Rich, Buddy 31
Rich, Freddie 74
Rich, Young and Pretty 69
Richards, Dick 21
Riddick, Clyde 79
Ride 'Em Cowboy 30, 126, 148
Ride, Ranger, Ride 169, 181
Ride, Tenderfoot, Ride 137
Riders of Pasco Basin 158
Riders of San Joaquin 103
Riders of the Black River 169
Riders of the Lone Star 46
Riders of the Northwest Mounted 25
Riders of the Rockies 182
Riders of the Santa Fe 151
Riders of the South 46
Riders of the Timberline 82
Riders of the Whistling Pines 37, 144
Ridin' Down the Canyon 170
Ridin' the Cherokee Trail 181

Riding High 128
Riding the Outlaw Trail 140
Riding Through Nevada 100
Rinker, Al 22
Rio Grande 169, 170
Rio Rita 67, 82
Riot on Sunset Strip 40, 62
Ripps, Don 35
A Ritmo de Twist 21
River of No Return 11
Riverboat Rhythm 72
Rivers, Joan 100
Rivers, Travis 20
Road Show 38
Road to Bali 24
The Road to Nashville 132, 137, 175
Road to Rio 11, 195
Road to Zanzibar 83
Roaring Rangers 125
Robbins, Pro 35
Roberts, Bud 8
Robertson, Bernard 51
Robin Hood of Texas 37
Robin Hood of the Range 103
Robison, Robbie 42
Rock All Night 23, 145
Rock Around the Clock 21, 63, 73, 145, 186
Rock Baby, Rock It! 18, 55, 66, 105, 146, 156
Rock 'n' Roll Revue 42. 51, 58, 117
Rock, Pretty Baby 101
Rock, Rock, Rock 41, 43, 67, 72, 101, 105, 130
Rockin' in the Rockies 35, 91, 171
Rockin' the Blues 66, 85, 92, 192
Roll Along Cowboy 32
Roll Along, Texas Moon 170
Rollin' Home to Texas 33
Rollin' Plains 20
Rollin' Westward 182
Romance on the High Seas 138, 158
Romance on the Range 170
Romano, Tommy 40
Rootin' Tootin' Rhythm 8
Rosales, Edgardo 34
Rosalie 69
Rose of Santa Rosa 91, 143
Rose of Washington Square 119
Rosica, Jim 29
Rosse, Bea 68
Rosse, Geri 68
Rosse, Marge 68
Rough Riding Ranger 104
The Rough, Tough West 140
The Roundup 111
Round-Up Time in Texas 33
Roustabout 107
Rovin' Tumbleweeds 138
Rowberry, Dave 12
Rubini, Jan 97
Rumble on the Docks 73
Run with the Wind 86, 133
Rustlers of the Badlands 8
Ruvio, Joe 29
Ryan, Phil 64

Saddle Pals 37
Saddle Serenade 71
Saddles and Sagebrush 25

Saga of Death Valley 103
Sailor Beware 54
St. John, Dick 53
Saint Louis Blues 83, 111, 124
Sally, Irene and Mary 29, 151
Salute for Three 55
Sanders, Ed 75
Sanders, Marty 98
San Fernando Valley 170
San Francisco 56
San Juan, Olga 78
Santa Fe Rides 164
Santiago, Herman 72
Santos, Mario 81
Saratoga 69
Sardinha, Anibal Augusto 15
Sarge Goes to College 96, 197
Sargent, Tommy 59
Sarong Girl 106
Satin, Arnie 56
The Satin Mushroom 124
Savitt, Jan 97
Scandal 120
Scarface 82
Scatterbrain 33, 124, 182
Schaeffer, John, II 68
Scheckter, Sam 35
Schwartz, Bernie 43
Scobey, Bob 25
Scoppettone, Dick 85
Scott, Shorty 32
Scraggins, Jad 20
Scream Free 27
Scream of the Butterfly 62
Screaming Mimi 152
Scroggins, Jerry 36
Seal, Bob 42
Seaside Swingers 73
Seckler, Bill 22
Second Chorus 14
Second Fiddle 29
Second Fiddle to a Steel Guitar 39, 90
The Second Greatest Sex 126
Secret Sinners 84
See My Lawyer 92, 110
Sellers, Paul 71
Sells, Paul 105
Selph, Jimmy 46
Senior Prom 24, 74, 115, 119, 159
Senorita from the West 171
Sensations of 1945 33, 43, 116, 197
Sepia Cinderella 50, 104, 114, 192
Seven Days Ashore 44, 74
Seven Days Leave 74, 115
Sex and the Single Girl 44
The Shadow of Silk Lennox 72
Shadow Valley 11
Shamblin, Eldon 25
Shantytown 124
Shaw, Artie 13
Shaw, Bill 23
She Has What It Takes 147, 189
Shea, Al 31
Shearing, George 77
Shelton, Billy 42
Shelton, Don 89
Shepherd of the Ozarks 193
Sherman, James 38
Sherman, Sidell 98
Sherman, Sidney 39

Sherwood, Bobby 26
She's for Me 61
Shine on, Harvest Moon 121
Ship Ahoy 82, 144, 185
The Shocking Miss Pilgrim 137
Shoot the Works 18
Short, Calvin 13
Short, Jimmy 62
Short, Leon 62
Show Boat 55, 145
The Show of Shows 180
The Showdown 111
Shroeder, Alan 23
Shrum, Cal 33
Sievert, Bud 71
The Silver Bullet 138
Silver City Raiders 25
Silver Skates 179
Silver Spurs 170
Silvestri, Louis 68
Simmons, Gus 49
Simms, Harry 11
Simpson, Mary Ellen 7
Sims, Artie 14
Sing a Jingle 70, 112
Sing a Song, for Heaven's Sake 23, 24, 40, 80, 93, 135, 147, 148, 172, 173, 177
Sing Another Chorus 142
Sing, Cowboy, Sing 182
Sing Me a Song of Texas 71, 83, 91
Sing, Neighbor, Sing 121, 128, 157
Sing While You're Able 29, 184
Sing Your Worries Away 9, 111
Singin' in the Corn 164
Singin' Spurs 91, 161
The Singing Buckaroo 100, 161
The Singing Kid 33, 198
Singing on the Trail 11, 52, 68, 91
The Singing Sheriff 171
Sioux City Sue 37
Sipes, Johnny 84
Sis Hopkins 24
Sitting Pretty 92, 144
Six-Gun Law 46
Ski Party 90, 97
Skidoo! 175
Skillet, Hank 20
Skirts Ahoy! 52
Skybound 21
The Skydivers 101
The Sky's the Limit 74
Slack, Freddie 74
Slaughter, Henry 93
Sleepy Lagoon 126
Sleepytime Gal 165
The Slender Thread 169
Slick, Grace 98
Slightly Scandalous 82
Slightly Terrific 61, 173
Sloey, Al 71
Smart Politics 35, 76
Smashing Time 186
Smith, Bud 84
Smith, Carson 39
Smith, Earl 63
Smith, Jessie 93
Smith, Jimmy 102
Smith, Mike 48
Smith, Paul 11

Smoking Guns 108
Smoky Mountain Melody 157
Smoky River Serenade 28, 91
Snow White and the Seven Dwarfs 72
Snyder, Dwight 71
Snyder, Eddie 36, 102
Snyder, Hal 84
So Dear to My Heart 154
Social Register 74
Solomon, Phil 35
Some Like It Hot 76
Somerville, Dave (David) 53, 69
Something for the Boys 15
Something to Shout About 181
Something to Sing About 189
Son of a Badman 57
Son of Inagi 174
Son of Roaring Dan 182
A Song for Miss Julie 155
A Song Is Born 28, 80, 138, 158
Song of Arizona 25, 170
Song of Idaho 91, 173, 176
Song of Mexico 107
Song of Nevada 170
Song of Russia 131, 141
Song of Texas 170
Song of the City 56
Song of the Gringo 107
Song of the Islands 86
Song of the Open Road 40, 89, 159
Song of the Prairie 46, 52, 91, 187
Song of the Range 105, 176
Song of the Saddle 169
Song of the Trail 148
Sons of the Pioneers 170
Sooter, Rudy 20
Sorci, Tony 38
So's Your Uncle 51, 96, 97, 178
Soul to Soul 66, 92, 93, 160, 173
Souls of Sin 85
South of Arizona 169
South of Caliente 157
South of Death Valley 186
South of Dixie 26, 39
South of Santa Fe 170
South of the Border 39
South of the Chisholm Trail 84
South of the Rio Grande 82
South Pacific Trail 153
Spangenberg, Bill 31
Spence, Skip 98
Spencer, Pete 21
Sperling, Sam 35
Spirit of Stanford 189
Spirit of Youth 45, 145
Spivak, Charlie 39
Spoilers of the Range 169
Spotlight Scandals (aka Spotlight Revue) 87, 147
Spree 41
Spriggins, Ace 13
Spriggins, Deuce 11, 52
Spring Is Here 30
Springs, Jimmy 66
Springtime in Texas 34
Springtime in the Rockies 15, 86, 102, 103, 165, 169
Springtime in the Sierras 170
Sprouse, Ed 23

Square Dance Jubilee 30, 61, 167, 171, 188
Square Dance Katy 100
Stabile, Dick 53
Stage Door Canteen 20, 74, 82, 108
Stage to Chino 138
Stagecoach Buckaroo 82
Stagecoach War 111
Stairway for a Star 50, 166, 182
Stakeout on Dope Street 113
Stampfel, Peter 75
Stamping Ground 32, 35, 99, 145, 160
Stand Up and Cheer! 148
The Star Maker 143
Star Spangled Rhythm 80, 166
Starlet 86
Starlight Over Texas 135
Starr, Ringo 16
Stars on Parade 18, 40, 143
Stars Over Texas 176
Start Cheering 106, 119
Stay Away, Joe 107
Steadman, Frances 41
Steel, John 12
Steinbeck, George 37
Steinberg, Lewie 27
Steinharter, Jack 88
Stevens, Dave 36
Stevens, Mark 56
Stewart, Carl 84
Stewart, Cecil 38
Stick to Your Guns 103
Stills, Stephen 45
Stokes, John 14
Stolen Heaven 71, 86
Stormy 13
Stormy Weather 33, 166, 187
Stout, John 59
Stover, Everett 25
Straight to Heaven 184
Strange, Glenn 13
Strange Justice 183
The Stranger from Ponca City 182
The Stranger from Texas 169
Strasen, Bob 89
The Strawberry Statement 152
Strazza, Peter 62
Street Girl 56, 82, 151
Streets of Ghost Town 137
Strevel, Burl 23
Stricklin, Alton 25
Strictly Dynamite 127
Strictly in the Groove 54, 100, 103, 114, 137
Strike Up the Band 140
The Strip 118
Strother, Cynthia 18
Strother, Kay 18
Sugar Daddy 47, 183
Sullivan, Niki 45
Sullivan's Empire 161
The Sultan's Daughter 44
Summer Lovers 101
Summers, Delrose 61
Summers, Jerry 56
Sumner, J.D. 23
Sun Valley Serenade 79, 129
Sunday Sinners 175
Sundown 56

218 Index

Sundown on the Prairie 132
Sundown Valley 181
Sunset Carson Rides Again 155
Sunset in El Dorado 170
Sunset in the West 71
The Sunset Murder Case 87
Sunset on the Desert 170
Sunset Serenade 170
Sunshine, Monte 40
Surf Party 14, 156
Susanna Pass 71
Suspense 26
Swanee River 55, 83
Swanee Showboat 61, 177
Sweet and Low-Down 20, 144
The Sweet Beat 66
Sweet Genevieve 8
Sweet Music 43, 71
Sweet Rosie O'Grady 25, 114
The Sweet Smell of Success 39
Sweet Surrender 7, 132, 188
The Sweetheart of Sigma Chi 72, 166, 179, 183, 184
Sweetheart of the Campus 70, 137
Sweethearts of the U.S.A. 87, 97, 143
Swing! 114
Swing, Cowboy, Swing 22, 192
Swing Fever 108
Swing in the Saddle 91, 103
Swing It, Professor 70
Swing It, Soldier 165, 175, 183
Swing Out, Sister 114
Swing Out the Blues 189
Swing Parade of 1946 119, 196
Swing Sister Swing 180
Swing the Western Way 45, 91, 99
Swing Your Lady 193
Swing Your Partner 121, 181
A Swingin' Affair 53
A Swingin' Summer 57, 75, 154, 155
Swingtime Johnny 11, 128
The Sword in the Stone 124
Sylvester, Terry 89
Syncopation 9, 73, 83
Szabo, Dave 36

Tahiti Nights 189
Take It Big 74, 137
Take It or Leave It 195
Take Me to Town 144
Taking Off 92
A Tale of Two Cities 56
Tales of Manhattan 50, 83
Talk About a Lady 173
The Talk of Hollywood 8
Tall Feller 20
Tall, Tan and Terrific 9, 189
Taxi! 44
The T.A.M.I. Show 15, 16, 22, 77, 97, 123, 156, 168, 177
Taylor, Dallas 42
Taylor, Fred 85
Taylor, Gil 90
Taylor, Larry 34
Teagarden, Jack 96
Teenage Millionaire 21
Templeman, Ted 85
Temptation 146
Ten Cents a Dance 7

Tender Is the Night 136
Tennessee Jamboree 107, 118
Tenting Tonight on the Old Camp Ground 103
Terror Trail 137
Terry, Joe 47
Tex Rides with the Boy Scouts 20
Texas Carnival 152
The Texas Marshal 13
Texas Stagecoach 170
Texas Stampede 169
Texas Terrors 103
Thall, George 39
Thank Your Lucky Stars 171
Thanks a Million 140, 198
Thanks for Everything 28
Thanks for Listening 29
That Girl from Paris 25
That Man of Mine 87, 94
That Night in Rio 15, 67
That Tennessee Beat 174
That Texas Jamboree 11, 52, 54, 91
That's My Baby 44, 82, 126
That's My Gal 82, 98
That's Right—You're Wrong 108
They Shall Have Music 141
This Could Be the Night 149
This Is Elvis—The Concert 178
This Is the Army 9
This Is the Life 18, 26, 150
This Is the Night 58
This Time for Keeps 198
Thomas, Frank 65
Thompson, Cotton 25
Thompson, George 15
Those Redheads from Seattle 18
Thousands Cheer 19, 24, 108
The Three Caballeros 14, 133, 188
Three Comrades 56
Thrill of a Lifetime 35, 198
Thrill of a Romance 111, 186
The Thrill of Brazil 62
Throw a Saddle on a Star 54, 71, 91
Thumbs Up 91
Thunder Alley 9
Thunder Over the Prairie 33
The Thundering Frontier 170
The Thundering West 170
Tiger By the Tail 125
Tilley, Jerry 21
The Timber Trail 71
Time Out for Rhythm 60, 78, 165
The Time, the Place and the Girl 36
Times Square Lady 101
Tin Pan Alley 29, 155
The Tioga Kid 11
Tish 56
Titterington, Steve 88
Tjader, Cal 33, 77
To Beat the Band 34
Tolby, Sean 20
Tonite Let's All Make Love in London 12, 145
Too Many Blondes 92
Toorish, John 69
Top Man 26, 27, 44
Top of the Town 16, 34, 69
Topper 184
The Torch 188
A Tornado in the Saddle 25

Tornado Range 11
Torrence, Dean 96
Tortilla Flat 25
Townson, Ron 65
Trace, Al 8
Trail of Robin Hood 71
Trail of the Rustlers 59
Trail to Gunsight 151
Trail to Laredo 37
Trail to Mexico 82
Trail to San Antone 37
Trailing Double Trouble 103
Tramp, Tramp, Tramp 27
Transatlantic Merry-Go-Round 28, 101
Trask, Walter 14
Traveres, Freddy 71
Traynor, John 98
Trietsch, Kenneth 90
Trietsch, Paul 90
Trigger, Jr. 71
Trigger Trail 151
Tripplehorn, Tom 75
Trocadero 61, 124, 147, 173, 197
Tropic Holiday 14, 159
Trotter, John Scott 104
Trouble at Melody Mesa 33
Trouble in Sundown 142
Trouble in Texas 182
The Trouble with Girls 137
True, Bobby 26
Tubb, Ernest 62
Tucson 37
The Tulsa Kid 103
Tumbledown Ranch in Arizona 189
Tumbleweed Trail 176
Tumbling Tumbleweeds 169
The Tunnel of Love 63
Turn Off the Moon 8, 143
Turner, Ike 92
Turner, Tina 92
Tuttle, Wesley 105
Tuxedo Junction 117, 193
Twenty Million Sweethearts 127, 179
20,000 Men a Year 28
Twilight in the Sierras 71
Twilight on the Prairie 61, 71, 96
Twilight on the Rio Grande 37
Twilight on the Trail 103
Twist All Night 159, 185
Twist Around the Clock 123
Two Blondes and a Redhead 186
Two-Faced Woman 111
Two-Fisted Rangers 170
Two Gals and a Guy 184
Two Girls and a Sailor 86, 198
Two Gun Man from Harlem 37, 87
Two Guys from Texas 143
Two Thousand Maniacs 145
Two Tickets to Broadway 24
Two Tickets to Paris 104

Under Arizona Skies 167
Under California Stars 170
Under Colorado Skies 71
Under Nevada Skies 170
Under Western Stars 122
Underwood, Loyal 13
Underworld 26, 84, 146, 165
Untamed Youth 89

Utah 170
The Utah Trail 182

Vacation Days 99, 171
Vacation from Love 111
Vaccaro, Rosario 68
The Vagabond Lover 43
Valentine, Hilton 12
Valentino, Sal 17
Vallee, Rudy 43
Valli, Frankie 70
Vance, Kenny 98
Varieties on Parade 26, 48, 113
Variety Girl 132, 171
Variety Time 72, 84, 99
Varsity Show 73
Vaughn, Jerry 71
Velarde, Bayardo 34
The Velvet Underground and Nico 190
Vestine, Henry 34
The Vigilantes Ride 26
Village Barn Dance 121, 183
The Village of the Giants 17
Vincent, Jean 76
Vitalich, Diane 7
Viva Las Vegas 36, 68, 107

Wabash Avenue 152
The WAC from Walla Walla 153
Waddy, Henrietta 41
Wade, Earl 33
Wagon Team 37
Wagon Wheels 164
Wagonmaster 170
Wake Up and Live 18, 28
Wakely, Jimmy 102
Wald, Jerry 99
Walk Softly, Stranger 56
Walker, David 75
Walking My Baby Back Home 129, 172
Walking on Air 122, 183
Wallace, Barbara 43
Waller, Jerry 75
Walls, Joe 15
Walter Wanger's Vogues of 1938 155, 191
Wanderlove 158
Ward, Alan 90
Ward, Clara 41
Ward, Jackie 36
Ward, Wayne 31
Ware, Edward 50
Waring, Fred 73
Warren, Quentin 102
Waters, Winnie 84
Watson, Deek 50, 94
Watson, Guy 68
Wattstax 173
A WAVE, a WAC and a Marine 74, 132
Way Down East 161
Way Down South 83
The Way of the West 9
Way Out West 14
Wayman, Leroy 50
Wayne, Chuck 77
Weathers, John 64
Weaver, Ken 75
Weber, Steve 75
Week-End at the Waldorf 198

Week-End Pass 51, 114, 172
Weekend Rebellion 178
Weeks, Anson 12
Weir, Bob 81
Weis, Danny 95
Welcome to My Nightmare 9
Wellborn, Larry 45
Wells, Cory 62
Welnick, Vince 81
Wenzel, Art 39
We're Not Dressing 82, 111
West, Art 13
West, Doug 98
West, John 75
West, Ricky 29
West of Abilene 170
West of Carson City 135
West of Cheyenne 169
West of Dodge City 132
West of Sonora 176
West of the Santa Fe 169
West to Glory 176
Western Caravans 169
Westward Ho 13, 164
The Westward Trail 11
Whalin, June 25
Whalin, Kermit 25
What a Crazy World 73, 103
What's Buzzin' Cousin? 74
What's Cookin'? 11, 197
What's Good for the Goose 147
What's Happening! 17
What's Up, Tiger Lily? 120
When Johnny Comes Marching Home 143
When the Boys Meet the Girls 88, 118, 159
When You're Smiling 24, 127, 129
When's Your Birthday? 122
Where Angels Go, Trouble Follows 93
Where the Buffalo Roam 120
Where the West Begins 142, 151, 164
Whirlwind Raiders 57
White, Dave 47
White, Steve 38
Whitsett, Carson 27
Whitwam, Barry 88
Whoopee! 77
Widner, Jimmy 84
Wife, Doctor and Nurse 28
Wild Country 176
Wild on the Beach 14, 96, 168
The Wild Party 31
The Wild Rebels 23
Wild Wheels 21, 160, 183, 184
Wild, Wild Winter 14, 17, 53, 96, 98
The Wild, Wild World of Jayne Mansfield 112
The Wild World of Batwoman 199
Williams, Billy 38
Williams, Curly 46
Williams, Ira 38
Williams, Joseph 46
Williams, Marion 41
Williams, Ray 64
Williams, Sanford 46
Williams, Willie 76
Williams, Winston 67
Williamson, Bill 21
Willing, Foy 71

Willingham, Johnny 33
Wills, Bob 25
Wills, Chill 14
Wills, Johnny Lee 25
Wills, Luke 25
Wilson, Alan 34
Wilson, Brian 16
Wilson, Carl 16
Wilson, Dave 36
Wilson, Dennis 16
Wilson, Orlandus 79
Wilson, Paul 66
Winburn, Anna Mae 94
Winfield, Clyde 85
Winfield, Jimmy 85
Winfield, Willie 85
Winley, Harold 42
Winter-a-Go-Go 135, 152
Winter Carnival 188
Wintertime 197
With a Song in My Heart 36
With Love and Kisses 39, 128, 142
With Six You Get Eggroll 81
The Wizard of Oz 49, 111, 158
Wood, Herman 66
Wood, Louis 66
Woode, Henri 87
Woods, Hosea 16
Woods, Thomas 42
Woodstock 35, 45, 46, 160, 162, 166, 181, 195
Words and Music 22
World by Night 72
Wright, Gil 12
Wright, Norman 51
Wrigley, Alan 88
WUSA 146
Wyoming Hurricane 26

Yachnin, Louis 98
Yanick, John 104
The Yanks Are Coming 87
Yellow Rose of Texas 170
Yellow Submarine 17
Yes Sir, Mr. Bones 44, 89, 99, 141
Yodelin' Kid from Pine Ridge 181
Yolanda and the Thief 56
You Are What You Eat 62, 65, 85, 191
You Can't Ration Love 48
You Were Never Lovelier 198
You'll Find Out 108
You'll Never Get Rich 51
Younce, George 23
Young, Audrey 78
Young, Neil 45
The Young Americans 199
Young and Beautiful 179
The Young Runaways 80
The Young Swingers 162
Yount, Dick 85
You're a Lucky Fellow, Mr. Smith 112
You're a Sweetheart 69, 135
You're in the Army Now 124, 133
You're the One 136
Youth Aflame 184
You've Got to Be Smart 15, 89

Zachariah 45
Zenobia 83
Ziegfeld Girl 132, 165